Postcolonial Theor
the Specter of Capital

Vivek Chibber

VERSO

London • New York

First published by Verso 2013
© Vivek Chibber 2013

1 3 5 7 9 10 8 6 4 2

Verso
UK: 6 Meard Street, London W1F 0EG
US: 20 Jay Street, Suite 1010, Brooklyn, NY 11201
www.versobooks.com

Verso is the imprint of New Left Books

ISBN-13: 978-1-84467-976-8 (PBK)
ISBN-13: 978-1-84467-977-5 (HBK)

British Library Cataloguing in Publication Data
A catalogue record for this book is available from the British Library

Library of Congress Cataloging-in-Publication Data
Chibber, Vivek, 1965-
 Postcolonial theory and the specter of capital / Vivek Chibber.
   pages cm
 Includes bibliographical references and index.
 ISBN 978-1-84467-977-5 (hardback : alk. paper) —
 ISBN 978-1-84467-976-8 (pbk. : alk. paper)
 1. Postcolonialism—Developing countries.
 2. Capitalism—Developing countries. I. Title.
 JV51.C475 2012
 325'.3—dc23

                    2012040848

Typeset in Minion Pro by Hewer Text UK Ltd, Edinburgh
Printed by in the US by Maple Vail

VIVEK CHIBBER teaches Sociology at New York University. He has contributed to, among others, the *Socialist Register, American Journal of Sociology, Boston Review* and *New Left Review*. His book *Locked In Place: State-Building and Late Industrialization in India* won the 2005 Barrington Moore Book Award and was one of *Choice*'s Outstanding Academic Titles of 2004.

For Nivedita

Contents

Preface

This is not a book I was especially keen to write. It was perhaps 2004 that Tariq Ali, during a visit to New York, suggested I write something on postcolonial theory for Verso. At the time, I demurred. The reason, I must admit, was not very exalted. I simply did not believe there was any point to it. The intellectual culture, in both the West and the East, did not have space for a serious engagement with postcolonial theory. To have presented a critique, no matter how careful, would probably have been to no avail. So I politely declined the offer and set about researching what, at the time, I regarded as more pressing subjects.

The change came around 2005, when I was approached by Rina Agarwala and Ron Herring to write a chapter on the decline of class analysis in South Asian studies, for a special issue of the venerable *Critical Asian Studies*.[1] I agreed to do so, focusing on the *Subaltern Studies* series as the emblem of both the turn away from class and the embrace of postcolonial theory. That essay was basically an exercise in the sociology of knowledge; it sought to foreground the social conditions behind the rise of postcolonial studies and its displacement of Marxism, but never actually engaged the arguments coming from the Subalternist camp. Still, as several readers pointed out to me, the tone of the article made clear that my view of the phenomenon was unfavorable. This created a dilemma. I had published an article suggesting that the eclipse of class analysis was regrettable, but had given no grounds for anyone to share my sentiments. If I thought Subaltern Studies was flawed as a theoretical project, then it seemed incumbent on me to explain why. Was it not possible that class analysis of the traditional kind had been eclipsed because it *should* have been? I began to feel that the publication of that article tied my hands. I would have to write the book I had been avoiding.

In 2007 I started working on it, expecting that the manuscript would be ready sometime in 2008. That year, however, witnessed the illness and death of my father and mother-in-law, both in Delhi, both of whom passed away within a month of each other from cancer. It was not until 2009 that I was able to return to the book. Once I started working on it, though, it became clear that it would have to be longer than I had envisioned. To criticize the core ideas of Subaltern Studies, and to do so in a way that took those ideas seriously, would require a substantial tome. Not until the end of 2011 did I finally finish.

During the years I spent working on this project, the support of friends and comrades has been essential. Jeff Goodwin, Robert Brenner, and Erik Wright

---

1 The article was published as "On the Decline of Class Analysis in South Asian Studies," *Critical Asian Studies* 38:4 (2008), 257–87. This was a special issue edited by Ronald Herring and Rina Agarwala, which they also published as an anthology under the title *Whatever Happened to Class? Reflections from South Asia* (London: Routledge, 2008).

read the whole manuscript. Jeff has been an ideal colleague at New York University, a constant source of good humor and a pillar of moral integrity. Bob, for years, has been both a friend and an interlocutor. He read every chapter but was especially vigilant and helpful with chapter 3. Erik had detailed comments, as usual, on the whole manuscript, and prompted a substantial rewriting of parts of chapter 7. Anwar Shaikh took time off from writing his own book to read my argument about abstract labor in chapter 6; Duncan Foley read that same chapter, and I am grateful to both of them for their help. I tease Anwar that, owing to his association with this book, his links with academics of South Asian descent will only become more tenuous—but it seems he is willing to take that risk. To Neil Brenner goes the lion's share of credit for the book's title. Over lunch, after I bemoaned my inability to think of a suitable title, he came up, within a minute, with *Postcolonial Studies and the Specter of Capitalism*. I tweaked it a bit, but the title is basically his. At the eleventh hour, a group of graduate students read the whole manuscript and willingly served as my own little "focus group"; hence, my thanks to Jonah Birch, Mark Cohen, Rene Rojas, Jason Stanley and Adaner Usmani—especially to Adaner for his very detailed, and very astute, written comments. Conversations with Leo Panitch and Greg Albo not only helped develop my thoughts but also kept my morale buoyed when the book's toll felt excessive. In Sebastian Budgen I have been fortunate to have not only a superb editor, but also a friend and comrade. Sebastian was among the first to suggest my writing this book, and waited patiently for me to come around. May every author be so fortunate. And Avis Lang was not only an exceptional copy-editor but an enthusiastic supporter.

I owe a special debt of gratitude to Bashir Abu-Manneh. During the past decade, Bashir has not only become a dear friend and comrade, but has insisted that I write this book. He read the whole manuscript with an eagle eye, bringing to it not merely his general knowledge of the field, but also his particular expertise on its instance in Middle East studies.

My daughter, Ananya, was mildly disappointed to learn that I would not be dedicating this book to her, but when I explained why, and informed her who the beneficiary of the dedication would be, she graciously offered her blessing. That beneficiary, of course, is Nivedita Majumdar, to whom I owe my greatest debt. One of the very first conversations we had, when we met in 1995, was on the subject of postcolonial studies. Nivedita's unshakable confidence in the same Enlightenment universals that the Subalternists denigrate has been like an elixir during the time I have struggled with this book. It is as a small token of my love and wonderment that I dedicate this book to her.

CHAPTER ONE

Postcolonial Theory and *Subaltern Studies*

1.1 POSTCOLONIAL STUDIES AS ANALYSIS AND CRITIQUE

Over the past two decades, postcolonial studies has acquired considerable visibility in academic circles. Its point of origin was in literary and cultural studies, where it started as a movement to transcend the marginalization of non-Western literatures in the canon. On this count, the campaign experienced enormous, and rapid, success. By the turn of the millennium, the conventional packaging of modern literary training had expanded—at least at many elite American universities—to include the works of authors as diverse as Ngũgĩ wa Thiong'o, Aimé Césaire, Salman Rushdie, and Gabriel García Márquez. This was a remarkable and salutary achievement in its own right, and had the influence of postcolonial studies been limited to this, it would have certainly merited real attention. But its significance would have been limited. Most likely it would have been understood as a current which, while no doubt important for widening the perspective of its field, nonetheless remained part of the internal story of an academic specialty—no more worthy of attention than any other scholarly trend. What set it apart—and continues to do so—were two additional facts about its trajectory.

The first was that postcolonial studies rapidly migrated beyond literary analysis, to find a happy home in other disciplines. It was most visible in history and anthropology, but its influence soon spread to other scholarly domains. This was part of a broader trend in academia at the fin de siècle, which has since continued apace and is often referred to as "the cultural turn."[1] The New Left's brief flirtation with Marxist materialism had, by this time, largely dissipated; in its wake came an abiding interest in culture and ideology, not merely as an object of study but as an explanatory principle that rapidly usurped the same exalted place that "class" or "capitalism" had occupied just a decade prior. As the shift toward cultural analysis gathered steam, it was not altogether surprising that intellectuals looked to literary theory for guidance on how to approach their subject. The frameworks and theories dominant in departments of literature thus found an audience in related fields—and among the exports was postcolonial studies. For area specialists in particular, whose focus was what had been known as the Third World, the turn

---

1 Some notable collections on this phenomenon include James W. Cook, Lawrence B. Glickman, and Michael O'Malley, *The Cultural Turn in U.S. History: Past, Present, and Future* (Chicago: University of Chicago Press, 2008); George Steinmetz, *State/Culture: State Formation after the Cultural Turn* (Durham: Duke University Press, 1999); an interesting and somewhat personal account is found in Geoff Eley, *A Crooked Line: From Cultural History to the History of Society* (Ann Arbor: University of Michigan Press, 2005).

toward cultural analysis naturally translated into a fascination with postcolonial studies as a framework. By the turn of the century, then, the approach was no longer a purely disciplinary phenomenon.

The second noteworthy fact about postcolonial studies was that it claimed not just to study colonial history but also to enable political practice. The ambition was not simply to generate scholarly output but, as Robert J. C. Young advised, to "foreground its *interventionist* possibilities."[2] Leading figures in the postcolonial field have often referred to it as more than just a theory; it is also presented as a form of practice or even a movement. In its early years, this impulse was naturally directed toward the structures of colonial and neocolonial domination. More recently, however, postcolonial studies has expanded its domain to the social sphere more generally. In a recent introduction to the field, it is described as a theory relevant to anyone "joined by the common political and ethical commitment to challenging and questioning the practices and consequences of domination and subordination."[3] The focus on imperial cultures and colonial rule thus occupies only one part of the field's universe. It now takes as its remit the gamut of social practices.

Postcolonial studies has thus positioned itself not only as positive theory but also as radical critique. In so doing, it has stepped quite consciously into the vacuum left by the decline of Marxism in both the industrialized West and its satellites. In part, this flows from the biographical trajectories of its leading lights, many of whom participated in the New Left's dalliance with Marxism. Figures such as Gayatri Chakravorty Spivak, Homi Bhabha, Ranajit Guha, Anibal Quijano, Partha Chatterjee, and Dipesh Chakrabarty emerged from the Marxist milieu of the 1970s, even if their immersion in it varied in intensity. It was only natural for them to take Marxism as their primary interlocutor as they made their way out of its orbit and forged the agenda for postcolonial studies. But while these biographical factors are certainly not irrelevant, the primary source of the engagement with, and rejection of, Marxism has been political: a sense that the world has moved on; that the dilemmas of late capitalism, particularly in the Global South, cannot be apprehended by the categories of historical materialism; even more, that the failure of liberation movements in the twentieth century was, in substantial measure, the result of Marxism's abiding theoretical inadequacies.

As a result, the challenge faced by postcolonial studies is strikingly similar to the one accepted by Marxism a century ago—to generate a theory adequate to the needs of a radical political agenda. There are differences, of course—the most obvious one being that Marxism's initial development and spread was almost entirely based in working-class organizations and political parties, while its

---

2   Robert J. C. Young, "Editorial," *Interventions* 1:1 (1998), 4. Emphasis added.

3   John McLeod, "Introduction," in McLeod, ed., *The Routledge Companion to Postcolonial Studies* (London: Routledge, 2007). 6.

foothold in universities was infinitesimally small. Postcolonial studies is its mirror image, having developed entirely within the university and, though drawing some inspiration from movements, rarely in more than symbolic contact with them. Still, in the universe of academic production, the success has been nothing short of remarkable. As even one of its critics has been moved to observe, "the most flourishing sector of cultural studies today is so-called postcolonial studies."[4]

But for any critic of postcolonial studies, the very success of the field raises formidable challenges to a proper assessment of it. Owing in large measure to their roots in poststructuralist theory and its anti-foundationalism, many postcolonial intellectuals have eschewed developing the kind of clearly constructed propositions that would normally accompany a research agenda. This would, perhaps, be considered too vulgar a display of truthmongering. Again and again, we find that the proponents of the field present it more as an intellectual orientation than as a theory. It is part of the move to what has been called *post*-theory.[5] In the inaugural issue of one of the journals dedicated to the field, Robert Young announces that "postcolonialism offers a politics rather than a coherent methodology. Indeed . . . strictly speaking there is no such thing as postcolonial theory as such—rather there are shared political perceptions and agenda [sic] which employ an eclectic range of theories in their service."[6] I believe that Young's characterization is quite accurate, and points to a central difference between postcolonial studies and the Marxist tradition it seeks to supplant. It is not that postcolonial studies is an assemblage of theories while Marxism was not—in fact, Marxism always comprised an eclectic range of theories, much as does the former. The difference is that Marxism always sought internal coherence and systematicity, while postcolonial studies resists any compulsion to bring together and assess its various strands. Thus, as its influence has spread, the variations in what falls under its rubric have tended to increase. From literature and cultural studies, to historiography, the philosophy of history, and anthropology, it is now possible to find postcolonial theory in all these areas and elsewhere besides, but with the common "theory" increasingly hard to discern.

The reluctance to strive for coherence has been overlaid with a phenomenon more typical of university culture. This is the eagerness among academics to appear *au courant*, at the cutting edge, to display familiarity with the very latest conceptual advances. The most common means of so doing is to troll for the latest neologisms in order to pepper one's work with them, even if only for symbolic purposes. The result is a kind of conceptual inflation, in which the substantive influence of a framework appears to extend far beyond its actual reach. Postcolonial studies has enjoyed this inflated popularity more than most others—hence the spread of terms

---

4 Terry Eagleton, *After Theory* (New York: Basic Books, 2003), 6.
5 See Eagleton's characteristically bracing discussion of this phenomenon in ibid., chaps. 1–4.
6 Young, Editorial, 5.

such as "subaltern," "hybridity," "the fragment," and "diaspora" across the scholarly landscape. Its conceptual repertoire can be found in works of many kinds, even when they are not committed to the same research agenda or to a common set of theoretical parameters. As a result, works that appear to fall within the domain of postcolonial studies may be committed to quite distinct theoretical agendas. What they will have in common is the field's style, not its substance.

If a field of research or intellectual practice becomes truly chaotic, it poses some special challenges for critics. Normally, in assessments of any research program, the first task is to locate its central theoretical propositions. These can then be judged with regard to consistency, empirical success, coherence, and so on. But in the case of a field as diffuse as postcolonial studies appears to be, critics run the risk of discovering counterexamples for every theoretical commitment they criticize. For every failure of the theory that critics might adduce, defenders can find exceptions and successes. The challenge is thus to examine whether, under the mountain of loosely connected scholarship, there lies a core set of commitments or propositions. If no such core can be discovered, the next task is to see whether there exists a strand of theorization within the field that has some coherence and makes explicit its commitments, even if these have not been adopted by the field as a whole.

Now, it seems reasonable to suppose that despite the "bandwagon effect" of its jargon, postcolonial studies does have some common political and theoretical commitments at its core. It is known for its critique of Eurocentrism, nationalism ("the nation form"), colonial ideology, and economic determinism. Its leading theorists claim to have excavated the sources of subaltern agency and reinserted culture as a central mechanism in social analysis; indeed, they are known for their insistence on the importance of the cultural specificity of "the East." These themes are quite commonly associated with postcolonial studies and are part of its attraction to intellectuals. Further, they are more than a set of political commitments. Serious proponents of these views presumably also carry a set of arguments in support of their positions. Perhaps these arguments are not accepted across the spectrum of those who call themselves postcolonial theorists, but as long as the arguments cohere, they do permit assessment. And so long as the influence of the arguments being assessed is real—even if not universal—then the critique is not only possible but also meaningful.

1.2. THE RISE OF SUBALTERN STUDIES

It happens that we can identify several strands of theorization within postcolonial studies. Some of them, particularly its cultural theory and some of its metatheoretical arguments, have already generated considerable discussion.[7]

---

7   Some notable engagements on the literary and cultural front are Aijaz Ahmad,

Although I intend to take up these issues to some extent in the following chapters, my central concern in this book is to examine the framework that postcolonial studies has generated for *historical analysis* and, in particular, the analysis of what once was called the Third World. There is little doubt that, had it not been for its spread into historical and anthropological scholarship, postcolonial studies would have enjoyed far less notoriety on the general intellectual landscape. Once exported into area studies and historical scholarship, however, the theory gained more general visibility. Moreover, scholars in these more empirically oriented domains have made efforts to enunciate their theoretical commitments. We are therefore able to analyze these historical arguments as well as the theory that they collectively comprise.

The most illustrious representative of postcolonial studies in the scholarship on the Global South is undoubtedly the Subaltern Studies project. Initially the term was merely a name, a proper noun that referred to an annual series published in India starting in 1982. But what began as an annual volume of essays on modern Indian history, inspired by Gramscian theory and critical trends within historical scholarship, had, by the turn of the century, morphed into something more generic. "Subaltern" now became a marker of a theoretical orientation, an adjective that characterized an approach to the analysis of colonialism, or imperial history, or even politics in general. Leading proponents of the project having announced its affiliation with postcolonial studies, it was, by the end of the twentieth century, widely regarded as the face of postcolonial scholarship in area studies. To be sure, there were and are theorists within the postcolonial fold who are not directly affiliated with *Subaltern Studies* or its theoretical agenda, but there is no more conspicuous exemplar of postcolonial theory in the relevant disciplines than the "Subalternists" themselves.

The contours of this story are well known.[8] When the annual series was launched in 1982, it was received in the scholarly world as the local avatar of

---

In Theory: Classes, Nations, Literatures (London: Verso, 1992); Neil Lazarus, *Marxism, Modernity and Postcolonial Studies* (Cambridge: Cambridge University Press, 2002), Neil Lazarus, ed., *The Cambridge Companion to Postcolonial Theory* (Cambridge: Cambridge University Press, 2004); Benita Parry, *Postcolonial Studies: A Materialist Critique* (London: Routledge, 2004); Neil Lazarus, *The Postcolonial Unconscious* (Cambridge: Cambridge University Press, 2011). The metatheoretical commitments of postcolonial theorists are a more complicated issue, since their professed views do not always jibe with their actual practice. For a critique of the boilerplate epistemology, see Christopher Norris, *Reclaiming Truth: Contribution to a Critique of Cultural Relativism* (Durham: Duke University Press, 1996).

8   The best sources for the story of *Subaltern Studies* are the sketches drawn by members of the collective. See Ranajit Guha, "Introduction," *Selected Subaltern Studies* (New York: Oxford University Press, 1988); Sumit Sarkar, "The Decline of the Subaltern in Subaltern Studies," in Sarkar, *Writing Social History* (Delhi: Oxford University Press, 1997), 82–108; Dipesh Chakrabarty, "*Subaltern Studies* and Postcolonial Historiography," *Nepantla: Views from South* 1:1 (2000), 9–32. See also David Ludden, "A Brief History of Subalternity," in Ludden, ed., *Reading Subaltern Studies* (London: Anthem Press, 2002), 1–39, and the introduction to Vinayak Chaturvedi's collection *Mapping Subaltern Studies and the Postcolonial* (London: Verso, 2000).

"history from below" as developed by the New Left. It was conceived by Ranajit Guha, a historian of modern India then based at the University of Sussex, together with a small group of younger scholars.[9] At the time they began meeting, in the late 1970s, most members of this group would have regarded themselves as Marxists. As with so many of their peers in the West, they were impressed by the achievements of the movement for a "history from below" and the turn toward popular consciousness as a research agenda. All of the sketches that group members have drawn up in later years recount the influence of E. P. Thompson, Eric Hobsbawm, and pioneers of popular history.[10] A natural accompaniment to this agenda was an abiding interest in the work of Antonio Gramsci, whose influence among social historians was growing rapidly during this period. Gramsci's scattered but powerful reflections on Marxist theory and Italian culture embodied, for this later generation, their dual concerns with popular history and matters of consciousness. The group that coalesced around Guha was no exception to this trend.

While the group internalized the turn toward popular movements and culture that was then pervading historical scholarship, it also took on board another set of concerns, of a more local character. These had to do with the trajectory of colonial and postcolonial India as set against the wider experience of global modernity. In initiating its project, the Subaltern Studies group proposed not just to ask new questions—about the history of subordinate groups, popular movements, peasant consciousness, and so forth – but also to provide new answers to old questions, especially questions about the Subcontinent's political evolution since Independence. All these concerns are in evidence in the first volume's prefatory document, which serves as a kind of manifesto. In it, the editors declared their intention not only to uncover the hidden history of the Subcontinent's laboring classes but also to provide some explanation for the historic failure of Indian nationalism, whether as an elite project or a popular aspiration for a national liberation struggle.[11] The editors thus committed themselves to developing an account of the broader political economy of the entire modern era in Indian history, a theme that had been at the center of debates in the Subcontinent in the preceding decades. The truly innovative dimension of *Subaltern Studies*, then, was to marry popular history to the analysis of colonial and postcolonial capitalism.

---

9 This group included Sumit Sarkar, Partha Chatterjee, David Hardiman, Gyanendra Pandey, and Dipesh Chakrabarty.

10 See Partha Chatterjee, "A Brief History of Subaltern Studies," in Chatterjee, *Empire and Nation* (New York: Columbia University Press, 2010), 289–301; Chakrabarty, "Subaltern Studies and Postcolonial Historiography," 14.

11 See Ranajit Guha, "On Some Aspects of the Historiography of Colonial India," in Guha, ed., *Subaltern Studies I: Writings on South Asian History & Society* (Delhi: Oxford University Press, 1982), 1–8.

While the intellectual agenda mapped out was no doubt exciting, it did not by any means constitute a radical break from the milieu that produced it. As had been promised, the early volumes of *Subaltern Studies* pursued the twin themes of history from below and colonial political economy. While the resulting output was exciting and in many ways innovative, it fit rather easily into the cultural Marxism in vogue at the time, and although it raised the hackles of some Marxists in India, the criticisms were not easily distinguishable from the reactions that typically accompany any departure from familiar nostrums.[12] Subaltern Studies was largely seen as an innovation *within* Marxist theory, not as a radical departure *from* it. This is not to downplay either the significance of the early work or the reactions—often hostile—that it elicited from more orthodox Marxists. But the flavor of these critiques, and of the Subalternists' responses to them, was that of a dispute within an epistemic community rather than a rupture within it.[13]

The more portentous departures came some years into the project, perhaps most famously with Gayatri Chakravorty Spivak's essay "Subaltern Studies: Deconstructing Historiography" in the fourth volume.[14] This was the first sign that the project might be making a transition from cultural Marxism to a more decidedly poststructuralist agenda. This was, of course, a familiar turn. From the start, *Subaltern Studies* had been closely aligned with intellectual trends in the New Left. Within this generation, poststructuralist theory was gaining in popularity by leaps and bounds. If the Subalternists now turned to Foucault and Derrida for inspiration, it would simply be keeping pace with broader shifts. One of the first signs of a shift within the Subalternist collective came in 1986, with the publication of Partha Chatterjee's *Nationalist Thought and the Colonial World*. In this work, while deploying some standard Marxist arguments about Indian nationalism, Chatterjee also offered an initial glimpse of themes he would revisit and deepen over the years—themes that evinced a decidedly postmodern suspiciousness of scientific thought, rationalism, and the larger Enlightenment project. Chatterjee's book was followed in 1989 by Dipesh Chakrabarty's *Rethinking Working-Class History*, which reflected a growing ambivalence toward Marxist frames for labor history, in particular their materialist and rationalist assumptions.[15] By the early 1990s, the traversal to a broadly postmodernist sensibility was more or less complete. While the annual volumes still published essays continuing the call for history from

---

12   For examples, see Suneet Chopra, "Missing Correct Perspective," *Social Scientist* 10:8 (Aug. 1982), 55–63; Sangeeta Singh et al., "*Subaltern Studies II*: A Review Article," *Social Scientist* 12:10 (Oct. 1984), 3–51.

13   For examples of such responses, see Partha Chatterjee, "More on Modes of Power," in Ranajit Guha, ed., *Subaltern Studies II* (Delhi: Oxford University Press, 1983).

14   Gayatri Chakravorty Spivak, "Subaltern Studies: Deconstructing Historiography," in Ranajit Guha, ed., *Subaltern Studies IV* (Delhi: Oxford University Press, 1985), 330–63.

15   Partha Chatterjee, *Nationalist Thought and the Colonial World: A Derivative Discourse?* (London: Zed Press, 1986); Dipesh Chakrabarty, *Rethinking Working-Class History: Bengal 1890–1940* (Princeton: Princeton University Press, 1989).

below, there was now an increasing preoccupation with textual analysis, with marginality rather than exploitation or domination as an axial concept, with the critique of "grand narratives," and so on.[16]

The turn toward a recognizably poststructuralist orientation certainly ensured the project's attractiveness outside the narrow circle of Marxist historians of South Asia. But perhaps equally important was the blue-ribbon reception that the series received in the West starting in the early nineties. The *Subaltern* series had attracted some attention in the West during its initial years, but this was largely confined to area specialists and a small circle of historians. To be sure, it was seen as a bracing development that Indian historians were taking up themes that had so enlivened scholarship in the West in the recent past. But this was happening across the spectrum in area studies—in African studies, especially in South Africa, among Latin Americanists, and also in some quarters of Middle Eastern studies.[17] There was nothing especially exotic or singular about the turn in Indian historiography. What made the Subalternists stand out was the incorporation of their project into the most dynamic trend in post-Marxist theorizing in the West, within which they found some powerful patrons. The first was, as mentioned, Gayatri Chakravorty Spivak, who parachuted into the project in 1985 with her essay in the fourth volume. Even more significant was the publication, in 1987, of *Selected Subaltern Studies*, which included a foreword, and hence endorsement, by Edward Said, an imposing presence on the intellectual scene by the late 1980s whose 1978 book *Orientalism* had already become a modern classic. As a result, the publication of *Selected Subaltern Studies* not only brought the project to Western academic circles, but delivered it with the imprimatur of two leading lights of cultural theory.

The marriage of Subaltern Studies to post-Marxian cultural theory was a dramatic success. It was from a reading of the early volumes that a leading American scholar of South Asia claimed, with no hint of irony or embarrassment, that "Indians are, for perhaps *the first time since colonization*, showing sustained signs of reappropriating the capacity to represent themselves."[18] The framework being developed by the collective soon became an object for more

---

16   Two examples of this turn are Gyan Prakash, *Bonded Histories: Genealogies of Labor Servitude in Colonial India* (Princeton: Princeton University Press, 1990); and Ajay Skaria, *Hybrid Histories: Forests. Frontiers, and Wildness in Western India* (Delhi: Oxford University Press, 1999).

17   It is interesting that South African historiography was moving in a direction largely parallel with that of India in the 1980s, with a strong turn to history from below and a kind of Gramscian Marxism. Key to this development were the works of Charles van Onselen, Belinda Bozzoli, Shula Marks, Dan O'Meara and others. The intellectual history is very ably charted by Martin J. Murray in "The Triumph of Marxist Approaches in South African Social and Labour History," *The Journal of Asian and African Studies* 23:1–2 (1988), 79–101. But these works never received the same attention in broader circles as did their Indian counterparts.

18   Ronald Inden, "Orientalist Constructions of South Asia," *Modern Asian Studies* 20:3 (1986), 445. Emphasis added. Better late than never, one might say . . .

general discussion among area-oriented scholars. A conspicuous marker of its impact was the decision by the *American Historical Review,* in 1994, to host a symposium on the project's importance to the historiography of the Global South.[19] But while the appearance of such a debate in the discipline's flagship journal was certainly noteworthy, it was only one example of the growing notoriety of Subaltern Studies as a theoretical tendency. Anthologies of not merely the group's essays but also of the surrounding debates began to appear.[20] By the turn of the century, there was even a Latin American Subaltern Studies group[21] and a journal devoted primarily to exploring the ramifications of the Subalternist approach for historical, cultural, and political analysis.[22]

1.3 SUBALTERN STUDIES AS THEORY

Subaltern Studies is a distinct, influential, and representative stream within postcolonial studies, perhaps more than any other. But can it be identified with the production of an interesting theory? If the phenomenon merely consisted in a revamped call for history from below, as seemed to be the case in its early years, or a jeremiad against the depredations of colonialism, or the celebration of Third World agency, then whatever else it achieved, it could hardly merit attention as a theoretical project. The matter is complicated somewhat by the fact that the obscurity of much poststructuralist theorizing resists easy delineation of its claims, and although *Subaltern Studies* is less given to such murkiness, the project is by no means free of it. No critic can approach the task of explicating its central theoretical commitments without trepidation. But, as it happens, members of the collective have, on a few occasions, offered a summary of the project's core theoretical agenda. One of the more recent of these, an essay by Dipesh Chakrabarty titled "A Small History of Subaltern Studies," is also the clearest and most comprehensive to date.[23]

One of the most striking revelations in Chakrabarty's presentation is that *Subaltern Studies* was, from the start, a fundamentally theoretical enterprise. In other words, in the collective members' own view, their work was oriented toward

---

19   See the symposium in the *American Historical Review* 99:4 (Dec. 1994), with essays by Gyan Prakash, Florencia Mallon, and Frederick Cooper.

20   Gyan Prakash, *After Colonialism: Imperial Histories and Postcolonial Displacements* (Princeton: Princeton University Press, 1995); David Ludden, *Reading* Subaltern Studies: *Critical History, Contested Meaning and the Globalisation of South Asia* (Delhi : Permanent Black, 2001); Vinayak Chaturvedi, ed., *Mapping Subaltern Studies and the Postcolonial* (London: Verso, 2000).

21   Representative essays from this genre are collected in Ileana Rodríguez, ed., *The Latin American Subaltern Studies Reader* (Durham: Duke University Press, 2001).

22   This was *Neplanta: Views from the South.* Apparently the journal was only in print from 2000 to 2003.

23   Chakrabarty, "Subaltern Studies and Postcolonial Historiography," republished as "A Small History of Subaltern Studies," in Dipesh Chakrabarty, *Habitations of Modernity* (Chicago: University of Chicago Press, 2002), 3–19.

producing not just a new historiography but also a challenge to the dominant theories that framed historical analysis. A second, equally striking element in Chakrabarty's account is that the theory taken by the Subalternist collective as its main interlocutor was not the mainstream, but rather the Marxism from which it emerged. Following a somewhat perfunctory initial account of nationalist and conservative historiography, which undoubtedly framed some early concerns of the collective, Chakrabarty settles into his essay's primary task, which is to show how *Subaltern Studies* engaged, and then overcame, the blinders imposed by Marxist theory. The elevation of Marxist theory to such a central place in the Subalternist theoretical project may not be entirely accurate, for there is no doubt that liberal political philosophy has taken quite a beating at their hands. But there is no denying that the shadow of Marxism looms very large over the collective's project, perhaps more so than any other framework. In what follows, I draw on Chakrabarty's account to lay out the main propositions generated by the project and also try to explain very briefly the reasoning behind them.

Lurking behind the positive theory developed by Subaltern Studies is a story—a "narrative," they would say—of political and economic modernization. This story forms the foil against which they develop their own theory. They often refer to it as Marxist in its essentials, though this is misleading. It is more an amalgam of liberal and Marxist elements, which cohere around a particularly Whiggish interpretation of the onset of modernity. The Marxism, therefore, is of a particular *kind*, and would scarcely be recognized by many contemporary Marxists. But that is another matter, and we will set it aside for now. The story appears in bits and pieces, not only in Chakrabarty's account but also in essays by other Subaltern Studies theorists. Its elements are introduced only to be knocked down, and yet if we piece together the various strands, we can glean the story's basic contours. Having a sense of its essential structure will help sharpen our understanding of what the Subalternists feel is novel about the framework they have developed.

THE CONVENTIONAL STORY

We will refer to the story against which Subaltern Studies frames its work as the Conventional Story. At its core is a set of claims about the onset and spread of capitalism: Modern society is the product of the rise of this economic system and its subsequent spread into the world. Capitalism struck its roots initially in Western Europe, coming to life through struggle—a political struggle against feudal rule, which constituted a block to bourgeois development. This political struggle was led by the bourgeoisie, a class of incipient capitalists functioning in the interstices of feudal society. In England and France, the bourgeoisie was able to gain a leading position in emerging political coalitions, because it was able to bring other social groups together under a common banner. In other words, capital succeeded in securing political hegemony over an antifeudal coalition.

This it accomplished because it was able to present its own interests as the basis for the furtherance of its partners' interests. Having established its leadership, the bourgeoisie led a struggle of increasing intensity against the monarchy, culminating in the classic bourgeois revolutions—the English in 1640, the French in 1789. These revolutions constituted the onset of bourgeois rule in the most advanced zones of Western Europe.

Once in power, the conquering bourgeoisie fundamentally transformed national economic and political institutions. It abolished feudal regulations in agriculture and, more haltingly, in cities, opening up the sluices for the spread of capitalism. On the political front, it did away with lordly despotism, established the rule of law, and most important, affirmed certain basic democratic rights for the people. In other words, it created the fundamental pillars of modern citizenship. This formed the basis for the emergence of modern politics—a politics organized around individual rights, the aggregation of different interests, and formal contestation in the public sphere. This was a politics fundamentally different from the premodern variety, which was confined to a narrow stratum of the lordly class and characterized by the dominance of religious discourse and the power of the courtly faction in matters of public contestation. What made all this possible was the emancipation of peasants and workers from feudal bonds, from the myriad sources of interpersonal domination around which the ancient regime had been organized. What took place was nothing less than a fundamental transformation of national culture. The entire structure of feeling, in the wake of bourgeois rule, was reorganized around modern citizenship and secular politics.

Having secured its rule in Western Europe, capital could not rest easy in its new domain. The new industrial masters fanned out into the world, searching for new avenues of profit. In much the same way that capital had established itself in the folds of the feudal economy, it now established beachheads in the New World and Asia. The Conventional Story predicted that the arrival of capitalists on the shores of these lands should set in train a process rather similar to that experienced in Europe. Finding local precapitalist social relations an obstacle to its ceaseless hunt for profits and markets, capital was expected to slowly drive out the local rulers and act as a solvent on local economic relations. That this process would occur under the auspices of formal colonial rule did not alter the fundamental direction of history. Colonialism would serve as the handmaiden of historical progress; if anything, it would enable an acceleration of the dynamic, as the European bourgeoisie would use the levers of state power to hasten the modernization of the local economy. As local economic relations morphed into modern capitalist ones, the colonial world would begin to be organized around modern political practices as well. The independence movements that drove imperial powers out of the South were the first real expressions of this political form, but it was also instantiated in the emergence of trade unions, political parties, and, of course, formal democratic institutions.

The upshot of the Conventional Story is that capitalist modernization was a global phenomenon, albeit one whose spread was temporally and spatially differentiated. Even though the colonized world came to it later, there was little doubt that it would track the grooves laid down by the advanced world. The engine that drove this process was constituted by industrialism and modern economic practices, and the accompanying political and cultural transformation was part of the package. This was capital's universalizing mission, as conventionally understood. It endowed the modern era with a recognizable Zeitgeist. This carried an important implication: namely, that it is possible to slot practices and even forms of consciousness into their appropriate places in the progression from premodern to modern. Europe showed the developing world a rough picture of its own future. Thus, if social agents in the latter regions were found to have exhibited forms of consciousness that did not conform to modern expectations, then it must be because they had not been fully subjected to the cleansing effect of capitalist relations. The cure, at least in part, would be simply to wait—to allow capitalism to do its work and imbue the agents with a modern orientation. Thanks to capital's ceaseless quest for hegemony, there would be a slow, but quite certain, global convergence around characteristically bourgeois forms of cultural and political reproduction.

THE SUBALTERN STUDIES RESPONSE

A central concern of the Subaltern Studies collective has been to reject central components of the Conventional Story, whether in Marxist or liberal guise. Much of their theorizing about the colonial and postcolonial world can be understood as a double movement—the rejection of core propositions of this orthodoxy, followed by an exploration of the implications of this rejection for our broader understanding of the colonial world and, more generally, of the Global South. And just as the Conventional Story begins with a thesis about the agent driving forward the modernizing project, so too do the Subalternists. The core arguments are summarized in the following two theses about the peculiarities of capitalism in the East.

The Specificity of Colonial Capitalism

- *Thesis 1: A Nonhegemonic Bourgeoisie*
The first source of the colonial world's divergence from the European trajectory is the character of its bourgeoisie. It is not that no capitalist class existed in the East. Rather, it is that the bourgeoisie under colonialism was either unable to, or chose not to, secure a leading position for itself in the struggle against the ancien régime. This is true for capitalists from the metropole, who went to the colonies under the patronage of the Europeans, as well as for local entrepreneurs who grew to maturity under colonial rule. These bourgeois classes, of course, exercised a great deal

of power. But they did not take up cudgels against dominant landed classes of the ancien régime. Instead, both segments of the bourgeoisie accommodated to the interests of the latter, thereby incorporating them into the modern political order. The result, Chakrabarty notes, was that "there was no class in South Asia comparable to the European bourgeoisie of Marxist metanarratives"—in other words, a bourgeoisie committed to eradicating the feudal order and capturing state power in order to revolutionize the political culture.[24]

Their eschewal of revolutionary ambitions meant, in turn, that there was little chance the capitalists would try to bring popular classes under their umbrella in a national-popular struggle against the traditional order, for they had sworn off taking on the feudal landed classes in a frontal assault. As a result, they would fail to appease the peasantry, since the main target of peasant animus was the landed overlord. Nor would the capitalists be able to promise workers a rising standard of living, since a backward agriculture would remain a drag on growth rates. Thus, Guha concludes, whereas the European bourgeoisie had come to power by forging a hegemonic coalition with workers and peasants, there would be no parallel experience in the colonial world. The bourgeoisie would exercise dominance, but not hegemony.

• *Thesis 2: The Derailment of Capital's Universalizing Drive*
The bourgeoisie's abrogation of a revolutionary course of action in India, its refusal to dismantle the pillars of feudal power, is taken to signify a deeper historical truth: that in its colonial venture, capital abandoned its "universalizing mission."[25] Universalization for the Subalternists seems to refer to two aspects of capitalism, the first of which is the ability of capital to present its interests as consistent with the interests of other classes, even those it exploits. This, for Guha, constitutes the key to the classic bourgeois revolutions in England and France. A rising bourgeoisie, in both cases, was able to overthrow feudalism because it successfully presented its own interests as congruent with those of peasants and workers, and in so doing, forged a social coalition under its leadership, a coalition it then mobilized to overthrow the feudal monarchy. In this instance, capital's universalizing drive refers to its ability to rise above the pursuit of its narrow sectional interests and make common cause with those of other classes.

The second aspect is the implantation of social institutions that reflect the politics and culture typical of bourgeois rule. These are taken to be those institutions that can be identified with liberalism and citizenship: formal equality, political freedoms, contractualism, secularism, and so forth. For the Subalternists,

---

24   Dipesh Chakrabarty, *Provincializing Europe* (Princeton: Princeton University Press, 2000), 15.

25   Ranajit Guha refers to the universalization of capital, sometimes as a "tendency", other times as a "drive." See Guha, *Dominance without Hegemony: History and Power in Colonial India* (Cambridge: Harvard University Press, 1997), 16, 19, 65, 102.

the link between capitalism and liberalism is very strong. It rests, perversely, on their acceptance of certain aspects of the Conventional Story, in which the bourgeoisie is understood to have fought not only for economic freedoms but also for political liberties. Once they had displaced the feudal ruling classes, the story goes, the bourgeoisie forged a social order based on both kinds of freedoms—the right to property, as well as political freedoms. This order of rights and liberties was granted to all, creating a national political community that overcame the localism and particularism of the ancien régime. Universalism is, in this instance, the spread of political liberalism as an accompaniment to the economic hegemony of capital.

The putative derailment of capital's universalizing drive is very significant for postcolonial theory, and for the Subalternist project in particular. Socially, it signals that the deep political and cultural transformations that accompanied the rise of capitalism were not in the East's cards—at least, not in any way that could fit into the standard liberal or Marxist framework. This is because the agent taken by the Subalternists as having ushered in these transformations—the emerging bourgeoisie—failed to demonstrate any such inclinations once it arrived on Eastern shores. From this sociological fact is derived a theoretical conclusion: if the social matrix and developmental arc of the modernizing Global South are not the same as those of early modern Europe, if their dominant political and cultural forms depart so radically from those of the modern West, then the theories imported from the West cannot be appropriate to the study of Eastern settings. As a result, the East needs its own, sui generis theoretical categories.

The Specificity of Colonial Modernity and the Dislodging of Eurocentrism

We move now to the implications of the argument from uniqueness. Theses 3 through 5 examine the consequences for political power and nationhood, while thesis 6 takes up the problem of Eurocentrism

- *Thesis 3: Colonialism and the Pluralization of Power*
Since colonial capitalism does not seek to overthrow the feudal landed classes, and instead merely accommodates them, it also backs away from eliminating the concomitant forms of domination. Unlike what took place in Europe, where an ascendant bourgeoisie swept away antiquated power relations even as it set about displacing feudal rule, the bourgeoisie in colonial and postcolonial settings learned to live with them. Thus one finds coexistence and active reproduction of classically bourgeois power relations—such as the wage relation—with forms of subordination typically associated with precapitalist social formations. It follows that modernity in such a setting will not keep to the same path as in Europe, with the same basic institutions, their verisimilitude increasing with time. Instead it will be an altogether different kind of modernity, one in which

apparently outdated power relations will be reproduced alongside more "modern" ones. This is an index of the fact that the bourgeoisie in colonial conditions failed "to live up to its own universalizing project."[26]

The immediate implication of this survival of antediluvian forms of social domination, Chakrabarty argues, is to force us to rethink the nature of power. In Europe, where the bourgeoisie was able to transform the social order, power came to be aligned with the rule of capital. Not so in colonial modernity. Guha's analysis, observes Chakrabarty, "fundamentally pluralizes the history of power in global modernity and separates it from any universal history of capital."[27] Hence, even while capital can be seen to expand around the globe, "the global history of capitalism need not reproduce everywhere the same history of power . . . [C]apital and power can be seen as analytically separable categories." Marxists are the primary targets of this admonishment, since they are held to assume a co-linearity between capital and power. If one accepts that a disjuncture between the two is possible, then the relevance of canonical Marxism cannot but suffer: the "traditional European-Marxist political thought that fuses the two [i.e., capital and power] is therefore always relevant but always inadequate for theorizing power in colonial-modern histories."[28]

- *Thesis 4: The Two Domains of Colonial Politics*

Colonial capital's refusal to take up its universalizing mission, its willingness to accommodate the ancien régime, has some important implications for political analysis. First, since it leaves untouched older forms of power, and therefore also the political idiom linked to those power relations, it means that the bourgeoisie does not integrate subaltern culture into its own modernizing discourse. A split between the two domains persists, so that the elite and the popular remain distinct social formations. This does not by any means suggest they are entirely independent of each other; it means rather that there is a recognizable "subaltern" domain of politics, related to, but distinct from, that of the ruling classes. This state of affairs is held to be in sharp contrast to Europe, where, claim the Subalternists, as an index of its hegemony a revolutionary bourgeoisie successfully integrated the popular into the domain of elite and organized politics.

Second, the persistence of this subaltern domain means that forms of political engagement typically associated with premodern politics will persist in modern times, as will the idiom in which the struggles of the poor and the oppressed have long been formulated. The language of a recognizably bourgeois politics will not be universal. Indeed, the assumption that politics is organized around the rational pursuit of individual interests becomes problematic. Often politics will be waged in

---

26   Guha, quoted in Chakrabarty, "Small History," 13.
27   Ibid., 12.
28   Ibid., 13.

religious language and around religious issues. Furthermore, the dominant axis will typically be community/ethnicity, not individual or class interests.

If peasant struggles in India are organized around caste or ethnic groupings, or are expressed in nonsecular terms, it is not a sign of their being "prepolitical," and hence premodern, as the Subalternists accuse Marxists such as Eric Hobsbawm to be claiming.[29] Instead, it shows they are thoroughly political and modern, for they reflect the fundamentally different character of colonial modernity. European political theory commits the error of equating modernity with recognizably bourgeois forms of power and political discourse. Colonial modernity, however, generates a break between these two; it produces a capitalism that *accommodates* to the hierarchies and the culture of the ancien régime. This is capitalism, yes, but without capitalist power relations and without a recognizably capitalist culture. Politics in such settings is therefore "heteroglossic in its idioms and fundamentally plural in its structure, interlocking within itself strands of different types of relationships that [do] not make up a logical whole."[30] If peasant political consciousness here does not resemble that of the Western laboring classes, it is because it cannot. The problem is not with the peasant, but with the expectations of the scholar, who brings to the table of analysis an unwarranted teleology.

- *Thesis 5: The Spuriousness of Colonial Nationalism*

Once it is accepted that, because of the absence of a universalizing bourgeoisie, there remained a gulf between the elite and popular domains within the culture, it cannot but affect our understanding of colonial nationalism. For colonial apologists, the colonial state was an agent of progress because it imported European culture into the conquered territories, a culture that lifted the native population from its rude state into modern civilization. It created a nation where once there was none. For nationalist historians, on the other hand, the rejection of colonial apologetics did not lead to a thorough critique of colonial capitalism. They replaced the flawed premise of colonialism's civilizing mission with a bland acceptance of a purportedly hegemonic domestic bourgeoisie. Nationalist historiography endowed the nationalist movement's leaders with a spurious legitimacy, since it is assumed that this leadership spoke for the nation.

An acceptance of the Subalternist critique of colonial capitalism requires a rejection of both the colonial and the nationalist theorizations of the independence movement and the state to which it gave birth. Chakrabarty concludes that the Subalternist theorization of nationalism calls for a "critical stance toward such official or statist nationalism and its attendant historiography."[31] The foun-

---

29 Ibid., 9–11. See especially p. 11 for Chakrabarty's characterization of Hobsbawm.
30 Ibid., 13.
31 Ibid., 14.

dation of their rejection of official nationalism was their observation that two spheres of politics persisted—the popular and the elite—the coexistence of which was the "index of an important historical truth, that is, the failure of the bourgeoisie to speak for the nation."[32] Because the bourgeoisie failed to integrate the elite and subaltern domains into one, there was no question of the nationalist leadership articulating a nation-building project akin to that of the European bourgeoisie, since "there was no unitary nation to speak for."[33] The real question, which the Subalternist historians now undertook to answer, "was how and through what practices an official nationalism emerged that claimed to represent such a unitary nation."[34] Subaltern Studies thus launched not only a critique of nationalist politics, but also of the historiography that endowed this nationalism with a spurious legitimacy.

- *Thesis 6: The Eurocentrism of Classical Theory*

Having examined the social implications of the bourgeoisie's putative abandonment of its universalizing drive, we turn now to the implications for theory. The upshot of the preceding theses is that the colonial and postcolonial social formations cannot be assimilated into the same general framework as those of the advanced West. Not only do they diverge in their basic structure, but they cannot be assumed to be moving along the same broad trajectory of development. From this premise, postcolonial theory draws a seemingly natural conclusion: if the reality of colonial social formations is fundamentally different from that of Western social formation, then theoretical categories generated from the experience of the West cannot be appropriate for an understanding of the East.

Hence, as Chakrabarty avers, "a history of political modernity in India could not be written as a simple application of the analytics of capital and nationalism available to Western Marxism."[35] These analytics are lacking because they are based on the assumption that colonial social formations are sufficiently similar to Western ones—or are on the same path of development—to justify reliance on the same theoretical framework. It is this basic congruence between West and East that the Subalternists deny, and it is this claim that is the basis for their conclusion that Western theories cannot be grafted onto Eastern realities. Two issues in particular stand out: *agency* and *historicism*.

Let us first address agency. For Subalternist theorists, the Eurocentrism of received theory is especially evident in its understanding of political movements. Their critique focuses on the matter of political psychology. Subalternists often accuse Western theorists of imputing a provincial and culturally specific psychology to peasants and workers in the East. Chakrabarty suggests that Marxist

---

32 Guha, quoted at ibid.
33 Ibid.
34 Ibid.
35 Chakrabarty, *Provincializing Europe*, 15.

analysis cannot appreciate the dynamics of labor struggles in colonial India, because it assumes that Indian workers function in a liberal, bourgeois culture. This assumption, he insists, is carried over from Marx's own work on the labor contract, insofar as the latter assumes that both labor and capitalists have internalized bourgeois norms.[36] The most egregious Eurocentric assumption is that workers are motivated by material needs. Chakrabarty takes Marxists to task for assuming that workers make choices based on their *interests*. This assumes that workers are motivated by what he calls a "utilitarian calculus," which he equates with a bourgeois culture. What Marxists fail to understand, he contends, is that workers in India were motivated by an entirely different kind of psychology, namely a psychology specific to their pre-bourgeois culture, wherein choices were not made on "rational" grounds to serve material interests. Rather, workers' choices reflected the premium they placed on community, religion, and honor.

Partha Chatterjee largely embraces the same strictures for the analysis of peasant politics. He warns that agrarian movements in colonial India cannot be subsumed under Marxist or liberal theories, which are organized around the Western notions of interest and rationality—common components in the theories imported from Europe. Among the culprits he lists are Marxism, modernization theory, Chayanovian theories, the disciplines of economics and sociology, and liberal theory more generally. Peasant agency must be understood "in its own constitutive forms,"[37] a mode of understanding that none of the approaches just listed can achieve. "We must," argues Chatterjee, "grant that peasant consciousness has its own paradigmatic form, which is not only different from bourgeois consciousness but in fact its very other."[38] Hence, since peasant consciousness is fundamentally different from the consciousness generated by bourgeois culture, we need new, indigenous categories. Only after Western theories have been set aside can we construct a proper sociology of peasant agency.

As for the second issue, historicism, this is perhaps the most elusive concept in the Subalternist arsenal. It appeared in some essays by Dipesh Chakrabarty during the 1990s, but did not take center stage for the Subalternists until the publication of Chakrabarty's *Provincializing Europe* in 2000. By assembling the earlier work, and providing Chakrabarty with the opportunity to develop the concept further, *Provincializing Europe* places historicism at the very heart of Subalternist theorizing. Unfortunately, being given pride of place has done little to clarify meaning. Chakrabarty not only fails to provide the reader with a clear understanding of historicism, but, as I shall show later in the book, seems quite committed to preserving the concept's opacity.

Chakrabarty identifies historicism with a cluster of arguments: that the

---

36   Chakrabarty, *Rethinking Working-Class History*, 3–5.
37   Partha Chatterjee, "The Nation and Its Peasants," in Chatterjee, *The Nation and Its Fragments: Colonial and Postcolonial Histories* (Princeton: Princeton University Press, 1993), 163.
38   Ibid., 164.

colonial world must follow in the steps of the West, and its future has therefore already been foretold;[39] that there are no discontinuities in historical processes, and thus all elements of a whole are tightly bound together, developing in quiet synchrony;[40] that any institution seeming to fit poorly with modern sensibilities is probably a relic or an anachronism;[41] that all the East need do in order for these unfamiliar elements to disppear is "wait," and they will melt onto the template set by the West.[42] All these assumptions are attributed to Marxism in particular, but viewed as extending back to the Enlightenment tradition. The critique of historicism therefore comprises a core element of Subaltern Studies' critique of Eurocentrism and encapsulates much of what the Subalternists find objectionable about Western political analysis.

Historicism is an outlook that illicitly subsumes local processes into a larger whole. This it does diachronically, in the form of historical teleology, or synchronically, in the form of structural essentialism. Closely bound up with the rejection of historicism, therefore, is the advocacy of what the Subalternists call the "fragment."[43] Fragments are those elements of social life that cannot easily be assimilated into dominant discourse or structures—minority cultures, dissident tracts, oppositional gestures. Fragments are thus part of social life. Social theory does violence to them when it ignores them, pretending that all that is worthy of analysis is the mainstream or the powerful, and also when it recognizes them but refuses to acknowledge their particularity, instead folding them into the mainstream. A postcolonial theory must, therefore, embrace the fragment, not only as a marker of resistance to dominant structures but as an analytical strategy. It is an antidote to the hubris of totalizing theories.

The arguments encapsulated in the preceding six theses do not by any means exhaust Subalternist social theory, nor do they cover all the issues to be taken up in this book. They do, nonetheless, cover much of the ground that the Subalternists have mapped out over the years, and a substantial portion of the claims now associated with their project. For the most part, since they largely follow Chakrabarty's own summation of the collective's contributions, they have the added benefit—especially with regard to the first five theses—of having been confirmed by one of the most active members of the collective. I have followed Chakrabarty fairly closely in my rendering of the theoretical project, in part to block a common response by postcolonial theorists when they come under scrutiny, namely to insist that their views have been misunderstood, distorted,

---

39   Chakrabarty, *Provincializing Europe*, 7.
40   Ibid., 23.
41   Ibid., 242–3.
42   Ibid., 8, 249–51.
43   Gyanendra Pandey, "In Defense of the Fragment: Writing about Hindu-Muslim Riots in India Today," *Representations* 37 (Winter 1992), 27–55

or exaggerated. Such lapses are certainly possible, especially given the turgidity of their prose. Chakrabarty's essay, by contrast, is noteworthy for its succinctness and lucidity, thereby facilitating the task of the critic.

Thesis 6, the final thesis summarized above, regarding the Eurocentrism of Western theories, is not only a well-known element of the postcolonial canon but perhaps its most famous. Indeed, it may surprise readers to encounter some of the more historical theses, especially thesis 1. It is a peculiarity of the Western reception of Subaltern Studies that these more sociological arguments—about capital's abandonment of its "universalizing drive," and the consequences thereof—have been passed over largely in silence, in favor of the conclusions that are derived from them. Yet as we have seen, the claims regarding capital's failed universalization are basic to the project as a whole and, indeed, comprise much of the work of several of its leading theorists, including its most senior member, Ranajit Guha. No assessment of the more well-travelled parts of the Subalternist landscape can afford to ignore the foundations on which they rest, and so, while we will in due course attend to the validity of these more meta-theoretical conclusions advanced by the Subalternists, we are obliged first to examine the historical sociology on which they rest.

1.4 ASSESSING SUBALTERN STUDIES

Mine is not the first critical engagement with Subaltern Studies. Over the years, there have been several careful and quite illuminating discussions of the project as a whole, and of work by individuals associated with it. A great deal of what I have to say in the following chapters will build on the available body of critique. It might be useful, however, to alert the reader to ways in which this book departs from existing treatments.

The first difference has simply to do with timing. Many of the more well-known critiques of the project were published during the early and mid-1990s, before some of its key arguments had been fully developed or had even seen the light of day.[44] This means that several of the more recent strands of its theoretical work have not been given the attention they deserve. Moreover, elements of

---

44   Chief among these were Rosalind O'Hanlon, "Recovering the Subject: Subaltern Studies and Histories of Resistance in Colonial South Asia," *Modern Asian Studies* 22:1 (1988), 189–224; C. A. Bayly, "Rallying around the Subaltern," *Journal of Peasant Studies* 16:1 (1988), 110–20; Tom Brass, "Moral Economists, Subalterns, New Social Movements, and the (Re-) Emergence of a (Post-) Modernized (Middle) Peasant," *Journal of Peasant Studies* 18:2 (1991), 173–205; David Washbrook and Rosalind O'Hanlon, "After Orientalism: Culture, Criticism and Politics in the Third World," *Comparative Studies in Society and History* 34:1 (1992), 141–67; Arif Dirlik, "The Postcolonial Aura: Third World Criticism in the Age of Global Capitalism," *Critical Inquiry* 20:2 (1994), 328–56; Sumit Sarkar, "The Decline of the Subaltern in *Subaltern Studies*," in Sarkar, *Writing Social History*, 82–108. Vinay Bahl, "Relevance (or Irrelevance) of Subaltern Studies," *Economic and Political Weekly* 32:23 (June 7–13, 1997), 1333–44.

the earlier work remained somewhat obscure—and thus their import was not thoroughly appreciated—until their fuller explication in later years. A salient example of this is Guha's argument about capital's abandonment of its universalizing mission, which was briefly outlined in the first volume and presented in bits and pieces over the next few years, but could not be properly grasped till the publication, in 1997, of *Dominance without Hegemony*. So, too, with Chakrabarty's critique of historicism, which was introduced in the early 1990s but did not then attract the attention it is now garnering.[45] Hence, there would seem to be a need for a fresh examination of the project, now that members of the collective have articulated its implications more extensively.

A second difference regards content. Several well-known engagements with Subaltern Studies have, between them, taken on different aspects of the project. One prominent theme has been the worry that the collective has not so much provided an alternative to the Orientalism of Western theories as *revived* it, repackaged as radical chic.[46] Another has been the claim that the agrarian analysis offered by the theorists is not an alternative to Western theories but rather an offshoot of the impeccably Western economics of A. V. Chayanov.[47] Others have noted that the early commitment to popular history was quickly replaced by an obsession with elite discourse, specifically the discourse of the Bengali elite.[48] Yet another theme has been the epistemological claims of the project and, in particular, its flirtation with relativism.[49] Finally, there is now a considerable literature on the Subalternist critique of secularism.[50]

In large measure, I agree with many of these critiques and will amplify some of them in the following chapters. And yet, even though certain aspects of Subaltern Studies have been effectively criticized, the actual theory produced by the

---

45   See the largely positive appraisals by Jacques Pouchepadass, "Pluralizing Reason," *History and Theory* 41:3 (Oct. 2002), 381–91; and Carola Dietze, "Toward a History on Equal Terms: A Discussion of *Provincializing Europe*," *History and Theory* 47:1 (2008), 69–84; for a somewhat more skeptical response, see Barbara Weinstein, "History without a Cause? Grand Narratives, World History and the Postcolonial Dilemma," *International Review of Social History* 50 (2005), 71–93.

46   See especially Sumit Sarkar, "Orientalism Revisited: Saidian Frameworks in the Writing of Modern Indian History," *Oxford Literary Review* 16:1–2 (1994), 205–24; Rajnarayan Chandavarkar, " 'The Making of the Working Class': E. P. Thompson and Indian History," *History Workshop* 43 (Spring 1997), 177–96; Achin Vanaik, *The Furies of Indian Communalism: Religion, Modernity, and Secularization* (London: Verso, 1997); O'Hanlon and Washbrook, "After Orientalism." For an incisive critique of Subaltern Studies' place within postcolonial theory more generally, see Aijaz Ahmad, "Postcolonial Theory and the 'Post' Condition," *The Socialist Register*, 1997, Vol. 33, 353–81.

47   Brass, "Moral Economists, Subalterns."

48   See Ramachandra Guha, "Subaltern and Bhadralok Studies," *Economic and Political Weekly* (Aug. 19, 1995), 2056–58; Sarkar "Decline of the Subaltern."

49   See Arif Dirlik, "The Postcolonial Aura."

50   Some of the articles on this subject are collected in Rajeev Bhargava, ed., *Secularism and Its Critics* (Delhi: Oxford University Press, 1998). The best engagement with Subaltern Studies on this issue is Achin Vanaik's brilliant *Furies of Indian Communalism*.

group has largely escaped scrutiny. Instead, the object of attention has more often been the politics of the project—its motivations, its implications, its place in the broader intellectual landscape. What has been given especially short shrift is the Subalternists' social and historical theory, on which they base the arguments that have drawn the greater part of the critical attention. One intended contribution of the present book is an analysis of these more foundational elements of the Subaltern Studies project and, by extension, the wider gamut of postcolonial studies. Here the primary focus will be the Subalternists' historical sociology, particularly their understanding of the East-West divergence—a subject crucial to their project, albeit one that has garnered very little attention. But I will also address more theoretical matters that have rarely been scrutinized in depth, and more rarely still in tandem with their broader historical claims.

1.5 THE FAILURE OF SUBALTERN STUDIES

Having signaled this book's goals, let me now describe its basic architecture. Readers will have noticed that the main thrust of Subaltern Studies is to stress *difference*. The project's basic message, which is consistent with the broad orientation of postcolonial studies, is that because Western theories are incapable of understanding the dynamics of non-Western societies, their inadequacy calls for a drastic overhaul of fundamental concepts or even the construction of an altogether new framework. The inadequacy of received theories stems from their inability to appreciate the fact that capitalism in the East turned out to have fundamentally different properties than did capitalism in the West.

In the six theses previously enumerated, it is possible to discern three domains in particular where Subalternist theorists stress a fundamental divide between East and West. The first is in the nature of the *bourgeoisie*: the Western bourgeoisie carried forth capital's universalizing drive while its descendant in the East did not. Second, the *power relations* produced by Western capitalism were unlike the power relations capitalism generated elsewhere. Third comes the question of *political psychology*: political actors are motivated by a different set of concerns in the East than they are in the West.

I will argue that the claims for a fundamental difference with regard to capital, power, and agency are all irredeemably flawed. I take up the question of the bourgeoisie in chapters 2 through 4; chapters 5 and 6 examine the issue of power; chapters 7 and 8 examine the problem of political psychology. Chapter 9 then addresses one of the main pillars of recent Subalternist theorizing, Dipesh Chakrabarty's arguments about historicism. I conclude with an assessment of Partha Chatterjee's theory of colonial nationalism.

The main thrust of the book, then, is to elucidate the failure of the arguments from difference, so central to postcolonial theory. Subaltern Studies has been the most ambitious attempt to demonstrate the various dimensions in which East and West diverge, but the attempt has not succeeded. The point is not to insist that there are no differences at all between the two; rather, that the differences, such as they are, are not of the kind described by the Subalternists. Now, this refutation of their historical and political sociology is important in its own right, but it matters also for its theoretical implications. Postcolonial studies has famously advocated an overhaul of the received frameworks of European thought. Again, the call to rethink the basic structure of Western theory is based on the prior claim that the structure of modernity in the East is so different from its structure in the West that the categories developed out of the European experience cannot possibly be adequate for analyzing the East. But if the sociology on which this argument rests is shown to be deeply shaky, then the grandiose claim that we must rethink our understanding of capitalism, politics, history, agency, and everything else is also called into question. If there does not exist a fundamental divergence between East and West—regarding the nature of their bourgeoisie, the power relations in place, and the subaltern groups' motivational structure—then we are permitted to consider the possibility that the theories emerging from the European experience might well be up to the task of capturing the basic structure of Eastern develop-ment in the modern epoch. Instead of being entirely different forms of society, the West and the non-West would, according to this perspective, turn out to be vari-ants of the same species. Further, if they are indeed variations of the same basic form, the theories generated by the European experience would not have to be overhauled or jettisoned, but simply modified.

In order to drive this point home, I complement the critique of Subalternist theories by developing an alternative analysis of the same phenomena they take up. Hence, in the chapters on the bourgeoisie, I show that Ranajit Guha's argu-ment is mistaken and also explicate the essential convergence of capitalist strategies West and East; in the critique of Chakrabarty's analysis of power, I explain how capitalism produces precisely the forms of authority that he deems departures from "bourgeois forms of power"; and in rejecting Chatterjee's and Chakrabarty's account of political psychology in the East, I provide positive evidence that it is the same as the political psychology of actors in the West, bolstering my argument with elements of a theory of rationality in political agency. So, too, with my critique of historicism and of Chatterjee's theory of nationalism. My hope is that readers will not only be persuaded of the weak-nesses of the Subaltern Studies project but that they will also see the strength of the very theories that the Subalternists impugn.

In the course of showing the flimsiness of their case, and offering an alter-native to their account, I hope to show that Subaltern Studies fails to deliver on its two basic promises—that it has developed an explanatory framework adequate for understanding the nature of modernity in the East, and that it is a platform for radical critique.

THE EXPLANATORY FAILURE

Subaltern Studies fails as an explanatory framework because it systematically misrepresents the relationship between capitalism and modernity, both in the East and in the West. It does so in two ways. First, it promotes a distorted understanding of what is distinctive about capitalism as a social system. Subalternist theorists take certain aspects of *twentieth-century* liberal *culture* as being defining characteristics of capitalism itself. Not surprisingly, once capitalism is defined so narrowly, it is easy to conclude that what we have in the East is not capitalism at all or that it is a bastardized version of the system. Recall that this is the perspective embodied in Theses 1–4, that capitalism mutated after its arrival in the colonies, losing its universalizing drive and generating a political order fundamentally different from the order established in early modern Europe. This argument, however, is based on a somewhat tendentious interpretation of the European experience and of capitalism's "universalizing drive." I will show that the arguments promoted by Subaltern Studies on both these issues are fundamentally flawed, because they build into their very definition of capitalism elements that are specific only to its very recent incarnation. Once we generate a more accurate analysis of European modernization, the apparent deviation of the East from some putative norm is revealed as chimerical. In other words, the political conflicts, institutional setups, forms of power, and other factors in postcolonial capitalism turn out to be not so very different from those of its European ancestor.[51] Hence, Subalternist theorists are simply mistaken in their insistence that the basic course of modernity in the East cannot be explained through the lens of capitalism. This is the fundamental thrust of my argument in chapters 2 to 6.

The second way in which the Subalternists misrepresent the relationship between capitalism and modernity is not by obscuring the role of the former but by denying it altogether. In other words, they evacuate capitalism from domains in which its influence has in fact been critical. I will demonstrate this in chapter 10, where I examine Partha Chatterjee's analysis of nationalist ideology. He notes, correctly, that a defining feature of colonial nationalism was a commitment to scientific and economic modernization. The ideology of nationalism thus tended to promote national modernization as a basic goal. Chatterjee

---

51   The Subalternist critique of the Indian bourgeoisie repeats many arguments from an earlier debate among historians about the course of German modernization. In that context, too, German capitalists were indicted for shortcomings based on a highly romanticized conception of the British and French experience. This line of argument was brilliantly criticized in Geoff Eley and David Blackbourn, *The Peculiarities of German History: Bourgeois Society and Politics in Nineteenth-Century Germany* (Oxford: Oxford University Press, 1984). The German debate was preceded by a similar set of arguments among British Marxist historians about England's path to modernity, touched off by E. P. Thompson's well-known article "The Peculiarities of the English," *Socialist Register* 2 (1965), 311–62. Surprisingly, in spite of their obvious relevance, none of these works finds mention in the Subalternist literature.

argues that the turn to modernization came about because national elites had internalized Western discourse, but I will show this argument to be entirely mistaken. Nationalist elites promoted modernization not because they were the victims of indoctrination but because of the pressures of governing in a capitalist world economy. What Chatterjee presents as an effect of discourse was in fact a recognition of real, material pressures from global capitalism. This is an example of how Subalternist theorists simply whisk capitalism out of the picture, even where it played a central role.

It is not that members of the collective pretend capitalism is irrelevant or has no material reality. Indeed, they invoke it constantly. They agree that any viable theory of the modern must take into account its connection to capitalism. The problem is that even while recognizing its importance, they obscure its dynamics—in some instances by endowing it with properties it does not have, in others by denying it powers it does indeed have, and in a few cases, such as Chatterjee's, by "disappearing" it altogether. The result is most curious: while claiming to theorize capitalism's global adventure, they separate the concept from its referent. It is shorn of any properties we might justifiably associate with it. Hence, far from illumining the peculiar trajectory of development in the East, Subalternist theorists shroud it in further mystery. They raise central questions about such matters as the course of political development, the structure of power, social agency, and nationalism but fail time and again to answer them properly, for the connections between these phenomena and broader structural transformations are simply lost from view. In sum, Subalternist theorists do not answer the very question they raise—namely, how the entry of capitalism into the colonial world affected the evolution of its cultural and political institutions.

THE CRITICAL FAILURE

Regarding the status of Subaltern Studies as critique, there are two dimensions of the failure on this front.

The less obvious, though by no means less important, dimension of the failure can be stated quite simply: one cannot adequately criticize a social phenomenon if one systematically misunderstands how it works. Subaltern Studies theorists cannot formulate a critique of globalizing capitalism if their theorization of its basic properties is mistaken. They are unable to separate those phenomena that are generated by capital, from those that are independent of it. Even more important, however, their arguments are not merely erroneous; in fact, they amount to a highly romanticized, even sanitized, presentation of capitalism. This is especially evident in Guha's work but also figures prominently in Chakrabarty's. The romanticization is not intended; it is simply a consequence of the fact that they identify capitalism with its newly minted *liberal* incarnations. Instead of taking liberal, democratic capitalism to be a recent phenomenon, brought about through centuries of struggle, they build its particular features into their bedrock definition of the system. Furthermore, not only do they build liberal freedoms into the definition of capital, they attribute the advent of those freedoms to the European bourgeoisie. Naturally, in a comparison between this idealized picture and the reality of postcolonial capitalism, the latter appears deformed and denatured. But when we replace the idealized picture with a more accurate one, it generates very different conclusions with respect to not only postcolonial capitalism but also the quality of modernity. This is a central pillar of my argument in chapters 3, 4, and 5.

The more obvious failing on the critical front is that, far from landing a blow *against* colonialist and Orientalist presentations of the East, Subaltern Studies has ended up *promoting* them. I show this especially in chapters 7 and 8, but it also arises in chapters 9 and 10. This is not true of all of the collective's members, though. Guha's work is largely free of Orientalism, wheras it is a central plank for both Chakrabarty and Chatterjee,[52] who both insist that laboring classes in India were motivated by fundamentally different conceptions of the self than were their counterparts in the West. Others have noted this aspect of the Subaltern Studies framework and have issued strong objections. I join in this criticism, but in a different vein. Many critics have urged that the Subalternist depictions of agency be rejected because of their Orientalism. The offensiveness of an argument, however, cannot be grounds for its rejection. The fact is, both Chatterjee and Chakrabarty go to considerable lengths to support their arguments empirically and theoretically. The bulk of chapters 7 and 8 is therefore dedicated to arguing that their Orientalism is not just objectionable but *wrong*—their own evidence undermines the claims they make about agency in the East. I augment this argument by offering a bare-bones, but I hope credible, theory of social agency, which is unabashedly universalistic while aiming to avoid charges of parochialism. To minimize accusations of cultural bias, I mainly use as evidence the empirical work of Guha, Chatterjee, and Chakrabarty themselves.

1.6 WHAT THIS BOOK IS NOT

So much for what the book is. Now some words on what it is not. This is not meant to be a history or intellectual biography of Subaltern Studies. I make no claim whatsoever to exhaustiveness or even comprehensiveness. My concern is to address components of the Subalternist project that have had real influence and have, in turn, been highlighted by members of the collective as their most important contributions. My intention is to examine the ideas that have become associated with the project in the broader intellectual culture, not to address the

---

52   Chatterjee tries to present Guha's arguments as coextensive with his own, but as I will show in chapter 8, the attempt is unsuccessful.

project in its entirety. As it happens, I do believe that I address most of the main arguments produced by members of the collective. Mainly because the book threatened to grow beyond a reasonable length, I have had no choice but to omit some. Perhaps the most conspicuous by its absence is Partha Chatterjee's recent work on political society in postcolonial formations. Also missing are Gyanendra Pandey's defense of the fragment and the overall debate on secularism. These are all important issues, but some of them have already received attention, and others will have to just be taken up at another time.

Moreover, this book largely avoids the task of tracing the theoretical lineage of the Subalternists' arguments. As a result, even though the influence of Gramsci and Althusser is evident to those familiar with the relevant literature, I do not analyze the nature of this connection. Nor do I assess how their ideas have been reconfigured at the hands of Subalternist theorists.[53] Again, this is partly because of the need to keep the book to a manageable size (and it is already longer than I had either wished or intended), but primarily because of my desire that the reader not be distracted by whether Subalternists have correctly interpreted a given theorist. What matters is not whether they are true to this or that theoretical tradition but whether they have produced sound arguments, and it is that final product—their arguments *as they stand*—that we need to assess.

Finally, I would like to say something about style. Readers will find that I rely a certain amount on direct quotations of passages—sometimes long ones— from the texts I subject to critique. As a reader, I find it distracting, choppy, even annoying. Normally I avoid it as much as possible, but I resort to it here in order to preempt charges of misrepresentation. I want the reader to be able to judge the merits of my arguments about key texts, and so I reproduce the relevant passages in full. But I also provide summaries for readers whose eyes, like mine, tend to glaze over in such circumstances.

However, there is another reason for this strategy. Several of the main theorists bury their arguments under a dense thicket of jargon, or present them so cryptically that the meaning is hard to nail down. The critic is therefore left with little choice but to interpret them to as best she can. Naturally this injects uncertainty into the argument. Here, again, the best antidote is to let the reader see the relevant texts so that she may form her own judgment about my rendering of them. No doubt there remains an element of interpretation in the task, but this is the case even when one deals with texts of exemplary clarity.

---

53   For an interesting set of arguments on Gramsci's incorporation into postcolonial studies and the Subalternist oeuvre, see Timothy Brennan, *Wars of Position: The Cultural Politics of Left and Right* (New York: Columbia University Press, 2006).

CHAPTER TWO

Dominance without Hegemony: The Argument Explained

Subaltern Studies is known for advocating—and, it is claimed, exemplifying—a rejection of Eurocentric theories inherited from the nineteenth century. If the theories they implicate are indeed Eurocentric, then they should be rejected outright. But first a relevant question presents itself: Are the characterizations accurate? We need to understand why, as Dipesh Chakrabarty contends, the modern experience of the East "could not be written as a simple application of the analytics of capital and nationalism available to Western Marxism."[1]

Chakrabarty and other Subalternist theorists acknowledge that many of the foundational historical arguments for this thesis were either developed in or inspired by the work of Ranajit Guha, who starting in the very first volume of *Subaltern Studies*, offered a historical sociology of colonial India that sought to establish the specificity of colonial modernity. His focus was the Indian experience, but the relevance of these essays is considered to extend far beyond the Subcontinent. Guha argued that while liberal and colonial ideology described Indian political development as coextensive with the European experience, in fact the modernization of India departed in basic ways from that of Western Europe. The differences were significant enough to create a qualitatively different kind of political culture in South Asia. It is on the basis of this argument that much subsequent Subalternist theorization proceeded.

The root cause of the East-West divergence is taken to reside in the peculiar nature of the colonial bourgeoisie. As summarized in theses 1 and 2 in the preceding chapter, it is the absence of a revolutionary bourgeoisie that accounts for the persistence of two parallel political domains, the elite and the subaltern. Had capital in the colonial setting not forsaken its "universalizing mission," it would have integrated subaltern culture into its own liberal worldview as part of its hegemonic strategy. In so doing, it would have generated a coherent culture, as was purportedly achieved in Europe. But in colonial India, Guha suggests, capital attained dominance without integrating the dominated classes into either its own worldview or the institutions characteristic of its rule in Europe. There thus remained a chasm between elite and subaltern domains. Hence, political culture in colonial and postcolonial settings did not and could not converge with the patterns observed in Europe. The subaltern domain

---

1 Dipesh Chakrabarty, *Provincializing Europe* (Princeton: Princeton University Press, 2000), 15.

continued to subsist as a distinct sphere, even though it could not remain hermetically sealed from elite influence. The persistence of this divide in the postcolonial world is what motivates the call for a new framework, because, the Subalternists declare, Marxist and liberal theories attain validity only in settings with a secure bourgeois culture.

This is a remarkably ambitious and exciting set of arguments. If successful, they would provide the Subalternist project with a powerful historical sociology on which could rest its more ambitious and widely known pronouncements. It is therefore remarkable how little attention these arguments have drawn. While his work has elicited a great deal of commentary, it is Guha's theorization of peasant rebellion in *Elementary Aspects of Peasant Insurgency in Colonial India* that has attracted the most attention (though, as I shall argue in Chapter 7, there has been a rather dramatic misrepresentation of the book, often by the Subalternists themselves).[2] Yet even while *Elementary Aspects* has attained a special status in postcolonial studies, it is not the site at which Guha developed his case for the two roads to bourgeois power. Initially he presented these arguments, albeit in highly telescoped form, in *Subaltern Studies'* debut collection in 1982.[3] He then developed them further in two essays published in 1989 and 1992, which were brought together in 1997 in the aptly titled *Dominance without Hegemony*.[4] It is this pair of essays that develop the arguments relevant to our discussion. In an important sense, even though Guha elaborated his views on this issue following the release of *Elementary Aspects of Peasant Insurgency*, the latter presupposes the basic framework laid down by the former. So, if the wider arguments in the Subalternist oeuvre are to be assessed, the first requirement is an appraisal of the historical sociology on which they rest, as developed by Guha. It is to this task that the present chapter, and the two that follow, are devoted.

2.1 SUBALTERN STUDIES IN CONTEXT

Subaltern Studies was born of crisis. In a retrospective look at the project's origins, Ranajit Guha recalls the sense of frustration and bewilderment felt by many Indian radicals, especially the younger ones, during the 1970s. In the latter half of the 1960s, India had descended into its deepest political crisis since

---

2 Ranajit Guha, *Elementary Aspects of Peasant Insurgency in Colonial India* (Delhi: Oxford University Press, 1983).

3 Ranajit Guha, "On Some Aspects of the Historiography of Colonial India," *Subaltern Studies I* (Delhi: Oxford University Press, 1982), 1–8.

4 Ranajit Guha, *Dominance without Hegemony: History and Power in Colonial India* (Cambridge: Harvard University Press, 1997), henceforth cited as *DH*. The volume also contained Guha's 1988 S. G. Deuskar Lecture. The two essays in question are "Dominance without Hegemony and Its Historiography," which was included in *Subaltern Studies VI* (1989), and "Discipline and Mobilize: Hegemony and Elite Control in Nationalist Campaigns," originally published in *Subaltern Studies VII* (1992).

Independence. The Indian National Congress (INC) had been through a bitter leadership battle after Jawaharlal Nehru's death in 1964, from which his daughter, Indira Gandhi, emerged as party leader and prime minster, but not before a bruising confrontation with regional party bosses. Furthermore, India had its second war with Pakistan in 1971, which also caused massive economic hardship for working people, triggering a significant upswing in industrial conflict and culminating in a historic strike by the Indian railway union, which, at its peak, involved well over a million workers. Although the strike lasted only about three weeks, its scope was enormous, shutting down much of the national rail system, and only massive state mobilization of the police and paramilitary forces achieved its defeat.[5] In the countryside, peasant actions in West Bengal and Andhra Pradesh were being organized by breakaway Communist activists, who soon came to be known as Naxalites, and who declared the bankruptcy of not only the Congress Party but the two major Communist parties as well. And in 1975, Indira Gandhi declared a nationwide state of emergency, suspending constitutional liberties and unleashing a wave of repression across the country. The Emergency lasted almost two years, and when, in a fit of hubris, Gandhi called for national elections in 1977, fully expecting to win, the outcome was an overwhelming defeat for the INC by a loose coalition of opposition parties. For the first time since 1947, the Congress had been ousted from power in Delhi.

This decade-long crisis formed the backdrop to the launch of *Subaltern Studies*. As Guha recalls, the events of the 1970s called into question the national mythology about Indian political culture. At the very least, the political maelstrom belied the Indian National Congress's claim to represent the masses. The ruling elite could not unleash its wave of repression while still claiming "the ascendancy of the Congress to power in independent India as the fulfillment of a promise of *rulership by consent*."[6] But the doubts did not stop there. The crisis years had exposed a chasm separating the political universe of the ruling elite from the culture of subaltern groups. The whole idea of a national political body, a new and encompassing ethos that bound the polity together at independence, seemed now to be no more than a shibboleth. "What came to be questioned," Guha writes, "was thus not only the record of the ruling party which had been in power for over two decades by then, but also the entire generation that had put it in power."[7]

If Congress rule had not in fact rested on the consent of the masses, then serious questions arose about its rise to power, its connection to the Indian population, its strategy during the independence movement, and so on. "One of

---

5   For a history and analysis of the strike, see Stephen Sherlock, *The Indian Railways Strike of 1974: A Study of Power and Organised Labour* (Delhi: Rupa, 2001).

6   Ranajit Guha, "Introduction," *The Subaltern Studies Reader* (Minneapolis: The University of Minnesota Press, 1997), xix. Emphasis added.

7   Ibid., xiii.

the many unsettling effects" of the 1970s, Guha continues, "was to bring the impact of the twenty-year-old nation-state's crisis to bear on a settled and in many respects codified understanding of the colonial past."[8] What the intellectual ferment called for was a new analysis of Indian politics over the previous half century or so, starting with the final decades of colonial rule. Guha summarizes the issue in two related puzzles:

1. What was there in our colonial past and our engagement with nationalism to land us in our current predicament—that is, the aggravating and seemingly insoluble difficulties of the nation-state?

2. How are the unbearable difficulties of our current condition compatible with and explained by what happened during colonial rule and our predecessors' engagement with the politics and culture of that period?[9]

The turbulent decade thus pressed into relief an intellectual project: to undertake a reexamination of late colonial politics, and thereby to generate an explanation for the political turmoil in which the nation was now embroiled, three decades after Independence. Central to this project would be an investigation of the real roots of Congress power, an explication of its inability to mold a cohesive nation-state, an exploration of its resort to coercion to maintain its rule, and a discussion of what this revealed about the dominant order. It is important now, three decades after the launching of *Subaltern Studies*, to recall that the inspiration was, at its core, political. It was geared to achieve an understanding of the roots of the political order that colonialism had bequeathed to the Subcontinent. The goal was to inaugurate a new historiography of colonialism, and of the nationalist response to British rule, as a step toward understanding the crisis of the postcolonial state.

2.2 THE ROOTS OF THE POSTCOLONIAL CRISIS

The core elements of the Subalternist collective's theorization of India's political crisis were offered in the inaugural volume of *Subaltern Studies*, in its opening pages.[10] It was Ranajit Guha who introduced the argument, and he did so as a set of numbered propositions, which captured the two axes that became central to much of his later work—the roots of the political impasse, and the failure of existing historiography to account for it. Guha began by noting that an encompassing political culture did not exist in India. Instead, the colonial era produced

---

8   Ibid.
9   Ibid., xi.
10   Guha, "On Some Aspects of the Historiography."

an enduring divide between the spheres of elite political and subaltern politics. Elite politics was coextensive with the domain of formal juridical institutions; this was the dimension of Indian political culture that had been modernized with the onset of colonialism, through which British administrative and juridical practices had been transplanted over the course of their rule. The elite political sphere was, of course, inhabited by the European elites who managed the colonial state apparatus; it also included, Guha seems to suggest, their Indian collaborators—those sections of the domestic ruling class that were recruited into the colonial order. To be sure, these new institutions were not entirely pristine replications of their European counterparts; of necessity, they had to be fused with elements of the precolonial state apparatus inherited from the Mughal state. Nevertheless, this domain of politics had its own integrity and its own practices.

While elite politics could be identified with the modern, formal institutions built around the colonial state, subaltern politics constituted a distinct domain, set apart from that of the ruling classes, with an idiom and practices of its own. Central to these was a reliance on informal, local networks that were based on kinship, local ties, and the primordial relations typical of traditional agrarian societies; occasionally, under certain conditions, this reliance on local networks also generated class association. Generally, however, whereas the elite domain was characterized by the discourse of law and juridical equality, the subaltern domain was suffused with traditional forms of hierarchy and subordination. The transformation that accompanied colonialism was thus of a certain kind: although it did transplant recognizably "modern" practices to the Subcontinent, these practices remained largely confined to the upper crust of the political system, leaving the culture of the subaltern classes largely intact.

Not only did each domain have its distinct idiom and reproductive practices, it also had its characteristic form of political mobilization. Elites relied on typically oligarchical, top-down strategies to elicit mass support for their campaigns—using parts of the state apparatus, patron-client networks, subtle forms of coercion, the mass media, and so on. Subaltern mobilization, on the other hand, was "horizontal" in its tactical deployment, relying on the same informal associational forms that were central to political reproduction in this sphere. Mainstream historiography, Guha charges, begins with the assumption that political culture under colonial rule was a seamless, integrated whole—it assumes that subaltern culture had become assimilated into that of the dominant classes. Hence, in its examination of elite political practice and discourse, it wrongly assumes that the conclusions derived from a study of this domain will also pertain to the political practice of subaltern groups. But the domains had not in fact been integrated, he reminds us, and the political practice associated with each was quite distinct. Subaltern political mobilization therefore warrants a historiography of its own, sensitive to its peculiarities, its distinctive moral universe—in short, its independence from elite political discourse and design. Only thus can we discover the roots of the present crisis, for it is in the persistent discontinuity between the two domains that we will find the key to the postcolonial state's crisis.

The fissure between elite and subaltern spheres was not preordained, nor was it the outgrowth of certain enduring cultural facts about India. It was, rather, the consequence of a very specific peculiarity of India's colonial experience, "the index of an important historical truth, that is, *the failure of the Indian bourgeoisie to speak for the nation*."[11] What Guha means by this is that the Indian bourgeoisie failed to successfully integrate the culture of the disparate groupings in Indian society into one all-embracing political community. Of particular relevance was its failure to assimilate the laboring classes into its political project, especially in the years leading up to independence from the British. As he observes, "There remained vast areas in the life and consciousness of the people which were never integrated into [the bourgeoisie's] hegemony."[12] The persistence of the two distinct domains is thus a direct consequence of the failure of a *particular* historical agent—namely, the bourgeoisie. And although in this synoptic presentation Guha focuses on Indian capitalists, we will see below that the failure belonged to capital as a whole in the colonial era, in both its European and Indian guises. Had the bourgeoisie secured hegemony, the process of national integration could have been successful, thereby generating a coherent national political culture rather than the fractured dualism that India actually inherited.

Now in this early essay, Guha does point to one other actor who might have been relevant for pushing India in the direction of an integrated political order: the working class. Toward the very end of the piece, he raises the possibility that the nationalist movement could have taken a different path, and produced a different outcome, had labor been able to assert itself more effectively. The bourgeoisie could have been pushed into a subordinate position, or could have been displaced altogether, in the style of a national liberation movement. The reason this did not take place was that "the working class was not sufficiently mature in the objective conditions of its social being and in its consciousness" to pull the movement in a different direction.[13]

This is a curious diagnosis of labor's failure. Was the Indian working class less mature in its objective conditions than the Chinese or Vietnamese? What, in any case, does it mean for conditions to be "mature"? Clearly, one could quibble with Guha's argument. But what is noteworthy is that, at this stage, he opens up the possibility of two distinct outcomes for the Indian nationalist movement,

---

11 Ibid., 5. Emphasis in the original.
12 Ibid., 5–6.
13 Ibid., 6.

and two actors relevant to its course: capital and labor. However, this is the only time that Guha—or his colleagues—contemplates two distinct paths. In his subsequent work, the focus is trained single-mindedly on the capitalist class— its nature, preferences, political strategy, and failings. We will see that this turns out to be a critical failing of *Subaltern Studies*, not just as historiography but also as analysis.

Let us return to the argument about the bourgeoisie's failure to achieve hegemony. For it to have any plausibility, Guha would need to provide two additional pieces of information. First, we would need a working definition of hegemony, to assess whether Indian capitalists did in fact fail at securing it. The concept is notoriously slippery, and if any verdict is to be rendered on the value of Guha's argument, then we need to have a working definition of what the term denotes. Second, and just as important, Guha would need to provide a specific kind of counterfactual, which established two claims implicit in his argument, the first claim being that the relevant agent capable of bringing about an integrated political culture is in fact the bourgeoisie, since it is to the politics and record of this actor that he directs his attention in the Indian case. For the bourgeoisie to shoulder the blame in India, it must have been appropriately successful elsewhere. We must be confident that this actor does have an interest in and capacity for the task Guha assigns it. Second, Guha needs to adduce cases in which this actor did indeed achieve hegemony over subaltern classes, so that not only can we be confident that hegemony is a real possibility but, even more so, have some sense of what hegemony looks like when it actually obtains. In other words, although Guha did not make much of this point when he penned the opening essay to *Subaltern Studies*, the argument for the Indian bourgeoisie's failure is intrinsically and unavoidably *contrastive*. To announce a failure in nation-building or in achieving hegemony simply makes no sense unless judged against historical cases that can be taken as standards of nation-building and genuine bourgeois hegemony. Absent a real historical benchmark, there is no way to assess whether the Indian record is one of relative success or failure—could it not be that the Indian experience just happens to be what hegemony looks like?

Guha took up neither of these challenges in *Subaltern Studies I*. He was content, at that point, to present his core propositions as the signposts of a new research agenda. It was in a series of later essays that he fleshed out what he had in mind when he characterized the bourgeoisie as having failed to gain hegemony; and it was in these essays that he offered some sense of where we might find successful hegemonic projects against which the Indian achievement could be judged. As indicated earlier in this chapter, the two key publications toward this end were first published as "Dominance without Hegemony and its Historiography" (1989) and "Discipline and Mobilize" (1992), and were conjoined as the core of his 1997 book *Dominance without Hegemony*. It was in this book that readers could view Guha's argument at its fullest, inasmuch as he provided both the ingredients missing from his opening salvo in *Subaltern Studies I*. It is to this larger work that we now turn.

2.3 THE TWO PATHS TO BOURGEOIS POWER

Dominance without Hegemony is structured not simply as history but as a critique of what Guha presents as liberal ideology. He argues that the dominant liberal historiography of India, in both its colonial and nationalist versions, suffers from a basic misconception. It assumes that the dominant classes and subaltern groups inhabited the same political and cultural universe. As a result, it blandly assumes that histories of elite strategies and preferences are an accurate stand-in for the political goals and contributions of the lower orders. But for such a state of affairs to have obtained, the dominant class in India—the capitalist class—would have had to establish its hegemony over society as a whole, which is exactly what Guha is concerned to deny. Since the bourgeoisie failed in this regard, the various and sundry political forces did not coalesce into one encompassing community. This was the failure of the nation to "come into its own." And this was what laid down the conditions for the political crisis of the 1970s. But what exactly is hegemony, and how does it generate an encompassing political sphere, bringing together all the disparate social groupings?

Guha defines hegemony as a state in which a class establishes its dominance by relying more on the consent of other classes than it does on coercion. As he presents it, "hegemony stands for a condition of Dominance (D), such that . . . Persuasion (P) outweighs Coercion (C)."[14] Hegemony does not imply the absence of coercion but rather its relegation to a minor role, relative to the importance of persuasion. A hegemonic class maintains its rule by eliciting the active consent of subaltern groups to its dominance in society. In so doing, it "speaks for all of society," as Guha frequently puts it. This ability to "speak for society" is what enables the bourgeoisie to tear down the walls separating elite culture from that of subaltern groups, and thus to incorporate the latter into the political nation. Capital wins over other groups to its rule by accommodating their interests to some significant degree, by creating a polity in which the pursuit of interests is no longer a zero-sum game.[15]

Notably, Guha argues that hegemony is an achievement entirely specific to modern, capitalist polities. It is a condition that was, he argues, impossible in precapitalist systems. Premodern ruling classes had neither the interest nor the capacity to incorporate laboring groups into the political culture. They did not

---

14   *DH* 23.

15   Guha clearly derives his argument from a certain reading of Gramsci, one that was very much in vogue among Marxists during the 1980s. As I indicated in Chapter 1, I will not comment on the merits of his interpretation of Gramsci's work, though I do believe that it is questionable.

strive to elicit subaltern consent, basing their rule instead on brute force or the threat of its application.[16] There was no attempt at persuasion, no "exchange at the level of culture," no process of political education. These polities were despotisms pure and simple. Guha concludes that, strictly speaking, formations such as this "did not have a ruling culture, although there was a ruler's culture operating side by side with that of the ruled in a state of mutual indifference."[17] The potential for their integration into an organic whole came about only with the rise of capitalism, as part of the political project of the rising bourgeoisie.

Now that we have a sense of what the concept of hegemony denotes, we come to the second challenge, namely, what are the cases of the successful attainment of hegemony against which the Indian case is being judged? The arena in which capital was able most clearly to establish itself as the hegemonic class was Western Europe, in particular England and France, and the period in which these advances were made was the early modern era. In fact, the time of capital's ascension to power can be pinpointed with some accuracy, for it was in two revolutionary explosions that the bourgeoisie established its rule: the English Revolution of 1640 and the great French Revolution of 1789. These revolutions marked the arrival of not only a new class but a new form of rule, an entirely new structure of class dominance. The modern bourgeoisie, as exemplified by English and French capitalists, maintained their power through the consent of the masses. In so doing, they also created the modern political nation.

This is the achievement against which the performance of the Indian bourgeoisie is judged. For Guha, the European experience established two things: first, that the bourgeoisie is the critical agent behind the establishment of the modern political nation, with its characteristic political idiom and institutions; and second, that the achievements are most clearly exemplified in the classic bourgeois revolutions of the early modern era. The capitalist class in India had the opportunity to construct its own nation, through a political mobilization of its own, when it participated in the nationalist mobilization against colonial rule. It could have charted a path parallel to the one taken by the classic capitalist classes in Europe, constructing a viable and consensual political order. But, Guha argues, the independence movement merely revealed the Indian bourgeoisie's utter inadequacy, its abject failure to attain real hegemony over the rest of society.

The standard set by the European achievement Guha refers to as the "competence" of the class—its potential as an historic agent; to this he contrasts the "performance" of the actual class, as it was found in India. The difference between its competence and its actual performance is what he is pressing in his later essays—the conditions under colonialism were such that the Indian

16   *DH* 63–4.
17   *DH* 64.

bourgeoisie's performance fell far short of its competence.[18] Indeed, the shortfall was so significant that it constitutes, for Guha, a fact of world-historic significance: it amounts to a "structural fault in the historic project of the bourgeoisie."[19] In other words, even though colonialism created a bourgeoisie on the Subcontinent and placed it on a trajectory that might have followed that of European modernization, this was not to be: the Indian capitalist class was committed to a political project fundamentally different from that of its European predecessors. Colonialism created a bourgeoisie, but one that would not, or could not, forge a recognizably modern political order.

The error of liberal historiography, then, is its assumption that the colonial order was built around real bourgeois hegemony, as was the case in Western Europe. It construes the colonial state as an extension of the liberal state of Great Britain. On the nationalist side, historians have assumed that the Indian bourgeoisie secured the ability to "speak for the nation," much as English and French capitalists had done during the classic bourgeois revolutions. Both of these formulations, however, fail to appreciate the "structural fault" between the bourgeois project as it took shape in Europe, and its local manifestation in the Subcontinent. What, then, explains this fault line separating the trajectory of the classic bourgeois transitions in the West from the bourgeois transitions in the colonies? To explain the disjuncture between the two experiences, Guha must proceed by first establishing the nature of the paradigmatic transformation in Europe and then by examining why a similar transformation was forestalled in India, even though actors of the same kind dominated the scene.

2.4 CAPITAL'S UNIVERSALIZING TENDENCY AND THE BOURGEOIS REVOLUTIONS

For Guha, Europe's political modernization issued from the same underlying forces as its economic modernization—the rise and subsequent ascendance of the capitalist class. Having arisen within the confines of feudal agrarian structures, the emergent bourgeoisie found its further economic expansion blocked by the ancien régime. In order to remove the obstacles to its further expansion, the capitalist class undertook a political struggle against the feudal monarchy. Once in power, the nascent capitalist class consolidated its economic program through legislation that enabled a more rapid spread of markets into the agrarian economy. They also initiated an ambitious program of political and cultural liberalization to round out the process of economic liberalization. As we will see, the central components of this dimension of European development were, for Guha, the creation of liberal political institutions and the eventual forging of

---

18   *DH* 4.
19   *DH* 5.

a national political identity. More to the point, because the construction of these institutions is an achievement attributed to the bourgeoisie, it constitutes the standard against which Indian capital's agency is measured.

Guha, as well as the Subalternists in general, insists that this modernizing project was in turn driven by a deeper structural force, namely, *the universalizing drive of capital*. This concept occupies a central place in their theoretical work; at times they refer to it as a drive, at other times as an urge or even a mission, and sometimes as a tendency. They do take the universalizing drive to have propelled Europe's political and economic transformation, but they also see it as having governed the emergence of the dominant ideologies of the era: liberalism, secularism, and socialism. Thus, while the bourgeoisie's political struggle is the proximate cause of the ancien régime's demise, the struggle is in turn the expression of a deeper motor force. It is necessary, then, to examine what Guha has to say about the connection between capital's universalization and the bourgeois-democratic transformation of Europe. This examination will enable an analysis of why a parallel process could not occur in India, and what the consequences were of this "structural fault" in the bourgeois project.

CAPITAL'S UNIVERSALIZING TENDENCY

At its core, capital's universalizing tendency is simply, for Guha, the drive by capitalists to expand their scope of operations. Although this is an economic imperative, it also brings along with it certain political and cultural transformations. Guha draws directly on Marx's theory in this regard, and his summary statement reads like an introduction to the Moor himself:

> This [universalizing] tendency derives from the self-expansion of capital. Its function is to create a world market, subjugate all antecedent modes of production, and replace all jural and institutional concomitants of such modes and generally the entire edifice of precapitalist cultures by laws, institutions, values, and other elements of a culture appropriate to bourgeois rule.[20]

We should note that the transformative urge has two distinct components for Guha: the economic, which pushes capital to expand into the world, create a global market, and then supplant antediluvian economic forms that stand in its way; and the politico-cultural, which refers to the construction of bourgeois norms and practices in areas where capital takes root. We will have more to say on this distinction later in the present chapter, and a great deal more in chapters 4 and 5. For now, it is enough to underline that Guha is aware of this distinction, and seems to suggest that the two dimensions should be coextensive.

---

20   *DH* 13–14. For Guha's approving quotes from Marx on this matter, see *DH* 14–15.

The propulsive force of capital's self-expansion has some important consequences. The first of these is that it creates an *interest* in overthrowing the ancien
régime. In the orthodox Marxist account, which Guha takes for granted, early
modern capitalists found their expansion blocked by the feudal nobility's political
and cultural dominance. Feudal lords used their influence within the state to
enact legislation that obstructed the further consolidation of capitalist production. Thus, through the use of state levers, premodern economic forms were kept
artificially alive —the protection of noble privileges, the grant of monopoly rights
to particular merchants and regional lords, the numerous price and quantity
controls allowed to guilds, and so on. The fact that such obstacles were encountered by the vast majority of capitalist economic units generated a corresponding
consciousness around a collective project, both political and cultural—a project
to seek state power in order to fashion juridical structures aligned with the needs
of the multiplying capitalist enterprises and to push aside the class of nobles kept
on life support by the state's protection. This is the sense in which capital's universalizing drive created, for the nascent bourgeoisie, an interest and motive to
launch a political struggle against the feudal order.

Another consequence of capital's universalizing drive was to complement the *interest* in initiating a political campaign with the *capacity* to
effectively wage the campaign. Drawing again on his reading of Marx, Guha
argues that it is

> [this universalist] drive which, as Marx argues in *The German Ideology*, makes
> the emergence of "ruling ideas" a necessary concomitant of capital's dominance
> in the mode of production and enable [*sic*] these ideas, in turn, to invest the
> bourgeoisie with the historic responsibility to "represent" the rest of society, *to
> speak for the nation.*[21]

In other words, the emergent bourgeois class is able to rise above its sectional
outlook and build upon its common interests with other classes—especially
workers and peasants—to forge a collective political project against the ancien
régime. Its interests are successfully represented as universal interests—indeed,
at the moment of struggle, they *are* universal, inasmuch as they are the condition for the furtherance of the interests of its allies.[22] This is the basis for
bourgeois hegemony in the antifeudal struggle. Having achieved this popular
hegemony, it mobilizes the broad political coalition of allied classes against the
feudal monarchy in order to replace it with the new bourgeois order.

---

21   *DH* 63. Emphasis added..
22   Ibid. Interestingly, Guha does not explain clearly how the universalizing drive should
enable the bourgeoisie to subordinate subaltern classes' interests to their own. Presumably it has to
do with the fact that a capitalist economy will provide a foundation for greater political freedoms
and for positive effects on the allies' incomes.

THE BOURGEOIS REVOLUTIONS

The dynamic described in the preceding section was, for Guha, most clearly captured in what he calls the "comprehensive character of the English and French revolutions respectively of 1648 and 1789."[23] Apparently he takes the social analysis of these revolutions to be uncontroversial. Despite their central place in his analysis, he expends little effort in explaining their origins; nor does he defend his interpretation of their significance. He seems to take the interpretation he offers as apodictic. This generates a stark imbalance in his presentation of the contrast between the European bourgeoisie's rise to power and that of colonial capital. While the latter is described in great detail, the former is relegated to condensed and rather cryptic statements. Nevertheless, the main elements of Guha's analysis are clear enough. To encapsulate his views, he approvingly quotes Marx's characterization of the revolutions as having heralded "*a new social order,* the victory of bourgeois ownership over feudal ownership, of nationality over provincialism, of competition over the guild, of the rule of landowner over the domination of the owner by the land, of enlightenment over superstition," and so forth.[24] The bourgeois revolutions thus represented nothing less than a complete social and cultural revolution. Guha considers three aspects to be central to their significance.

Dismantling Feudal Landed Power

The revolutions were launched by the bourgeoisie in order to dismantle feudal agrarian relations. This follows naturally from the premise that capital is propelled to expand its zone of operation. In predominantly agricultural economies, as long as the peasantry remained in possession of its land and was subject to feudal rent, capital would come up against hard limits to its expansion. The central task in 1640 and in 1789, therefore, was to eradicate feudal lordly power. It was only with the abolition of feudal property that the bourgeoisie could fulfill its historic mission—to overturn the rule of the landowner, create a national market, overcome localism, forge a national community, and so on. The critical place of this element of the classic revolutions emerges even more clearly when Guha explains the reasons for Indian capital's failures. Above all for him, the roots of failure lie in the compromises made with landed classes, so that instead of overthrowing them, capital acceded to their continued rule in the countryside.

Securing Hegemony over the Antifeudal Coalition

Even though the bourgeoisie was committed to overthrowing feudal power, it could not do so alone. It was still a minor actor in the broader political

---

23   *DH* 17. Guha uses the date 1648, but readers should not be confused by this. The revolution he has in mind is the same one that began in 1640.

24   *DH* 17–18.

landscape, lacking the means to assault the dominant order on its own. Hence, it had to bring other classes—primarily the peasantry, but also subordinate urban classes—to its side. It could do so either by various authoritarian and coercive means, or by soliciting their consensual participation. Guha maintains that one of the crowning achievements of the bourgeoisie in the great revolutions of 1640 and 1789 was that it secured broad-ranging *consent* to its leadership. This is an important part of his argument: he regards a central contrast between the bourgeois revolutions and the Indian nationalist movement to have been that elite leaders in the former movements secured compliance from subaltern classes through consent, while those in the latter could do so only through coercion.

Guha contends that the leaders of the bourgeois revolutions achieved consent by genuinely accommodating subaltern interests within their political programs—an instance of capital's universalizing tendency—though he does not detail what those concessions might have been. What he seems to have in mind is peasants and workers being won over on the promise to dismantle seignorial power, and, equally important, the promise of political liberties. The effectiveness of bourgeois leadership issued from the fact that the concessions they made were real, not empty slogans. Their assumption of leadership thus had a genuine basis: "it was initially as an acknowledgement of the connection between its own interests and those of all the other nonruling classes that the bourgeoisie had led the struggle against feudalism and established its hegemony over the peasantry."[25]

The bourgeoisie, then, acquired social consent to its leadership through recognition of subaltern interests. The reliance on consent, as against coercion or discipline, is what Guha takes to be the defining characteristic of political hegemony. He often discusses hegemony not only in terms of consent, but as the ability truly to represent the interests of others, to "speak for" other classes; in the bourgeois revolutions, he writes, "the bourgeoisie in the West could speak for all of society in a recognizably hegemonic voice, even as it was striving for power, or had just won it."[26] A hegemonic class can "speak for all of society" because it recognizes, and represents, the interests of subordinate groups. In so doing, it can relegate coercion to a secondary or even peripheral role in the maintenance of its power. Its strategy is to integrate the other classes into one encompassing community of interests, albeit one in which power imbalances are preserved.

---

25   *DH* 134.

26   Guha uses this very expression—"to speak for all of society"—at least twice in discussions of the bourgeoisie's role in the classical revolutions. See *DH* 19 and 134. On p. 19, he then links this capacity with the acquisition of hegemony, and hegemony itself as "rule based on the consent of the subject population."

From Coalitional Hegemony to Social Hegemony

The third critical feature of the bourgeois revolutions was their outcome: the construction of a social order in which the bourgeoisie was hegemonic, not merely dominant. What this means is that, just as it did during the antifeudal mobilization, capital maintains its power by relying more on consent than on coercion. We move now from hegemony as a characteristic of a political movement to hegemony as a means of social integration.

In his discussion of how the bourgeoisie secures popular consent to its rule, Guha returns to the language of representation: the dominant class secures its power by "representing all of the will of the people."[27] So, the achievement of the British and French bourgeoisie was that it anchored its rule not on coercion or force, but on its willingness to represent wider social interests. In this way, it embarked on the creation of an entirely new political community, unlike anything witnessed before the advent of bourgeois rule. The bourgeoisie created a new political nation, based on universal principles and issuing from its universalizing drive.

While this characterization of the new political order does describe its functional form, it does not tell us much about the institutional mechanisms through which hegemony is reproduced. If the new ruling class committed itself to the represention of wider social interests, there must have been an institutional matrix through which it achieved this end. Unfortunately, Guha does not identify the institutional supports of hegemony in the new order. We must resort, therefore, to a more interpretive strategy, pulling together his scattered remarks on the matter.

As discussed above, Guha often describes hegemony as the ability to "speak for all of society" or to "represent the will of the people." What he seems to have in mind as the specific embodiment of this principle is that of *liberalism*, political and economic, both as a set of institutions and as the language of political contestation. Capital gains its legitimacy, its ability to speak for the nation, by opening a space for subaltern groups to articulate and pursue their interests— albeit within the limits of bourgeois property relations. The basic rights and freedoms associated with liberalism and political democracy are the means by which they achieve these ends. The formal freedoms associated with liberal democracy greatly expand the scope of political practice for the laboring classes. Moreover, in allowing for new political practices, they also create an entirely new political idiom. This means that the institutions of liberalism are not the only factor in the building of hegemony. The bourgeoisie also enables the creation of a new discursive form, what Guha calls a "political idiom," through which interests are expressed by social actors. This idiom is that of rights, liberties, equality, universal principles. The political actualization of rights, freedoms,

---

27   *DH* 20.

and the rule of law thus brings social classes into one encompassing political order and becomes the basis of a new political discourse.[28]

The significance of the bourgeois revolutions, then, was that they embodied the universalizing tendency of capital. This tendency initially took shape as a broad, antifeudal social coalition led by the bourgeoisie and became a new liberal political order based on universal rights and formal equality. In so doing, it created, for the first time, an encompassing political community that brought together dominant and subaltern classes into the same political domain. This was, for Guha, the historic achievement of the British and French bourgeoisie. As was said above, it set the standard against which the performance of colonial and national capital in India is measured.

Having examined the significance of capital's universalizing drive in Europe, we now turn to its frustration in modern India.

2.5 UNIVERSALIZATION ABANDONED: CAPITAL'S COLONIAL VENTURE

Two forms of capital are relevant for understanding Indian political evolution: the capital that rested in European hands during the years of British rule, and the capital that belonged to Indian entrepreneurs. The very presence of these two forms—the fact that they successfully reproduced themselves over the course of two centuries and even swelled enormously in scale—might suggest that the universalizing tendency did materialize in the Subcontinent. But Guha resists any such conclusion. While capital did migrate to the Indian

---

28   There are two contexts in which we can discern Guha's commitment to this view—in direct discussions of the postrevolutionary regimes and in discussions of the nonhegemonic order of South Asia, in which Britain and France are used as counterfactuals. He is quite consistent across both. Textual support for his association of bourgeois hegemony with the discourse and institutions of liberalism can be found throughout *Dominance without Hegemony*. The evidence for the colonial order being nonhegemonic is its *autocratic* character, which Guha contrasts to the British state, which is hegemonic in that it is *democratic* (*DH* xii, 4, 65–6). He characterizes British capital's stance as championing self-determination in Europe while crushing any such aspirations in its colonies (*DH* 4); hence, capital's orientation where it is hegemonic is to recognize national rights, while the evidence of its having abandoned hegemonic aspirations in India is that it denies Indians the right to self-determination. Later Guha argues that colonialist ideologues tried to legitimize British rule by gathering "evidence for the essentially *liberal* character of the Raj" (*DH* 31, 33). Here again, hegemony is tied to liberal institutions. Guha finds that what was most laudable in British political culture, and lacking in the political culture of colonialism, was "Liberalism, Democracy, Liberty, the Rule of Law, and so on" (*DH* 67). James Mill's attempts to present the Indian state as an extension of the British state—and hence as being based, as was the British state, on the consent of the governed—failed because "*liberal* culture hardly managed to penetrate beyond the upper crust . . . while the ideal of *liberal government* persisted only as idle and empty cant until the end of the raj" (*DH* 80). The marker of colonialism's inability to achieve hegemony was the "failure of *liberalism* to overcome the resistance of entrenched feudal customs and belief systems" (ibid.). Again and again, the marker of a truly hegemonic bourgeois order is linked with liberal ideology, representative democracy, political liberties, and the like.

Subcontinent, it did not instantiate its universalism in the relevant way. What Guha has in mind is the political and cultural transformation that was unleashed in Europe. Judged by this standard, he announces, both groups failed. Neither segment of the class had any inclination to play the transformative role of their counterparts in early modern Europe. Hence, "the universalist project we have been discussing hurtled itself against an insuperable barrier in colonialism."[29] Let us, then, examine Guha's arguments for the dimensions of bourgeois failure—both British and Indian—within colonial India.

THE MYTHOLOGY OF LIBERAL COLONIALISM

Guha begins with the observation that elite historiography assumes a basic continuity between the liberalism of British domestic culture, and the structure of colonial rule. It "regard[s] the colonial state as an organic extension of the metropolitan bourgeois state and colonialism as an adaptation, if not quite a replication, of the classic bourgeois culture of the West in English rendering."[30] Taking as its model the European experience, liberal historiography assumes that

> capital, in its Indian career, succeeded in overcoming the obstacles to its self-expansion and subjugating all precapitalist relations in material and spiritual life well enough to enable the bourgeoisie to speak for all of society, as it had done on the occasion of its historic triumphs in 1648 and 1789.[31]

This view, generated by the bourgeoisie itself and propagated by its intellectual representatives, has sustained liberal apologetics for both the colonial and the post-colonial political order. Given this core assumption, notes Guha, it is hardly surprising that colonialism "was regarded by [bourgeois apologists] as a positive instance of the universalizing instance of capital"[32] or that a basic continuity was assumed between the colonial era and the regime that followed it. Guha affirms that there was, in fact, a deep continuity between the two, but not in the fashion suggested by liberal ideology. On the contrary, in neither era was either segment of capital inclined to carry out the mission to which both claimed fidelity.

COLONIAL CAPITAL

There were two indices of the colonial bourgeoisie's abrogation of its historic mission in India: the first was its willingness to impose an autocratic order rather than a liberal one, and the second was its resort to an alliance with, rather than the destruction of, the ancien régime.

---

29   *DH* 19.
30   *DH* 4.
31   *DH* 19
32   *DH* 4.

Guha takes the political order established in India by the colonizers as direct evidence that the British bourgeoisie was not committed to the same project it had launched at home. He points to the anomaly of "the metropolitan bourgeoisie, who had professed and practiced democracy at home, but were quite happy to conduct the government of their Indian empire as an autocracy."[33] But while he frequently refers to this disjuncture as a paradox or anomaly, he understands that it is not entirely surprising.[34] The fact that the colonial state "[was] created by the sword made this historically necessary."[35] It was, after all, a forcible imposition of alien rule on a subject population. The very idea of its transmutation into a liberal order was therefore problematic. Since the state had to be autocratic, there was no possibility of incorporating the laboring classes into the broad political culture in the way that had been accomplished in Europe. They remained an external force, with their own culture and interests, and while they no doubt had to be accounted for, they were not an active part of the political process. In sum, for Guha, the nature of the state presented the first and perhaps most important obstacle to the colonial bourgeoisie's construction of a hegemonic order.

Another significant obstacle to the implantation of a liberal order in the colony was the kind of alliance system that the British had to forge. Of necessity, even while pushing aside the established ruling classes, colonial authorities were forced to enlist them as junior partners in the state. A few thousand colonial administrators from an alien culture could hardly hope to achieve stable rule without bringing into the fold some local sources of power. Again in contrast to the European precedent, the new elite therefore reached out to precapitalist ruling groups. A natural concomitant was the preservation of these groups' sources of income and power, and thereby the idiom of local politics—with the result that "feudal practices, far from being abolished or at least reduced, were in fact reinforced under a government representing the authority of the world's most advanced bourgeoisie."[36] This underlines the point that the colonial bourgeoisie's "antagonism to feudal values and institutions in their own society made little difference . . . to their vast tolerance of precapitalist values and institutions in Indian society."[37]

The preservation of these institutions further solidified traditional power relations and, in so doing, prevented the creation of a hegemonic bourgeois regime. There was no drive to create a singular people-nation. Instead, the heritage of colonial rule was the reproduction of archaic power relations and,

---

33 *DH* 4–5.
34 For references to the absence of a liberal colonial order as a paradox or anomaly, see *DH* xii, 4, 19, 26, 64–5.
35 *DH* 64.
36 *DH* 26–7.
37 *DH* 4–5.

through that, the distinctiveness of subaltern culture—in contact with, but separate from, the culture of its rulers. Herein lay the structural fault separating the bourgeois project in Europe from that in India. British capital exchanged its historic mission for the opportunity to secure power in its new zones of conquest. Guha concludes that "colonialism could continue as a relation of power in the subcontinent only on the condition that the colonizing bourgeoisie should fail to live up to its universalist project."[38]

THE INDIAN BOURGEOISIE

If we turn now to the domestic bourgeoisie, we find that the Indian counterpart to the bourgeois revolutions in Europe was the nationalist movement for independence. The British and French capitalist classes came to power by overthrowing the feudal monarchies; Indian capital in its turn had to confront the power of feudal landed classes. But in taking them on, capital came up against not a feudal state per se but rather a colonial state that was patronizing these classes. In some respects, capital's task paralleled that of its European predecessors—it still had to confront traditional classes but could do so only by crafting a broad political coalition. As Guha puts it, it would still have to "express its hegemonic urge in the form of universality."[39] But the form taken by this universalism would have to differ somewhat from the European version. It would have to be not just an antifeudal coalition, but a *nationalist movement*. "Thanks to the historic conditions of its formation," declares Guha, "the Indian bourgeoisie could strive towards its hegemonic aim only by constituting 'all the members of society' into a *nation* and their 'common interest' into an 'ideal form' of a *nationalism*."[40]

Any verdict on the Indian bourgeoisie's competence at its historic mission thus derives, above all, from its performance in the nationalist movement. And the verdict is severe indeed. Guha's summary assessment is that Indian capital failed on all three fronts that he considers central to the classic bourgeois revolutions.

The Accommodation to Landlordism

First, and perhaps foundationally, Indian capital never launched a frontal assault on the traditional landed nobility as had British and French capitalists. Instead, it tried to reach an accommodation with them. Says Guha: "Fostered by colonialism and dependent on the latter for its very survival during its formative phase, it had learned to live at peace with those pre-capitalist modes of production and culture which made the perpetuation of British rule possible."[41]

---

38   *DH* 64.
39   *DH* 101.
40   Ibid. Emphasis added.
41   *DH* 132.

The bourgeoisie thus subsisted in a "symbiosis with landlordism and complicity with many forms of feudal oppression"[42] rather than in tension with it, as was the case in Europe, according to Guha. The result was that an attack on traditional classes simply was not on the cards for the nationalist movement.

The Failure to Hegemonize the Nationalist Movement

Indian capital's reluctance to attack landlordism placed severe limits on the bourgeoisie's ability to represent the common interest. One critical manifestation of this inability was the failure to bring the laboring classes under its leadership. As long as it refused to break with traditional landed elites, it could not accommodate even the basic demands of the peasantry, such as the call for rent reductions.[43] Instead of mobilizing the peasantry against the landed classes, the bourgeoisie sought the latter's patronage.[44] The working class quickly discovered that, since capital had placed strict limits on its own political vision and ambitions, it would have little patience for integrating workers' interests in its strategy.[45] As a result,

> by the time they were called upon to mobilize in the campaigns initiated by the nationalist leadership at the end of the First World War, both these groups [i.e., workers and peasants] had already developed class aims which it was not possible for the bourgeoisie to accommodate in any program sponsored exclusively under its own auspices.[46]

The consequences of this failure to incorporate the class interests of subaltern groups lie at the heart of Guha's overall argument. The first and more direct consequence was that the bourgeoisie could not legitimately claim to represent "the nation." Guha seems to rely here on a counterfactual, though he does not explicitly say this—that the evidence for genuine leadership of a movement would appear to be the absence of contending claims to that leadership.[47] But

---

42 Ibid.

43 "With all its concern to involve the peasantry in nationalist politics, [the bourgeoisie] could not bring itself to include the struggle against rents in its programs" (*DH* 132).

44 See Guha's biting critique of Mahatma Gandhi's political philosophy on this count, which he correctly characterizes as dedicated to preserving landlordism (*DH* 35–9). In fact, Guha's attitude to Gandhi throughout *Dominance without Hegemony* is quite critical.

45 *DH* 133.

46 *DH* 132, 133. Guha also points to the communal front as a site of bourgeois failure. It was never able to displace the All-India Muslim League as representative of the Muslim population, nor was it able to sideline the Hindu Mahasabha as the voice of devout Hindus (*DH* 131–3). But while Guha gives due attention to this phenomenon, he prioritizes the class problem: "much of the specificity of Indian politics of this period [the 1920s and 1930s] derives precisely from the failure of nationalism to assimilate the class interests of peasants and workers effectively into a bourgeois hegemony" (*DH* 133).

47 See *DH* 131–5.

because the Indian National Congress had been unable to acquire the working masses' consent to its leadership, that space came under challenge by other political forces—socialists, communists, and other radicals, as well as other nationalist parties. This was the glimmer of an alternative hegemony to which Guha alluded in his inaugural *Subaltern Studies* essay, a hegemony that, if successful, would have been based in the working class and its allies.[48] These forces were not, of course, able to displace the INC from the helm of the movement. But neither was the INC able to drive them out. They remained, throughout the movement's later phases, a visible and contending force. So, while the European capitalists had been able to win a hegemonic position over its mass movements, "in India there was always yet another voice, a subaltern voice, that spoke for a large part of society which it was not for the bourgeoisie to represent."[49]

Having failed to secure their active consent to its leadership, the bourgeoisie had no choice but to keep the laboring classes in line by resorting to coercion. They turned to traditional forms of authority, both material and ideational, to maintain their place at the helm of the movement. Instead of appealing to their common interests with the masses as an incentive for the latter's participation, they leaned instead on subtle or overt threats and on traditional notions of duty, obligation, and station.[50] The means used by the Indian bourgeoisie to assert control, which Guha takes as paradigmatic of a nonhegemonic leadership, were of two functional kinds: mechanisms to ensure conformity within the ranks of Congress, cadre or crowds participating in public events such as rallies, and measures to ensure wider social compliance with political initiatives such as boycotts and political campaigns. The main difference between the two was that the former pertained to a narrower band of social groups, namely those that were already within the INC or were in close contact with it, and the latter pertained to a far wider set of strata, many of which had no direct contact with the INC as an organizational body.

Guha takes the use of these disciplinary measures as proof that the INC had failed to elicit genuine consent from the masses and thus had failed to emerge as the authentic voice of subaltern aspirations. It is noteworthy that he does not say it was the *degree* of coercion or the *kind* of disciplinary measures that signaled the failure of consent. He simply points to the *fact* that discipline was used and then interprets this as a signal that the bourgeoisie and its political organ had failed to emerge as the nation's genuine representative. It is a somewhat surprising argument. Undoubtedly, an organization that relies on intimidation and terror over its own base cannot lay claim to representing that

---

48   See above, 33–34; see also Guha, "On some aspects of the historiography," 7.
49   *DH* 134.
50   *DH*, chap. 2.

base. But Guha provides no evidence whatsoever that matters had reached this stage for the Congress—which, of course, they had not. To persuade us that the INC's coercive measures fell outside the range of measures used by organizations that can safely be regarded as "hegemonic" would require some accounting: what is the permissible range of disciplinary measures for a "hegemonic" leadership, and what kinds of measures fall outside that range? But Guha gives us not even the smidgen of an argument in this direction. We are offered only two elements—the fact that coercion was used, and the conclusion that this demonstrates a failed hegemony.

The Failure of Bourgeois Liberalism

We now arrive at the third dimension of the Indian bourgeoisie's failure. Unwilling to attack landlordism, having compromised with feudal interests, refusing to acknowledge the authentic interests of labor and the peasantry, and unconfident in its political legitimacy—the bourgeoisie failed to establish its hegemony over the new order. In sum, "the indigenous bourgeoisie, spawned and nurtured by colonialism itself, adopted a role that was distinguished by its *failure to measure up to the heroism of the European bourgeoisie* in its period of ascendancy."[51] Again Guha's characterization of its failures reverts to the language of liberalism and representation:

> The *liberalism* they [the Indian bourgeoisie] professed was never strong enough to exceed the limitations of the half-hearted initiatives for reform which issued from the colonial administration. This *mediocre liberalism*, a caricature of the vigorous democratic culture of the epoch of the rise of the bourgeoisie of the West, operated throughout the colonial period in a symbiotic relationship with the still active and vigorous forces of the semi-feudal culture of India.[52]

The bourgeoisie's "mediocre liberalism," which Guha contrasts to the "heroism of the European bourgeoisie" and in particular to the "vigorous democratic culture" that it helped cultivate, was the direct expression of its refusal to shape its program in ways that would accommodate the interests of the subaltern classes. It reflected capital's inability, or unwillingness, to secure their consent to its leadership.

Capital's half-hearted liberalism meant, finally, a failure to integrate subaltern culture into its own. Having no organic link to the masses, resorting to becoming allied with traditional classes, and mobilizing traditional cultural tropes and forms of power to keep the masses in line during the independence movement, the bourgeoisie succeeded only in giving further life to the autonomy of subaltern

---

51 *DH* 5. Emphasis added.
52 Ibid. Emphasis added.

culture. Instead of incorporating them into a new, inclusive, and expansive world-view, it preserved their traditional political practices and idioms. The consequence was the phenomenon which *Subaltern Studies* took as the defining feature of post-colonial India: the existence and reproduction of a distinct subaltern domain, a separate political culture that exists parallel to and in contact with, but has never been absorbed into, modern bourgeois politics. As Guha concludes, the failure of the bourgeoisie to "speak for the nation" during its nationalist phase carried over into the postcolonial era:

> That failure is self-evident from the difficulty which has frustrated the bourgeoisie in its effort so far at winning a hegemonic role for itself *even after half a century since the birth of a sovereign Indian nation-state.* The predicament continues to grow worse, and by current showing should keep the students of contemporary South Asia busy for years to come.[53]

Thus, the ultimate expression of India's failed bourgeois revolution was the fail-ure to build an integrated political culture, which would have been possible only if the capitalist class had recognized the real interests of the laboring classes. This it did not do, because as it entered India, capital—in both its Euro-pean and Indian guises—abandoned its historic tasks. In exchange for power, capital relinquished its universalizing mission.

2.6 CONCLUSION

At the heart of the Subalternist project, and of postcolonial theory more generally, stands the claim that there is a deep fault line separating Western capitalist nations from the postcolonial world. The importance of Ranajit Guha's work is that it offers a historical sociology that seeks to explain how and why this fault line came into being. The power of his argument lies in the fact that he does not derive it from the kind of essentialism that can some-times be found in postcolonial theory or in the writings of other Subalternists. He relies, instead, on a historical argument about the different biographies of capital in the two zones. Central to Guha's explanation is the claim that the kind of modernization that capital wrought in the West was not on the agenda as it travelled to the colonial world—that in colonial social formations, capital abandoned its universalizing drive.

Having unpacked in some detail the specifics of this argument, we are now in a position to make some observations about its peculiarities. The first has to do with what Guha means by capital's universalization. Recall that he begins by locating the drive to universalize in the economic logic of capitalist

---

53   *DH* xiii.

production—in what he calls the "self-expansion of capital," which propels it to "create a world market [and] subjugate all antecedent modes of production."[54] But, while Guha bases the expansion of capital's ambit on its economic logic, this soon recedes into the background of his analysis. What begins to loom larger is the notion that, as it expands, capital must also transform the political and cultural matrix of traditional societies. Indeed, for Guha, the true test for whether capital has established itself in a region—what he refers to as its universalization—is the extent to which it replaces the local culture with "laws, institutions, values, and other elements of a culture appropriate to bourgeois rule."[55]

Although this shift might appear minor, its consequences are significant. In Marx's rendering, the expansion of capital's sphere does not carry any direct implication for the form of political rule. The spread of its characteristic economic relations is consistent with, and might even require, coercive state structures. For Guha, however, since the universalizing drive is identified with acquisition of the consent of subaltern groups, his framework generates a distinct cultural criterion for testing the extent of capital's universalization: insofar as capital fails to promote a liberal polity, it fails in its universalizing mission. With admirable clarity, Guha brings together the three phenomena— capital's universalization, bourgeois hegemony, and hegemony as the ability to represent the general will—in a passage denouncing liberal apologetics:

> [T]here is no acknowledgement in [liberal] discourse that in reality the universalist project we have been discussing hurtled itself against an insuperable barrier in colonialism. Hence the attempt, in colonialist writings, to make the rule of British capital appear as a rule based on the consent of the subject population—*that is,* as hegemonic—and correspondingly to construct, in nationalist writings, the domi-nance of the Indian bourgeoisie as the political effect of a consensus representing the will of the people—*that is,* as hegemonic again.[56]

The evidence for the failure of capital's universalization is that the bourgeoisie failed to garner the consent of those it was exploiting or, even more, that it was unable to represent "the will of the people." This strongly suggests that for the universalistic project to have successfully unfolded, capital needed to have emerged as spokesman for the general will. Where liberals err is not in their acceptance of this as a criterion for universalization, but in their claim that the Indian story embodies just such a project.

Two issues are involved here. The first is the suggestion of a very tight fit between the economic dimension of capitalist expansion and the generation of

---

54   *DH* 13.
55   *DH* 14.
56   *DH* 19–20. Emphasis added.

a new cultural and political environment. Such a claim may not appear contro-versial, since it would seem natural to assume that a drastic change in economic institutions should call forth at least some changes in culture and politics. But it is one thing to argue that economic changes are likely to generate pressures for corresponding shifts in culture and politics; it is quite another to use particular institutional and cultural changes *as a test* for whether the economic transfor-mation is in fact taking place. Guha not only argues that the universalization of capital induces the rise of new cultural forms, but he takes the dissemination of particular instances of these as a litmus for whether or not capital has been universalized. Hence his insistence that, in failing to transform subaltern culture, to break down its obduracy and integrate it into a national culture, capital abandoned its universalizing mission. He never considers the possibility that the expansion of capital's economic logic simply may not require the kind of deep cultural transformations that he thinks it does. He does not consider that capital might be able to meet its basic needs by relying on the very cultural forms he thinks are inimical to it—those typical of traditional political econo-mies, suffused with outdated forms of social hierarchy and subordination. So, while there could certainly be some shifts in politics and culture, they may not be of the kind that Guha assumes are necessary.

And just what are the institutions Guha points to as evidence for capital's universalization? Not only does he insist that capital must revolutionize the political culture; he seems also to have a very clear idea of just what the *content* of the new culture must be. Again and again, he links capital's universalization with the rise of *liberal* political and cultural institutions. If the colonial bour-geoisie failed in its mission, it is because of having turned its back on the liberalism it professed in the West; if the Indian business houses were found wanting in their mettle, it is because of their "mediocre liberalism," which was a "caricature" of the liberalism of their Western counterparts. If capital in India failed in its transformative mission, it is because it did not replace the political idioms of the traditional order with those of modern bourgeois society—the rule of law, formal equality, self-determination, and so on. Capital's aborted universalization is inferred from the fact that these notions did not become institutionalized in the broader political culture. Guha does not consider that the shift to capitalist social structures might actually fit quite well with the idiom of traditional politics. If this is indeed the case, then the perpetuation of what he calls precapitalist institutions might not constitute evidence for an aborted universalization after all.

Guha's argument about capital's universalization rests on his understanding of the bourgeoisie as historic actor. He takes the notions of *bourgeois* democracy and *bourgeois* liberalism quite literally—these political forms do not simply arise in the capitalist *era* but are, for him, desired and fought for *by* the bour-geoisie. Capitalists are, at least in the classic cases, the vectors of these ideals, and it is bourgeois agency that implants them in the political culture. As in the case for capital's universalization, Guha shifts the focus from the economic—such as the imperative of profit maximization—as the sine qua non of bourgeois goals, to the pursuit of certain political and cultural ends. The bourgeois revolutions are significant for him because they crystallize what he takes to be the real achievements of the bourgeoisie as a historical actor—not merely the establishment of capitalist economic relations, but the universalization of the class's political and ideological commitments.

It is surprising that Guha does not entertain the possibility that the spread of the cultural and political forms he associates with the British and French bourgeoisie might have issued from other sources; hence, while they might have become established in the capitalist *era*, they would not have been brought about by capitalist *design*. This is surprising only because, by the time Guha published *Dominance without Hegemony*, there was a veritable mountain of historical literature pointing precisely in this direction.

We now turn to the historical evidence on the course of the so-called bourgeois revolutions.

CHAPTER THREE

Dominance without Hegemony: The Argument Assessed

As I have noted, Ranajit Guha's argument regarding the bourgeois paths to power in Europe, and then in India, is foundational to the Subalternist enterprise. It cannot be regarded merely as a component specific to the early years of *Subaltern Studies*—as a residue of the Subalternists' immersion in Indian Marxism which was then abandoned in later work. *Dominance without Hegemony* was released in 1997, very much in the mature phase of the Subalternist project, and its arguments were clearly intended to elaborate the highly compressed declarations of the inaugural volume in the series. In its essentials, the book is entirely faithful to the earlier propositions and thereby upholds a powerful line of continuity across the career of *Subaltern Studies*. Moreover, in subsequent work Guha has said nothing to suggest a deviation from the book's conclusions. Finally, his assessment of the "structural fault" separating the Indian bourgeoisie from its early modern predecessors in Europe is endorsed by other leading members of the collective, in particular by Dipesh Chakrabarty in his summation of *Subaltern Studies'* theoretical commitments.[1] Having elaborated in some detail the structure of Guha's argument and the evidence he marshals in its defense, we are now positioned to offer an assessment.

In this chapter, I examine the British and French experience in far greater depth than does Guha. His version of the story occurs in highly compressed statements scattered across three essays and always presented in the form of assertion, never as argument. By contrast, I heap attention on the two cases. The level of detail I bring to the subject might strike the reader as incongruous, even excessive, but I would urge that it is warranted. As I suggested in the previous chapter, Guha's argument about the peculiarity of colonial modernity rests on a deeper claim about the departure of the Indian bourgeois revolution—the struggle for independence from British rule—from the classic experiences of early modern Europe. He does not simply rest his case on a descriptive account of how India was transformed by colonial rule. Instead it is a comparative story about how India's experience embodied a departure from other experiences, which the current historiography has been unable to capture because it subsumes the Subcontinent into the same general narrative as Europe. In

---

1 Chakrabarty also endorses the argument in his *Provincializing Europe* (Princeton: Princeton University Press, 2000), where it forms a premise for some of the author's own conclusions. See the discussion below in Chap. 5, 103–9.

stressing the specificity of the colonial experience, Guha's argument is essentially and unavoidably *contrastive*.

A good indication of the contrastive nature of Guha's argument is that one could accept his factual descriptions of India's colonial history and the nature of the independence movement, while denying his conclusion that they constituted a historical break from the experience in Europe. Our judgment on whether capital abandoned its universalizing mission depends entirely on our standard for what such a mission entails, and that standard can only be based on our understanding of other, baseline cases. The claim that the bourgeoisie abandoned its mission to transform society cannot be upheld *except* in comparison to other cases. Without a defensible understanding of the story that forms the comparison, all we know is that *something* happened in India—that the Indian National Congress came to power, that it had a particular orientation toward the laboring classes, that industrialists had their own views and certain priorities. But for all we know, these facts about India could be the norm. It is perfectly possible that they could be in line with other experiences of state formation or political modernization. Perhaps the Indian experience is just what modernity looks like. If we are to accept Guha's conclusions regarding the peculiarity of India's ascent into modernity, we cannot avoid taking a deeper look at the cases that form his baseline: England and France.

I contend that the case Guha builds for the contrast between the classic bourgeois revolutions and the Indian experience is untenable. The episodes he has in mind—the English Civil Wars of 1640–8 and the French Revolution of 1789—were simply not driven by the forces he thinks were at work, nor did they directly produce the consequences he assigns to them. *In fine*, neither can be defended as a "bourgeois revolution" *in the sense that Guha uses the term*. The reasons they cannot be so described are different in each case, and so must be addressed each in turn. But in both instances the end point of the analysis is the same.

The significance of this finding is profound, not only for Guha's argument but for the larger verdict tendered by *Subaltern Studies* for Indian history and beyond. It turns out that once the two European cases are properly described, the Indian experience no longer appears as a deviation from some classic norm. Indeed, the bourgeoisie's road to power in the Indian Subcontinent now appears quite consistent with the European experience and settles comfortably into the grooves laid down by them. If this is so, a central plank for the Subalternists' insistence on a chasm—a "structural fault"—separating the Indian postcolonial formation from Europe will have been dismantled. What this means, and just how significant it might be, is to be explored in the chapters to follow.

3.1 THE ENGLISH REVOLUTION[2]

The basic facts about the English Revolution are not in dispute. In 1640, the Stuart monarch Charles I convened Parliament for the first time since having dissolved it eleven years earlier. He did so reluctantly, largely in order to raise funds to push back an advancing Scottish army. For much of his reign, Charles had been straining to break free of parliamentary controls on his power. The goal had been to concentrate financial and military initiative in the hands of the monarchy, much as Spain and France were doing across the English Channel. The onset of a new cycle of interstate conflict in the 1620s had made this seem something of an imperative to the Stuarts, who were acutely aware that, on a geopolitical scale, England was still no match for the Catholic powers on the Continent.[3] The prospects of following suit, in the direction of an Absolutist monarchy, must have seemed necessary if England were to hold its own against more powerful rivals. The problem was that any attempt to centralize power in this fashion brought the Stuarts into tension with England's landed classes, who had to agree either to new taxation or to less control over fiscal policy. And the landowners had at their disposal a powerful instrument in the form of the English parliament, an institution largely under their control.

So, when Charles convened Parliament in 1640, after having cast it into the wilderness for eleven years, his agenda unleashed a storm of controversy. Parliament wished to reassert its authority in matters of state, against what it took to be a grasping and incipiently autocratic king, while Charles wished to defend what he took to be his legitimate authority as monarch. The intensity of the conflict between Parliament and king only deepened over the course of the following months, until, in the summer of 1642, civil war broke out. In 1649, after more than seven years of conflict, the New Model Army, under the leadership of Oliver Cromwell, finally won a decisive victory over Royalist forces. It marched triumphantly into London in December 1648, and on January 30, 1649, Charles I was beheaded, the monarchy overturned, and England declared a republic.

For those who have interpreted these events as a bourgeois revolution, the two sides in the war have been taken as representatives of two classes and two

---

2   I refer to the events of 1640 as a revolution, mainly in deference to Guha's preferred language. They are also often called the Civil Wars, which, in many respects, is a more accurate encapsulation of the conflict. For a limited defense of its characterization as a revolution, see Barry Coward, "Preface," *The Stuart Age: England 1603–1714* (New York: Longman, 2003), 3rd ed., xxix–xxxiii; for a somewhat more skeptical view, see Clive Holmes, *Why Was Charles I Executed?* (London: Hambledon Continuum, 2006), 175–201.

3   For a recent and quite illuminating discussion of the connection between war-making and state breakdown in the seventeenth century, see Geoffrey Parker, "Crisis and Catastrophe: The Global Crisis of the Seventeenth Century Reconsidered," *American Historical Review* 113:4 (2008), 1053–79.

antagonistic economic systems. The parliamentary forces, especially the House of Commons, have been viewed as agents of the rising capitalist class, while the royalist side has been viewed as the recalcitrant feudal nobility, standing by the greatest of all feudal lords: the king.[4] The victory of Parliament and its New Model Army is naturally presented as the triumph of the bourgeoisie over a decrepit feudal order. This is the interpretation Guha evidently draws on, and apparently regards as so self-evident that he does not feel pressed to offer any evidence on its behalf. His disregard of the matter is curious, for by the late 1980s—the years in which he was developing his initial formulations into the full-fledged essays that comprise *Dominance without Hegemony*—this interpretation of the English Revolution was almost universally understood as being unsustainable. Even Christopher Hill, perhaps the most illustrious defender of the "bourgeois antifeudal project" view, had beaten a tactical retreat.[5] The problem starts with the basic claim that the revolution was launched by a capitalist class to dismantle a feudal political economy.

THE PROBLEM OF FEUDALISM

The fundamental flaw with the view that Guha reproduces is that, by 1640, there was no structural division in the landed class, with a rising capitalist gentry on one side and a refractory feudal nobility on the other. Indeed, by the early decades of the seventeenth century, the English countryside had been largely transformed, so that feudal agrarian relations were a thing of the past all across the kingdom.[6] Rural surplus appropriators were, in general, committed to market-dependent forms of production, feudal dues having been replaced by capitalist rent or profits. Hence, there was simply no question of the revolution being antifeudal, since there was quite simply no feudalism to shift away from. The conflict that unfolded and then spiraled into civil war after 1640 took place entirely *within* a class of agrarian capitalists. The rural magnates that organized Cromwell's New Model Army as well as those lined up against them on the

---

4 This interpretation was advanced among Marxists by Christopher Hill, "The English Revolution," in his *The English Revolution 1640: Three Essays* (London: Lawrence and Wishart, 1940), 9–82. Hill's essay was the visible tip of an intense subterranean debate in the 1940s among historians associated with the Communist Party of Great Britain about the character of the English Revolution. The various positions have been conveniently collected in one volume, with a useful introduction by the editor; see David Parker, ed., *Ideology, Absolutism, and the English Revolution: Debates of the British Communist Historians, 1940–1956* (London: Lawrence and Wishart, 2008).

5 See Christopher Hill, "Parliament and People," *Past & Present* 92 (Aug. 1981), 100–24.

6 This argument draws on the work of Robert Brenner, especially his essays in T. H. Aston and C. H. E. Philpin, eds., *The Brenner Debate: Agrarian Class Structure and Economic Development in Pre-Industrial Europe* (Cambridge: Cambridge University Press, 1985); and his massive study *Merchants and Revolution: Commercial Change, Political Conflict and London's Overseas Traders 1550–1653* (Princeton: Princeton University Press, 1993). My understanding of not only the English case, but also the contrasting French experience, owes an enormous debt to Brenner's pathbreaking scholarship.

Royalist side were all capitalists. To be sure, differences in size and status still existed. But these did not map onto divergent modes of surplus appropriation. The war was not waged to install a capitalist order; rather, it was waged over what *kind* of capitalist order England ought to have.

The issue that brought so much of the landed class to loggerheads with the Stuart monarchy was not the need to transform rural economic relations, but the monarchy's apparent push toward absolutism. It was a fight over the political order. Over the course of the sixteenth century, the rural gentry had secured its power at the local level. It dominated the Justices of the Peace, the county courts, the religious institutions, and so on, much as the feudal classes had done in medieval times. Now, however, these institutions were turned to the protection of absolute rights in landed property and, through that, the rule of the agrarian bourgeoisie. The Tudor monarchy had, both directly and indirectly, aided the stabilization of gentry rule at the local level. While this did have the effect of underwriting a gradual uptick in rural economic growth, making it possible for England to emerge as perhaps the most dynamic economy in Europe by the turn of the seventeenth century, it also generated a structural dilemma.[7] Unlike its rivals on the Continent, the English monarchy had not been able to develop its own apparatus for revenue collection. It relied instead on the domestic landed classes to collect and deliver up its tax revenues.[8] This meant that as the pressures of war intensified and the Stuarts felt obliged to ratchet up the intensity of rural taxation, they came into continual conflict with agrarian elites, who viewed this as an encroachment on their own power. What especially rankled was not just the pitch of taxation, but the gentry's sentiment that their pivotal role in the generation and disbursement of revenue was not matched by a corresponding power within the state. The thrust toward absolutism was thus viewed by the landed classes as an attack on their freedom to rule.[9]

For the monarchy, the solution to the problem was to reduce its dependence on lordly cooperation in all matters of state, by building new instruments of fiscal and legislative autonomy, centralizing power in the Crown, and reducing the power of Parliament. For the rural lords, the imperative was to reassert their sovereignty as masters of the political nation, to defend the

---

7   By the seventeenth century, England was probably growing faster than the Netherlands, which had been the most dynamic regional economy in the preceding decades. See David Ormond, *The Rise of Commercial Empires: England and the Netherlands in the Age of Mercantilism, 1650–-1770* (Cambridge: Cambridge University Press, 2003), 9–27; and E. A. Wrigley, "The Divergence of England: The Growth of the English Economy in the Seventeenth and Eighteenth Centuries (The Prothero Lecture)," *Transactions of the Royal Historical Society*, 6th ser., vol. 10 (2000), 117–41.

8   Conrad Russell, *The Fall of the British Monarchies, 1637–-1642* (Oxford: Oxford University Press, 1991), 72–5; see also Brenner, *Merchants and Revolution*, 655, 668.

9   The connection between continental warfare and domestic tensions is well analyzed in Jonathan Scott, *England's Troubles: Seventeenth-Century English Political Instability in European Context* (Cambridge: Cambridge University Press, 2000), 27–31, 57–8, 141–2.

rightful power of Parliament, and in so doing, to beat back the Stuart monar-chy's centralizing ambitions. Their reaction to the centralizing drive did not in any way entail a revolutionary break from, or transformation of, the larger social system. Indeed, the gentry largely understood its mission to be the *pres-ervation* of the political order from Charles's grasping hand. After all, this economic and political system served their interests well. They were the only lordly class in Europe to have won absolute property rights in land; they dominated county and parish juridical institutions; they had carried through the Reformation and hegemonized the local Church; and they had real national representation. As long as the national-level institutions could be kept in line with the basic conditions of lordly domination at the local level, the rural gentry's position would be unassailable for the foreseeable future.[10] The lords' goal was, in effect, reformist: to bring the state back into line with earlier patterns of rule by dismantling the instruments that gave Charles increased power over them. This was not a trivial matter, to be sure. It entailed a direct confrontation with the Crown. But it did not impel them to launch an assault on the social order—since it was *their* social order.

THE POLITICAL COALITION

If Guha's characterization of the conflict as antifeudal is misleading, so is his understanding of its political base. In his account, the bourgeoisie launches its confrontation with the feudal state by building a coalition with other classes, including peasants and urban labor—and they agree to its leadership. He takes this consent to have rested on the parliamentary leadership's construction of a program that represented the authentic interests of popular forces. The central planks of the program were the dismantling of feudal economic restrictions and the expansion of political rights for the lower orders. Guha credits the bour-geoisie for initiating these elements, and this is the basis for his criticism of the Indian capitalist class, in that they refused to promulgate a similar program. But here, too, his presentation steers wide of the facts.

It is true that the revolution unleashed an avalanche of popular initiatives, which, for a while, did expand the political order. This was not, however, because of a bourgeois commitment to cobbling together a broad social coalition. In fact, the intention of parliamentary leaders in 1640 was to keep the social coali-tion on their side as narrow as possible. What they wanted was to push Charles into accepting their demands for parliamentary and religious reform *without*

---

10   Brenner puts the matter very well: "All that was necessary for the full realization of their [i.e., the landed classes'] potential power was to put an end to the limitations on these mechanisms that were set by overarching centralized hierarchies in church and state. Once the encrustation of . . . independent monarchical and Episcopal administration had been torn away, or at least brought under control, the powerful aristocratic structures of governance that had grown up beneath it could function unimpeded." See *Merchants and Revolution*, 320.

having to mobilize popular forces. It was to be an elite pact. Within the House of Commons, gentry support for reform in 1640–1 was widespread, and given Charles's desperate situation with regard to the invading Scottish forces, a unified opposition was quite effective in pressing its demands. By the summer of 1641, the parliamentary opposition had achieved most of its political objectives by legislative means. Hardly a sword had yet been drawn. If anything, the early and easy success of the parliamentary initiative was evidence that a revolution was unnecessary. There is considerable evidence that the leadership wanted to complement legislative changes with positions for John Pym and a few other MPs on Charles's Privy Council, the immediate body of advisors on whom the king relied for policy. This was not revolution; it was reform backed by a change in the power elite.

The matter could have perhaps ended there, but for the fact that Charles gave every signal that although he had agreed to the anti-absolutist measures as a temporary expedient, he would likely move to reassert his power once the balance swung back in his favor. That this was a real danger was made clear in the fall of 1641, as evidence mounted that he was plotting a military coup against the parliamentary opposition. Parliamentary forces led by Pym saw little choice but to press for further powers, if only to defend themselves, and so, by the end of 1642, they were demanding greater control over the military as well as ministerial appointments. In addition, and perhaps most important, the opposition began to respond to rapidly building popular pressure in London, which was mobilizing to defend the measures passed during the early phase of the rebellion, and also pushing for greater haste and ambition in the reform process—by force, if need be. London quickly became the center of a powerful mass movement, buoying the spirit and strength of the opposition.[11]

The entry of the London crowds unalterably changed the character of the conflict. Thus far, Pym and his colleagues had kept it an elite affair, intended to shift the balance from king to Parliament, but with no serious ambitions beyond that. The arrival of the popular classes forced a shift in the rebellion's entire structure—but the change was double-edged. While it emboldened some parliamentary leaders to press their demands further, their confidence bolstered by the acquisition of a new mass base, the movement also had the effect of diluting support for the rebellion within the ruling class. As long as the "meaner sort" had been kept out of the conflict with Charles, the parameters of the negotiations could be carefully managed, so that the reforms under consideration did not reach beyond the balance between two distinct segments of the ruling class—the monarchy and the landed classes. Now, however, demands made on

---

11   The classic modern history of the urban mass movement is Brian Manning, *The English People and the English Revolution* (London: Heinemann, 1976). For another account, stressing the role of popular classes in London, see Keith Lindley, *Popular Politics and Religion in Civil War London* (Aldershot: Scolar Press, 1997).

the leadership by the swelling crowds raced ahead of the leadership's initial designs.[12] A victory by Parliament could thus betoken a deep transformation of the existing religious, political, and social hierarchies.

For much of the parliamentary leadership, such an outcome was beyond the pale. They now had to weigh which outcome was the more detestable—the possibility of Charles's emerging from the conflict unscathed, though perhaps weaker, or the likely losses in the event that a radical mass movement took power. For most of the aristocrats in Parliament, the prospect of the former was distinctly preferable to the latter. Even while a resuscitated Stuart rule would be obnoxious, it would at least defend lordly dominance over the rabble. As a result, in 1642 a large section of the parliamentary leadership defected from the rebellion. They did not all go over to the Royalist side. In fact, most seem to have settled into an anxious neutrality as the conflict escalated. But there is no doubt that a substantial number preferred to join the Royalist camp against the rising power of the popular forces. Hence, in the summer of 1642, as it became clear that Charles was assembling an armed force to march into London, 302 MPs remained with the opposition to prepare for its defense while 236 MPs left London altogether, most of whom probably joined Charles.[13] Whereas the members of Parliament had been almost totally united in the early months of the conflict, they were now almost evenly split. Thus, the London crowds saved Pym and his colleagues from Charles's military coup, but at the cost of driving other members into the arms of the monarchy.

As for those who remained committed to the parliamentary cause, their willingness to lean on popular forces in its defense did not by any means suggest an embrace of radical demands. Indeed, even though their disdain for "the meaner sort" was less intense than that of the defectors to the Royalist side, opposition leaders still regarded the mass movement as a necessary evil at best. The core strategy of the gentry leadership over the duration of the conflict was to push for victory while simultaneously containing the spread of radicalism. These leaders had never wanted a revolution, had never countenanced taking up arms against the monarchy, and had certainly not intended to unleash the fury of mass radicalism. What they had wanted was to push back the drive to an absolutist state, and they had achieved that goal in 1641. It was Charles's obstinacy that had forced them to turn to the crowds for support. Now the key was to restore the balance, suitably modified by anti-absolutist legislation.

In the earlier phase of the war with Charles, the preferred route to this end

---

12   David Wootton has argued that highly articulate presentations of radical ideas can be traced to the earliest stages of the conflict, at least as far back as the winter of 1642-3. See Wootton, "From Rebellion to Revolution: The Crisis of the Winter of 1642/43 and the Origins of the Civil War," *The English Historical Review* 105:416, 654–69.

13   Lawrence Stone, *The Causes of the English Revolution 1529–1642* (London: Routledge, 1986), 141.

was to reach a settlement with the deposed monarch as quickly as possible. As long as he agreed to the measures passed by Parliament in the early months of the conflict, his return to the throne was the best way to restore order. For months, the parliamentary leadership sent out feelers to the Royalist forces seeking just such a truce—but Charles would have none of it. The war thus continued to its gruesome end as Cromwell finally secured victory in the fall of 1648. Meanwhile, as the opposition gained strength and radical forces extended their influence, gentry support for the opposition grew correspondingly thinner. By the time Cromwell ordered the beheading of Charles, parliamentary power rested on a wafer-thin section of the English ruling class. [14]

The relationship of the bourgeois leadership to the laboring classes was thus quite different from Guha's presentation of it. The opposition leadership had never intended to lead a revolution; what it had hoped for was an elite pact, pushed through on the strength of Parliament's unity and Charles's desperation. What turned the conflict into civil war, and then a potential revolution, was the combination of Charles's recalcitrance and the entrance of the London masses onto the scene. The opposition leadership did accept the support of the mass movement, but only reluctantly, and at the cost of driving more and more sections of the ruling class into the Royalist camp. There was no commitment to fashioning a political program that respected the authentic interests of the laboring classes. On the contrary, the energy of the leadership was directed to finding ways of securing victory while conceding as little as possible to the lower orders.

THE REVOLUTIONARY SETTLEMENT

Guha attributes the genesis of modern political liberalism to the struggle of the bourgeoisie against feudal rule, and traces the genealogy of this liberal culture to the incorporation of subaltern interests into the political program of the revolutionary bourgeoisie. This is the "heroism" he attributes to British capital. At a formal level, his surmise is correct—there was a connection between the revolutionary strategy of British elites and the kind of political order they subsequently constructed. But its substance was rather different from Guha's understanding of the matter. The continuity between the two phases of their ascent to power—the revolutionary struggle and the construction of the new state—was marked by the landed class's efforts to *constrict* the political arena to the greatest extent possible, so that subaltern groups would be frozen out of the emergent political nation. This began in the course of the Civil Wars and accelerated after the Restoration in 1660. [15]

---

14   Coward, *Stuart Age*, 236–7.
15   David Underdown, *A Freeborn People: Politics and the Nation in Seventeenth-Century England* (Oxford: Oxford University Press, 1996), 120–5.

Civil war unleashed an explosion of popular energy, which found expression above all in a phenomenon relatively new to British political culture—tens of thousands of pamphlets, petitions, magazines, leaflets, and handbills that expressed the aspirations of the popular classes.[16] To a certain extent, the landed classes and their elite allies shared in this new discourse. In so violent a struggle, in which each side was trying to muster public support for its position, there was a need to justify the actions taken and for each camp to make the case that its interests were identical with the public interest. In this broadened space for ideological contestation, the elites could not prevent the eruption of popular demands for political rights. It was in this context that groupings such as the Levellers and Diggers came to the fore—groups regarded by many scholars as the first modern proponents of an egalitarian political ideology.[17] Radical ideas spread rapidly across the realm, particularly in cities, but their strongest base was probably within the army.

The influence of radical ideas—by which we mean here the demand for political and religious liberalism—was handicapped by two main weaknesses. The first was that their currency remained limited. To be sure, they found a significant mass base in London and other urban centers,[18] but outside the cities they found nowhere near the same level of popular support. This made the political balance in England quite different from what obtained in France at the time of its own revolution, where peasants constituted an authentic force for radical change.

The second weakness was that, being the sharp end of the popular movement for inclusion, the spread of radical ideas only further galvanized the sentiment within the landed classes that the optimal course of action was to restore order as soon as possible. Over the course of the Civil Wars, gentry domination of local institutions had been challenged—though by no means eclipsed—by the entrance of new groupings into positions of authority. [19] This

16   See David Zaret, *Origins of Democratic Culture: Printing, Petitions, and the Public Sphere in Early-modern England* (Princeton: Princeton University Press, 2000), 217–64; Mark Knights, *Representation and Misrepresentation in Later Stuart Britain: Partisanship and Political Culture* (Oxford: Oxford University Press, 2005). Knights's book is interesting in that it takes a longer sweep on the rise of print culture in the Stuart period and beyond.

17   A classic presentation of the Levellers as forerunners of modern socialism is H. N. Brailsford, *The Levellers and the English Revolution*, ed. Christopher Hill (Nottingham: Spokesman, 1976). An illuminating analysis of the content of Leveller ideology and its social context is David Wooton, "Leveller Democracy and the Puritan Revolution," in J. H. Burns, ed. (ass't. Mark Goldie), *The Cambridge History of Political Thought, 1450-1700* (Cambridge: Cambridge University Press, 2008), 412–42; a good recent collection is Michael Mendle, ed., *The Putney Debates of 1647* (Cambridge: Cambridge University Press, 2001).

18   Phil Withington, *The Politics of Commonwealth: Citizens and Freemen in Early Modern England* (Cambridge: Cambridge University Press, 2005).

19   This is brilliantly examined by David Underdown in his *Revel, Riot and Rebellion: Popular Politics and Culture in England, 1603-1660* (London: Oxford University Press, 1985).

was a direct blow to the very order that the gentry had sought to protect from Charles's encroachments, and for the sake of which it had launched its struggle. The growth of radicalism threatened not only to give ideological license to these developments but to further empower new challengers. The solution that parliamentary forces sought to institutionalize was a new political order that would restore old social hierarchies, minus the drive to an absolutist state—much along the lines of what they thought they had secured in 1641, before Charles began to amass his forces. After the beheading of Charles, the landed classes' support for Cromwell rested on their confidence that he would stamp out radical ideas but would also respect their own anti-absolutist commitments.[20] It would be a mistake to underestimate the importance of the former—namely, the need to eradicate the demands for subaltern political inclusion. Its weight was such that the gentry showed itself willing to revive monarchical rule less than one year after Cromwell's death, when the Stuarts were restored to the throne in the person of Charles II.[21] Clearly, by 1660 the ruling class regarded the need to push back popular forces—to roll back liberal gains—as its most pressing concern.

We must be clear about what was happening. The English Civil Wars had generated a new concept of political legitimacy. Whereas in medieval political doctrine, sovereignty had rested in the monarchy, it now was seen to reside in the nation. This was an epochal shift in the understanding of the political community. But while legitimacy was now transferred to the nation, the groupings or classes that *constituted* the nation was not yet settled. Gentry strategy after 1649 was to ensure that the popular classes were kept out of the new concept of the nation. As David Loades has concluded,

> The bitter ideological strife of the 1640s produced a reaction which lasted many years and was not repeated in the next crisis of 1688–89. At the same time, the aristocracy had received a sharp lesson. "Posterity will say," a royalist writer had declared in 1649, "that we overthrew the king to subject ourselves to the tyranny of the base rabble." Thanks to Cromwell, this had not happened, but it had come close

20   Barry Coward, "The Experience of the Gentry, 1640–1660," in R. C. Richardson, ed., *Town and Countryside in the English Revolution* (Manchester: Manchester University Press, 1992), 198–223; Steve Hindle, "The Growth of Social Stability in Restoration England," *The European Legacy* 5:4 (2000), 563–76, esp. 570, 572.

21   The Restoration did not, of course, give Charles II carte blanche to continue centralizing power. The understanding was that he would respect the legislation passed in 1640–1. In fact, he did—to the exclusion of everything that followed. When he was placed on the throne, one of his reign's first pieces of legislation stated that all laws promulgated during the Long Parliament which did not have the Crown's approval were null and void—meaning all laws passed after 1641. This effectively cemented the early anti-absolutist legislation and nullified everything that came later, during the Civil Wars' more radical phases. The Restoration was thus a return to 1641, not to 1639. See Coward, *Stuart Age*, 290, and John Miller, "Politics in Restoration Britain," in Barry Coward, ed., *A Companion to Stuart Britain* (London: Blackwell, 2003), 410.

enough to constitute an unmistakable warning of the dangers which could follow if the "lower orders" were called in to settle quarrels within the ruling class. The experience was never to be forgotten and was not to be repeated in this country until the eve of the present [i.e., twentieth] century.[22]

The rebellion had never intended that power devolve beyond members of the ruling class. The time had come to bring the rabble back into line. In this effort to restore order, the landed classes largely succeeded. For a brief moment, from 1689 to the first decade of the next century, political space expanded, as both the electorate and the frequency of elections increased in number.[23] But this opening was short-lived. The ascension of George III in 1714 inaugurated a long and suffocating process of political constriction. In essence, the Crown forged a modus vivendi with the bourgeois aristocracy, allowing them to consolidate their power in the localities in exchange for their support of far-reaching financial and administrative reforms.[24] It was these reforms that enabled the construction of England's fiscal-military state, by mid-century the most fearsome military apparatus in the Western world. The flip side of this state-building process, however, was the long-term disenfranchisement of the lower orders. As David Underdown notes, the Restoration unleashed an ongoing *constriction* of the political nation—not, as Guha suggests, its expansion.[25]

The most glaring element of the regime's oligarchic nature was its narrow electoral base. By the time of George III's ascension, the landed classes had begun a slow strangulation of the political arena, adding one obstacle after another to lower-class participation. Over the course of the eighteenth century, the nascent and increasingly vital electoral arena came under the tightening grip of the Whig oligarchy, only to be followed by decades of Tory hegemony. Expansion of this domain of politics did not occur again until the Reform Act of 1832, and it is sobering to contemplate that by the time it passed, the franchise in England was smaller and narrower than it had been in 1630.[26] But the exclusion of the popular classes went far beyond the electoral arena. The entire structure of the political system was punitive. Trade unions did not get legal

---

22 David M. Loades, *Politics and Nation: England 1450–1660* (London: Basil Blackwell, 1999), 392.

23 W. A. Speck, *Stability and Strife: England, 1714–1760* (Cambridge, MA: Harvard University Press, 1976), 16, 21. J. H. Plumb shows that this political vitality began earlier, being visible as early as the 1630s; see Plumb, "The Electorate in England from 1600 to 1775," *Past and Present* 45 (Nov. 1969), 90–116. Plumb's argument is reinforced by Derek Hirst in *The Representative of the People? Voters and Voting in England under the Early Stuarts* (Cambridge: Cambridge University Press, 1975).

24 J. H. Plumb, *The Growth of Social Stability in England, 1675–1725* (Boston: Houghton Mifflin, 1965). See also the more recent analysis in Richard Price, *British Society 1680–1880: Dynamism, Containment, and Change* (Cambridge: Cambridge University Press, 1999), 234–44.

25 Underdown, *Freeborn People*, 112–25.

26 Plumb, "Electorate in England," 111.

protection until 1871; indentured labor was a common practice well into the late nineteenth century (as I show in chapter 5); the legal system imposed draconian penalties, even capital punishment, for petty theft.[27] The radical promise of 1640, embodied in the demands of groups such as the Levellers and the Quakers, was driven underground by the 1720s, reappearing periodically in bursts of militancy; exported to the Continent, radical ideas took root in France and elsewhere but achieved little institutional anchorage in England, where they originated.[28] The enduring political consequence of the English Civil Wars was a bourgeois oligarchy, not a new and expansive political nation.

We can safely conclude that the English Revolution did not substantively resemble Guha's depiction of it in any of the three dimensions he cites as evidence of the "heroism" of the bourgeoisie—its putative antifeudal, antiland-lord objectives; its creation of an inclusive, hegemonic coalition, constructed to recognize and reflect subaltern aspirations; or its creation of a liberal social order after the acquisition of state power. In each of these domains, as we have seen, the actual practice of the English bourgeoisie was at odds with Guha's portrayal. It was not antifeudal because there was little left of the feudal agrarian structure; it was either indifferent to or contemptuous of subaltern interests in the actual conflict, accommodating them only when absolutely unavoidable; and its political strategy, during the campaign and after, was to exclude the lower order from politics. These facts are very well known. What is remarkable is that Guha seems unaware of them, and even more so, that the historical profession has allowed these misconceptions to pass uncontested.

3.2 THE FRENCH REVOLUTION

Guha would seem to be on surer ground in his characterization of the French Revolution than of the English. For most of the twentieth century, the events of 1789 were taken as paradigmatic of the bourgeoisie's revolutionary capture of power. If any revolution was antifeudal, devoted to liberalism—indeed, was it not inspired by Enlightenment ideas?—and paradigmatically modern in its political discourse, surely it must be the French. But in fact, here too the histo-riography has not been kind to Guha's interpretation. To be sure, the revolution did culminate in the end of centuries-old seignorial rule in the agrarian

---

27   The literature on the penal culture of eighteenth-century England is enormous. An excellent example is Peter Linebaugh, *The London Hanged: Crime and Civil Society in the Eighteenth Century*, 2nd ed. (London: Verso, 2006). Linebaugh is carrying forward the program of his mentor, E. P. Thompson, who, along with his students, produced a series of important works on the subject. Some of this collaborative work was presented in E. P. Thompson et al., *Albion's Fatal Tree: Crime and Society in Eighteenth-Century England* (New York: Pantheon, 1976).

28   The importation of radical republican ideas to France, and to the Continent more generally, is described by Jonathan I. Israel in his monumental study of the Enlightenment. See Israel, *Enlightenment Contested*, (Oxford: Oxford University Press, 2006), 326–371.

economy, and, in that sense, yes, it was genuinely antifeudal. And true, it also opened up the space for political contestation in the direction of liberalism to a greater extent than any preceding revolution. In these respects, the French Revolution was a decidedly epoch-making event. But while these characteristics of the revolution do make it unarguably significant, closer inspection reveals little to confirm Guha's specific propositions concerning its significance: namely, that it was led by a rising capitalist class, that this class launched the conflict in order to install a liberal economic and political order, and that it did so by attracting the peasants and workers to its program.

THE REVOLUTION AND THE BOURGEOISIE

The English Revolution could not be antifeudal because it occurred after the transition to capitalism had already been completed. In France, capitalism had barely begun to sprout by 1789. Hence, there was every possibility for the revolution to be antifeudal, and in fact, this was one of its defining characteristics. The problem is that it was not led by actors who in any sense could be described as capitalists.

In some respects, the background to the French Revolution is remarkably reminiscent of the English experience of a century prior. Much as was the case with the Stuarts, the ruling Bourbon dynasty was confronted with a catastrophic imbalance between the military and geopolitical demands being made on the state, on the one hand, and the revenues available to fund them, on the other. In the course of the eighteenth century, France had been locked in almost perpetual conflict with England, the most recent of which—the Seven Years' War—had resulted in humiliating defeat. The root of the fiscal weakness was an agrarian economy still encased in precapitalist property relations, unlike the more dynamic English agriculture. Backward agriculture, of course, made for a slow-growing revenue base, a situation aggravated by the fact that the French nobility was largely exempt from taxation. Over the centuries, the French state had been able to expand its reach only through the expedient of reaching an accommodation with regional landed magnates, granting them state office and exemptions from taxation in exchange for their political support. Consequently, the flow from an already low revenue base was reduced even further, as monies that could have buoyed the exchequer went instead into the nobility's coffers. By the end of the century, what had originated as an expedient had turned into a curse. The panoply of exemptions and perquisites had locked the state into perpetual fiscal crisis.[29]

---

29 For a recent overview, which also compares the French political economy with early modern England, see David Parker, *Class and State in Ancien Régime France: The Road to Modernity?* (London: Routledge, 1996); the standard source in English for the fiscal crisis is J. F. Bosher, *French Finances 1770–1795: From Business to Bureaucracy* (Cambridge: Cambridge University Press, 1970).

Faced with a treasury verging on collapse, the Crown had no choice but to push for greater revenue. The most feasible approach was to reconsider the myriad privileges and tax exemptions that had been granted to the nobility over the centuries. But the landed magnates would hardly relinquish their prerogatives without a struggle. Faced with a serious crisis of governance, Louis XVI agreed to convene the Estates-General, a national assembly that brought together representatives of all three orders—the nobility, the clergy, and the so-called Third Estate, the 97 percent of the population that belonged to neither. The twelve hundred delegates were chosen through a national electoral process and converged on Versailles in May 1789. Within days, it was clear there would be no simple way out of the crisis. The delegates found themselves at loggerheads.[30]

At the heart of the impasse was a divergence of goals among the delegates to the Estates-General. On some basic points regarding the desired direction of reform, opinion did converge. Virtually all the delegates agreed on the need to scale back the arbitrary use of power by the monarchy—in other words, that Bourbon absolutism needed to be dismantled. But beyond this, the vision of the new order fractured. For the nobility, the goal was to pare down the Crown's powers while retaining as many of their own privileges as possible; their desired new regime would be a constitutional monarchy, but geared to the preservation of noble power and dominance. For representatives of the Third Estate, reform would be pointless if noble privileges were left untouched. Louis XVI certainly had to accept a diminution of his powers, but this would be of little use if not accompanied by more opportunities for professional and social advancement for non-noble moneyed groupings—the strata represented at the convention under the rubric of the Third Estate.[31] So, while the latter rallied to the nobility's call to hem in monarchical arbitrariness, they also raised the cry for equality before the law and an end to noble privilege, thus directly pitting themselves against most of the noble delegates.

What had begun as a call to discuss avenues for fiscal reform rapidly turned into a campaign to dismantle the absolutist state. It is important to stress, however, that almost none of the delegates construed this goal as a call to revolution. There was a commitment to political change, to be sure, but even the most radical of the delegates imagined nothing more drastic than turning France into a constitutional monarchy.[32] Certainly, the bourgeois delegates of

---

30   There are innumerable histories of these early weeks of the convention, but a particularly good one—in part because of its brevity—is Peter McPhee, *The French Revolution, 1789–1799* (Oxford: Oxford University Press, 2002).

31   The divergent goals of the nobility and the Third Estate are well covered in William Doyle, *Origins of the French Revolution* (Oxford: Oxford University Press, 1999), 101–11.

32   The most extensive study of the delegates to the Estates-General is Timothy Tackett, *Becoming a Revolutionary: The Deputies of the French National Assembly and the Emergence of a*

the Third Estate showed no *ex ante* commitment to popular sovereignty.[33] Much as in the English case, the horizons of even the most refractory elements in the reform coalition were confined to expanding their own power. This amounted to a diminution of arbitrary use of power by the state and an expansion of political space for whichever elite group the delegate happened to represent. For the Third Estate, reform thus meant greater political and social scope for themselves, but with no commitment to greater rights for subaltern groups. Indeed, in the most famous tract to emerge from the Third—Abbé Sieyès, *What Is the Third Estate?*—there was an explicit rejection of political rights for those without property.[34] Nobody came to Versailles in 1789 carrying a program for bourgeois revolution.

If the Third Estate was not revolutionary, neither was it capitalist. For purposes of assessing Guha's argument, this is perhaps the central point. Of those who represented the Third Estate, from whom would emerge the leaders of the French Revolution, the overwhelming majority had nothing to do with capitalist production. There were 610 representatives of the Third Estate, and only ninety of them had anything to do with commerce. Even here, most of the ninety were petty bourgeois—shopkeepers, merchants, and so on. Only about ten were involved with industrial production, and most of these were from traditional, heavily protected sectors. Even more damaging, those who would later emerge as the Jacobin faction were among the poorest of the delegates, closer to the plebeian world of the Parisian masses than to the glitter of the moneyed classes. The vast majority of the delegates who came representing the Third Estate were people who today would be called the salaried middle class. In fact, of the 610 delegates, some five hundred were associated with the legal profession.[35] If the social background of the delegates to Versailles is relevant to the characterization of the revolutionary coalition—and surely it must be— then there is little to warrant labeling it as "bourgeois" in the modern sense of the term.

The lack of correspondence between the use of the word and its current meaning was also true in the larger society. The delegates of the Third Estate were often referred to as "bourgeois" only because their occupations were assimilated within that category. It is well understood in the historiography of the ancien régime that "bourgeois" was a nebulous term, referring not to capitalists per se but to a cluster of occupations that had in common only what they were not: neither peasant nor laborer, these persons belonged to moneyed strata

---

Revolutionary Culture (1789–1790) (Princeton: Princeton University Press, 1996).

33   Ibid., 104–5.

34   See the analysis in William H. Sewell, Jr., *A Rhetoric of Bourgeois Revolution: The Abbé Sieyès and* What Is the Third Estate? (Durham: Duke University Press, 1994), 19–47.

35   Ibid., 145–94.

outside the nobility.[36] They could be industrialists, merchants, shopkeepers, urban professionals. In fact, the typical bourgeois in eighteenth-century France belong to the last category, simply because of its growing importance in the political economy. Hence, it comes as no surprise that in the contemporary histories of the French Revolution, the leaders were often referred to as bourgeois, since the strata to which they belonged were typically subsumed under that banner.[37]

Given the task of this book, the French leadership's middle-class origins is no small matter. Guha repeatedly castigates the Indian bourgeoisie for falling short of the boldness and revolutionary ardor of the "bourgeois" leaders of the French Revolution. Yet the Indian counterparts to the Jacobins, or delegates of the Third Estate more generally, are not the Birlas or Tatas. They are, rather, the middle-class elements of the Congress leadership. It is not semantic nitpicking to say that French predecessors to the Birlas simply did not exist in the late eighteenth century. In comparing the two groups—the French "bourgeoisie" and the Indian bourgeoisie—we are in fact looking at strata in two very different sets of social relations. The Indian bourgeoisie was a class that obtained its income and wealth by commanding the labor of others; the French groupings were either themselves the employees of others, or were independent producers. One group (the Indian) is, in the Marxian framework used by Guha, an exploiting class, while the other (the French) is not. It would therefore be quite astonishing if the Indian capitalists turned out to be as revolutionary as the French lawyers.

Even while the Third Estate was not itself a dominant class, it showed no inclination in the early weeks of the convention to overthrow the monarchy, much less unleash a social revolution. As noted earlier, its basic goals were to turn the absolute monarchy into a constitutional monarchy and to drastically scale back or even abolish the privileges granted to the nobility. Its agenda was thus primarily to increase the political and social space for its own advancement. In the initial weeks of the convention in the summer of 1789, these goals seemed to have been achieved. In June the Third assumed leadership of the three estates represented at Versailles, declaring the formation of the National Assembly. It was joined quickly by the clergy and a plurality of the noble delegates. The newly formed assembly quickly declared that it—not Louis—most directly represented

---

36   The literature on this matter is legion. For a succinct overview and guide to the literature, see T. C. W. Blanning, *The French Revolution: Aristocrats versus Bourgeois?* (New Jersey: Humanities Press, 1987). A more recent summary is in Sarah Maza, *The Myth of the French Bourgeoisie: An Essay on the Social Imaginary, 1750–1850* (Cambridge: Harvard University Press, 2003).

37   Perhaps the most careful theoretical analyses of this question are by Ellen Meiksins Wood and her students. For Wood's most elaborate statement, see *The Pristine Culture of Capitalism: A Historical Essay on Old Regimes and Modern States* (London: Verso, 1996). See also two excellent books by her students: George Comninel, *Rethinking the French Revolution* (London: Verso, 1987), and Colin Mooers, *The Making of Bourgeois Europe* (London: Verso, 1990).

the French nation and could not be dissolved without the nation's consent. By so doing, it pronounced the death of the absolute monarchy. Once a significant segment of the nobility came over to the National Assembly, Louis had no choice but to concede defeat. In late June, he agreed to recognize the assembly, rescind unpopular taxes, and confer with the Estates-General on future taxation; he also promised freedom of the press and individual liberties.[38] The delegates had achieved their goal. Absolutism was dead.

It is important to be clear, however, about what did *not* change in June 1789. Louis had expressly preserved seignorial rights, and so feudalism had not been abolished; basic liberties had been promised but not yet enumerated; more directly, there had been no extension of the franchise to the workers and peasants. Neither the abolition of feudalism nor the extension of democratic rights to subaltern classes had been demanded by the Third Estate. What they had demanded, and been granted, was greater rights for *themselves*. What they had garnered, therefore, was an elite pact, much as the English gentry had forged in the winter of 1640–1. And this, really, was all that the vast majority of delegates in the National Assembly had aspired to. There was no call to go further.

THE POLITICAL COALITION

What drove the events in France from being merely an elite pact to being a true revolution was, as in England, the combination of a recalcitrant monarch and the intervention of the popular classes. It was not, as Guha would have it, driven by elites reaching out to producers and soliciting their participation in a social mobilization. It was not, in other words, part of an elite hegemonic strategy, in Guha's terms. Rather, the subaltern classes *forced* their concerns onto the elite project—a project that had been based largely on the exclusion of those interests. Further, the representatives of the Third Estate only reluctantly acted on popular demands for inclusion and reversed some of the central legislation as soon as threats from below subsided.

In late June 1789, Louis agreed to recognize the National Assembly as well as a battery of civil liberties. Within days, however, it became clear that this might well be only a temporary concession, as news reached the assembly that he had begun to amass thousands of troops outside Paris and Versailles. He seemed to be preparing a military strike to disperse the National Assembly. It was at this point that the popular classes intervened in Paris, most famously in the capture of the Bastille. France became engulfed in popular uprisings. In urban centers across the country, local committees quickly formed in defense of the National Assembly. Perhaps even more significant was the coalescence of

---

38 Significantly, while Louis exhorted nobles to reconsider their fiscal privileges, he did not abolish them. This was part of his strategy of using the nobility against the Third Estate. See William Doyle, *The Oxford History of the French Revolution*, 2nd ed. (Oxford: Oxford University Press, 2002), 106.

this urban movement with a massive rural uprising that spread across much of the country.

The rural revolts did not come out of the blue. Episodic, though noticeable, unrest had been in evidence since 1775, driven at least in part by a squeeze exerted on the peasantry by landed proprietors.[39] The uptick in peasant actions amounted to something of a counterattack against the seignorial regime, remarkably consistent in tempo. Peasant insurgency was further fueled by a failed harvest in 1788-9 and the inevitable deprivations that followed in its wake. Already in early 1789, before the Estates-General had met, peasant actions had begun to escalate, with demands not just for a reduction in seigno-rial dues but also for the opening of food stockpiles in lordly granaries. There was widespread suspicion that landed proprietors, both secular and ecclesiasti-cal, were hoarding grain. By summer, rumors of grain hoarding mingled with fears of violent migrants and of aristocratic plots against the Third Estate.[40] These rumors added yet more fuel to the fires of rural insurrection, and by late July 1789, much of France was gripped by a spiraling peasant revolt.

The immediate effect of the popular intervention was that it once again forced Louis to retreat. He hastily announced the withdrawal of the troops amassed outside Paris, thereby appearing to abdicate power to the National Assembly. The more fundamental consequence of the national uprising, however, was to impel the assembly to more radical measures. In the country-side, peasant actions had taken on an explicitly antiseignorial character, and the months of June and July saw something of a crescendo in the uprising.[41] While the delegates to the assembly were overjoyed to have the revolution come to their rescue, their relief gave way to a deepening apprehension as news of the movement's escalating radicalism surfaced. The initial response from most of the delegates was consternation, bordering on revulsion. But as the days went by and word of the movement's episodic violence reached them, the apprehen-sion turned to fear and panic.[42] By early August, it seemed as though the mass movement might spin out of control.

---

39   John Markoff, "Peasants Help Destroy an Old Regime and Defy a New One: Some Lessons from (and for) the Study of Social Movements," *American Journal of Sociology* 102:4 (Jan., 1997), 1117. The thesis of a seignorial reaction, originally advanced by Georges Lefebvre and Camille-Ernest Labrousse, fell into disrepute in the 1960s and 1970s but has recently been revived by Peter Jones and others. See P. M. Jones, *The Peasantry in the French Revolution* (Cambridge: Cambridge University Press, 1988), 42–8.

40   The classic study is, of course, Georges Lefebvre, *The Great Fear of 1789: Rural Panic in Revolutionary France*, 1st Amer. ed. (New York: Pantheon Books, 1973).

41   Whereas in the initial phases of the rural revolt, it was taxation that loomed large for peasants, by the summer this had been replaced by an attack on the myriad exactions of the local seigniors. This is brilliantly analyzed by John Markoff in his *The Abolition of Feudalism: Peasants, Lords, and Legislators in the French Revolution* (University Park: Pennsylvania State University Press, 1996), chap. 6.

42   Tackett, *Becoming a Revolutionary*, 165–9.

Up to this point, more than a month after Louis XVI had conceded defeat, little had transpired in the National Assembly. Delegates had agreed in principle on the need for reform but drew back from crafting the needed legislation—partly because of the deep divisions between them and partly because of the sheer overwork of running the new regime. The exploding mass movement shook them out of their torpor. In a matter of days during the first half of August, the assembly issued two sets of declarations that seemed to dismantle the pillars of the social order: the abolition of feudalism and the Declaration of the Rights of Man and of the Citizen. The first promised to dismantle the entire seignorial regime, and the other to incorporate the laboring classes into the political order.

What are we to make of the promulgation of these revolutionary decrees? Were they evidence of a bourgeoisie finally coming into its own and embracing its historic project, as Guha suggests? Apparently not. Recall that although the delegates were of privileged, moneyed origins, there was virtually no capitalist grouping in the National Assembly. Even if the delegates had come with a fully formed agenda to dismantle the feudal regime, it would be of limited relevance for Guha's attempted parallels between the "bourgeois" representatives to the Estates-General and the Indian capitalist class. But even if we admit the possibility that there may have been a real capitalist presence in the assembly, the course of events belies any notion that there was an elite, antifeudal and liberal project, or that the delegates reached out to the masses by crafting a program that represented their interests.

In fact, it was the reverse: the popular movement imposed the revolutionary agenda on the delegates. As we have seen, there is no evidence that the Third Estate had any inclination to dissolve feudalism or to extend political rights to laboring classes. They moved in this direction only under pressure from the movement. Possibly the mere fact that the decrees followed a mass rebellion is not conclusive evidence that the latter caused the former. Reform might have been coming anyway, and perhaps only the timing was affected by mass pressure. But even this argument cannot be sustained: consider the actual content of the legislation that followed the issuance of the general decrees, and the continuing association between reform legislation and the popular movement.

Had the delegates been genuinely committed to a revolutionary program, they would certainly have tried to squeeze maximal leverage from the mass pressure. Instead, their strategy was to craft legislation that *minimized* the blows to the existing power structure. By the fall of 1789, the peasant revolt had subsided somewhat, giving legislators the sense that the immediate threat of violence, too, had subsided. Their reaction was to skew the laws *toward* the status quo, not against it. When antifeudal legislation finally emerged in March 1790, it was clearly intended to minimize the blow to seignorial power. Both the legal and the financial burden of freedom was placed on the peasants, making it highly difficult for them to wrest free of feudal obligations.[43] And, on the political front, when the Rights of Man were translated into actual law, it turned out that the non-propertied would have distinctly fewer rights than their betters. The Assembly refused to allow universal suffrage. A minimal property requirement was mandated for voting rights, and even more demanding preconditions for the right to hold office. In the end, only around 45,000 French men were given the right to hold high office.[44] Democratic rights were thus made conditional on being propertied.

The legislation around the abolition of feudalism and the Rights of Man revealed the assembly's priorities. Its members were committed, much as the English revolutionaries in 1640 had been, primarily to rolling back royal power; their attitude toward popular power was decidedly less enthusiastic, even hostile. It was a force they leaned on only because it was the sole available counter to royal malfeasance. Had they been committed to popular power, they would have used the mobilization of summer 1789 as a means to dismantle the ancien régime. Instead, they tried their best to preserve it, but with greater latitude for the propertied Third Estate. As Albert Soboul incisively summarizes:

> The new political institutions had one aim and one aim only, that of ensuring the peaceful, uninterrupted rule of the middle classes in their hour of victory, free from the threat of a counter-revolution and monarchy on the one hand, and of the any attempt of the people on the other.[45]

The National Assembly's goal was to strike a fine balance between rolling back the threat of royal counterrevolution while also keeping the subaltern classes out of the political nation. But just as in the English case, no such equilibrium was possible. Above all, there was no direct control over the popular movement. And as mass uprisings erupted across the country, more and more segments of the elite reformist coalition defected to the side of reaction. As their base within the ruling classes contracted, the remaining reform-minded delegates had no choice but to increase their reliance on the mass movement—which only prompted further defections from the reform coalition, forcing it to embrace the revolution.

It was this pressure from below that forced the assembly to return to the promises they had made in the August declarations. The antifeudal measures were redrawn—but only after the assembly was confronted yet again, in 1791–2, with a tidal wave of rural unrest. Indeed, John Markoff has shown an uncanny correspondence between spikes in rural upheaval and the issuance of new

---

43   Jones, *Peasantry in the French Revolution*, 86–90.
44   Doyle, *Oxford History of the French Revolution*, 123–5.
45   Albert Soboul, *A Short History of the French Revolution, 1789–1799*, trans. Geoffrey Symcox (Berkeley: University of California Press, 1977), 182.

antifeudal legislation.[46] Political rights were extended to the laboring masses in 1792, giving France universal suffrage for the first time—but here, too, only under enormous pressure. The defections of aristocratic elements from the reform coalition did not result in civil war, as in England in 1640. Instead, the malcontents emigrated to friendly neighboring states, whose rulers were aghast at the scenes unfolding in Paris and the provinces. Soon France was engulfed in war, as its neighbors combined to attack the revolution and restore the ancien régime. The National Assembly had no choice but to constitute a National Guard. However, peasants and workers would not willingly populate it without being granted political rights. And so, in fall 1792, the Jacobins relented and promulgated a law extending universal suffrage—again, only under duress. The revolution had finally become antifeudal and democratic, but not because of a "bourgeois project." The "bourgeois" legislators of the Third Estate had to be dragged kicking and screaming to assume their role as revolutionaries.

Thus, contrary to Ranajit Guha's argument regarding the antifeudal commitments of the bourgeois leadership of the French Revolution, the leaders were neither bourgeois nor antifeudal. True, they were "bourgeois" in the parlance of the time, but were not capitalists; they finally abolished feudal obligations, but did so literally at the point of a sword. Similarly, the extension of democratic rights to the subaltern classes, primarily through the expansion of suffrage, was thrust upon the National Assembly, initially by mass rebellions, and then by the need to raise a citizens army to defend against foreign aggression. If there was a "project" at all, it was the more limited one of dismantling absolutist rule and increasing the Third Estate's scope for professional advancement. Guha's presentation of the dynamic—with the leadership forging a coalition by reaching out to the laboring classes and accommodating their interests— is therefore largely imaginary. It was in fact the *peasants* who had to reach out to the dignitaries in order to get the reform coalition to turn into a revolutionary one.

THE REVOLUTIONARY SETTLEMENT

The final element in Guha's mythologizing of the "bourgeois project" is his contention that it entailed a commitment to establishing an encompassing liberal order that would transcend the gulf separating elite culture from subaltern culture. This was what the bourgeois-democratic revolution was meant to achieve—the nation-building exercise that the Indian bourgeoisie either abandoned or never undertook. Just as the aftermath of the English Revolution was a far cry from an encompassing liberalism, so too, in the French case, the outcome was not as Guha depicts it.

The extension of universal suffrage in the heady days of autumn 1792 was an

---

46 Markoff, *Abolition of Feudalism*, 487–9.

epochal event, but it was not the culmination of a political project nurtured by the Third Estate. It was, instead, an expedient they had to accept as a condition for establishing the National Guard. Support for the measure was thus never very deep. As the revolution progressed and its mass base expanded, its elite support contracted. The fall of the Jacobin dictatorship in 1794 to a more conservative coalition sealed the fate of the democratic measures. In the fall of 1795, only three years after it had been passed, the law for universal suffrage was rescinded— "abandoned as impractical as popular pressure on the Convention eased," observes William Doyle—as France returned to a limited franchise based on property requirements.[47] The result was a far-reaching reassertion of elite power, "defining the political nation in effect as the Notables," in Doyle's summation.[48]

This contraction of the political nation was not to be challenged again for more than two generations, until 1848. In the meantime, the social order that the new regime set about building was designed to reassert the boundaries between elite and subaltern prerogatives, not to dissolve them. Thus electoral rights were not extended to adult men until midcentury; the right to strike was not granted to workers until 1864 and the right to form trade unions until the mid-1880s; so, too, the right to free and universal education did not come until the 1880s. More broadly, as Eugen Weber argued in his classic study, regional rural society remained largely separate from the urban, modernizing French culture for almost a full century after the French Revolution. There was no question of the subaltern domain being integrated into a larger bourgeois culture, since rural France maintained its distinct ways of life until the process of integration finally took root in the 1880s.[49] As for the larger polity, it is sobering to recall that France underwent another three revolutionary upheavals—one every three decades—after the Napoleonic Wars. This was no stable, integrated polity. It was, like its British predecessor, a narrow oligarchy, designed to cement the power of the ruling classes, an oligarchy bent on dominating the subaltern sphere, not integrating it into a consensual order.[50]

3.3 CONCLUSION

The events that transpired in the British Isles in 1640s and in France in 1789 certainly deserve to be called revolutions. The critique of the "bourgeois

---

47   Doyle, *Oxford History of the French Revolution*, 419; see also Soboul, *French Revolution*, 467–74.

48   Doyle, ibid.

49   Eugen Weber, *Peasants into Frenchmen: The Modernization of Rural France, 1870–1914* (Stanford: Stanford University Press, 1976).

50   See the excellent discussion in Ronald Aminzade, *Class, Politics and Early Industrial Capitalism: A Study of Mid-Nineteenth Century Toulouse, France* (Albany; The State University of New York Press, 1981), 269–89.

revolutions" developed in this chapter is not intended to deny their social significance. What I suggest is simply that they were important in ways rather different from those proposed by Guha or by the historical tradition on which he draws. The classic understanding of these revolutions was that they were instrumental in the development of capitalist economic structures and the rise of liberal political regimes. These attributions are not entirely wrong; both revolutions did have significant economic and political effects. But the effects were not as dramatic as is often supposed and, in many ways, entirely different from those perhaps expected.

If we turn to the economic effects of these two revolutions, it should be clear that their contribution to the development of capitalism was either weak or redundant. In England, where the agrarian structure was already capitalist, there was no question of the revolution's creation of a bourgeois economy. At best, all it did was to accelerate trends that were already firmly in place. In the case of France, it was no doubt important that the revolution abolished some of the bulwarks of seignorial power and thus contributed to the eventual development of capitalism. But the causal link is weak. The French Revolution's most direct economic consequence was the strengthening of peasant property, not the creation of an agrarian bourgeoisie. In effect, the revolution weakened the feudal prerogatives of the nobility but without giving them new, more properly capitalist powers. The immediate gains with regard to property rights were made by the peasantry.[51] While this, in principle, laid the foundation for rural accumulation, it was necessary to wait another few decades for the advent of a dynamic, capitalist agrarian economy. The short-term result of strengthened peasant property rights was to amplify the risk-averse and conservative economic strategies typical of smallholders. The agrarian base of the French economy remained mired in very slow growth till the second half of the nineteenth century.[52]

As for the political effects of the revolutions, it ought to be clear that their contribution to the birth of modern liberalism was weak. At their radical peak, they unleashed, for the first time, truly democratic impulses into the body politic. But the emergent dominant classes quickly suppressed the greater part of these radical impulses. As with the contribution to the rise of capitalism, we need to deflate the revolutions' significance as harbingers of political liberalization. What they bequeathed was an oligarchic state with an expanded scope for political participation—but only for members of the ruling order who had hitherto been excluded.

---

51 For a recent assessment, see Jean-Laurent Rosenthal, *The Fruits of Revolution: Property Rights, Litigation and French Agriculture, 1700–1860* (Cambridge: Cambridge University Press, 1992).

52 For an overview, see Roger Price, *The Modernization of Rural France: Communications Networks and Agricultural Market Structures in Nineteenth-century France* (New York: St. Martin's Press, 1983).

If there was a direct contribution made by these two upheavals, it was to the growth and strengthening of the *state*, not capitalism or democracy. In this, the English Revolution's contribution must be recognized as a modern catalyst. Until the seventeenth century, England could only look nervously, and not a little enviously, at the emerging military behemoths on the Continent. The Crown viewed the emerging absolutisms in Spain and France as the primary dangers to British security; to compensate for its own geopolitical weakness, it crafted a delicate system of alliances with other Continental powers. Even while the agrarian sector slowly accelerated its growth rate and made it possible for England to pull away from its rivals, the state could not capitalize on the expanding agrarian surpluses, because it lacked the fiscal instruments to capture them.

It was the long revolutionary transformation between 1640 and 1688 that installed a revamped fiscal apparatus, thus enabling the construction of Britain's "fiscal-military" state.[53] Over the course of the eighteenth century, England emerged as not only the most dynamic economy in the European arena but also the most formidable military power. Its military prowess was based critically on the Crown's compromise with the landed oligarchy, giving the latter control over state finances and local governance in exchange for the monarchy's retention of executive privileges. This was the political nation that the revolution created—narrow, grasping, highly authoritarian, and increasingly belligerent in its dealings with the world.

France had already embarked on a centralizing project in the seventeenth century, as it constructed Europe's most formidable absolutism. But unlike postrevolutionary England, where state-building was fueled by an increasingly dynamic economy, the drive to strengthen the state in prerevolutionary France strained against an archaic and stagnant economic base. It was, in fact, the relentless pressure coming from across the Channel, from Great Britain, that impelled the Bourbons to make unsustainable demands on the domestic power structure. By the time of the revolution, most members of the ruling class understood that whatever else the outcome, France would have to build and maintain a political apparatus capable of competing with British power on a global scale. Hence, from the early stages of the Thermidor through Napoleon's rise to power, the centralizing efforts of the French Revolution were not disturbed, even as its radical and democratic impulses were rolled back.[54]

---

53   The standard analysis of this process is John Brewer, *The Sinews of Power: War, Money, and the English State, 1688–1783* (New York: Alfred A. Knopf, 1989). For a more recent synthesis, which builds on Brewer, see Michael J. Braddick, *State Formation in Early Modern England, c. 1550–1700* (Cambridge: Cambridge University Press, 2000).

54   For the domestic face of state centralization, see the recent analysis by Howard G. Brown, *Ending the French Revolution: Violence, Justice, and Repression from the Terror to Napoleon* (Charlottesville: University of Virginia Press, 2006).

France emerged from the revolution with an even more formidable state apparatus than was in place on its eve.[55]

We can safely say, then, that the major immediate achievement of the bourgeois revolutions was the building of new and more powerful states, authoritarian in their internal dealings, narrow in their social bases, and aggressive in their external policies. Nation-building did follow in train, but the development of national consciousness and national identity was in large measure a *consequence* of state-building, not its antecedent condition. For the European powers, the fact of England's geopolitical ascension in the eighteenth century, its repeated defeat of the vaunted French military machine, and its pivotal role in defeating Napoleon, served as tocsins for an uncertain future. The message was clear—to have a future, rival Continental powers would have to construct political economies that measured up to the looming juggernaut across the Channel. England had managed to achieve both a dynamic capitalist economy and a cohesive, stable and fiscally sound state structure. European rivals would have to follow suit. Through the first half of the nineteenth century, Continental powers embarked on ambitious projects of domestic economic transformation and state-building. In all these cases, state-building was the first order of business; the construction of national identities either followed in train or was embarked upon in service of the drive to build more powerful states. This is a point to which I will return in chapter 10, when we examine Partha Chatterjee's analysis of colonial nationalism.

We now have an assessment of the counterfactual against which Guha assesses the advent of Indian nationalism, insisting that the Indian bourgeoisie falls short of the standard set by its British and French predecessors. We have seen that in neither England nor France did any of the three critical dimensions of the revolutions resemble his depiction of them. We are now positioned to assess the implications of our findings for his larger project—placing Indian modernity in a global context and drawing the necessary theoretical and practical conclusions.

---

55 The continuity in state-building from absolutism to the Napoleonic era is stressed by Wood, *Pristine Culture of Capitalism*, 24–7.

CHAPTER FOUR

Dominance without Hegemony: The Argument in Context

Now that we have reviewed the actual record of the British and French upheavals, it is time to take anew the measure of the Indian bourgeoisie, which, as we know, Ranajit Guha regards as having failed in its assigned mission to transform the political order in the direction taken by England and France. This chapter offers an assessment of Guha's argument about India's path to political and economic modernity, using as a backdrop the findings of chapter 3. I have signaled the relevance of the main findings along the way in the previous pages, and this chapter serves as an opportunity to bring them together and assess their implications. But, in addition to placing the Indian experience in a systematic comparison with Guha's baseline cases, I also expand the comparative frame. After all, it might be that the reason Guha fails to convince is that he has relied on the wrong historical cases. Perhaps the bourgeoisie in other instances, or other historical periods, did perform as Guha thinks they did in early modern Europe. It could be that, given the proper comparison, there are indeed grounds for maintaining that Indian capital failed to live up to standards set elsewhere. Maybe capital did abandon its universalizing mission, not in comparison with England and France, but in comparison with its achievements in other regions. As it happens, however, the heroism and boldness that Guha mistakenly assigns to the British and French are hard to find anywhere, for any bourgeoisie. The Indian experience, I will argue, is consistent not only with the two cases Guha leans on but also with the generality of modern experience.

Guha's mistaken view of the European experience does not simply undermine his analysis of the postcolonial polity. It also has grave implications for his more ambitious project of political critique. He presents his argument as something more than a diagnosis of the postcolonial political crisis. He takes it as the foundation for a far-reaching critique of liberal historiography, and ultimately of liberal theory itself. Other Subalternist theorists have similarly trumpeted Guha's achievements as a critic of Enlightenment universalism, a judgment that they base in part on the arguments we are now considering. It is my intention to show that the grounds for this claim are even weaker than for his empirical analysis, because Guha's rendering of the European experience is itself a wholesale reproduction of liberal fictions. He bases his analysis on a Whig historical tradition that was born, in the early nineteenth century, as an apologia for capital. It is the bourgeoisie's own vision of its past—cleaned up, beautified, and perfumed. It does, no doubt, also have a Marxist pedigree, but Guha's version of the theory is much closer to the Whig historians of the nineteenth century than it is to Marx's.

In the first part of this chapter, I place the Indian bourgeoisie's orientation against the practice of the French and British elites during their bourgeois revolutions, focusing on three dimensions central to Guha's analysis: the dismantling of landlordism, the creation of a hegemonic antifeudal coalition, and the implantation of a consensual, liberal post-revolutionary order. I then revisit the crisis of the 1970s—the events that led Guha and his colleagues to surmise that something had gone terribly askew in India's modernization—and see how, based on the argument I have developed, that crisis might be reinterpreted. Finally, I examine the historiographical lineage of Guha's conception of the bourgeois revolutions and its ideological implications.

4.1 BOURGEOIS INTERESTS AND LAND REFORM

Judged in terms of space or of word count, Guha does not devote much attention to the fortunes of the landed classes, either in the European bourgeois revolutions or the Indian nationalist movement. The real focus of his attention is the issue of leadership. Still, the bourgeoisie's relation with traditional landed classes occupies a central place in his analysis, even if this is not reflected in the number of pages he devotes to it. He traces the root of what he calls the "structural fault" between the two modernizing projects—that of Western Europe and of India—in the bourgeoisie's divergent orientations to landed property. Whereas the British and French elites launched their revolutions as a frontal assault on the feudal nobility, the Indian bourgeoisie accommodated to it. From these contrasting origins springs the specificity of colonial modernity, a modernity without recognizably capitalist cultural and political forms—or so claim the Subalternists.

The problem with the argument is threefold. First, in only one of the revolutions was there any attack at all on traditional landlord power, for in only one of the cases did such power exert significant social weight. By the onset of the revolution in 1640, feudal landed relations in England had largely been reduced to the status of a historical relic. There was a landed aristocracy, to be sure, but for the most part it was by now a class of capitalist landlords, not feudal magnates. The bourgeoisie did participate in the revolution, but its ambition was not to *transform* the social order so much as to *preserve* it against the encroachments of an overly ambitious monarchy and its drive to absolutism. It was only in France that the revolution took on a somewhat antifeudal character, in that there was a legislative drive to dismantle seignorialism in the countryside.

But this is where the second problem arises for Guha. It may be argued that even though the English Revolution was not antifeudal, the French surely was. Yet even though there was a strongly antifeudal complexion to the upheaval in France, it cannot help Guha's case, for it was by no means a *bourgeois* project.

For one thing, the revolutionary leadership included virtually no bourgeois presence; what was referred to as the "bourgeoisie" was overwhelmingly a group of urban professionals, mainly from the legal realm. Even more important, however, this leadership showed no ambition to dismantle seignorial power of its own volition. Antiseignorialism did not figure prominently in its stated goals prior to the revolution, and when the revolution started to unfold, elite leaders showed no inclination to push it in that direction. Much as in the English case, the ambition of elite leaders was more or less limited to asserting their rights against the state, not to extinguishing feudal landed power.

This brings up the third problem. Insofar as the elites in France turned against seignorialism at all, it was only because of overwhelming pressure from the peasantry, whose rural revolution evoked great consternation among the notables in the National Assembly. Even if it is established, through a miracle of historical research, that the members of the Third Estate were in fact capitalists, it would still not sustain Guha's argument. Whatever the class background of the Third Estate, the crucial fact is that its radicalism was produced through the use of force and was by no means an index of the liberalism or antifeudal fervor of the bourgeoisie. It is crucial to recall that, even in the face of peasant revolution, the elite leadership dragged its feet and sustained feudal rights as long as possible.

How, then, can it be claimed that the Indian bourgeoisie departed from a standard set by its Western European predecessors? Clearly it did not, at least with regard to its attitude to landlordism. But perhaps Guha's admonishment would have some traction if we changed the reference frame from the classic bourgeois revolutions to other cases. Could we not look to other regions or times, when capitalist classes might have taken up cudgels against their landed oligarchies, leading an antifeudal revolution of the kind Guha ascribes to the British and French? This would certainly preserve the basic structure of his argument, even if the historical referents would now be different. The Indian bourgeoisie could still be found wanting when set against its counterparts elsewhere.

The problem is that it is hard to think of *any* historical experiences that conform to Guha's account of the classic bourgeois revolutions—cases of agrarian reform being pushed through by a domestic class of capitalists at the helm of a broad and inclusive social coalition. Broadly speaking, the routes to agrarian reform in the modern epoch have been of three sorts, none of which are friendly to Guha's theory. The first, of which Stein-Hardenberg reforms in Prussia and the Russian reforms of 1861 are examples, were state-led and imposed from above. They were not driven through by a modernizing capitalist class, but rather by a modernizing *state*, with some support from the highest echelons of the rural aristocracy.[1] In the case of Russia, the aristocracy had little recourse against the state

---

1   For Prussia, see Robert Berdahl, *The Politics of the Prussian Nobility: The Development of a Conservative Ideology 1770–1848* (Princeton: Princeton University Press, 1988), chap. 3–4. An older

initiative since it was, in the European context, one of the weakest landed elites vis-à-vis the central state; in Prussia, they were carried out with the support of some segments of the nobility, a tactic to which the state had to resort because of the comparatively greater power of the landed classes. But in both cases, the initiative came from above and lacked even a hint of the hegemonic or liberal political commitment that Guha associates with bourgeois revolutions. Twentieth-century analogs to this strategy are hard to find, but the limited reforms of Ataturk in Anatolia and Nasser in Egypt are perhaps the closest.

A second route to reform has been the revolutionary one, embodied most conspicuously in the great peasant revolutions of the twentieth century—in Mexico, Russia, China, Vietnam, and so on.[2] It goes without saying that these cannot serve as stand-ins for the bourgeois revolution. These were revolutions from below, led primarily by the peasantry. Guha might have carried out a comparison here with the Indian experience had he not abandoned his query, raised in his inaugural essay in *Subaltern Studies 1*, about why national integration in India took a bourgeois path instead of one led by an alliance of workers and peasants. It would have been interesting to ask why Indian statehood came into being under elite leadership and did not break out onto a revolutionary path as it did in Mexico or Vietnam. But Guha chose not to pursue this analytical track, opting instead to focus single-mindedly on the question of the bourgeoisie.

The third route has been through military imposition, typically by occupying powers. For decades, historians took Napoleon's expansion into Europe to be the first instance of agrarian reform from above. No doubt this was partly influenced by his own propaganda, which presented his campaigns as extensions of the revolution outward, against reactionary nobilities on the Continent. Recent scholarship has been somewhat less credulous with respect to Napoleon's claims, showing that he was in fact quite willing to reach an accommodation with rural elites in exchange for their support.[3] The pillars of rural class power

but still useful work is Walter M. Simon, *The Failure of the Prussian Reform Movement, 1807–1819* (Ithaca: Cornell University Press, 1955). For Russia, a standard analysis in English is Alexander Gerschenkron, "Russia: Agrarian Policies and Industrialization, 1861–1917," in his *Continuity in History and Other Essays* (Cambridge: Harvard University Press, 1968), 140–248. Gerschenkron approaches his analysis with the mind-set of an economic historian, more concerned with the reforms' effects than their causes. For an illuminating and influential analysis of the emancipation declaration of 1861, see Larissa G. Zakharova, *Autocracy and the Abolition of Serfdom in Russia, 1856–1861*, trans. in *Soviet Studies in History* 26:2 (Fall 1987).

2   For Mexico, the scholarship is immense. The works of Alan Knight, John Mason Hart, and Friedrich Katz stand out. See Knight's two-volume *The Mexican Revolution* (Cambridge: Cambridge University Press, 1986), Hart's *Revolutionary Mexico: The Coming and Process of the Mexican Revolution* (Berkeley: University of California Press, 1987), and Katz's excellent *The Secret War in Mexico: Europe, the United States, and the Mexican Revolution* (Chicago: University of Chicago Press, 1981).

3   However, it must be said that in English-language historiography, research on the details of Napoleon's imperial structure is still somewhat thin. For some good overviews, see Michael Broers, *Europe under Napoleon 1799–1815* (London: Arnold Press, 1996), Charles J.

were shaken, but not destroyed, through Napoleon's policies. In more recent years, it was the American occupation of Japan and Korea in the aftermath of the Second World War that occasioned militarily imposed agrarian reforms. In these instances, the reforms were quite far-reaching, especially in Korea, where they effectively destroyed rural landed elites.[4] Whatever the story of these reform episodes, they do not support Guha's argument. If anything, they further undermine it, because in these cases reform was imposed by occupiers—showing the utter inability, or unwillingness, of domestic elites to attack landed power. Reforms had to come from the outside, because no internal force was able to implement them. These cases cannot, therefore, bolster Guha's case for the under-performance of the Indian bourgeoisie.

If we take a sweep of all three of these reform strategies, we see that they have one thing in common—they do nothing toward reviving Guha's faith in the capitalist class as antifeudal protagonist. The reforms were all initiated and led by social forces *other* than the capitalist class. Guha is correct in his observation that the capitalists in the Indian nationalist movement did not lead the charge against traditional landed classes; he is incorrect, however, in his assertion that this set them apart in any way from their counterparts anywhere else, or even from the nonbourgeois leaders in the so-called bourgeois revolutions of Western Europe. Indeed, bourgeois reluctance to attack landed property has been the rule throughout the modern epoch, even in countries that experienced agrarian reform. We can safely conclude that, in its preference to cement an alliance with local landed classes over the prospect of an antifeudal coalition, the Indian bourgeoisie did not stand out in any way at all. To use Guha's language, its performance was very much in line with its competence.

4.2 THE BOURGEOISIE AND SUBALTERN CLASSES

We turn now to the matter of whether or not the bourgeoisie achieved ideological hegemony—in Guha's terms—over the revolutionary coalition. Recall that, in his presentation, the leadership of the revolutions attained hegemony because it incorporated the real interests of subaltern social classes into its revolutionary program. Through representing their aspirations, it thus "spoke for all of society." The key elements of this program were liberation from feudal exploitation and

---

Esdaile, *The Wars of Napoleon* (New York: Longman, 1995), and the collection in Michael Rowe, ed., *Collaboration and Resistance in Napoleonic Europe: State-Formation in an Age of Upheaval, c. 1800–1815* (New York: Palgrave Macmillan, 2003).

4   For Japan, see R. P. Dore, *Land Reform in Japan* (Oxford: Oxford University Press, 1959); and for Korea, see the summary account in John Lie, *Han Unbound: The Political Economy of South Korea* (Palo Alto: Stanford University Press, 1998). In both cases, peasant uprisings played an important role in pushing reforms forward. But pressure from the United States as an occupying power seems to have been the critical factor.

the bestowal of political liberties. The litmus test for having secured hegemony is the fact that European elites sustained their leadership of the revolutionary forces without having to resort to coercion. In the Indian nationalist movement, by contrast, the bourgeoisie did not willingly internalize subaltern demands. It resisted placing them on the political agenda, and hence failed to elicit subaltern consent to its leadership. Having failed to secure its hegemony over the movement, it had to utilize coercion to keep its mass base in line. The disciplinary measures were an index of its inability to win mass consent to its leadership.

Upon examination, these arguments can be seen to break down. As for the leadership's commitment to subaltern interests, we saw in the previous chapter that, in neither the English nor the French case, was this part of the story. In both, the leaders' intention, far from incorporating mass demands, was to marginalize them as much as possible, and to keep the political agenda confined to the preferences of the elite groupings. In both, the design had been to just beat back the Crown's absolutist ambitions and to expand the political space for landed classes and urban elites. The goal was to force through an elite pact, not to transform the condition of the lower orders. To the extent that the demands of the latter were brought on board, it was because mass mobilization *forced* the issue. Furthermore, once mass pressure subsided, the very same elite leadership moved to push subaltern groups back out of the political arena and confine its scope to the privileged classes. Hence, insofar as the Indian bourgeoisie was reluctant to incorporate subaltern demands into its program, it was no different from European elites in the classic revolutions. In both cases, ruling classes reacted similarly to subaltern mobilization—by trying to minimize its claims on their own power.

If we turn now to the use of discipline in the movements, and whether this signaled a hegemonic failure for the Indian capitalist class, the results are even more damaging to Guha's argument. The critical point here is that his case for Indian capital's failure rests entirely on the implicit contrast with the European elites' practice. When we examine the course of the English and French Revolutions, however, we find not only that their leaders resorted to a vast spectrum of disciplinary devices to control and mobilize their base, but that the measures were, in all likelihood, far *more* coercive than anything the Indian National Congress ever attempted. Both revolutions turned into civil wars, in which the revolutionary side had to resort to measures such as conscription, billeting, and requisition of supplies, which make anything done by the INC pale in comparison. So, if the INC was not a hegemonic leader of its political coalition, neither were the English and French elites. Guha, however, has stipulated that the later *were*—which would mean that the INC, too, must be deemed hegemonic. Either way, the case for its exceptionalism collapses.

Perhaps his argument can be saved by changing the contrastive frame. As we tried in the preceding section, perhaps his case will fare better if we look to other countries as possible benchmarks with which to compare the Indian experience. Perhaps the European cases are inappropriate as comparisons, because they were real revolutions, while the Indian one was not. We could try to look to other movements where bourgeois leaderships did not resort to discipline, at least not of the kind highlighted by Guha. The problem is, it is hard to think of any mass political mobilization in modern history in which leaders did not use disciplinary devices, of the kind Guha mentions, over their mass base. The kind of tactics Guha points to—social boycotts, psychological pressure, ostracism, crowd control—have been central to every modern social mobilization we know of. Whether we turn to the great anticolonial movements, or social reform struggles, or trade union movements, there has never been a social struggle in which such measures were not used.[5]

In sum, there seems to be scant justification for the view that the INC's practice is an index of relative failure in acquiring hegemony. Guha's argument thus seems to land us in a dilemma. If we accept his insistence that the European experience is a benchmark of hegemonic success, then we must reject his categorization of Indian capitalists as having failed. Whereas if we accept his judgment about Indian capital as failing to attain hegemony, then the European leaderships must also be so judged, and what is more, the leadership of just about every successful modern movement must also be deemed nonhegemonic—surely a perverse conclusion. Either way, there is no basis for an insistence on a "structural fault" between the bourgeoisie of Europe and that of India.

4.3 THE BOURGEOISIE AND NATION-BUILDING

We now come to the final element in Guha's argument about the bourgeois revolutions, which focuses on the nature of the political settlement they generated. Guha believes that the liberalism of the revolutionary bourgeoisie issued in the construction of an inclusive and encompassing social order. Capital had acquired hegemony by successfully articulating the interests of subaltern classes in the antifeudal coalition; it then built upon its success as a mobilizing agent in creating, after its victory, a political nation that bridged the gulf that had thus far separated subaltern politics from elite politics.

---

5   The most plausible rendering of his case is that what made the INC's use of discipline stand out was its reliance on traditional symbols and practices such as caste membership, Hindu doctrine, etc. This gave sustenance to nonbourgeois ideology and social institutions. Such an argument would rest on two implicit claims: that capitalists typically refrain from resorting to traditional symbols and practices to stabilize their hegemony, and that we can enumerate the proper components of "bourgeois" ideology, so that elements like Hindu doctrine must be placed outside it. Neither assumption is sustainable, and both are examined in great detail in chaps. 5 and 6 below. In those chapters, I show that the bourgeoisie has resorted to "traditional" discursive forms as well as power relations with great regularity in the West, that is, in regions that Guha takes as bastions of bourgeois hegemony. Hence, if the INC resorted to such mechanisms in its mobilization, that would not set it apart from the exemplars of successful "hegemony."

What disappoints Guha when he considers the Indian experience is "the mediocre liberalism" of its capitalist class, which "failed to measure up to the heroism" of its European predecessors. Recall that he regards this failure as lying at the root of the crisis-ridden political culture of postcolonial India. Because it did not create an encompassing political culture, based on the consent of the subaltern classes, the bourgeoisie could not stabilize its rule. It had, perforce, to continue its reliance on discipline and coercion, much as it had done during the independence movement. Whereas the European capitalists had rested their dominance on the consent of the masses, the Indian ruling class settled for dominance without hegemony.

In assessing this argument, let us again assume that Guha's facts about the Indian experience are correct. I will not challenge him in his surmise that the Indian bourgeoisie's liberalism was mediocre, or even negligible; that it had no deep desire to build an encompassing political community; or that it did not strive to "speak for the nation." Even if we accept all these descriptions, however, the evidence adduced in the previous chapter shows that Guha's claim of the existence of a "structural fault" between the Indian bourgeoisie and the leaders of the classic bourgeois revolutions is deeply flawed, not because he has his facts about India wrong but because, once again, he dramatically misconstrues the European experience.

Recall that the priority of the elite French and English coalitions after their victories was to exclude subaltern classes from the political nation—not to strengthen their incorporation. In both of these revolutions, the opposition leaderships' own agenda had no place for the construction of an inclusive political community. The intent was to install a political regime with an expanded set of rights for non-noble *elites*, but with no real intention of enfranchising laboring groups. The vision was for a constitutional monarchy, with even limited political rights for the "meaner sort" a matter of great ambivalence, if not consternation, for the antimonarchical forces. And in both England and France, the immediate consequences of the revolutions were not at all friendly to the poor. The polities that arose in the wake of the classical bourgeois revolutions were oligarchies, not liberal orders. They were more open than absolutist states, to be sure; they were not, however, encompassing political communities. For more than a century after the new states were installed, laboring classes had to wage unceasing struggle to gain any substantial political rights—the very rights that Guha seems to associate with a hegemonic order. On his own terms, it would be hard to maintain that the chief means of stability in this period was the active consent of the poor to their place in the world. A hegemonic order, as Guha defines it, took more than a century to form.

Compared to the realities of the bourgeois revolutions, the Indian experience seems, if anything, a relative advance. The political order installed in 1947 was not what most progressives had hoped for, especially on matters of minority rights. But the new state offered a great deal more political space than had either of the European models. This is not because the Indian bourgeoisie was especially enlightened. Guha is entirely correct that the Indian business community was, on the whole, deeply suspicious of a fully enfranchised and empowered working class. But it had little choice in the matter. While the European elites were able to suppress subaltern political aspirations in their revolutions, the Indians were not. Having had to abide a massive social movement as its ticket to power, the Indian bourgeoisie did not have the means of disenfranchising it. The movement was too strong, too well-organized, and had too many supporters in the nationalist leadership. While the bourgeoisie may not have wanted to endow laboring classes with power, it was something they had to accept.

This point is worth stressing. Guha is entirely justified in impugning the liberal credentials of Indian capitalists. They were no lovers of democracy or of the empowerment of the laboring classes. Indeed, their early reaction to the transformation of the Indian National Congress into a mass, mobilizational organization in the 1920s was to make moves toward organizing a rival party to represent the propertied classes.[6] It was only with some hesitation that they maintained their partnership with the INC. Only after an initial experiment with limited home rule after 1935, when the INC took over the reins of government in several provinces, did their attitude soften. And this was not because the captains of industry had suddenly become proponents of popular power. It was because, upon winning office in the provinces, the INC moved swiftly to subdue and subordinate the popular forces, especially labor. The bourgeoisie solidified its relationship to Congress because Congress proved it could be trusted: Nehru, Patel, Gandhi and other leaders showed they could contain the Left within the organization, leaving no doubt that vital capitalist interests would be prioritized once Congress secured full power.[7] And once Independence was attained in 1947, Nehru moved to demobilize and then marginalize the trade unions and the Left in the party and in the political scene more generally.[8] All this justifies Guha's criticism of the Indian bourgeoisie and the INC.

---

6   See Sumit Sarkar, *Modern India, 1885–1947* (Delhi: Macmillan, 1984), 279–81.

7   For the Congress provincial ministries, the basic work is Claude Markovits, *Indian Business and Nationalist Politics, 1931–39: The Indigenous Capitalist Class and the Rise of the Congress Party* (Cambridge: Cambridge University Press, 1985). For relevant material on the INC's orientation away from the mass movement during its tenure in the provinces, see also Sujata Patel, *The Making of Industrial Relations: The Ahmedabad Textile Industry, 1918–1939* (Delhi: Oxford University Press, 1987); Vinita Damodaran, *Broken Promises: Popular Protest, Indian Nationalism, and the Congress Party in Bihar, 1935–1946* (Delhi: Oxford University Press, 1992); Amit Kumar Gupta, *The Agrarian Drama: The Leftists and the Rural Poor in India, 1934–1951* (Delhi: Manohar, 1996). Although it covers a slightly earlier period, also valuable is A. D. D. Gordon, *Businessmen and Politics: Rising Nationalism and a Modernising Economy in Bombay, 1918–1933* (Delhi: Manohar, 1978).

8   I describe these dynamics in Chibber, *Locked in Place: State-Building and Late Industrialization in India* (Princeton: Princeton University Press, 2003), chaps. 4–6, and in Chibber, "From Class Compromise to Class Accommodation: Labor's Incorporation into the

Nevertheless, none of these facts distinguishes Indian capitalists from the elites of the British or French revolutions. Guha's argument is entirely contrastive—it is not about the deficiencies of Indian capital per se, but their deficiencies *relative* to their forbears. So, too, with the political economy more generally. The political order India inherited was no doubt flawed, but it was, in many ways, also more democratic, more integrated, and more inclusive than was England's in 1720 or France's in 1815.

In sum, on this third and final dimension, there was no "structural fault" between the Indian bourgeoisie and its predecessors. The Indian business class was disdainful of subaltern agency, to be sure; but so were the Europeans. There was a difference in the kind of political regimes that the two epochs generated— but what emerged were two oligarchies in Europe and electoral democracy in India. It took European subaltern classes more than a century to achieve what the Indians acquired at the very birth of the postcolonial state. Even this difference, while certainly real and inimical to Guha's claims, cannot be attributed to any significant polarities in the political preferences of ruling elites. It arose, instead, because of variations in the political *capacities* of the other actors— even though the preferences of capitalists in India were much like those of the British or French elites, they were not in a position to impose them on the rest of the nation. Subaltern agency took care of that.[9]

4.4 THE POSTCOLONIAL CRISIS REVISITED

What motivated Guha to undertake his analysis was, as mentioned, the political crisis of the 1970s. It is now clear that our conclusions cast these events in a very different light than do his conclusions. To Guha and the Subalternists, the political upheavals of these years were symptomatic of a deep structural weakness of the postcolonial order, namely, the chasm separating elite political culture from that of subaltern groups. These phenomena were viewed as deviations from the route to modernity taken in early modern Europe and as the legacy of a weak and illiberal bourgeoisie that itself fell short of the heroic performance of the British and French capitalist classes. The failure of Indian capital was declared on three interrelated grounds: their refusal to confront landed property, their inability to achieve hegemony over the national movement and thus their resort

---

Indian Political Economy," in Raka Ray and Mary Fainsod Katzenstein, eds., *Social Movements in India: Poverty, Power and Politics* (Lanham, MD: Rowman & Littlefield, 2005). See also the very valuable dissertation by Suhit Sen, "The Transitional State: Congress and Government in U.P., 1946–1957" (Ph.D. diss., University of London, SOAS, 1998).

9   Of course, this still leaves the issue of why so much of the political culture in the Subcontinent was, and continues to be, overtly coercive. I will address this issue in chaps. 6 and 8, showing that the answer lies not in the political orientation or the capacities of the bourgeoisie, as Guha would have it, but in that of the laboring classes.

to coercion, and their failure to build a binding social order and thereby bridge the gap between the two domains.

The arguments of the present and preceding chapters suggest that not only is Guha's explanation for the crisis-ridden polity flawed, but the significance he attaches to the crisis must also be revised. He takes the political crisis of the post-colonial order to be an indicator of a failed bourgeois revolution; it is viewed as pathological and, had the path to modernity been of a standard type, avoidable. If the modernization process had been shepherded by a competent bourgeoisie and political leadership, the expected result would have been very different. In what ways? Presumably it would have looked something like what Guha takes to have occurred in Europe. He thinks that the bourgeoisie's ascension was coeval with the installation of a liberal and consensual political order. The implication is that a polity of this kind would have been far more stable and harmonious, and, most important, would have rested on the consent of the governed.

I have argued that, to the contrary, the bourgeois revolutions created what was essentially an oligarchy of the propertied classes—riven with conflict and wracked with political instability. Indeed, in the French case, it culminated in two further revolutions within half a century. Against this backdrop, what Guha considers a deviation from Europe's story—the creation of a fractured political nation, the exclusion of the dominated groups, the gap between elite and subaltern—is in fact directly aligned with it. Indeed, we can safely say that the postrevolutionary regimes in Europe were more oligarchic and less consensual than India's in 1947.[10] Hence, what Guha takes as pathological should instead be seen as normal in the construction of bourgeois political orders. What Guha takes as a sign of a failure in political modernization is in reality what political modernization has looked like for much of the world. His premise that postcolonial India deviated fundamentally from the norm established by early modern Western Europe is thus quite dubious.

If the very premise of the project is questionable, so is the explanation he offers. Guha claims that the exceptional features of Indian political culture are the consequence of the many shortcomings of its capitalist class. These he measures against the virtues of the British and French bourgeoisies. The implication is that, had the Indian bourgeoisie been more akin to capital during its rise to power in the classic revolutions, the outcome in India would have been very different. Once again, the premise—that the capitalist classes in the two eras had very different political orientations—falls flat. The English bourgeoisie and French "capitalists" were no more interested in building an encompassing political nation than were

---

10   This is not, of course, to deny the resort to coercion by the Indian state, especially in its project of political centralization. Of particular relevance is the violence with which Nehru and his successors have maintained order in Kashmir and the Northeast. But the measures they have used are no less coercive than those used by Britain in Ireland. They establish a continuity with the bloody history of state formation in the West, not a deviation from it.

the Birlas or Tatas in India. They had no more animus against feudalism than did the Indians, nor were they any more solicitous of subaltern interests. There were good reasons that Indian political modernization exhibited a gap between elite and subaltern political domains: this was exactly what the "bourgeois" orders of early modern Europe looked like, as long as the new ruling classes were able to impress their preferences onto the political order.

In sum, dominance without hegemony—as Guha defines it—is not an aberration associated with the postcolonial world or the sign of a failed bourgeois revolution. It is, and has been, the normal face of bourgeois power.

4.5 CRITIQUE OR APOLOGIA? SUBALTERNISTS AS THE NEW WHIGS

At this point, we should pause and reconsider Guha's conviction that he has provided a critique of, and alternative to, liberal historiography. He uses the appellation "liberal" pejoratively, taking it as an intellectual enterprise committed to obscuring the real history of capitalist expansion, especially its expansion into the colonial world: "A bourgeois discourse par excellence, it helped the bourgeoisie to change or at least significantly to modify the world according to its class interests in the period of its ascendancy, and since then to consolidate and perpetuate its dominance."[11] Liberal historiography is thus complicit with the dominance of the modern bourgeoisie. In fact, Guha continues, "the function of this complicity is . . . to make liberal historiography speak from within the bourgeois consciousness itself."[12] Thus, the liberal interpretation of history not only extends the interests of the dominant class, but actually reflects that class's own views of itself and of the world. The arguments developed in *Dominance without Hegemony* are meant to be an antidote to such apologetics.

THE LIMITS OF GUHA'S CRITIQUE

What are the elements that, to Guha, make liberal historiography an expression of the bourgeoisie's own worldview? For him, what makes liberals complicit with bourgeois ideology is the claim that the mission launched by capital in the East is the same one that it had successfully carried out in Western Europe. In the West, capital had established a political order based on the consent of the governed—on the acquisition of hegemony. Liberal intellectuals misrepresent actual history when they depict the colonial and postcolonial polities as resting on similar foundations:

> The essential point about that misrepresentation is that dominance under colonial conditions has quite erroneously been endowed with hegemony. This is so because

---

11   Ranajit Guha, *Dominance without Hegemony: History and Power in Colonial India* (Cambridge: Harvard University Press, 1997), 6–7. Henceforth cited as *DH*.

12   Ibid.

liberal historiography has been led to presume that capital, in its Indian career, succeeded in overcoming the obstacles to its self-expansion and subjugating all pre-capitalist relations in material and spiritual life well enough to enable the bourgeoisie to speak for all of society, as it had done in England and France in 1640 and 1789.[13]

This argument has two significant components. One is, as we have stressed, that the litmus test for capital's having overcome the obstacles to its self-expansion is that it is able to "speak for all of society"—to base its rule on the masses' consent. The test is not whether capital is able to establish its economic dominance or its political supremacy. No doubt these are important to Guha, but the real indication of capi-tal's having carried out its mission is that it becomes an agent for expressing the general will. The second noteworthy point, again, is that Guha takes just such an outcome to have occurred in England and France after their revolutions. To him, these revolutions embody the liberal commitment of the bourgeoisie.

The problem with liberal ideology, for Guha, is that it illicitly *generalizes* the European experience onto capital's Eastern career. It therefore masks or obscures the class's *failure* to carry out its mission. He does not dispute its self-descrip-tion in the European context. He accuses it of acting in bad faith. This is why his criticism of colonial capital is colored with a distinct sense of disappointment—it did not bring to India the same political commitments that drove it on its home turf. He charges the bourgeoisie with failing to live up to standards embodied in its own practice. This is exemplified with great clarity in one of his most powerful denunciations of British capital's misdeeds in India. I excerpted it in chapter 2 but present it again here, with the relevant passages highlighted:

> [T]he metropolitan bourgeoisie, *who professed and practiced democracy at home* . . . were quite happy to conduct the government of their Indian empire as an autocracy. *Champions of the right of the European nations to self-determination*, they denied the same right to their Indian subjects until the very last phase of the raj . . . Their *antagonism to feudal values and institutions in their own society made little difference* . . . to their vast tolerance of pre-capitalist values and institutions in Indian society.[14]

We must pay attention to the italicized passages, for Guha takes them to collec-tively embody the "paradox" of colonial rule—the paradox being the dramatic contrast between British capitalists' political practice at home as opposed to its actions in India. But this is a paradox only if one accepts as one's premise a largely mythological account of European history. If we inject, instead, the *real* history of capital's ascension into Guha's account, the putative paradox evaporates. An

---

13   Ibid., 19
14   *DH* 4–5. Emphasis added.

accurate rendering of the European experience would generate, instead, the following paragraph to replace his original one, with the italicized passages in the original quotation replaced by new passages, more reflective of actual history:

> [T]he metropolitan bourgeoisie, *who fought against and suppressed democracy at home* . . . were quite happy to conduct the government of their Indian empire as an autocracy. *Wary of the right of the European nations to self-determination*, they denied the same right to their Indian subjects until the very last phase of the raj . . . Their *accommodation to feudal values and institutions in their own society was paralleled by* . . . their vast tolerance of pre-capitalist values and institutions in Indian society.

This is what Guha *ought* to have said; had he done so, it would have generated a very different framework for understanding the dynamic of colonial rule in India. In a sense, the liberal historians whom Guha castigates were correct—the colonial state *was* a product of the same impulses that drove state formation in Great Britain. It is just that the content of these impulses was not as they described it, on either side. The bourgeoisie strove to install an oligarchic form of rule at home, no less than it did in India. It follows that the despotic character of colonial rule, far from being a fundamental departure from the bourgeoisie's political preferences in England or France, was simply a *concentrated and more brutal expression of those preferences*. Guha merely faults the liberal historians for getting the Indian side of the story wrong. But he accepts *in toto* the liberal description of the European experience. Hence, using Guha's own definition of the term, his account is not only wrong, but ideological. It not only obscures the real history of European modernization, but does so in a fashion that white-washes capital's real objectives, which were to set up a polity narrowly committed to its particular interests. It is a story that substitutes capital's self-serving vision of its past for the real one.

THE WHIG ORIGINS OF GUHA'S CRITIQUE

The ideological character of Guha's construction is still more evident if we examine its pedigree. The notion that a progressive and liberal bourgeoisie launched the classic revolutions was crafted in post-Napoleonic Europe by liberal intellectuals fighting against a rising tide of Royalist sentiments. In both England and France, the 1820s witnessed a powerful recrudescence of conservative ideology, at the heart of which lay an effort to delegitimize not only the French Revolution but the very idea of popular power. In England, historical debates had, for decades, been structured by the political struggle between two parties, Tory and Whig, both captured by dominant classes and both hostile to popular classes. The origins of the Whig version of the English Revolution can be traced to the propaganda that parliamentary leaders crafted during the revolutionary years, and thereafter. It portrayed the antimonarchical leaders as driven by the defense of liberty against arbitrary power; more to the point, this historiography depicted the revolutionary goals as a defense of popular and national interests, not the interests of a particular class. Herein lay the origins of the notion that the bourgeois leadership of the movement expressed the interests of the broader nation. In this Whig interpretation, the Civil Wars were not only justified but necessary in the forward march of freedom and liberty. The Whigs laid claim to be the lineal descendants of the revolutionary forces, and thereby to be defenders of liberty.

In the Whig tradition as handed down to the 1820s, parliamentary leaders in 1640 carried the banner of liberty, but they were not yet identified as bourgeois.[15] They were seen as enlightened leaders committed to the idea of freedom. The identification of freedom with bourgeois leadership was imported into the story more by French historians, also writing in the wake of Napoleon's fall.[16] Fighting against the restoration of Bourbon rule, when the revolution of 1789 was under attack as an orgy of excesses, progressive liberals developed an interpretation that not only portrayed the French Revolution as a defense of popular liberties, but added to it the argument that the bourgeoisie had been at the helm of the struggle. In their highly influential works, published over a span of more than three decades, Augustin Thierry, François Guizot, François Mignet, Henri de Saint-Simon, and others laid the foundation for what has come to be known as the liberal interpretation of the French Revolution. But the basic elements of this interpretation eventually congealed into a general framework for *both* of the great revolutions, British and French. Guizot and Thierry both projected the analysis of 1789 back to the Civil Wars in England. Within this view, both revolutions were the product of a rising bourgeoisie, fighting for modern liberties and overthrowing the feudal order in their defense.

French liberal historiography was the first to portray the revolution as a product of class struggle. But in their interpretation, the struggle was between the Third Estate as a whole and the parasitic nobility. They accepted Sieyès's dictum that the Third Estate was "everything"—that it comprised virtually the entire nation. Hence, its bourgeois leadership literally "spoke for the nation"; there was no question of conflicting interests between the leadership and its mass base. This formulation reached its sharpest expression in the work of Augustin Thierry, which was very influential at midcentury. In his early writings, Thierry regarded the very idea of a conflict between the bourgeoisie and the masses as absurd, because the former was just another way of describing the

---

15   See the overview in R. C. Richardson, *The Debate on the English Revolution Revisited*, 2nd ed. (London: Routledge, 1988).

16   Shirley M. Gruner, "Political Historiography in Restoration France," *History and Theory* 8:3 (1969), 346–65; Shirley M. Gruner, *Economic Materialism and Social Moralism: A Study in the History of Ideas in France from the Latter Part of the 18th Century to the Middle of the 19th Century* (The Hague: Mouton Press, 1973).

latter—the bourgeoisie *was* the nation.[17] Later he allowed for the possibility of antagonism but pointed to its doubtfulness, because the bourgeoisie was now identified with the universal aspirations and interests of the people.[18] This basic identification of the bourgeoisie with the aspirations of the populace, and hence of the nation, became the bedrock on which liberal historiography was built over the course of the nineteenth century. It carried over into Guizot, Michelet, and Marx, and, later, to the progressive historians of the early twentieth century.

The French liberal historians had a long-term impact on how the revolution of 1789 was interpreted. They also had a most immediate impact on the interpretation of the English Civil Wars. In order to legitimate their case for the French Revolution, Thierry and Guizot reinterpreted the events of 1640-8 in England as a precursor to 1789. English Whigs had already gone to some lengths to defend the Civil Wars as a victory for the forces of liberty. The French liberals now handed them an argument to further strengthen their case. Whereas the earlier historiography had seen parliamentary opposition in 1640 as motivated by religious and moral convictions, the newer vintage anchored these motivations to the agenda of a social class. For Guizot, the religious discourse used to justify the rebellion in 1640 "was a screen for the social question, the struggle of various classes for power and influence."[19] The English Revolution was in this fashion recast as the victory of the bourgeoisie against a reactionary landed aristocracy, and the French upheavals celebrated as the lineal descendant of the English.[20] By the middle of the nineteenth century, both revolutions were firmly ensconced in a historiographical tradition that identified their protagonists as the bourgeoisie, whose mission was to speak on behalf of the people-nation, and who were credited with having constructed a liberal political order based on the people-nation's consent.

The Marxist Inflection . . .

It should be clear that Guha's argument rests squarely on a Whig interpretation of British and French modernization. As we will see, this is also the tradition that informs his conceptualization of the logic of capitalism. Perhaps this seems a curious claim, given that Guha draws explicitly on Marx in his construction of the bourgeois revolutions, and his conceptual vocabulary looks to be directly derived from Marx. How, then, is it justifiable to present him as a modern-day Whig?

17   Shirley M. Gruner, "The Revolution of July 1830 and the Expression 'Bourgeoisie,' " *The Historical Journal* 11:3 (1968), 462–71

18   Lionel Gossman, "Augustin Thierry and Liberal Historiography," *History and Theory* 14:4 (Dec. 1976), 3–83; see esp. 28–32.

19   Guizot, The English Revolution, 9–10.

20   See Richardson, *English Revolution Revisited*, 56–64; Alastair MacLachlan, *The Rise and Fall of Revolutionary England: An Essay on the Fabrication of Seventeenth Century History* (London: Macmillan, 1997), 12–14.

Such a characterization is defensible on two grounds. The first is that Marx himself incorporated substantial elements of the Whig story into his analysis of the early modern revolutions. Guizot, Thierry, Mignet and other prominent liberal historians were among his main sources for the history of these events. Furthermore, he took their analysis to be quite compatible with his materialist approach to history. Marx insisted, on more than one occasion, that the progressive liberals had preempted him in recognizing the importance of class forces in historical development.[21] Indeed, he found the notion of the bourgeoisie's leadership of the revolution especially appealing, in that it converged with the idea that history was a progression of societies from one mode of production to another. Marx simply took the idea of a bourgeois revolution and imported it into his larger theory of historical evolution—thus internalizing, along with it, many weaknesses of the liberal analysis. Hence, to the extent that Guha borrows from Marx on these questions, he internalizes the same liberal nostrums, and the same infirmities, as did Marx.[22]

But, while Marx did digest substantial elements of the Whig analysis, it would be misleading to collapse his work into the Whig tradition. First, on the narrow question of the bourgeoisie's role in the revolutions, Marx was far more alive than were the liberal historians to the ambivalence of the elite leadership toward popular forces. He excoriated Thierry for trying to deny the existence of antagonism between elite and subaltern in the revolution, for forgetting that the "bourgeoisie" succeeded only when it decided to make "common cause with the peasants."[23] There are several instances in which he admits that the revolutions went beyond their initial timid thrusts, not because of the bourgeoisie's embrace of a radical program but because of pressure from below.[24] As François Furet has noted, Marx was never able to reconcile his acceptance of Whig myths about the rising bourgeoisie with his recognition of bourgeois timidity during the actual course of events.[25] Still, the importance Marx gives to the role of

---

21   See Marx's statement in his letter to Joseph Weydemeyer, where he declares that it was the liberal historians, and not he, who discovered the history of classes, and advises "democratic gents" to "study the historical works of Thierry, Guizot, John Wade and so forth, in order to enlighten themselves as to the past 'history of the classes.' " Karl Marx and Frederick Engels, *Collected Works*, vol. 39 (London: Lawrence and Wishart), 58.

22   For an especially clear formulation of this argument, see George Comninel, *Rethinking the French Revolution* (London: Verso, 1987), 53–75.

23   Marx to Engels, July 27, 1854, in Marx and Engels, *Collected Works* vol. 39, 472. I have placed the word "bourgeoisie" in scare quotes because the term is misleading in the French context, as shown above in chap. 3.

24   As Marx observes in *The Eighteenth Brumaire of Louis Bonaparte*, the French Revolution moved forward only as it escaped the grasp of its leadership. Every time it seemed to stall, the existing leadership "was pushed aside by the bolder ally standing behind it and sent to the guillotine." Karl Marx, *Political Writings, vol. II: Surveys from Exile*, ed. and trans. David Fernbach (New York: Vintage, 1974), 169.

25   "Introduction," in François Furet, *Marx and the French Revolution*, trans. Deborah Kan Furet (Chicago: University of Chicago Press, 1988), 46.

popular pressures sets his analysis apart from Whig historiography, even if he cannot escape its basic weaknesses.

A second, and more important, reason to resist assimilating Marx into the Whig tradition is that, for him, the significance of the bourgeois revolutions lay in the thrust they gave to the spread of capitalism as an *economic* system. No doubt he exaggerated their significance for the development of capitalism, as I argued in chapter 3.[26] By 1640, England was already largely capitalist, whereas France did not experience a significant shift to the new economic system until the final quarter of the nineteenth century, almost a full century after its own revolution. Nevertheless, though Marx may have exaggerated the bourgeoisie's economic achievements in the two revolutions, there is little doubt that he was far more circumspect about their liberal and communitarian commitments. He did emphasize, in his early writings, the importance of capitalism in allowing for the emergence of civil society as a distinct sphere; however, while according great significance to bourgeois *civil society*, he was far more guarded in his praise for the bourgeois *class*. The class was, he argued, far more concerned with strengthening the *state*—especially its repressive apparatus—than it was with the deepening of liberal freedoms. The decisive statement of this view appears in his commentary on the Paris Commune, where he comes back to this theme in each of his three drafts, searching for the proper formulation of his insight. The French Revolution did sweep away the ancien régime, Marx observes, but in so doing, it established a parliament "under the direct control of the propertied classes," giving the state the character of "a public force organized for social enslavement, of an engine of class despotism."[27] This is a far cry from the idyllic version of history found in Guha's narrative.

. . . to a Fundamentally Whig Argument

Even though the immediate referent for Guha's work is Marx, then, his interpretation of the revolutions harkens back to its Whig roots. Two points in particular deserve notice. First, there is almost no recognition in Guha's analysis of the role played by popular forces in radicalizing the political agenda. He places all his weight on the bourgeoisie's revolutionary ardor and expansive vision. This shows up on the other side of his counterfactual, in the Indian case. Had Guha recognized the importance of popular forces in the classic revolutions, he would have been forced to deemphasize the heroism of the bourgeoisie as a causal factor. The framework would have had to include the analysis of popular mobilization as a core element in explaining the course of bourgeois revolutions. Transferring this framework to the Indian case would have meant a correspondingly reduced

---

26   This is more so with regard to France than England. Marx recognized that landed property in England was capitalist by the time of the revolution. See his review of Guizot's *Pourquoi la Révolution d'Angleterre a-t-elle Réussi?* in *Surveys from Exile*, 250–5.

27   "The Civil War in France—Final Draft," in ibid., 207.

emphasis on the "mediocre liberalism" of Indian capitalists as an explanatory mechanism. Indian capitalists would no longer be seen as mediocre relative to British, but in fact very much like them. The conservative character of Indian nationalism would then have to be seen not simply as a consequence of the short-comings of Indian capital, but of the failure of the subaltern classes in the nationalist movement. This would require an independent analysis of workers and peasants movements, for purposes of explicating their inability to garner the kind of power that might have been able to extract greater concessions from the INC, much as the popular movements did in Europe.

But in *Dominance without Hegemony*, the subaltern classes rarely emerge as an actor, as a "historical subject." Throughout the analysis, they are always the *object* of the bourgeoisie's strategy. Guha never takes up the question of why popular forces failed to gather enough strength to push the INC in a more radi-cal direction. This reflects his commitment to taking the bourgeoisie as the central actor for explaining the quality of Indian nationalism and, following that, the postcolonial state. He never asks the relevant question, because in his framework the course of the revolution reflects the qualities of its bourgeois leadership. This derives from an internalization of the Whig interpretation of the classic revolutions, in which a heroic bourgeoisie ushers in a new era, inde-pendent of popular pressure, thereby generating Guha's distorted counterfactual.

Second, Guha's focus on *consent* as the hallmark of bourgeois rule also sets him firmly in the Whig tradition. It is difficult to find a suggestion in Marx's work that the new order established after 1640 or 1789 expressed an abiding social consensus. He is far more aware than were his liberal sources of the narrow base of the bourgeois oligarchies. With Guha, this caution is absent. For him, the hallmark of the postrevolutionary polity is that elites and subalterns are integrated into the same consensual order. This is how the chasm between the political cultures of dominant and dominated classes is obliterated. As a result, the concept of hegemony, as mobilized by Guha, becomes an expression of national integration. The bourgeoisie not only brings the laboring classes into the same political coalition, but effectively "speaks for the nation." This under-standing descends from Thierry, not Marx. For Marx, the new political order cannot prevent the persistence of class antagonism and class struggle, whereas for Guha, the eruption of class conflict—as in India in the 1970s—is a patho-logical development, sign of a failed bourgeois revolution. Guha's formulation thus represents a decisive regression toward Whig historiography.

In sum, Guha's argument in *Dominance without Hegemony* cannot provide a critique of liberalism, because he has internalized so many of liberal histori-ography's central precepts. He agrees that the bourgeoisie was the main protagonist in the classic revolutions; he also agrees that this class crystallized, in its outlook and program, the aspirations of "the nation"; and he endorses the view that, once in power, its main achievement was to install a political order based on the consent of the masses. Indeed, Guha builds these outcomes into his definition of capitalist development itself. Capital's universalization, he insists, issues in a political order in which the bourgeoisie successfully delivers these ends. What capital universalizes is political rule based on consent. Insofar as it fails to do so, what has been installed is a bastard child. Thus Guha's criticism of liberal ideology is of a minor order. He does not question the basic liberal conceptualization of capital, nor does he reject the mythology about capital's role as an historic actor He merely questions whether capital has carried out its so-called mission—its "striving toward self-realization"—in India.[28]

4.6 CONCLUSION

For the past three chapters, we have examined Ranajit Guha's central claim regarding Indian political formation, viz., that its pathologies are attributable to its bourgeoisie having failed to lead a proper bourgeois revolution. Guha's judgment rests on his conviction that the revolutions of 1640 and 1789 generated a novel form of social power, unique to the modern bourgeois epoch—power based on the consent of the governed. The British and French bourgeoisie based their rule on hegemony, while in India the capitalist class attained dominance but not hegemony. The task I have thus far undertaken is to show that hegemony—defined as reliance on consent rather than on coercion—was never the anchor of the bourgeois revolutions.

Hegemony has two relevant dimensions in Guha's argument: its role as the glue that held the revolutionary coalition together and, subsequently, its contribution to the establishment of an encompassing political order. Our evidence has shown that, in neither of these dimensions, did the elite leaderships of the revolutions seek or establish hegemony, thus defined. In the revolutionary period, they tried their best to contain and suppress subaltern demands for representation, administering a significant dose of outright coercion, certainly more than the leadership of the INC used over its own base in the nationalist movement. Once in power, they pushed the laboring classes out of the political arenas, thereby establishing a narrow, oligarchic form of rule—far more restricted, in fact, than in the Indian case. The result was a constriction of the political nation, to encompass only the ruling classes and a small sliver of the general population. Far from being marginal to political stability in the new order, coercion was central to it. So, if the hallmark of hegemony is the promotion of persuasion—rather than coercion—as the main instrument of stability, then the bourgeois revolutions cannot be associated with hegemonic leadership

---

28 "[Liberal] historiography has got itself trapped in an abstract universalism thanks to which it is unable to distinguish between the ideal of capital's striving toward self-realization and the reality of its failure to do so"(*DH* 19).

These findings bolster my broader conclusion: that there was no "structural fault" in the political ambitions of the Indian bourgeoisie as compared with the leadership of the classic bourgeois revolutions.

The task now is to examine what remains of the deeper theoretical argument used by Guha to justify his understanding of the bourgeoisie's historical mission. Recall that for Guha, the capitalists' struggle for hegemony, as well as their success in achieving hegemony, are both expressions of a deeper force, the universalizing tendency of capital. If it turns out that capital did not in fact strive for hegemony—as Guha defines it—and indeed was not even especially interested in it, perhaps the very idea of a universalizing drive is mistaken. We might conclude that capital not only failed to subsume the colonial world under its logic, but that it has no internal motor to universalize. And if that is so, then surely the theories that have been developed over the past century, which place a general conception of capitalism at the core of their conceptual framework, are even weaker than we thought. Each part of the world would then have to generate theories derived from its cultural and social specificity. The postcolonial rejection of European Enlightenment theories would extend far beyond the colonial world.

As it happens, the consequences of my empirical critique are not quite so dire. Guha works with a very particular understanding of capital's universalization. As we have seen, what is universalized is the bourgeoisie's construction of a very specific kind of political order—one in which the dominant class bases its rule on the consent of the governed. For Guha, as for other Subalternist theorists, there is a clear criterion by which to judge the matter: for capital to have universalized, it must be the case that the bourgeoisie acquired hegemony, and hegemony is defined as rule based on consent. Insofar as these conditions are not in evidence, the universalizing dynamic can be deemed a failure.

In the next chapter, I will propose a different definition of capital's universalization, one that is more consistent with the bourgeoisie's actual practice. I will argue that Guha was correct to suggest that capital has a universalizing tendency but that he wrongly identified its content—in other words, he was right in his claim that capital has a universalizing drive but wrong in identifying *what* is actually universalized. It was not a particular normative order, but rather the subordination of economic agents to the competitive pressures of the market. Capitalism universalizes market dependence. We will see that this process is perfectly consistent with the phenomena that Subalternist theorists claim is specific to the colonial world but deem inconsistent with capital's universalizing tendency—the persistence of a subaltern domain, distinct from that of the elites and suffused with social hierarchies, traditional power relations, and political idioms.

CHAPTER FIVE

Capital's Universalizing Tendency

The main conclusion of the preceding chapters is that India's "bourgeois revolution"—its independence movement—did not, as Ranajit Guha maintains, diverge from the classic European revolutions. The reason Guha's reading of this history cannot be supported is not that he has his facts about India wrong; his reading of the Indian experience is unobjectionable, even conventional in many respects. The reason his argument fails is that his understanding of the European experience is fatally flawed, and all his conclusions about India ride on his European counterfactual.

The fact is, the European bourgeoisie was no more enamored of democracy, or contemptuous of the ancien régime, or respectful of subaltern agency, than were the Indians. In terms of actual achievement, the Indian nationalist movement created a state that was, if anything, closer to Guha's ideal of a hegemonic order than were the oligarchies established by the classic bourgeois revolutions. So the divergence that Guha imagines as central to the postcolonial predicament simply does not exist. Indeed, not only is his argument wrong, but it dusts off and repackages one of the hoariest traditions of bourgeois apologetics. It cannot generate a critique of liberal historiography because it relies fully on that very historiographical tradition, on its apologia for the emerging capitalist class.

While the empirical critique settles the question of Indian capitalists' divergence from the Europeans, its implication for Guha's deeper theoretical argument is uncertain. There are two main components to the argument: that the European bourgeoisie championed, and then established, a consensual and liberal political order; and that the bourgeoisie's willingness to base its rule on popular consent was itself an expression of a deeper force, namely capital's universalizing tendency. Guha takes the former as evidence of the latter. Hence, the fact that the colonial and Indian bourgeoisie showed no interest in an encompassing political order indicates that capital abandoned its universalizing mission.

The issue now is, What are the implications of the discovery that nowhere did capitalists ever try to "speak for the nation"? If the European bourgeoisie at home was no more interested in a consensual order than was Indian capital at home, it could be taken to mean that not only did the Indian capitalist class eschew its universalizing mission, but so did its European predecessors. Does this not suggest that the very idea of capitalism having a universalizing tendency might have to be abandoned? Does my critique of Guha justify the conclusion that the very idea of capitalism's universalizing drive is fatally flawed? Perhaps his mistake lay in attributing any such tendency to capitalism at all?

In this chapter, I offer a defense of the idea that capital does have a universalizing tendency, even if Guha's conceptualization of it is incorrect. In the conclusion to Chapter 4, I suggested that Guha's doubts about capital's universalization rest on a very specific understanding of what is being universalized—he takes it to be the spread of ideological hegemony, narrowly defined. In this chapter, I propose that there is little warrant for Guha's definition. He settles on it more or less arbitrarily, even though there are grounds for another rendering of it, grounds with which he is quite familiar. Furthermore, as we have seen, Guha's construal of the concept seems to have very little support from the historical record. It is hard to find any instance of a bourgeoisie committed to the kind of universalization that Guha's rendering of it requires. Hence, I offer a different definition of universalization, and I show that this definition is both more consistent with the actual practice of capitalists. Having shown that my alternative definition is more in line with the historical record, I then argue that universalization, properly defined, is quite consistent with the very phenomena that Subalternists think are evidence against it.

For Guha, the main evidence for incomplete universalization is that the bourgeoisie does not base its rule on the consent of the governed. We have clearly seen the flaws in this whole line of reasoning. Now I will address another of the putative indices of failed bourgeois hegemony: the persistence of certain kinds of power relations, which Subalternist theorists see as different from bourgeois forms of power, and thus see as more evidence of the stalled universalizing drive. Here, too, their basic sociology is mistaken. The power relations they regard as signs of a failed or abandoned bourgeois project are, in fact, entirely compatible with a dominant bourgeois political culture. Once again, this proposition gains support from the historical record in capitalism's heartland, Western Europe and the United States. I show that, in all of the zones where capitalism took root, its political practice undermines Guha's characterization of its basic tendencies, but upholds the definition that I have offered. In other words, the evidence suggests that capital does show a consistent universalizing tendency, just not in the manner understood by Guha.

Taken together, chapters 4 and 5 show that the phenomenon Guha takes to be symptomatic of a stalled universalizing drive by capital—the existence of a distinct subaltern domain, with its own idiom, embedded in antiquated power relations, and with its own political culture—is quite consistent with the universalizing process, but only if this process is redefined. We thereby reject Guha's historical sociology while retaining the idea that capital is driven to universalize itself.

5.1 WHAT IS AT STAKE

In two separate essays published in the same year, Dipesh Chakrabarty explains his view of the deep implications of Guha's analysis.[1] He affirms Guha's thesis concerning the bourgeoisie's failure to base its rule on the consent of the governed, quoting approvingly Guha's verdict that "vast areas in the life and consciousness of the people' escaped any kind of 'bourgeois hegemony."[2] He also agrees that the failure to hegemonize was itself a symptom of the universalizing dynamic coming to a halt. But he places additional emphasis on another consequence, which was also present in Guha's analysis but receives greater prominence in Chakrabarty's own work. This is the failure, in capital's bid for supremacy, to transform relations of *power*.

The fact that capitalism did not dissolve the separate subaltern domain did not just mean that the lower orders remained outside the influence of bourgeois ideology; it also implied that they were subject to forms of power very different from those established by capital in Europe, where it undertook a thorough social transformation. Chakrabarty explains it thus in *Provincializing Europe*:

> South Asian political modernity, Guha argued, brings together two noncommensurable logics of power, both modern. One is the logic of the quasi-liberal legal and institutional frameworks that European rule introduced into the country . . . Braided with this, however, is the logic of another set of relationships in which both the elites and the subalterns are also involved. These are the relations that articulate *hierarchy through practices of direct and explicit subordination of the less powerful by the more powerful.*[3]

In another essay, Chakrabarty produces a very similar description of Guha's analysis but describes the form of power in the subaltern domain a little more sharply, as one in which "hierarchy was based on direct and explicit domination and subordination of the less powerful through *both ideological-symbolic means and physical force.*"[4] He later continues, "Social domination and subordination of the subaltern by the elite was thus an everyday feature of Indian capitalism itself. This was capitalism of a colonial type."[5]

The peculiarity of Indian modernity was that its capitalism left intact the political domain of subaltern groups and the forms of power peculiar to it, in which elites exercised "direct and explicit subordination" of the lower orders,

---

1   The essays are the introduction to Dipesh Chakrabarty, *Provincializing Europe* (Princeton: Princeton University Press, 2000), 3–23, henceforth cited as *PE*; and "*Subaltern Studies* and Postcolonial Historiography," *Nepantla: Views from South* 1:1 (2000), 9–32.

2   Chakrabarty, "*Subaltern Studies* and Postcolonial Historiography," 21.

3   *PE* 14. Emphasis added.

4   Chakrabarty, "*Subaltern Studies* and Postcolonial Historiography," 17, emphasis added.

5   Ibid., 20.

often involving the use of physical coercion. In itself, this is not an uncommon observation. Virtually every social analysis of colonial development has noticed that Indian modernization has left older forms of domination intact. But this is where Chakrabarty wishes to distinguish the *Subaltern Studies* analysis and conclusions. Whereas for many analysts, the obduracy of antediluvian power relations was a symptom of an incomplete transition to capitalism, Chakrabarty argues that any such inference would be mistaken. The persistence of these forms of power was not an index of an incomplete capitalism, or even a backward capitalism. They did not persist because feudal remnants lingered in the countryside or because labor had only been "formally subsumed" under capital. In fact, he chastises Guha for occasionally attributing the persistence of subordination and political coercion to an incomplete capitalist transition.[6] They persisted, Chakrabarty argues, because a nonuniversalizing variant has social dynamics rather different from the original, universalizing capitalism. So, Guha and Chakrabarty are united in their view that colonial capitalism, even in its most developed form, produces distinctive forms of power.

> Guha goes beyond the argument that reduces questions of democracy and power in the subcontinent to propositions about an incomplete transition to capitalism. He does not deny the connections of colonial India to the global forces of capitalism. His point, however, is that the global history of capitalism need not produce everywhere the same history of power.[7]

Thus, capitalism can spread around the globe, but the relations of power it establishes will not be identical. This claim seems fair enough. But it is at this juncture that the more interesting parts of Chakrabarty's argument start to emerge. Even though these forms of power are thoroughly modern, and coeval with the development of capitalism, he resists describing them as capitalist. In other words, Chakrabarty does not want to designate them as *bourgeois* forms of power. Guha's work enjoins us, he argues in the essay, to recognize "differences in the history of power in colonial India and in Europe. The gesture is radical in that it fundamentally pluralizes the history of power in global modernity and *separates it from any universal history of capital.*"[8] In *Provincializing Europe*, Chakrabarty reproduces the passage but adds a clause:

> [Guha's analysis] fundamentally pluralizes the history of power in global modernity and separates it from any universalist narratives of capital. Subaltern

---

6   Ibid., 18; *PE* 13.
7   Chakrabarty, "*Subaltern Studies* and Postcolonial Historiography," 20.
8   Ibid., 19.

historiography *questions the assumption that capitalism necessarily brings bourgeois relations of power to a position of hegemony.*[9]

Chakrabarty is making a significant and distinctive argument here. Colonial capitalism implanted certain power relations in India, which cannot be subsumed under a "universal history of capital"; that is, they cannot be taken as an instance of the same capitalist power relations that emerged during European modernization. The reason is that in no meaningful way were they "bourgeois forms of power," because the bourgeoisie in India never achieved hegemony, did not penetrate the subaltern domain, and could not do so because capital had abandoned its universalizing drive. As he concludes, "this was capitalism *but without capitalist hierarchies*, a capitalist dominance without a hegemonic capitalist culture—or, in Guha's famous term, 'dominance without hegemony.' "[10] That is to say, a nonuniversalizing capital produces a bourgeoisie without hegemony, as well as a capitalism that does not produce recognizably capitalist forms of power or specifically capitalist hierarchies.

Let us clarify what kinds of authority Chakrabarty is referring to. In the essays where he makes this argument, he does not provide many concrete examples, but he does tell us where we can find them. In a footnote, he points the reader to his earlier work, a history of labor in Indian jute mills during the interwar years,[11] where he describes in some detail the power relations he has in mind. In this earlier book, Chakrabarty explored the forms of authority that managers wielded over their workers in the jute industry.[12] He argues that the power relations used by managers departed from the kind Marx identified with capitalism. In capitalism, power is supposed to be exercised "through an articulated body of rules and legislation that have the effect of ensuring an economy in the use and exercise of managerial power."[13] In other words, the exercise of power must be transparent, predictable, and clearly demarcated. But in the jute mills, Chakrabarty observes, managers' authority over their workers was highly arbitrary, personal, often violent, and excessive.[14] Managers could hire and fire at will, they could use terror as a form of labor control, and they arbitrarily set wages at levels they deemed fit. They ensnared workers in debt obligations, confiscated wages, intimidated or beat workers who defected to other mills, and, of course, used violence against suspected union organizers.

In order to exercise their authority, managers often relied on workers'

---

9   *PE* 14. Emphasis added.
10   Ibid., 21.
11   See *PE* 14n46.
12   See Dipesh Chakrabarty, *Rethinking Working Class History: Bengal 1890–1940* (Princeton: Princeton University Press, 1989), chaps. 3, 5.
13   Ibid., 172.
14   Ibid., 170–7.

preexisting notions of deference and hierarchy, which stemmed from their rural cultures. Chakrabarty describes the various forms of paternalism that managers enacted, and even promoted, to secure obeisance. Central to this was the concept of the *Ma-Baap*, a traditional Indian notion that authority figures assumed something akin to parental responsibility for those under their control. Hence, managers "claimed that they were *in loco parentis* to the workers."[15] Workers, correspondingly, had a responsibility to accept the authority of managers and to perform as directed. When punishment was meted out, it was justified as " 'parental' justice."[16] Existing caste hierarchies and social divisions made fertile ground for the implantation of such ideas, of course. Managers keyed on these aspects of worker consciousness and remobilized them to suit their own ends.

Here Chakrabarty draws on the premise that truly bourgeois forms of power rely on a unique and clearly identifiable set of mechanisms, which do not include the kind he found in Bengal's jute mills. What he probably has in mind is the notion that, with the advent of capitalism, ruling classes need not rely on direct coercion to extract a surplus from laboring groups. In feudalism, because the peasantry had direct access to the means of production, they did not rely on lords for their productive activities. Lacking any leverage to induce a surplus from peasants, lords had no choice but to rely on threats and intimidation to extract rents from them. This made power in feudalism highly arbitrary, very violent, and interpersonal in form. Coercion thus was built into the class structure, as was direct subordination.[17] But in capitalism, surplus extraction does not have to depend on outright coercion. Employers can rely instead on the "silent compulsion of economic relations," to use Marx's famous formulation.[18] Direct coercion fades away, and power is then exercised through the impersonal force of structural pressures. Rather than appearing as their direct oppressors, capitalists can present themselves as the workers' benefactors. The system turns out to be perfectly compatible with formal equality in the political realm, even as the bourgeoisie exercises economic dominance. So, the unstated premise on which Chakrabarty bases his designation of colonial power as nonbourgeois seems to be that formal equality and impersonal power relations appear as the quintessential forms of capitalist power. If capitalism had truly universalized, without distortions, into the colonial world, it would not have had to rely on the forms of coercion Chakrabarty found in the Calcutta jute mills of the 1920s. It would have generated forms of authority closer to the impersonal coercion typical of European capitalism. The managers found in the East certainly do reproduce capitalism, but they rely on nonbourgeois forms of power, namely, forms that deviate from those practiced in classical capitalism.

---

15   Ibid., 163.
16   Ibid.
17   See Marx's comments in *Capital,* vol. III (New York: Vintage Books, 1981), 926–7.
18   Ibid., vol. I, 899.

From the preceding argument, Chakrabarty derives certain important theoretical implications. The first is that the analysis of social hierarchies in India cannot draw on the categories of political economy, which rely on capital as an explanatory mechanism. Since the Indian power relations were not part of the universal history of capital, they cannot be explained through the logic of capitalism. Any theoretical framework that would try to link subordination and dominance to the logic of capital cannot but fail to illuminate postcolonial realities. The chief victim here is Marxist theory. Chakrabarty explains it thus:

> In the calculus of modernity, power is not a dependent variable, with capital playing the role of an independent one. Capital and power are analytically separable categories. Traditional European-Marxist thought, which fused the two, would therefore always be relevant, but inadequate for analyzing power in colonial-modern histories.[19]

It is not entirely clear how European-Marxist thought *fuses* capital and power. Chakrabarty seems to suggest that these theories construe every form of power as an expression of capital—a remarkable claim, advanced without argument or evidence.[20] But let us leave that matter aside for now.

The next conclusion he extracts is that, for the theoretical renaissance to take off, a new set of categories must be crafted. It is in this context that he calls for "provincializing" Europe:

> My argument for provincializing Europe follows directly from my involvement in this project. *A history of political modernity in India cannot be written as a simple application of the analytics of capital and nationalism available to Western Marxism.* One could not, in the manner of some nationalist historians, pit the story of a regressive colonialism against an account of a robust nationalist bourgeoisie seeking to establish a bourgeois outlook throughout society. For in Guha's terms, there was no class in South Asia comparable to the European bourgeoisie of Marxist metanarratives, a class able to fabricate a hegemonic ideology that made its own interests look and feel like the interests of all ... *This was capitalism indeed, but without bourgeois relations that attain a position of unchallenged hegemony*; it was capitalist dominance without a hegemonic bourgeois culture—or, in Guha's famous terms, 'dominance without hegemony.'[21]

---

19   Chakrabarty, "*Subaltern Studies* and Postcolonial Historiography," 20.

20   Chakrabarty's claim ignores the entire gamut of Marxist theorizing since the 1960s, which strove mightily to establish the relative *autonomy* of the political from the economic. This was certainly true of the political theorists influenced by Althusser, such as Nicos Poulantzas, Göran Therborn, and Bob Jessop, but also of some of Althusser's fiercest critics, such as Ellen Meiksins Wood, as well as theorists such as Fred Block, who came out of the American New Left.

21   *PE* 15. Emphasis added.

Several points need highlighting here. The first is that Chakrabarty reproduces, *in toto*, Guha's argument about there being a structural fault separating the Indian bourgeoisie from the European. He affirms that the nationalist movement cannot be told as a story of capital's ascension, because capital did not behave as it should have—it did not try to "speak for the nation," as British capitalists did in their revolution. Social theory therefore needs to craft a new set of categories, which will have to be very different from those mobilized to explain the European dynamic. This is just an extension of Guha. But, as an added inflection, he gives special emphasis to the kind of power relations that colonial capitalism produced: they were not, he categorically asserts, capitalist power relations, and they cannot be so regarded, because they are relations of interpersonal domination. Guha had taken hegemony to mean rule by consent. Chakrabarty adds to this the criterion that power relations should also be transformed, presumably away from personal domination and toward a more formal, impersonal variety.

Chakrabarty further endorses Guha's view that the modern nation, resting on bourgeois hegemony, was brought about by the bourgeoisie, and that the Indian bourgeoisie did not follow in those footsteps. So capital in India failed to implant its own form of domination—through impersonal means—and also failed to generate a genuine political community under its hegemony. This is why Marxist theory as a "metanarrative" loses relevance for India: Marxist theory is the child of European reality. It presumes that history unfolds in a certain way—the bourgeoisie is born; it recognizes its interests; it overthrows the traditional order, imposes its own vision of society, creates a viable nation, and exercises power through formal and impersonal means. Since this did not happen in India, Marxist theory—and its liberal cousin—must be replaced by theory attuned to Indian realities and freed of European assumptions. This is how Europe is to be provincialized.

We can now appreciate what is at stake, for the Subalternist collective, in the universalization of capital: the appropriateness of European categories (at least as bequeathed by the Enlightenment tradition) to Indian reality and, by extension, to the rest of the postcolonial world. Chakrabarty's desire to provincialize Europe stems from his conviction that any comparisons with the European story will be misleading, because, once capital traveled to the colonies, the latter were subjected to a very different set of economic and political dynamics than those experienced in Europe. A proper apprehension of these dynamics will require the construction of a new set of categories, sensitive to the peculiarities of this new form of modernity—a modernity that sustained a capitalism that refused to produce the power relations it implanted in the West. A specifically *postcolonial capitalism* demands specifically *postcolonial categories*.

Two pillars support Chakrabarty's conclusion that Western categories must be abandoned for new, indigenous ones: the claim that the bourgeoisie did not establish its ideological hegemony in the form of rule by consent, and the claim that it did not displace older power relations with its own. Both are dimensions of Guha's metaconcept—the universalization of capital. If capital successfully universalizes, so the argument goes, it will exercise its rule by consent and will displace older power relations with recognizably bourgeois forms of power. We have already seen that the first of these two axioms is, for the most part, a fantasy, a myth accepted by Guha and his followers with alacrity. No gulf separates the rise of the European bourgeoisie from that of its Indian descendants. The political and social vision of capital in its European incarnation was fairly similar to the vision that shaped its course in India. Whichever analytical framework is appropriate to explaining the former, then, will be just as appropriate to explaining the latter, as we have demonstrated in chapters 3 and 4. So, if part of the justification of abandoning "the simple application of the analytics of capital and nationalism" is that the story will simply make no sense, since Indian capital did not act on the same interests or with the same goals as it did in Europe, then we can safely conclude that the worries lack foundation.

It now remains to be seen if the second pillar can withstand the weight that the Subalternist collective places upon it. Are the reproduction of interpersonal hierarchies and the dependence on coercion impossible to explain through the "narrative of capital"? Or, to translate this bit of jargon: Is the exercise of personal domination consistent with capitalist exploitation? Should we expect that as capital expands its scope in an economy, it will abjure a reliance on such forms of power? Is the resort to such domination by capitalists an anomalous development? If so, then we must accept Chakrabarty's conclusions that capital did not implant "bourgeois relations of power" and that traditional Marxian categories are inadequate to Indian reality. But if it can be shown that interpersonal coercion is perfectly consistent with capitalist employment relations, then we will be forced to reject these conclusions, in which case, the history of power—of this kind—can indeed be assimilated into the "narrative of capital." And if this is so, we will have demonstrated that capital's historical path to dominance, as well as the persistent social hierarchies to which Chakrabarty now refers, are explicable through the very categories that he urges us to reject.

5.2 WHAT DOES CAPITALISM UNIVERSALIZE?

To assess whether capital abandoned its universalizing mission in its colonial venture, we first must ask, what it is supposed to universalize? Whatever capital supposedly universalizes, it must be something that can be tied quite closely to its intrinsic features. We must have good reason to believe that wherever capitalist social relations appear, so must these attendant phenomena.

Having rejected Guha's argument, the burden falls upon us to provide an alternative. As it happens, an alternative candidate for universalization is not hard to find. Guha refers to it in his own discussion. Recall that he describes capital's tendency to universalize thus:

> This [universalizing] tendency derives from the self-expansion of capital. Its function is to create a world market, subjugate all antecedent modes of production, and replace all jural and institutional concomitants of such modes and generally the entire edifice of precapitalist cultures by laws, institutions, values, and other elements of a culture appropriate to bourgeois rule.[22]

As noted in chapter 2, this passage contains two distinct elements associated with the universalizing tendency—the "self-expansion of capital" on one side, and its attendant political and cultural transformations on the other. Guha never defines capital's self-expansion, presumably because he assumes the reader will take it to carry Marx's meaning. For Marx, it referred to both a micro- and a macro-level phenomenon. At the macro level, it referred to the tendency of capitalism as a system to expand its zone of operation—to find new markets, to create new ones if needed by displacing existing economic forms, to reach into every part of the world and incorporate it into a world market. But for Marx this macro-level tendency derives from the micro-level action of individual firms. Capitalism expands geographically as producers seek out new buyers for their products and new inputs to go into the production process. But capital's self-expansion also means the increasing scale of operations for individual producers, as part of the competitive battle between firms. In order to drive out rival firms, producers constantly search for ways to lower the market price of their product. One way to do so is to expand their productive capacity, to throw greater quantities of the product onto the market so as to lower its unit cost. This requires a greater scale of operations, bigger units, and larger production runs, thereby using more labor, consuming more inputs—and demanding yet bigger and deeper markets to absorb the goods. Hence, as capital expands its geographical zone of operation, it also expands the size of its units, its scale of production, the baseline size of operations for market entrants, and so forth. The system not only widens, it deepens.

An economic system that tends to quicken its tempo and spread around the world could certainly be described as expanding. But it is not immediately clear why it should be described as *self*-expanding. The choice of words here goes beyond Marx's Hegelian pedigree. What the term is meant to convey, I would suggest, is that capital is driven to expand because of mechanisms internal to its reproduction; that capitalists are driven to expand simply by virtue of being

---

22   Ranajit Guha, *Dominance without Hegemony: History and Power in Colonial India* (Cambridge: Harvard University Press, 1997), 13–14. Henceforth cited as *DH*.

capitalists—not because of their personal idiosyncrasies, or their ideological predilections, or their cultural background. The agents who run firms in a fully monetized economy do not need any inducements to accumulate capital other than those generated by their structural location. The compulsions, Marx notes, "assert themselves as the coercive laws of competition, and therefore enter into the consciousness of the individual capitalist as the motives that drive him forward."[23] The imperative to survive in the market—to repel the threat of other producers' displacement of them unless they grow, unless they constantly expand their revenue base and productivity—is all the motivation they need. Capitalism grows as firms take their revenues after every cycle of production and plow them back into acquiring ever more capital, in order to strengthen their position in the market. Marx refers to this process as the accumulation of capital.

What capitalism universalizes, then, is a particular strategy of economic reproduction. It compels economic units to focus single-mindedly on accumulating ever more capital. Economic managers internalize it as their goal because it is built into the structural location of being a capitalist; it is not something capitalists have to be convinced to do. Wherever capitalism goes, so too does this imperative. Guha is aware of the economic dimension, but although he begins with it, he sets it aside when he defines universalization as the bourgeoisie's creation of an encompassing political order. Insofar as the capitalist class does not base its rule on consent, it can be said to have abandoned its universalizing drive. Notice, however, that based on the new definition I have offered, we can accept that capital has universalized *even if* its political mission is not devoted to winning the consent of laboring classes. By our criteria, the universalizing process is under way if agents' reproductive strategies shift toward market dependence.

Our new definition has effectively decoupled universalization from the phenomena that Guha associated with it. The issue now is to assess what kind of power relations are implied in the new definition of universalization. We first need to judge whether capital can be expected to generate the kind of power relations that Chakrabarty found in the jute mills. This might seem an odd question. After all, those were power relations in *capitalist* jute mills, which were in the business of accumulating capital. It thus seems rather obvious that capitalism can rely on power relations of the kind Chakrabarty describes. But we must remember that Chakrabarty's argument is that what makes Indian capitalism generate such forms of power is its specifically *colonial* character. A special kind of capitalism produces a special kind of power:

> [T]he manager's authority was *essentially colonial*. It derived more from the colonial situation than from *any other factor internal to the production*

---

23   Karl Marx, *Capital*, vol. I (London: Vintage, 1977), 433; see also 381.

process . . . The Scottish manager in a Calcutta jute mill was something he could never have been at home.[24]

In other words, arbitrary power, the use of terror, the mobilization of traditional hierarchies, the creation of debt obligations—the multifaceted reliance on inter-personal power—were phenomena peculiar to colonial capitalism.

The issue, then, is whether capitalists' direct authority over workers—both on and off the shop floor—is an artifact unique to colonial capitalism, or generic to all forms of capitalism. If the drive to dominate their laborers is general, shared by capitalists everywhere, then Chakrabarty's argument fails. If the experience of capitalism in Europe and the Americas shows that managers strove to extend their control over workers, that they resorted to interpersonal forms of authority, used violence, terrorized workers, relied on state backing, ensnared workers in debt, mobilized traditional cultural roles whenever they could—if all this is true of capitalism in the West as well as the East, then Chakrabarty loses his basis for arguing that when such strategies are employed in colonial India, they pose a challenge for theory. When capitalism in the East relies on such power forms, it can no longer be seen as evidence of capital's failed universalization. To the contrary, it will be good evidence for its having successfully universalized.

In the next section, I will show that the drive to dominate labor above and beyond the impersonal coercion of economic relations is indeed generic to capitalism, and that there is therefore no reason to exclude interpersonal domi-nation from the category of "bourgeois relations of power." Regardless of geographic location, it is rational for capitalists to dominate workers in this fashion. The historical record shows that, well into the twentieth century, domi-nation of this kind was the norm in Europe and the Americas. Managers used the very same kinds of practices in England and the United States as they did in Bengal. As a result, there is no basis to insist that these power relations were an exception, and no justification for the view that they pose a fundamental chal-lenge to theory.

5.3 CAPITAL AND POWER

Capital came to the colonial world in a form that many theorists have associated with highly coercive and even brutal forms of domination. In agriculture as well as in industry, colonial capitalism tended to rely on backward technology, labor-inten-sive production processes, and high ratios of capital to output (i.e., low productivity). All these elements combined to make for low growth and low profit margins. Because production was so labor-intensive and producers' profits so slim, even

---

24   Chakrabarty, *Rethinking Working-Class History*, 166. Emphasis added.

small increases in wages could be devastating to employers. Labor-*intensive* production was thus tightly linked with labor-*repressive* economic regimes.[25]

The repressive nature of employment had several dimensions. One, of course, was the establishment of a host of institutional mechanisms to discourage economic demands from employees—draconian anti-union laws, airtight supervision on the shop floor, private armies to terrorize local labor. But employers complemented these measures with more individualized ways to ensure the supply of cheap and docile labor. Hence, they commonly ensnared workers in debt and even reduced some to the status of bonded laborers; in addition, employers often reduced individual laborers to varying degrees of servility, both to discourage economic demands and to tie them down to their particular location. Whereas the first set of institutional mechanisms was directed at labor as a whole, the latter was mobilized at the level of the individual. Jointly, they created the highly coercive forms of exploitation that Chakrabarty associates with colonial modernity.

Such regimes of labor-repressive production were very much part of capital's spread into the colonial world, and they have been explicitly theorized by many scholars as capitalist production. For those based in a Marxian tradition, such regimes are conceptualized as relying on the production of absolute surplus value; for those based in more mainstream approaches, they are understood as interlocking markets. But in both cases, they are seen as forms of capitalism—as instances of capital's universalization. Hence, one way to answer the challenge from postcolonial theorists would be to argue that the highly coercive regimes of exploitation in the South are attributable to the particular form in which capital entered those parts of the world. If we used Marxian language, for example, we could offer the following formulation: in the colonial world, the reliance on producing absolute surplus value rendered capitalism highly coercive and violent, while in the advanced world, it was the production of relative surplus value that caused a switch to less personalized, more formal regimes of profit making.

Although it would be legitimate to link the persistence of coercive exploitation to the prevalence of backward technology and labor-intensive production of the kind just described, I will adopt another strategy here. The sorts of power relations discussed by postcolonial theorists are certainly coincident with the extraction of absolute surplus value. But they are not confined to such conditions. Indeed, one phenomenon that motivates postcolonial theorists' worries about the relevance of Marxian categories, and of Western categories more generally, is the persistence of caste and status hierarchies, and of coercive

---

25   Two classic discussions of the connection between labor-intensive production and political repression are Barrington Moore, Jr., *Social Origins of Dictatorship and Democracy: Lord and Peasant in the Making of the Modern World* (Boston: Beacon Press, 1966); and Jeffrey M. Paige, *Agrarian Revolution* (New York: Free Press, 1975).

relations of exploitation, even in the more modern sectors of the economy. Hence, it will not do to explain such power relations as the product of outmoded production techniques. If we wish to show that such forms of power are consistent with capital's universalization, then we are obliged to demonstrate their possibility even in the extraction of relative surplus value—that is, in the more capital-intensive, technologically dynamic conditions of bourgeois employment relations.

WAGE LABOR AND DOMINATION

There is a superficial plausibility to the belief that capitalist production ought to dispense with interpersonal coercion in class relations. In feudal economies, peasant producers had secure access to the means of production—chiefly land—which ensured that they could reproduce their families through their own labor, with some cooperation from the village community. Peasants had no material need for lordly patronage or lordly assets. Moreover, lords were obligated to respect peasants' customary rights to their holdings; evicting recalcitrant producers from their land was typically not a viable option, even if they resisted the lords' rental demands. In such a situation, lords could make demands on peasants' surplus but had to back up those demands by the threat of force, for they lacked any other means to motivate peasants to relinquish their surplus. For a lord's threat of force to be effective, it could be leveled only against his own peasants; it had to be specific to the village communities in the lord's reach, and in cases where the same village was divided between several manors, the threat had to be specific to the families under the lord's jurisdiction. Peasants were thus exploited by a particular lord, in a particular region.

With the advent of capitalism, the logic of exploitation underwent a transformation. Peasants who once had customary rights to the land found themselves thrown off their holdings and forced to seek employment, either from capitalist farmers or from urban manufacturers.[26] In one sense, peasants experienced this new dispensation as liberating. They were now emancipated from the personalized rule of their lords and free to dispose of their labor as they wished. Crucially, however, though they were free to decide whom to choose as an employer, they no longer had the option of rejecting employment per se. Expropriation meant the loss of livelihood, and hence of independent production based on family labor. Lacking the means to reproduce themselves, they had to seek out employment as a basic condition for physical survival. They had escaped subordination to the personal rule of their overlord only to find themselves subject to the impersonal coercion of their economic circumstances. This is what Marx had in mind when he referred to the "dull compulsion of economic relations."

---

26   I ignore here the logic of tenancy under capitalist conditions.

In this scenario, it is true that the locus and even the form of coercion have changed. In feudalism, the agrarian overlords had to seek out peasant communities and impose demands on them; as their ability to impose direct rule over the peasant community receded, so did the stream of rents flowing into their coffers. In capitalism, the employer does not have to seek out and then threaten the worker with violence in order to compel him to offer his labor. The locus of compulsion has shifted from the person of the overlord to the workers' structural situation, and so has the form: no longer is the laborer threatened with bodily harm or violent death; now he is threatened simply with compromised well-being or, at worst, death by starvation. None of this is delivered on the sharp point of a lance or from the barrel of a gun. It is transmitted through the impersonal force of the laborer's situation.

Yet while it is correct to insist that the labor-extraction process in capitalism does not rest solely on interpersonal domination, it does not follow that interpersonal domination becomes redundant. In fact, it occupies a central place in capitalist economies. What changes is its location in the production process. In feudalism, coercion is used in order to induce the peasant to offer his labor services. Lords compel their wards either to work on their demesnes for a stipulated duration each week, or to surrender a portion of their crop if they work on their own plots for the entire duration. Either way, coercion is used to compel them to work for the lord. But the actual work effort—the labor process, in which peasants grow and attend to the crops—is essentially under the peasant's control. The lord exercises little or no authority over the peasant in this dimension. Force is thus mobilized outside the labor process, not within it. In capitalism, the employer does not have to compel the worker to offer his labor services. This is taken care of by the worker's economic circumstances. But once the laborer appears at the work site, the employer has to mobilize some degree of authority or power in order to extract the needed labor effort from him. There is a need for the exercise of interpersonal domination, but its locus has shifted from outside the labor process, as was the case in feudalism, to within it.

DOMINATION AND THE LABOR PROCESS

There are two basic reasons for the capitalist to wield a measure of personal authority over his workers, whether he is located in an advanced or a colonial economy. The first has to do with employers' compulsion to extract maximum labor effort from employees. Capitalists need not compel workers to show up for work, as we have seen. The inducement to sell their labor power is imposed on workers by their economic situation. When they offer to work for an employer, however, what they agree to is the simple fact of work for a stipulated period of time. The intensity and dexterity of that work cannot be specified. How hard they will work is a matter subject to constant manipulation and adjustment, and can only be settled in situ. For the employer, the goal of production is set very clearly—to maximize his profit, in order to expand his market share and market power. To achieve this, his most powerful weapon is minimization of unit costs, in order to increase the margin between his product's costs and its selling price. But, in order to minimize his unit costs, he must increase labor productivity—he has to induce his employees to produce more goods in the same amount of time, which translates into insisting that his employees work at the highest level of intensity they can sustain. The employer thus organizes his workplace to extract the maximum quantum of labor effort from his workers, as a condition for his own success as a capitalist. This goal is imposed on him by the demands of competition.

The compulsion to extract the maximum work effort would not be a problem were the capitalist's labor force to offer it willingly. His problem arises from the fact that while the employees will indeed offer him their working time, they will have good reason not to work at the intensity he deems fit. For the employer, profit maximization is the primary motive, as well as the goal, of his activity. For workers, the firm's profitability is a second-order concern, accepted only because it is a condition for the fulfillment of their primary goal, which is to secure their material welfare. But their material welfare depends not only on the profits of the firm. It also hinges on other dimensions of their experience at work—its demands on their health, on their autonomy in the production process, on the proportion of their waking time it consumes, and so on. The call to ratchet up the intensity of their work—to surrender the maximum amount of labor in a given period of time—collides with these other dimensions. Workers may, and often do, find that the increasing intensity of labor comes at the cost of their well-being.

If all the returns from increased labor effort went to the workers, they might be induced to comply with employers' wishes. But this would of course be a groundless expectation, for two reasons. First, the employer sets the basic terms on which any increased revenues are divvied up between him and his labor force—if at all. It is entirely possible that all extra income from the increased efficiency will go to him. Just as important, though, is the fact that every jump in the efficiency of production will increase the likelihood of job loss for any given worker, because as each worker is able to produce more goods in less time, the employer can afford to shed some of his labor force. The economic uncertainty generated by rising productivity merely adds to the workers' list of reasons to resist the demand for greater effort. Hence, when the call comes to ratchet up the intensity of their labor, workers have good reason to push back. They perceive it as a call for sacrificing other of their genuine interests for returns that are, at best, highly uncertain. While they will certainly have an interest in maintaining a certain level of labor effort in order to keep their firm afloat and hence keep their jobs, they do not share the goal of maximizing its returns.

Capitalists cannot, therefore, leave it to their employees to work at an intensity consistent with profit maximization. The natural inclination of workers will be to shirk—to work at a pace they deem consistent with their manifold interests, a pace that will most likely be at a lower level than desired by their employer. To extract the needed work, capitalists must thus wield some degree of authority over their employees in the labor process. This is why, in capitalism, the place of coercion shifts from outside the labor process to within it. Employers have to institutionalize direct authority on the shop floor, or within the office, as an intrinsic component of work organization. It can be wielded directly by the owner or parcelized across layers of intermediate management. Its organizational form notwithstanding, what is clear is that, in capitalist production, there is a powerful inducement for employers to exert interpersonal coercion over workers.

While managerial authority constitutes an important mechanism for surplus extraction, its effectiveness is undermined if labor is able to wield a countervailing power of its own, either through individual efforts on the part of workers or through organized resistance. What ensues on the shop floor, therefore, is a struggle to exert power, by both labor and capital, in order to control the tempo and direction of work. A critical component of the power game is for management to ensure that workers cannot build organizations for collective action.[27] If they are permitted to do so, the resultant leverage can be wielded to place limits on the demands that employers can make. One of the chief means of ensuring that employees remain weak in their bargaining position is to heighten the divisions between them. Where employers find that labor is already riven with caste, cultural, or ethnic divisions, they can and often do find ways of using these divisions to their advantage.

THE LABOR PROCESS AND SOCIAL HIERARCHIES

Employers can capitalize on social divisions or hierarchies in two distinct ways. The first is by mobilizing them in a divide-and-conquer strategy, which deepens social divisions within labor, thereby tilting the balance of power toward employers. Social divisions do not have to be invented by capital: often they already exist within the population as it is proletarianized and absorbed into the labor process. Recruitment patterns ensure that workers arrive at the work site already sorted into culturally or socially distinct occupational groupings. For much of the nineteenth and twentieth centuries, employers depended on various "jobbers" to find and enlist labor for their factories. Typically, these jobbers tapped into ethnic or community networks to recruit fresh workers, and these communities, for their part, often concentrated on certain occupational specializations.[28] New

---

27   The classic analysis of the structure of capital-labor conflict is Claus Offe and Helmut Wiesenthal, "Two Logics of Collective Action: Theoretical Notes on Social Class and Organizational Form," *Political Power and Social Theory* 1 (1980), 67–115.

28   I offer here only a smattering of the references to labor recruitment, because the

employees were thus filtered into the plant as ethnically or racially segregated occupational clusters. For employers, this meant that these segregated groupings of workers had already borne some of the costs of training that would otherwise have had to be absorbed by the employer. It also divided the workforce into distinct communities, and thus increased the difficulty of collective action if they tried to organize across community boundaries—which, of course, they typically had to do. What all this shows is that the divisions in the divide-and-conquer strategy do not have to be invented by capital—even though it often does try to create them. Labor typically comes to capital already riven by social hierarchies, which capital finds it can turn to its advantage.

But divide-and-conquer need not be an artifact of transitional societies. It is also built into the fabric of more developed incarnations of capitalism. One source of division in the working class, even in the advanced world, is the unceasing competition for jobs. The labor market in capitalist economies is a site of generalized insecurity. Individuals have no guarantee of finding employment, nor do they have any promise of retaining a job once they find it. The traditional instrument for reducing uncertainty and increasing security has been reliance on familial and social networks, which tend to be ethnically or racially homogenous. Workers depend on their extended families, friends, caste networks, regional links—any and all social ties that are available—so as to insulate themselves from the vagaries of the labor market.[29] The result of this reliance on networks is that it hardens lines of divisions within the working

---

literature is so vast and the phenomenon is fairly well understood. For its prevalence in a variety of national settings, see, for example, Andrew Gordon, *The Evolution of Labor Relations in Japan: Heavy Industry, 1853–1955* (Cambridge: Harvard University Press, 1988); Gunther Peck, *Reinventing Free Labor: Padrones and Immigrant Workers in the North American West, 1880–1930* (Cambridge: Cambridge University Press, 2000); Rajnarayan Chandavarkar, "The Decline and Fall of the Jobber System in the Bombay Cotton Textile Industry, 1870–1955," *Modern Asian Studies* 42:1 (2008), 117–210.

29   A superb explication of this dynamic can be found in Edna Bonacich, "A Theory of Ethnic Antagonism: The Split Labor Market," *American Sociological Review* 37:5 (Oct. 1972), 547–59; and Edna Bonacich, "Advanced Capitalism and Black/White Race Relations in the United States: A Split Labor Market Interpretation," *American Sociological Review* 41:1 (Feb. 1976), 34–51. See also Patrick L. Mason, "Race, Competition and Differential Wages," *Cambridge Journal of Economics* 19:4 (1995), 545–67; and Randy Albelda, Robert Drago, and Steven Shulman, *Unlevel Playing Fields: Understanding Wage Inequality and Discrimination*, 3rd ed. (Boston: Economics Affairs Bureau, 2010). An excellent field study of workers' reliance on their ethnic and racial networks is Deidre Royster, *Race and the Invisible Hand: How White Workers Exclude Back Men from Blue-Collar Jobs* (Berkeley: University of California Press, 2003). An important implication of this body of work is that racial divisions are generated by the capitalist system itself, not by the idiosyncrasies of individual capitalists within the system. These hierarchies will persist even if capitalists abstain from actively deepening them. This is because they are the product of a structural feature of the system—the generalized insecurity that workers experience in labor markets. Any solution to the pervasiveness of such divisions will therefore have to address the structural causes that generate them. It will have to recognize that the divisions are not simply the result of "false consciousness" on the part of workers, since workers do enhance some aspects of their well-being by relying on them.

class, simply as a result of competition in the labor market. Workers coalesce around their racial or ethnic identities, as these identities become a means for enhancing their material security. Employers therefore do not have to *create* social hierarchies as a conscious strategy—they find the hierarchies already constructed through the reproduction of capitalism itself. But having found workers already segmented along racial or ethnic lines, employers will often use these divisions to their advantage in their ongoing power struggles with labor.

A second, more direct device by which employers can benefit from social divisions or hierarchies is by relying on them to reinforce their interpersonal authority over the workers. Hierarchies often produce their own norms of deference and obeisance as part of their reproductive logic. Dominated groups learn, over time, to include displays of submission as part of their repertoire of survival in the face of authority. Where such norms of deference are an important component of community relations, and where employers are from communities that command such deference as part of the culture, employers can and do mobilize these norms to demand compliance from employees. Employers belonging to dominant ethnic or racial groups can rely on workers' habits of obeisance as a part of the labor extraction process. And in order to ensure the stability of such norms, they often give support to the institutions that bolster them—religious, cultural, or educational. The Birlas in India will find good reason to endow massive Hindu temples, as they in fact have done, and billionaires in the United States will funnel massive funds into evangelical churches. Capitalism, in these instances, will not only fail to dissolve the traditional culture of the subaltern classes, but will give it added strength and substance.

DOMINATION AND THE POLITICAL DOMAIN

As we can see, capitalists mobilize all available means to increase their power in the organization of work, even in labor processes characterized by regular technical change.[30] That is, even in the more advanced sectors of capitalist production, employers find it necessary to exercise direct authority over their labor force in order to extract work at the needed intensity. But the degree to

---

30   Marx expresses the dynamic of the situation very well. Even though the worker freely contracts to sell his labor power to the employer, " . . . the social position of the seller and the buyer changes in the production process itself. The buyer takes command of the seller . . . there comes into being, outside the simple exchange process, *a relation of domination and servitude*, which is however distinguished from all other historical relations of this kind by the fact that it only follows from the specific nature of the commodity which is being sold by the seller." Karl Marx, *Collected Works*, vol. 30, 106; emphasis added. See also ibid., 37, 93. In *Capital*, Marx observes that insofar as capitalists coordinate the division of labor on the shop floor, "in form [this coordination] is necessarily *despotic*" (vol. 1, 450). Later in vol. 1 of *Capital* he continues, "Division of labour within the workshop implies the *undisputed authority* of the capitalist over men," so that "anarchy in the social division of labour and *despotism* in the manufacturing division mutually condition each other" (477). Emphasis added in all.

which authority is successfully imposed within the labor process cannot be unaffected by the distribution of power outside it.[31] To impose his will on his employees, the capitalist uses whatever leverage his greater social power may afford him. The main such source of power is the structural advantage he wields over his workers—the fact that he can deprive them of their livelihood. The fear of being sacked is perhaps the main inducement felt by workers to submit to his authority and his demands. Employers are therefore wary of measures that decrease their workers' dependence on their waged work—hence business groups' often intense resentment of the decommodification of sundry goods by the welfare state. The broader political rights and social privileges afforded to workers also become a matter of concern to employers. Workers are far less able to resist authority at the workplace if they lack social and political equality outside it. If employers also have monopoly power over the state apparatus, cultural production, political parties, and so on, these institutions lie beyond the reach of the laboring population and thus cannot be used to protect their interests at the workplace. Consequently, the drive to impose their authority in the production process inclines employers also to establish their dominance in the broader political and social sphere.

This is why the bourgeois revolutions in Europe yielded a political nation that was in fact a bourgeois oligarchy. The established capitalist class in England and the emerging capitalists in France both had a direct interest in a social order in which they could use their political dominance to intensify their power on the shop floor. This ambition is what drove their hostility to the laboring classes' demands for universal suffrage, the legalization of trade unions, and so forth. Capitalists' resistance to political liberalization was in part occasioned by the fact that, even into the mid-nineteenth century, manufacturers across Europe were still heavily dependent on low-wage, labor-intensive production, and therefore had much to lose from an enfranchised and organized working class. Any increase in unit labor costs was perceived as a body blow to profit margins. Employers' preferred means of surplus extraction was still through absolute means—keeping wages at subsistence levels and extending each shift to its maximum duration[32]—and yet the preference for such strategies extended well into the latter decades of the nineteenth century and even into the twentieth. In other words, the reliance on labor repression was maintained even as British manufacturing shifted to a more technologically driven production regime.

There is no better evidence of the resort to state-sanctioned coercion than

---

31   The connection between workplace and societal power is one of the themes explored in Michael Burawoy, *The Politics of Production: Factory Regimes under Capitalism and Socialism* (London: Verso, 1985).

32   A comprehensive survey is provided in Richard Price, *British Society, 1680–1880: Dynamism, Containment, and Change* (Cambridge: Cambridge University Press, 1999).

in the extraordinary longevity of contract labor in England and the United States, under the master and servant laws.[33] For most of the nineteenth century, in both countries, workers employed in manufacturing did not have the freedoms typically associated with free labor. A common form of employment in industry was contract labor, in which workers agreed to commit to their employer for a stipulated period of time, often several years, at a fixed rate of remuneration. Any attempt to renege on the bargain, either by quitting or by insisting on renegotiating the wage rate, was punishable by law. Employers were free to terminate the contract at any time, but workers lacked a symmetrical privilege. A worker who gained employment under these terms had forfeited the right to dispose of his labor power as he wished. He was now his employer's man, in a manner reminiscent of feudal Europe, even though the relation differed in content. But the employer's power over his employees was not confined to a right to their labor power; it extended also to the effort that the workers expended. Workers could be drawn up on charges not just for quitting, but for unexcused absences from work—as in cases of illness—or for unsatisfactory performance, which was deemed an encroachment on the employer's proprietary use of the employee's labor power.

In spirit, the legislation that provided capitalists with this power over their workers could be traced back to the fourteenth century. But it is critical to note that most legislation stretching back to that era had been repealed over the intervening centuries, and that the actual laws governing contract labor were drawn up at the height of the Industrial Revolution, in the early decades of the nineteenth century.[34] The legislation was thus revived and resuscitated *explicitly* for the sake of modernizing capitalists. Furthermore, its incidence was widespread across sector and region. The actual frequency with which it was used to intimidate workers is, of course, difficult to assess. But it was widely used even in the advanced manufacturing sectors.[35] Indeed, it was particularly attractive to employers in more advanced industries, where on-site training was important in the labor process. Employers were especially keen in these cases to

---

33   The scholarship on contract labor in the nineteenth century is of surprisingly recent provenance. A pioneering essay was Daphne Simon, "Master and Servant," in John Saville, ed., *Democracy and the Labour Movement: Essays in Honor of Dona Torr* (London: Lawrence and Wishart, 1954), 160–200. The most extensive survey in recent years is Robert J. Steinfeld, *Coercion, Contract and Free Labor in the Nineteenth Century* (Cambridge: Cambridge University Press, 2001); see also Steinfeld's earlier book, *The Invention of Free Labor: The Employment Relation in English and American Law and Culture, 1350–1870* (Chapel Hill: University of North Carolina Press, 1991). More recent is Christopher Tomlins, *Freedom Bound: Law, Labor and Civic Identity in English America, 1580–1865* (Cambridge: Cambridge University Press, 2010), 342–59. Tomlins's analysis does not go much beyond the early nineteenth century; for later decades, Steinfeld is superb.

34   See Douglas Hay, "England, 1562–1875: The Law and Its Uses," in Hay and Paul Craven, eds. *Masters, Servants and Magistrates in Britain and the Empire, 1562-1955*, (Chapel Hill: University of North Carolina Press, 2004), 59–117.

35   Steinfeld, *Coercion, Contract, and Free Labor*, 39–84. See esp. 76–9.

avoid losing the investment they made in worker training if their employees walked away with the valuable skills they had learned on the job. British capitalists thus pressed legislators to protect their control over workers—their own particular workers—by giving them legal grounds to prosecute.[36] And in this they were entirely successful.

The means used to bind workers to their employers were not confined to master and servant law. Well into the twentieth century, employers also resorted to debt peonage. In the United States, the nineteenth century witnessed the emergence of private militias as a means of intimidating workers, and these, too, operated well into the 1930s. Moreover, in much of the American industrial economy, workers were pressed into "company towns," in which much of their daily reproduction was directly under the influence, if not control, of their employer, and where all the instruments just enumerated were enforced with brutal tenacity. All of these forms of coercion were deployed across industrial sectors in the most advanced capitalisms in the world, well after mass production had emerged. They were different in content from feudal coercion, to be sure. But they were even more different from Chakrabarty's idealized picture of "bourgeois forms of production." Indeed, they were almost exactly like the coercive relations he points to in India, which he regards as departures from capitalist power relations and therefore as symptoms of capital's failed universalization.

CAPITAL AND POWER REVISITED

The foregoing examples of domination show two things. First, the oligarchies established in modernizing Europe were geared, in substantial measure, to intensify the power of employers over their labor force. The hostility evinced by capitalists to universal suffrage, during and after the bourgeois revolutions, is explicable only through the arguments developed in the preceding section. The legal sanctions I have described—the resistance to the franchise, the resort to various forms of servitude—all these were developed in order to facilitate the task of labor extraction. It was understood that greater power for labor in the political arena would dilute capital's authority in the labor process, over matters of distribution, and over the power struggle between labor and capital more generally.

Second, the practices just discussed were instances of direct, interpersonal coercion in the employment relation—the very sort of coercion that Subalternist theorists present as a departure from bourgeois power. This again undermines Chakrabarty's claim that relations of interpersonal coercion

---

36 For large and modernizing employers' defense of coercive contract law, see Mark Curthoys, *Governments, Labour and the Law in Mid-Victorian Britain: The Trade Union Legislation of the 1870s* (Oxford: Oxford University Press, 2004), 185–6, 215.

endure within Indian economic structures because India is burdened with a form of capitalism qualitatively different from the one that took root in Europe. We now see, however, that Chakrabarty's argument is based, much as was Guha's, on an imaginary history.[37] European elites' resort to interpersonal coercion, backed by state power, endured for centuries across the Western world and lasted well into the twentieth century. This was true even in England and the United States, surely cradles of bourgeois modernity. The persistence of such coercive relations in India during the sixty years since Independence is thoroughly unremarkable.

It is not clear, therefore, why Indian capital's reliance on coercive extraction should be seen as a departure from "bourgeois forms of power" at all. Chakrabarty is wrong to assert that the power relations in Calcutta jute mills were "derived more from the colonial situation than from *any other factor internal to the production process*."[38] In fact, as just shown, power relations of precisely that kind are derived from factors internal to the capitalist production process, whether colonial or not. The resort to such forms of coercion should be viewed as entirely consistent with capitalism, not a departure from it. All forms of capitalism, whether backward or advanced, generate some measure of personal subordination of workers to their employers. This is written into the labor process. What the Western experience shows is that, if its degree is left to the discretion of employers, they will reinforce their baseline level of dominance over the labor process by whatever means they can mobilize—legal, extralegal, financial, cultural, and so on. The fact that Western capitalism eventually moved away from these forms in its heartland should be viewed as an *achievement*, as the product of very specific circumstances. What these circumstances were, I will address in the next chapter. For now, the point to highlight is that if and when such forms of authority are found in the colonial or postcolonial world, they do not automatically signal a radical break between the practices of capital in the West and the practices during its subsequent Eastern sojourn. Capital, in both East and West, has never been content to rely on the "dull compulsion of economic relations" to enforce its diktat.

Chakrabarty, then, is mistaken in his analysis of power. But our analysis here has additional implications for postcolonial theory, especially with regard to its status as social criticism. Subalternists have gone to great lengths to avoid lapsing into economic reductionism. In this, they fall in line with much postcolonial theorizing, which is so sensitive to this accusation that it often whisks economic analysis out of the picture altogether. True, it is surely problematic to see capital lurking behind every social phenomenon, but it is no less

---

37 Chakrabarty has a ready defense against the charge that he romanticizes European history: that he is referring to Europe only as a "hyperreal" entity. In the postscript to this chapter, I show that this is a notable instance of special pleading.

38 Chakrabarty, *Rethinking Working-Class History*, 166.

objectionable to deny its salience where it is in fact a relevant causal agent. The core elements of *Subaltern Studies* theorizing have served just this function since its inception. The arguments examined in the preceding chapters systematically obscure the real dynamics of capitalist development. Thus far we have encountered two theorists, and there are more to come. Both Guha and Chakrabarty accept some of the oldest and most hallowed myths about the heroic struggle of the bourgeoisie, its championing of popular rights, its commitment to consensus, and so on. They do so because they ignore and obscure the real compulsions that drive capitalist political and economic practice.

This makes the Subalternists vulnerable to a second weakness, which is that they ignore the mechanisms that make it rational for capital to sustain and reinforce power relations resembling those of the feudal past. Hence, in their analysis of capital's rise in Europe, Subalternist theorists insist that the bourgeoisie was an important actor, but they misdiagnose its real interests and its practice; in the case of power relations within a capitalist economy, they simply deny that the myriad forms of coercion exercised by capital are capitalist all. These power relations are ruled out by Chakrabarty as "bourgeois forms of power." Chakrabarty, like Guha, thereby only obscures capital's reproductive dynamic in the colonial world. Instead of theorizing how capitalism reproduces status and caste hierarchies, he detaches these hierarchies from capital. These arguments are instances of Guha's and Chakrabarty's acceptance of a highly romanticized conception of capitalism—one in which the bourgeoisie's inclination to dominate, coerce, and utilize traditional discourses is ruled out *tout court*, in favor of a conception that capitalism's defenders have promulgated for more than two centuries. We will encounter several other instances of this weakness in the chapters to come.

5.4 CONCLUSION

Subaltern Studies launched its research agenda on the back of an observation: that the political development of the East seems to have diverged in crucial respects from that of the West. Whereas the West has experienced the development of a stable, integrated political culture, the East continues to be burdened with a poorly integrated and unstable polity. This constitutes the premise for the entire Subalternist project, and I have not disputed its validity. What I have questioned is the set of propositions that Ranajit Guha has mobilized to explain the East-West divergence. According to Guha, political modernization in the West has been a consequence of the universalization of capital. Capital's universalizing drive was carried through by the modern bourgeoisie in England and France, who launched the revolutions of 1640 and 1789 and then established, for the first time, political orders founded on the consent of the governed. This is what the bourgeoisie in the East failed to do. Moreover, Guha contends that the bourgeoisie's failure was indicative of another, deeper lacuna, which is that when capital entered the colonial world, it abandoned its universalizing mission.

I have argued in this chapter that there are no grounds for concluding that capital gave up its universalizing mission once it came to the Subcontinent. Guha arrives at his conclusion based on an idiosyncratic notion of what universalization entails. Not only is his an unusual definition of the term, but it has scant support from the historical record. If the West is where capital successfully universalized, then the bourgeoisie's political practice in that region ought to be consistent with what the theory predicts. But it was not, as we observed in chapter 3. Neither British capitalists nor French elite leaders showed any inclination to pursue the ends that Guha asserts they did.

If, however, we replace Guha's definition of universalization with the one I have offered, then the tension with the historical record disappears. What is universalized under the rule of capital is not the drive for a consensual and encompassing political order, but rather the compulsions of market dependence. For capital, this amounts to a compulsion to produce in order to sell—production for exchange value, not for use. This, in its turn, makes it rational for capitalists to seek political power over their workforce—both at the microlevel on the shop floor, and in broader political institutions outside the production process. My account leads to the prediction that, far from seeking to accommodate the ambitions of the subaltern classes, capital should view their independence with suspicion; instead of fighting for a liberal political order, as Guha would have it, a universalizing capital ought to prefer a narrower, more exclusionary regime. These predictions are far closer to actual historical experience than are the ones generated by the Subalternist account. What is more, they are consistent with the experience of both East and West.

Two conclusions follow from the argument thus far. The first is that the peculiarities of the Subcontinent—and much of the postcolonial world—are not generated by capital's having *failed* in its drive, but of its having *acted* on that drive. The continued salience of archaic power relations, the resort to traditional symbols, the resilience of caste and kin-based political coalitions, and so forth— all this can be shown to be consistent with the universalizing tendency.[39] So, too, are the preferences and practices of Indian capitalists in the independence movement perfectly consistent with this same process of universalization. Hence, even if we allow that the kind of power exercised by capital in the East is different from that in the West, they can both be explained as instances of capitalist dynamics. They express capitalists' different responses to different settings.

------

39 This does not mean that all political forms are expressions of capital. There continue to be pockets and regions where capitalism has not yet made many inroads, and where social relations continue to be governed by older economic structures. It is thus an empirical question whether any given form of authority is genuinely independent of capital or has been given new life by it.

All this I have already pointed out. But I repeat it here because it is the basis for our second conclusion: that, if my critique is accepted, we can safely reject Dipesh Chakrabarty's insistence that the actual course of political modernity in India cannot be viewed as part of the "universal narrative of capital" and cannot be explained through an "application of the analytics of capital and nationalism."[40] In fact, the arguments of the present chapter, if successful, do precisely that—they show the *relevance* of the "universal narrative of capital" to the advent of political modernity, not just in the West but also in the East.

Thus far my argument has addressed only a part of Chakrabarty's challenge. Recall that his claim was twofold: that capital's failure to universalize, the bourgeoisie's inability to attain hegemony, produced forms of power and authority that are inconsistent with the logic of capital. Hence his call to "pluralize" the analysis of power. The second claim was that such noncapitalist forms of power resist scrutiny through the lens of Marxian categories. Both claims have been addressed in the current chapter—but not exhaustively. We have seen that a different conception of capital—a conception true to Marx's formulation, but by no means unique to him—is capable of explaining the persistence of the very forms of power that Chakrabarty presents as anomalous. Yet the worries about Marxism's "universalizing" categories run deeper.

In the next chapter, I will address additional concerns that universalizing categories cannot explain the diversity of power in the postcolonial world. I will then take up a second issue, rounding out our engagement with Guha's and Chakrabarty's analysis of the elite-subaltern split. Although I have already shown that the persistence of a distinct subaltern sphere is perfectly consistent with a universalizing capitalism, I have not addressed the next looming puzzle: if the bourgeoisie is not driven to integrate the subaltern sphere into one encompassing polity, then why, in Europe, did such integration nonetheless take place? Why, despite the centuries-long persistence of authoritarian, oligarchic rule in Europe, did the Continent experience a wide-ranging democratization of the culture by the mid-twentieth century? On both counts, as we shall see, the answers reveal further weaknesses in the *Subaltern Studies* project.

5.5 POSTSCRIPT: THE BOGEY OF A "HYPERREAL EUROPE"

In the preceding chapters I have pointed out that much of the Subalternist argument for the uniqueness of the East is based on a false depiction of the European experience with capitalism. Now, one possible response available to Chakrabarty is that he never intended to describe Europe as it really was. At several places in *Provincializing Europe*, Chakrabarty warns that he refers to Europe only as a "hyperreal" entity.[41] For him, hyperreal concepts "refer to certain

---

40 See above, 107.
41 *PE* 27, 40, 45.

figures of imagination whose geographical referents remain somewhat indeterminate."[42] This is the closest he comes to a definition.[43] Seemingly, then, his argument is about an abstraction, an *idea* of Europe—not the actual entity. There is some connection, of course, between the hyperreal Europe and its actual referent, but Chakrabarty apparently prefers to make no commitment to its verisimilitude.

This claim is worth considering. Several commentators seem to view Chakrabarty's defense as a credible description of how he actually uses Europe in his analysis. In addition, the defense could be used against the accusation that he misdescribes the real history of capitalism in Europe. He can simply counter such accusations by reminding us that he is concerned only with how a certain notion of Europe is used to marginalize the East—not with Europe as it actually was, but merely how its fictive stand-in is put to use. If this is the case, it might also insulate him from certain aspects of my criticism, such as when I charge him with presenting a highly romanticized construal of the history of capitalism.

So, we may begin by asking whether the argument in *Provincializing Europe*—or in any of the other works examined in this book—can be understood as referring only to a *idea* of Europe, rather than to actual experience. I find this a rather fantastic claim. When Chakrabarty says that power relations in India are different from those in Europe, clearly he is referring to the real history of Europe; when Guha claims that the Indian bourgeoisie fell short of the heroism exhibited by its European counterpart, he has in mind the actual British capitalists, not their imaginary representations. In Guha's case, this is quite clear—if he did not think there was a real difference between early-stage British capital and early-stage Indian capital, then it would be nonsensical for him to castigate the Indian bourgeoisie for its failings. His excoriation of Indian capital assumes that European capital really did undertake the mission to overthrow feudalism, and really did establish a consensual political order. Moreover, Chakrabarty explicitly endorses Guha's balance sheet, as I showed above.[44] He agrees that India lacked a counterpart to the revolutionary bourgeoisie in Europe and that this was why the subaltern sphere and the elite sphere remained separate. This is a real comparison, not a comparison of two concepts.

As for Chakrabarty's own work, I have described him as misrepresenting European history in his claim that the power relations in India depart fundamentally from those witnessed in Europe. Is he referring here only to the idea of Europe? Clearly not. Recall that he motivates his call for a new theory of power by a claim about the real history of capital, reminding us that "the

---

42   *PE* 27.

43   He mentions having borrowed the expression from Jean Baudrillard, but also warns that his use of it differs from the latter's (*PE* 265n2). Baudrillard may not be a beacon of lucidity, but this means that even referring to his work for guidance is rendered out of the question.

44   See above, 103–8.

global history of capitalism need not produce everywhere the same history of power."[45] This is a contrast between actual histories, not two different concepts of the history. Because capitalism does not produce the same power relations everywhere, we might need to come up with concepts and new theories of how power works. Exactly where might we find this real difference in the global history of capitalism? Again, Chakrabarty is clear. Urging that we note "differences in the history of power in colonial India and in Europe,"[46] he is drawing attention to the difference between India and Europe. There is no hint, nor is there reason to believe, that he has only their hyperreal counterparts in mind.

We may also turn to Chakrabarty's argument in *Rethinking Working-Class History*, from which he draws in *Provincializing Europe*. There, too, his discussion of power relations on the shop floor, his designation of the violence and discipline as "excessive," is an explicit comparison with the exercise of power in British industrial relations as he understands them to have actually been. It is a real comparison, however mistaken it turned out to be. It is not a comparison between Calcutta jute mills and the *idea* of capitalist domination.[47] It is safe to say, then, that the motivation to rethink the sundry categories of Enlightenment thought can only arise from the putative *real* difference in their experience. Only if the history of power in India *really does* depart from that of its European predecessor must we reject narratives based on the European experience.

To put the point another way, Chakrabarty asks us to believe that whenever he claims there to be a difference between the European experience and that of the East, we should take Europe to denote an abstract concept—that we should place invisible scare quotes around it, reading it as "Europe." Yet he cannot reasonably mean this. If he does, it radically destabilizes his call, as well as the call from postcolonial theory more generally, to reject "grand narratives." The justification for the rejection of totalizing or grand narratives, and the resultant need to construct categories tied to the specificity of the East, presumes the existence of real differences between the histories and structures of West and East. Everything I have quoted in the preceding paragraphs is consistent with this commitment. If we now suddenly deflate that commitment, and insist that we are only comparing the East with "Europe"—which may or may not accurately present Europe as it actually was—then we also remove the justification for rejecting grand narratives. What if it turned out that European history and structures are in fact much like those of the East? On what basis should we then reject grand narratives? To the contrary, we would now have good reason to *embrace* theories that viewed West and East as part of the same basic story, that

---

45   Chakrabarty, "*Subaltern Studies* and Postcolonial Historiography," 20.
46   *PE* 14.
47   See above, 105–6.

construed them as variants of the same universal history. Chakrabarty cannot have it both ways. He cannot enjoin us to recognize the specificity of the East, while also claiming that he is making no claims about the actual history of Europe and India.[48] If he really does think that grand narratives are misleading, he must admit this is because the East really is different from the West.

---

48   In a response to Carola Dietze, who offers a perfectly sensible interpretation of his argument, he denies that a "hyperreal" Europe refers only to a *concept*. It is, Chakrabarty says, "something *less* than a concept." And what does it mean for something to be *less than a concept*? Chakrabarty clarifies it thus: "By using the adjective 'hyperreal' . . . I wanted to refer to something less determined than a concept, something like an imaginary entity that has some relation to the real but is also at the same time phantasmal and that, as I said, is part of everyday representations in a place like India." But what does it mean to be *less* determined than a concept and yet also have *some* relation to the real? He does not explain. All this seems a rather deliberate exercise in evasiveness—someone trying very hard to be so vague as to immunize their view from criticism. But the problem remains: either the hyperreal is a (more or less) defensible account of Europe, or it is not. Making it less than a concept, more than a fiction, or a smidgen short of a conjecture—none of these circumlocutions succeeds in neutralizing the challenge. See Chakrabarty, "In Defense of *Provincializing Europe*: A Response to Carola Dietze," *History and Theory* 47 (Feb. 2008), 85–96, esp. 86–7.

CHAPTER SIX

Capital, Abstract Labor, and Difference

The previous chapter established that capitalism can directly generate many varieties of power relations, including interpersonal domination—the very kind of power that Chakrabarty presents as evidence of a failed universalization. Relations of direct authority and subordination can quite readily be folded into the "universal narrative of capital." Some postcolonial theorists grant that the reliance on interpersonal domination, and on existing racial and cultural divisions, is not alien to class relations in capitalism; their worry is that the phenomena cannot be explained through the theoretical frameworks bequeathed by the Enlightenment. Here, too, the most common target is Marx, although the criticisms extend to Enlightenment thought more generally. Capitalism may generate a highly diverse landscape of labor extraction and domination, the argument goes, but Enlightenment thought cannot provide us with a conceptual vocabulary to understand this diversity, because the theories handed down from Europe are relentlessly homogenizing and universalizing, and thereby incapable of appreciating complexity. So, while the actual history of capitalism may be uneven and diverse, the frameworks handed down by European thinkers will be inadequate for the task of capturing its dynamics.

Postcolonial theorists have fastened onto Marx's concept of abstract labor as a prime example of the deficiencies of universalizing theories. Since the concept appears quite frequently in postcolonial theorizing, and since postcolonial theorists point to it as an exemplar of the problems associated with universalizing concepts, I would like to examine their case for its flaws. I do so with some reluctance, since this endeavor involves a descent into some of the more arcane dimensions of Marx's value theory. But I believe that even though the concept is associated with the labor theory of value, it actually captures some important aspects of the labor extraction process, which can be defended independent of the more controversial aspects of value theory. More important, I intend to show that postcolonial theorists have thoroughly misunderstood its significance. Far from blinding us to the heterogeneity of the working class, or being unable to accommodate the persistence of caste-based, racial or ethnic divisions within it, the concept of abstract labor powerfully illuminates these very phenomena. Hence, while the preceding chapter showed that a universalizing capitalism does not have to homogenize all power relations, this chapter will show that concepts like abstract labor are fully capable of apprehending the resulting social diversity.

But this raises a further question: if capitalism, even in its zone of origin, was not driven to transform the political culture and to integrate the elite and subaltern domains, if it could have happily accommodated an ongoing political exclusion of the laboring classes, then why did the European polity in fact move away from exclusion and toward an integrated political culture? Europe could have remained dotted with bourgeois oligarchies, but it did not. Locating the real source of this transformation will enable us to pose the counterfactual that Guha ought to have posed. If it was not the bourgeoisie's failure that accounts for the political maladies of the postcolonial world, then what kind of political project might allow the empowerment of laboring classes? What I will show is that it was not the heroism of capital that liberated the subaltern classes, but their own political struggles. That finding necessitates a research agenda different from the one launched by Guha, and yet the theoretical commitments of Subaltern Studies make it difficult for them to pursue such an agenda. The reasons for this will be addressed at the end of this chapter.

6.1 THE PROBLEM DEFINED

Within the Subalternist collective, it is Dipesh Chakrabarty who has most directly addressed the status of abstract labor. He sees it as an instance of Marx's reliance on "Enlightenment ideas of juridical equality and the abstract political rights of citizenship."[1] More specifically, he sees in the concept a dilemma from which Marx was never able to escape—that, while the notion of abstract labor illuminates some crucial dimensions of capitalism's reproduction, Marx's reliance on it forces him to ignore the myriad differences between social formations and among real human beings. Focusing on labor's abstract qualities comes at the expense of suppressing the matter of historical differences—and it is those differences that make us human. Hence, for Chakrabarty, critical historians must approach concepts such as abstract labor with caution, for they impose a univocal grid on the diversity of social experience and of human existence. Accordingly, the task at hand becomes to "try to open up Marxist narratives of capitalist modernity to issues of historical difference."[2]

The idea that abstract categories are incapable of explaining the genesis of historical diversity is very common among postcolonial theorists. We have just seen that it is central to Chakrabarty's critique of Enlightenment theories. We must wait till chapter 9 to fully address his critique, since a comprehensive response will require a few intermediate steps. In the present chapter, we will begin by taking up the criticism developed by postcolonial theorists who are motivated by the same concerns as Chakrabarty but whose arguments are somewhat distinct from his.

---

1   Dipesh Chakrabarty, *Provincializing Europe* (Princeton: Princeton University Press, 2000), 50. Henceforth cited as *PE*.
2   *PE* 19.

One of the most influential statements of the critique of abstract labor has come from Lisa Lowe's work on the assimilation of Asian immigrants into the United States. Lowe charges that political economy—particularly Marx's work—cannot make sense of the manner in which Asian Americans have been incorporated into American capitalism over the past century. She does not claim, as does Chakrabarty, that the persistence of racial hierarchies somehow undermines the idea of capital's universalization. She agrees that capitalists will readily utilize racial hierarchy where they find it and, in so doing, will reproduce racial differences. She also allows that this will often involve interpersonal domination in the employment relation as well as between workers. Her criticism is thus not identical to Chakrabarty's.[3] What concerns her is that while Marxism can recognize the historical reality of racial hierarchies within the labor force, it cannot adequately *theorize* this phenomenon with the framework Marx generated. For her, the reality of racial difference is inconsistent with the theoretical structure of Marxian political economy.

What supposedly makes a racialized labor force, and racialized work relations, difficult for Marxian theory is the central place it accords to abstract labor. Like many postcolonial theorists, Lowe never offers a detailed explication of the concept, so the source of her concern is not immediately apparent. But the basic thrust of her critique seems clear enough. She takes Marx to have argued that capitalism makes labor abstract by rendering it increasingly *homogeneous* over time. Lowe sees Marx's theory as having been clearly overturned by the historical record, by the fact that "in the United States, capital has maintained its profits not through rendering labor 'abstract' but precisely through the social production of 'difference,' of restrictive particularity and illegitimacy marked by race, nation, geographical origins, and gender."[4] Capitalism's production of "difference" is thus taken to be anomalous for Marxian theory, particularly for its understanding of the labor market.

For Lowe, "Marx remains committed to Enlightenment universalisms, through which we can neither account for the specificity of racialized Asian immigrant labor within the U.S. economy nor for the role of colonialism and imperialism in the emergence of the political nation."[5] The reason these universalisms cannot illuminate the specificity of immigrant labor or the workings of imperialism is that according to these theories, of which Marx's is a prime example, "capital accumulates through *universal homogenization* rather than through differentiation."[6] Yet persistent diversity—differentiation—is central to the history of American capitalism. Hence, Lowe concludes, "Asian immigrants and Asian

---

3   Cf. Chap. 5 above, 103–5.
4   Lisa Lowe, *Immigrant Acts: On Asian American Cultural Politics* (Durham, NC: Duke University Press, 1996), 27.
5   Ibid., 28.
6   Ibid. Emphasis added.

Americans have been neither 'abstract labor' nor 'abstract citizens,' but have been historically formed in contradiction to the economic and political spheres."[7]

The equation of abstract labor with homogeneous labor runs through the gamut of postcolonial theory.[8] In chapter 9 we will see that Chakrabarty bases his arguments on essentially the same premise. Its acceptance even extends to several theorists hailing from the Marxian tradition, such as David R. Roediger. In recent work, Roediger has explicitly endorsed Lowe's view regarding the incompatibility of Marx's abstract analysis with the reality of racial differentiation. And, like Lowe, he takes abstract labor to be homogeneous labor. "Marx's logic," Roediger avers, "held that capital homogenizes society because it sees a world made up of units of labor, rather than of races, nationalities or genders." Marx incorporated this view into his basic framework, accepting "the idea that labor is abstract and that mature capitalism is, or should be, colorblind."[9] The problem is that the actual path of industrialization "produced no firm drive to make labor abstract, raceless, and subject to a level playing field."[10] Since the reality of capitalist development has departed so significantly from what Marx's theory would predict, this cannot but be a blow to its universalizing pretensions.

The argument offered by Lowe and Roediger differs from the one presented by Chakrabarty, who takes the sheer fact of historical diversity as symptomatic of capitalism's failed universalizing mission and builds an entire theory around this supposed failure. Lowe and Roediger do not see diversity as a departure from capitalism, but rather as a refutation of a particular theory of how capitalism works—Marx's theory. They believe that the system necessarily generates social difference, but they also believe that an abstract theory, such as Marx's, cannot adequately theorize how it does this.

6.2 CAPITALISM AND ABSTRACT LABOR

Lowe and Roediger build upon a real ambiguity in Marx. The fact is, he never systematically developed an argument about social identities in capitalism. There are pithy and sometimes provocative passages suggesting that they would dissolve—for example, the *Communist Manifesto* describes the revolutionary impact of capitalist production, whereby "all fixed, fast-frozen relations, with

---

7   Ibid.

8   Apart from Lowe's and Chakrabarty's work, see Lisa Lowe and David Lloyd, "Introduction," in Lowe and Lloyd, eds., *The Politics of Culture in the Shadow of Capital* (Durham: Duke University Press, 1997), 13; Vijay Mishra and Bob Hodge, "What Was Postcolonialism?" *New Literary History* 36:3 (2005), 397; Paul K. Eiss and David Pedersen, "Values of Value," *Cultural Anthropology* 17:3 (2002), 285; and Michael Denning's qualified endorsement of Chakrabarty and Lowe in Denning, "Representing Global Labor," *Social Text* 92 (Fall 2007), 141.

9   David R. Roediger, *How Race Survived U.S. History: From Settlement and Slavery to the Obama Phenomenon* (London: Verso, 2008), 66.

10   Ibid., 68.

their train of ancient and venerable prejudices, and opinions, are swept away . . . [and] all that is solid melts into air."[11] Passages such as this lend credibility to the view that Marx expected old social identities and roles to evaporate as capitalism developed.[12] But while this characterization of his view is somewhat justified, the expectation that old roles will dissolve does not warrant the further claim that the end result will be social homogenization. In only a very few instances does Marx predict that social differences will simply disappear in capitalism. Even if we focus on the passage just quoted, Marx is merely claiming that old relations and prejudices will be swept away—there is no basis for concluding that what will take their place is a homogeneous social landscape. The dissolution of traditional roles is perfectly consistent with the construction of new roles that preserve a baseline heterogeneity of the social sphere. Keeping our focus on Marx, there are numerous instances where he points to the rationality, for capitalists, of promoting racial differentiation—hence his description of the use of Irish labor by British capitalists as a means of weakening the trade union movement in England.[13] Not only can heterogeneity survive in capitalism; Marx also deems it rational for capitalists to actively engineer it. The textual evidence regarding his views points in both directions.

Pasting conclusions onto scattered remarks buried in popular writings is not the best way to develop a theory. A more promising avenue is to look at Marx's more systematic arguments, especially those focusing on social reproduction. In this respect, Lowe, Roediger, and the Subalternists are on the right track, in their focus on the part of Marx's theory that seems to address directly at least one aspect of role differentiation—the place of labor in the creation of surplus value. Nevertheless, as I am about to show, the conclusions that follow from Marx's theory are in fact quite different from those derived by these critics. It turns out that the persistence of racial or ethnic divisions within the labor force is consistent with the concept of abstract labor. Whatever the failings of this theory, blindness to the facts of racial hierarchy is not among them. The criticisms leveled against it by Lowe and Roediger are baseless.

CONCRETE AND ABSTRACT LABOR

Critics like Lowe often charge that Marx failed to acknowledge the heterogeneity of labor. As shown above, she seems to understand abstract labor to be labor

---

11   "The Communist Manifesto," in Karl Marx, *The Revolutions of 1848*, ed. and trans. David Fernbach (New York: Vintage, 1974), 70.

12   I would like to thank Erik Olin Wright for pressing me to be clearer on this issue.

13   See Karl Marx and Frederick Engels, Collected Works, Vol. 34, *The Economic Manuscripts of 1861-63*, (New York: International Publishers), 296;see also Marx's widely cited letter in which he describes the position of Irish workers in England as being analogous to that of Black workers in the United States: Marx to Siegfried Meyer and August Vogt, April 9, 1870, in Marx and Engels, *Selected Correspondence*, Progress Publishers, 1975, 220–4.

that is homogenized over time—taking Marx to have held, typical of Enlightenment thinkers, that capitalism imposes a "universal homogenization" on society. The homogenization of labor is seen as emblematic of this larger dynamic, and it is through this process that labor becomes abstract. But there is scant textual evidence for this claim. To the contrary, Marx's argument seems to be that labor is *irreducibly* heterogeneous.[14]

When he first introduces the concept of abstract labor, Marx presents it as possessing two properties. First, it comprises a dimension of all actual, concrete labors that go into the production of commodities. All use-values in capitalism are just "congealed quantities of homogeneous human labor, i.e. of human labor-power expended without regard to the form of its expenditure."[15] The form of its expenditure, of course, is the particular, concrete labor associated with the specific good produced. So, abstract labor is the common element—the "residue," as Marx calls it—in all concrete labors. The second property of abstract labor is that it endows the commodity with its exchange-value: "A use-value . . . has value only because abstract human labor is objectified or materialized in it."[16] The magnitude of its value is regulated by the quantity of this abstract labor that has gone into its production—with one crucial proviso, that it be labor that is socially necessary, a fact to which I will return presently. For now, let us focus a bit more on the relation between concrete and abstract labor.

The central point for our purposes is that even while it is the abstract quality of labor—its property of being labor power pure and simple, without regard to its particular qualities—that endows the commodity with its exchange-value, this does not liberate labor from its concrete form. Labor never becomes something other than concrete labor. It is impossible to separate concrete labor from abstract labor, except as an abstraction. As Marx explains,

> work is not done twice over, once to produce a suitable product, a use-value . . . and a second time to generate value and surplus value. Work is contributed only in the definite, concrete, specific form, manner, mode of existence in which it is the purposive activity that can convert the means of production into a specific product, spindle and cotton, for instance, into yarn. All that is contributed is the labor of spinning etc.[17]

---

14   Marx does, on a few occasions, describe value-creating labor as homogeneous. When he does, he is clearly referring to it as a quality of laboring activity, not of the laborer him- or herself. See *Capital*, vol. I (London: Vintage, 1976), 128, 134, 136.

15   Ibid., 128.

16   Ibid., 129.

17   Ibid., 991. Also, "Use-values cannot confront each other as commodities unless the labour contained in them *is qualitatively different in each case*" (ibid., 133; emphasis added). See also ibid., 137.

The reason labor does not escape its embeddedness in particular activities is that it *cannot*. Laboring activities must remain differentiated because they are tied to the differentiation of the use-values that they create. And use-values are desirable precisely because they satisfy very different needs and must therefore be endlessly ramified. As long as use-values remain distinctive, so must the labor that produces them. The separateness of every concrete labor is thus built into the very process of creating use-values. It does not have to cease being concrete labor, in order that it might take the form of abstract labor.[18] What this means is that postcolonial theorists are mistaken in thinking that Marx expects a "homogenization" of labor, if they take it to mean that labor ceases to be instantiated as particular, concrete activities carried out by differently skilled and differently endowed workers.

ABSTRACT LABOR AND DESKILLED LABOR

Some theorists within the Marxist tradition have tried to accommodate this observation by insisting that, although labor was distinctive in capitalism's earlier stages, it becomes increasingly homogenized over time. The mechanism for this homogenization is the progressive deskilling of labor that accompanies mechanization, as through the introduction of Taylorism and the production line. The most influential of these arguments was formulated by Harry Braverman in his classic study of the labor process under capitalism. Braverman showed in great detail that in order to take control of the labor process, managers in early twentieth-century capitalism sought to break down the skill levels of their labor force and to progressively deskill workers over time. In so doing, they reduced worker autonomy on the shop floor, thereby also reducing workers' control over the pace and direction of work. An added benefit for the capitalists was that as workers became less skilled, they also became more easily replaceable. Nowhere was this more evident than in the advent of Taylorism as a form of work organization. Workers employed in plants using Taylorist methods found that they were reduced to little more than appendages of the gigantic automated machines they operated, and that the dull, repetitive nature of the work also made it simple to replace them if they resisted managerial directives. Braverman took this to be an enactment of labor's increasingly abstract character in capitalism. As he concluded, the "mechanical exercise of human faculties according to motion types which are studied independently of the kind of work being done, brings to life the Marxist conception of 'abstract labor.' "[19]

---

18   As Marx notes, even though the capitalist cares only about labor's expansion of exchange-value, "[i]t [labor] naturally provides this quantity *in the particular form* appropriate to it as a specific kind of useful labour, as the labour of spinning, of weaving, etc." Marx, *Collected Works*, vol. 34, 135. Emphasis in original.

19   Harry Braverman, *Labor and Monopoly Capital: The Degradation of Work in the Twentieth Century* (New York: Monthly Review Press, 1974), 125. A more explicit connection of

While Braverman's argument is attractive, it is hampered by two weaknesses. The first is that even while the skill level of work in any given occupation might be lowered, this does not make that work indistinguishable from other kinds of work. A deskilled auto worker, for example, cannot be taken to be engaged in the identical laboring activity as a deskilled software engineer. No doubt, the distance between them might have shrunk compared to the situation a century ago, but the labors themselves remain distinct. Each occupation still requires job-specific training, even if workers can acquire those skills in less time than in the 1920s. The second weakness is that within capitalism, there is no fixed set of occupations that are progressively deskilled over time. The dynamism of the system keeps producing new products, which call for new skills and new forms of laboring activity. So capitalism continues to generate new, high-skill concrete labors even as it deskills older vintages. It is difficult to maintain, as a Bravermanesque argument must do, that the labor force is becoming more homogeneous over time. There is a dual process underway: the uneven deskilling of existing occupations, alongside the appearance of new and highly skilled ones—which might, of course, be subject to deskilling over time, as even newer skilled occupations emerge.

6.3 FROM SOCIALLY NECESSARY LABOR TO ABSTRACT LABOR

Labor in capitalism thus never ceases to be concrete labor, because it cannot avoid being directly connected to particular use-values. This conclusion steers the discussion back to the original question: What is abstract labor and how do we explain its emergence in capitalism? We have seen that labor does not become more "homogeneous" over time; we have also seen that deskilling should not be conflated with abstract labor. Wherein, then, lies the source of abstract labor?

Recall that Marx defines abstract labor as having two characteristics—that it is a dimension of actual, concrete labor, and that it constitutes the "substance" of exchange-value. All labor, everywhere, is concrete labor. But abstract labor emerges only in conditions where the goal of production is the maximization of surplus value—in capitalist conditions. Hence, the key to understanding abstract labor is to examine those features of capitalism that conduce to the creation of value, and in particular, surplus value. Something happens to the place of labor in the economy when production is carried out under capitalist conditions, so that, for the first time in history, it is no longer just concrete labor, but also abstract.

We have seen that the defining characteristic of capitalist production, and what sets it apart from other economic systems, is that it forces producers to

abstract labor with deskilling appears in David Gleicher, "A Historical Approach to the Question of Abstract Labor" *Capital and Class* 7:3 (Winter 1983), 97–122.

submit to the competitive pressures of the market.[20] In order to survive this pressure, firms have to orient their economic activities to the maximization of profit. Survival in the market requires that firms capture a large enough share of total demand to allow them to recoup their outlays and also to make a surplus over and above the initial expenses. It is this surplus that allows them to fund the acquisition of new technologies, new machines, workplace reorganization, or other measures that increase productivity and drive down unit costs. This drive to continually intensify surplus extraction and continually lower production costs is what is "universalized" in capitalism.

In order to produce their goods, firms must hire labor—and this labor must have particular skills, with particular aptitudes or abilities, suited to the manufacture of the specific goods that the firm produces. A textile producer mobilizes the concrete labor needed for the production of his particular textile, and a watchmaker engages labor with the skills needed to produce his specific watches. To produce any use-value at all requires that the labor process be designed to the requirements of the particular use-value in question. Now, this aspect of production is not specific to capitalism. In any economic system, whenever a good is produced, the labor that is utilized, and the labor process that actually manufactures the good, is constrained by the good's specific attributes. For capitalist producers, these constraints are just as operative as they are for producers in earlier epochs. What is specific to capitalism is that, while the goods produced must be use-values, simply making them available for consumption is not the fundamental goal of those who produced them. For the capitalists who manufacture the goods, it is the goods' potential as sources of *profit* that is relevant. Hence, while production must cater to the commodity's particular properties, it must also be organized to maximize its profitability. The real attraction to the capitalist is thus its exchange-value.

Precisely because the real goal of production is exchange-value, not use-value, capitalism forces an epochal shift in the utilization of labor. If the goal of production were simply the creation of a use-value and nothing more, with no other binding constraints, then the labor that the employer mobilizes would be judged on this one quality—that it be good enough to produce the item in its desired form and make it available for consumption. But under capitalism, employers feel a pressure to judge labor on other grounds as well. Labor cannot, in capitalist conditions, merely be good enough to produce the use-value. It has to produce the use-value in such a fashion that the employer can sell it on the market at a price that garners a surplus, at an acceptable rate of return.

In order to sell the commodity at a price that will yield a steady and acceptable rate of return, the labor must be at least as good—as productive and dexterous—as the labor employed by his competitors. The employer is thus

---

20   See above, Chap. 5, 110–11.

compelled to judge his labor force not just on its ability to produce the good in accordance with the specifications he has set out, but to produce it at competitive levels of productivity. This is a direct response to the fact that the market judges commodities on this very dimension—their costs relative to other, similar commodities. If the employer pays no attention to the relative efficiency of his labor, then even though he has successfully produced a use-value at the end of the labor process, consumers will gravitate to the goods made by his competitors, which are sold at lower prices because they were made with more productive labor and at lower unit costs. This brings about the tectonic shift, mentioned above, in how labor is viewed. Marx explains it thus:

> [R]eal work [concrete labor] creates value only if it is performed at a *normally defined rate of intensity* (or in other words it only *pays* as long as it achieves this) and if this *real work* of given intensity and of given quantity as measured in terms of time actually materializes as a product . . . Therefore, the labor process becomes a valorization process by virtue of the fact that the concrete labor invested in it is a quantity of *socially necessary labor* (thanks to its intensity), = a certain quantity of *average social labor*.[21]

So, once goods change from being use-values pure and simple, to carriers of exchange-value, the producers of those goods are forced to change the way they utilize labor. Their labor inputs are now rewarded not simply on the quality of the use-value they produce, but on whether or not they produce it as well and as efficiently as other producers. This means that the labor itself has to be offered at benchmark levels of efficiency. And the main measure of this efficiency is labor *time*. Marx refers to labor time of this benchmark intensity as *socially necessary* labor.[22]

What capitalists seek, then, is concrete labor that works at socially necessary levels of efficiency. But calling this kind of labor "concrete" is, for Marx, misleading. It remains labor of distinct kinds, to be sure, because it is tied to distinct use-values. Nevertheless, the market does not reward the labor on the basis of particular characteristics. It is rewarded on its *relational* properties— how well it performs *relative* to those of its competitors, and in particular, how productive it is compared to other labors. These are dimensions of the labor that are comparable to others, that it has in common with others, and that can be measured by a common metric. Labor, in other words, is rewarded in the market on its *general* features, not its particular ones. It is rewarded as *abstract*

---

21   Marx, *Capital*, vol. 1, 991–2. Emphasis in original. This passage is best read in the context of Marx's broader discussion of socially necessary labor (ibid., 986–94).

22   "Socially necessary labor time is the labor-time required to produce any use-value under conditions of production normal for a given society and with the average degree of skill and intensity of labor prevalent in that society" (ibid.,129).

labor—labor as such, general labor, average labor—even though it must be mobilized in its concrete forms.

Hence, abstract labor is not a distinct kind of labor. It is not another species of labor called "homogeneous labor," as postcolonial theorists imply. It is simply a *dimension* of *concrete* labors; it refers to properties that the latter have in common, properties which can be compared with one another and which are rewarded by the market. The most important such property is labor's productive efficiency, which can be measured in its throughput. Marx's argument is that the emergence of abstract labor is specific to capitalism because capitalism creates a social mechanism that takes the dispersed, disparate laboring activities of producers, and forces them onto a common metric. That mechanism is market competition, and that metric is labor time. Competition pushes producers to expend no more time on making a product than is socially necessary. Since producers are rewarded solely on this dimension, employers also shift their focus from the myriad qualities of their laborers' work, to a single quality which they consider in abstraction—the laborers' productive efficiency. This is the dimension that enables them to stay in business. Capitalism forces employers to treat labor abstractly, because the market demands it.

6.4 ABSTRACT LABOR AND SOCIAL HIERARCHIES

Now that we have derived the concept of abstract labor from the dynamic properties of capitalism, what remains to be seen is how it relates to social hierarchies such as race, caste, ethnicity, or gender. The drive to treat labor abstractly is consistent with the persistence of social hierarchies in two distinct ways.

First, employers might use racial groupings as a *sorting mechanism* within the labor process, if distinct skills map onto different racial or caste communities. As observed above, capitalists often find labor clustered into distinct occupational specializations, associated with particular communities.[23] The employer hires them as laborers of a particular kind, with particular skills that are handed to him for free, absolving him of some of the costs normally involved with training his labor force. This represents the community's socialization of part of his labor costs—what Marx refers to as "variable capital." The capitalist therefore assimilates this social division into the technical division of labor of his plant—he sorts the workers into the labor process by their community identity, because this sorting brings along their skill sets. Hence, communal identities are protected and reproduced because they seem, to the capitalist, to assist in the incessant drive toward cost reduction. In the language of value theory, the

---

23   See above, Chap. 5, 118-9. For the Indian setting, see Rajnarayan Chandavarkar, *The Origins of Industrial Capitalism in India: Business Strategies and the Working Classes in Bombay, 1900-1940* (Cambridge: Cambridge University Press, 1994), 316-26; Chitra Joshi, *Lost Worlds: Indian Labour and Its Forgotten Histories* (Delhi: Permanent Black, 2003), 82-4.

drive to extract those abstract qualities of labor that are needed to make profits leads the capitalist to validate and reproduce traditional identities—and thereby promote social differences within the labor force.

Now, it should be noted that there is plenty of room for error by employers. Conditions might allow capitalists to sort labor along communal lines, even if their judgments are mistaken about the efficiency gains from such a device. One such condition is when the firm in question happens to be in a healthy competitive position, with ample profit margins. Fat margins give employers a cushion capable of absorbing the cost of all manner of racial or communal fantasies—about which communities are harder workers, or more dexterous, or more intelligent, and so on.[24] More subtly, however, employers can indulge their racial fantasies by creating "racial attributes" out of whole cloth, thus seemingly affirming their prior prejudices. Imagine members of three ethnic communities vying for employment in a particular plant, each equally willing to work and each equally capable. The local employer harbors the conviction that Community A is more pliant, has better work habits, and is better equipped genetically. He then acts on his conviction, placing workers from Community A in all the most important or most demanding positions within his plant. Of course, being willing to work and having every reason to impress their employer, these workers provide labor at the levels of efficiency he demands. To the employer, this outcome confirms all his racial preconceptions about workers' abilities and fuels the legend that workers belonging to Community A are best suited to this kind of work—even though members of the other two communities would have worked just as well and just as hard. The employer succeeded in two things here: he has indulged a racial stereotype, and he has deployed it in a way that will confirm his racial prejudices. He has created "difference"—but as part of the drive to extract maximum labor, at levels of efficiency demanded by market competition. In treating labor as an abstract input, then, capitalists can use race as a sorting mechanism in their pursuit of increased productivity, and they can do so while virtually creating racial differences and reinforcing their racial fantasies.

A second connection between social hierarchies and abstract labor is that racial or communal differences can be mobilized to elicit work effort from employees beyond the level they would ordinarily offer. Recall that in order to stay competitive, capitalists must seek out labor that is not just willing to work, but also willing to do so at a baseline or "normal" level of intensity. This is what is meant by capitalists treating labor as abstract labor—its quality is judged in comparison to that of other labors in the market. However, what counts as

---

24 Good examples of this are provided in Elizabeth Esch and David R. Roediger, "One Symptom of Originality: Race and the Management of Labour in the History of the United States," *Historical Materialism* 17:1 (2009).

"normal" work effort at one point will often be deemed insufficient at a time in the near future; moreover, the skills that are deemed appropriate at time X will often be obsolete by time Y. Thus, while employers must seek out labor with particular skills at any given point, they cannot be *bound* by these skills or these capacities. They have to be able to extricate themselves from the concrete laboring activities of their workers, so that the labor process can be remolded to the demands of new production techniques as these techniques become available.[25] The employers will then mobilize a new set of concrete labors, which will operate at newly defined levels of intensity and will come with their own particular benefits and constraints. These particular capacities will remain in place until the social standard shifts yet again, compelling the employer to redesign his work organization once more. Capitalists have to find ways of imposing these new standards, and new demands, on their labor force.

Communal differences have been a powerful mechanism for allowing an upward revision of what counts as normal. Even while Community A is favored in the employment relation at a certain time, its members might settle on a certain pace of work that they regard as normal or acceptable. As competition ratchets up the demands on the working day, employers who meet resistance from workers belonging to Community A can instead threaten to use, or rely on using, workers from Community B in order to compel greater effort from the former. In this dynamic, workers need not be goaded into undermining the livelihood of other communities; what happens instead is that the insecurity of the labor market impels them to offer their services at a lower price and to develop whatever skills or capacities will make them more attractive than their rivals. As a result, they offer themselves as an exploitable labor force, using their communal identities as markers, or guarantees, of their reliability. Communal identities are thus reinforced as employers pit workers against one another in a bidding war—in the drive to make labor produce at rates demanded by market competition.

Finally, it is a small step from the use of social divisions as a means of increasing intra-labor competition, to using such divisions as a means of weakening labor's capacity to resist managerial authority. We thus, in an important sense, return to the discussion in the preceding chapter, where, in the process of discovering what it is that capitalism universalizes, I argued that capitalist competition makes it rational for employers to mobilize social divisions in order to extract maximal labor effort from their labor force.[26] Our discussion of abstract labor here has arrived at the very same endpoint. The force of market competition compels employers to treat their workers as carriers of abstract laboring activity and to structure the labor process so as to maximize their extraction of this

---

25   This is another way of saying that abstract labor is not a distinctive kind of labor, since its content—its particular mix of skill, speed, stamina, etc.—cannot be specified. It is a set of formal properties, the content of which keeps changing as conditions of work change.

26   See above, Chap. 5, 118–20.

laboring activity from their employees. The drive to maximize the extraction of work effort is nothing other than the drive to maximize the extraction of abstract labor. Hence, we inescapably derive the same conclusions as were derived above: racial hierarchies—and by extension, social hierarchies of the kind that worry Ranajit Guha and Dipesh Chakrabarty—are consistent both with the dynamics of capital accumulation and with the concept of abstract labor.

6.5 CAPITALISM AND SOCIAL HIERARCHIES

The upshot of the preceding section is that social hierarchies cannot be inconsistent with abstract labor, because labor is often rendered abstract through the mobilization of these very hierarchies. In other words, capital is able to induce, or compel, labor to perform at socially necessary levels of efficiency by utilizing, and hence reinforcing, various social divisions. Having examined the actual meaning of abstract labor, we might find it useful to return to the postcolonial critiques. Theorists such as Lisa Lowe and David R. Roediger are well aware that employers can benefit from, and even create, racial or caste divisions in the manner already discussed. They assert, however, that these practices run counter to the logic of abstract labor, as defined by Marx. One of Roediger's formulations offers a hint as to why they think there is a tension between the two. In an illuminating article coauthored with Elizabeth Esch, which traces in some detail the employers' use of racial divisions in a manner quite consistent with the argument I have developed above, Roediger concludes that

> *far from reducing labor to abstract and faceless inputs* into the labour-process, capital and management helped to reproduce racial differences over long stretches of U.S. history, and to divide workers in ways that compromised labour's efforts to address race—or class—inequalities.[27]

For Esch and Roediger, employers' mobilization of racial identities or racial stereotypes is evidence *against* the relevance of abstract labor. This is because abstract labor supposedly reduces labor to "abstract and faceless inputs." And what does "abstract and faceless" mean here? It suggests a state of affairs in which one worker is no different from, or is interchangeable with, any other worker. This is consistent with Roediger's formulations elsewhere, which I quoted earlier, to the effect that capitalism, following Marx's logic, ought to be color-blind. It should treat workers simply as "units of labor, rather than races, nationalities, or genders."[28] This is the argument from homogeneity—the reasoning that, for labor to be

---

27   Esch and Roediger, "One Symptom of Originality," 35.
28   Roediger, *How Race Survived U.S. History*, 66.

abstract, it has to be homogeneous and interchangeable. Employers should therefore be indifferent to the identity of their laborers, since, in an abstract and faceless labor force, any given unit of the input ought to be replaceable by any other. The recruitment of labor should be more or less random with respect to their racial or ethnic identities. This is the promise of abstract labor—that in its indifference to identity, in its consideration of labor abstractly, it makes labor "raceless, and subject to a level playing field."[29]

It is true that, for Marx, all the capitalist cares about is labor's capacity to produce value. So why does this obsession not lead to an imperviousness to race? It does not because workers' laboring capacities cannot be separated from their *persons*.[30] And the distinct qualities attached to their personal identities—such as their race, or caste, or gender—often have a direct bearing on the quality of their laboring capacity. This is what the discussion of this section has sought to establish. Capitalists have no direct interest other than maximizing their rates of return, for which they seek to extract a maximal labor effort from their workers; this is the outcome they seek. What they find is that among the mechanisms that produce this outcome is the mobilization of workers' communal or racial identities. In looking for the abstract entity that they need—workers who are willing to labor at the socially necessary level of efficiency—they find that this *abstract* labor input comes clothed in *concrete* identities. The search for this abstract entity thus leads directly to a valorization of the historically specific identities that enable its acquisition. It does so because "abstract labor" does not exist as a separate substance. It is a dimension of concrete labor, which is performed by concrete labor*ers*, who belong to particular racial or ethnic or caste communities and who carry particular capacities. The extraction of the abstract capacity to labor comes from a negotiation with these concrete identities.

The discussions in the previous and present chapters lead us inexorably to the following conclusion: *capital can reproduce social hierarchies just as readily as it can dissolve them.* Certain properties of the system can and will, under certain conditions, level out the social landscape; but the system is equally capable of reproducing, and even solidifying, existing forms of social domination or differentiation. Marx's theory of exploitation does not point firmly in one direction or the other. Depending on the background conditions, the drive to produce surplus value can generate either result. The resort to interpersonal coercion by employers, or the persistence of social divisions among subaltern classes—both of which, as has been underscored here, are taken by Guha and Chakrabarty as evidence for a failed capitalism—might very well be a *consequence* of capital's universalization, not an index of its failure. Whether or not

---

29   Ibid., 68.

30   The classic statement of this argument, though developed for a different theoretical purpose, is Claus Offe and Helmut Wiesenthal, "Two Logics of Collective Action: Theoretical Notes on Social Class and Organizational Form," *Political Power and Social Theory* 1 (1980), 67–115.

this is so is, of course, an empirical matter. It is entirely possible that various coercive relations, where found, might constitute evidence for precapitalist production relations. But whether it is the former or the latter that is producing the interpersonal coercion must be ascertained through detailed empirical examination. What we can safely conclude is that the *mere existence* of social domination cannot be taken as evidence that some fundamental break in capital's mission occurred when it entered the non-Western world.

This, in turn, undermines at least a part of Chakrabarty's case for the abandonment of Enlightenment theories—as described in Chapter 5—in so far as they rely on universalizing categories of political economy. Some categories might of course be misleading, or deserving of criticism. But no one has ever doubted that. What is at issue is whether there is something about the deep structure of Enlightenment theories that prevents them from coming to terms with social heterogeneity, especially in the Global South. It is this latter claim that we can reject. Based on the arguments I have developed thus far, rooted in an Enlightenment tradition, there is no warrant for concluding that in order to theorize the constellation of power in postcolonial nations, we need to construct entirely new theoretical frameworks. As we have seen, the most abstract category of all, abstract labor, is perfectly capable of explaining the enduring social heterogeneity of the working class—its postcolonial detractors notwithstanding. To be sure, we are not yet finished—there are more arguments to consider. But we have made some headway against two of the main ones: that capital's universalization stalled in the East, as evidenced by the persistence of social hierarchies; and that the dynamics of these hierarchies lie outside the purview of Enlightenment, especially Marxian, thought.

6.6 THE REAL ENGINE OF DEMOCRATIZATION

Capitalism, as we have now demonstrated, does not have to dissolve social differences—even though it can and often does just that. The fact that postcolonial social formations are riven by such differences cannot, therefore, justify the conclusion that these formations lie outside the ambit of capital's functioning or that their capitalism is any less robust than the West's. The power relations that Chakrabarty sees as signs of capitalism's failure might well be its direct consequence. What is more, for centuries after its advent, capitalism in the West valorized the same kinds of interpersonal coercion that Chakrabarty and Guha take as indexes of its nonuniversalization in the East. But while these findings compel us to recognize that India's postcolonial modernity might be[31] no less

---

31 I say "might be" because whether or not Indian capitalism is fully established, with a dynamic accumulation strategy, is an empirical question. My point is not to insist that India was fully capitalist by 1947, or even now. It is to say that the mere presence of social domination is not evidence for a nonuniversalizing capitalism. All sorts of coercive social relations are perfectly

capitalist than Western modernity, they nonetheless force us to confront a final issue: even though such practices were reproduced in the West long after capitalism became the dominant economic system, the fact is that the European order *did* undergo a deep transformation—from oligarchy to democracy, from hierarchical to socially egalitarian. The Western polities *have* generated an integrated political culture, with more democratic norms of social infraction and a diminution of interpersonal coercion, even if Guha and other Subalternists may romanticize the end result. The basic intuition driving the Subalternist project and postcolonial studies—that there is a significant difference between the political culture of the East and the West—cannot be dismissed as mere fiction. The difference is real, even if *Subaltern Studies* has misdiagnosed its cause.

What, then, are the real roots of the political transformation of Europe, and can this slice of history be consistent with capital's universalization? There is good reason to suggest the presence of a link between capital*ism* and democratization.[32] What I have questioned is whether the connection is made through the agency of capital*ists*. For much of the nineteenth and twentieth centuries, the elision between capitalism and capitalists was common among historically oriented scholars, including, as we have seen, Marx. By the late 1960s, this current had probably reached its peak. Among Marxist scholars, the influence of orthodox, Stalinized Marxism had hardened this view into a semiofficial line, so that even among the more academically oriented Marxists such as Christopher Hill and Albert Soboul, the bourgeoisie was seen as the crucial actor in the rise of modern political culture.[33] Outside the domain of Marxist scholarship, modernization theory advanced a similar view, in which the urban middle-class and entrepreneurs were seen as the critical agents behind political modernization;[34] even among more critically oriented scholars, Barrington Moore's highly

---

compatible with a robust capitalism. Of course, they are also compatible with traditional economic systems, such as feudalism. So what kind of economic formation they signify, if they are found in India, will have to be established by examining their economic logic. And that, indeed, is an empirical issue.

32   See the brilliant discussion in Ellen Meiksins Wood, *Democracy against Capitalism: Renewing Historical Materialism* (Cambridge: Cambridge University Press, 1995), chaps. 6, 7.

33   Neither Hill nor Soboul accepted a version as one-dimensional as the one Guha promotes. But their views did hew rather closely to the orthodox line. For Hill, see his essay "The English Revolution" in *The English Revolution 1640: Three Essays* (London: Lawrence and Wishart, 1940), 9–82. By the 1970s, Hill was beginning to modify his argument, trying to defend a broadly social interpretation of the English Revolution while downplaying the revolutionary aspirations of the capitalist class. See his reconsiderations in "Parliament and People in Seventeenth-Century England," *Past & Present* 92 (Aug. 1981), 100–24. Soboul's analysis evinced a hard-nosed realism about French elites' contempt for plebian rights; but he was never able to break from the basic orthodox view. See his classic, *A Short History of the French Revolution, 1789–1799*, trans. Geoffrey Symcox (London: Verso, 1974).

34   A classic exposition of modernization theory, which attributed democratization to elite and middle-class sectors, is Seymour Martin Lipset, *Political Man: The Social Bases of Politics* (New York: Doubleday, 1960).

influential analysis of the social origins of democracy came to similar conclusions. As Moore famously put it, "No bourgeoisie, no democracy."[35]

But doubts regarding the role of the bourgeoisie were in evidence even before the *Subaltern Studies* series was launched. In a path-breaking essay published five years before the inaugural volume, Göran Therborn argued that it was the organized working class, not the bourgeoisie, that had played the pivotal role in European democratization.[36] Indeed, to the extent that capitalists were relevant at all, it was typically as opponents of democratic rights, fighting against the popular reform movements.[37] On the other hand, Therborn also pointed out that labor organizations were rarely able to push through democratic reform on their own; workers typically had to recruit allies to their movements, often from the producing classes in the countryside, but also from the urban middle classes and occasionally even from dominant groups. What it took to achieve reform, in other words, was a coalition of classes, lined up against elite oligarchies. In fact, labor was often defeated in democratic struggles when it was the sole protagonist or even the numerically preponderant component of the democratic movement. But while the actual movement for democracy was rarely a labor movement outright, it was still the case that the working class "was the only consistent democratic force in the arena."[38] Labor and labor parties spearheaded the drive for democracy, forming its center of gravity and giving the movement its crucial leverage, because of labor's strategic location within the growing capitalist economy. Subsequent research has rendered considerable support to Therborn's thesis, confirming the critical role of the working class as well as the observation that success typically depended on the construction of a broader, but labor-led, coalition.[39]

Popular pressure thus played a crucial role in the rise of democratic institutions, even if the triggers for actual reform may have been different, and the routes to democratization diverse. The same principle was at work in the

---

35   Barrington Moore, Jr., *Social Origins of Dictatorship and Democracy: Lord and Peasant in the Making of the Modern World* (Boston: Beacon Press, 1966).

36   Göran Therborn, "The Rule of Capital and the Rise of Democracy," *New Left Review* I:103 (May–June 1977), 3–41

37   Ibid., 17, 24.

38   Ibid., 24.

39   The most important and ambitious recent work on democratization has been Dietrich Rueschemeyer, Evelyne Huber Stephens, and John D. Stephens, *Capitalist Development and Democracy* (Chicago: University of Chicago Press, 1992). See also John Markoff, "Where and When Was Democracy Invented?" *Comparative Studies in Society and History* 41:4 (Oct. 1999), 660–90; and Ruth Berins Collier, *Paths toward Democracy: The Working Class and Elites in Western Europe and South America* (Cambridge: Cambridge University Press, 1999). Both Markoff and Collier uphold the view that labor was critical to democratization, though they offer some modifications with regard to the degree and modalities of its centrality. A brilliant and wide-ranging analysis of democratization that puts popular struggles and elite resistance at the heart of the process is Adam Przeworski, "Conquered or Granted? A History of Suffrage Extensions," *British Journal of Political Science* 39:2 (2009), 291–321.

deepening of civil rights and the dismantling of various forms of social coercion discussed earlier—indentured servitude, contract labor, company towns. Most such phenomena owed their existence, in large measure, to the penury of the typical industrial worker and his resulting dependence on the patronage of his employer. But with the establishment of trade union rights, the unions' demands for better wages and working conditions, the greater financial stability that they afforded working families, vulnerability to predation by employers radically decreased. In the United States, company towns and long-term indebtedness to employers fell drastically soon after the passage of the Wagner Act of 1935, which legalized trade unions.[40]

It was not the bourgeoisie that brought about what Guha, Chakrabarty, and other postcolonial theorists call "bourgeois relations of power"—the reliance on impersonal forms of domination, the recognition of formal equality, the extinction of status hierarchies, and so on. These forms of power are not built into the logic of capital, even though they can be forced on capitalists, and the latter can be made to live with them. They are *compatible* with capitalism, but no less than are the kinds of authority relations that Chakrabarty takes as *anomalous* for capital. Both categories are forms of capitalist power, and both are explicable through the abstract logic of capital accumulation.

Emergence of the more benign relations, which relied less on personal coercion, required decades of struggle by the laboring classes. The irony is that, precisely because popular classes were able to push their way into the political arena as active participants, bending public institutions to their will, forcing elites to respect their civil rights, the *effect* of their success was to integrate those classes more fully into a *bourgeois* order. Politics ceased to be a monopoly of the dominant classes. Throughout the course of the twentieth century, politics became a mass phenomenon, and the political culture increasingly came to reflect the newfound power of groups hitherto excluded from it. In other words, it was as a consequence of mass movements that elite political culture and elite institutions were forcibly integrated with those of the laboring classes, forging one integrated sphere. The key to the dissolution of the subaltern domain, then, was not a bourgeoisie following through on the promises it had made to workers and peasants as it recruited them into its coalition; it was the mobilization of the lower orders, forcing the dominant class to relinquish its monopoly over social and political power.

It would seem, then, that the key to the emergence of an integrated political order—the question that animated Guha's entire research project—is not the bourgeoisie, but rather the subaltern classes. Left to the whims of the capitalist class, the universalization of capital is more likely to lead to coercive and

---

40 Margaret Crawford, *Building the Workingman's Paradise: The Design of American Company Towns* (London: Verso, 1996), 201–3.

exclusionary regimes than to rule by consent. Hence, if in India the political sphere has not undergone the sort of integration that the West experienced in its modernization, then the explanation would seem to lie primarily in the structural, or organizational, or even cultural facts about the working class and the peasantry. Why have they been unable to amass the needed organizational capacity? Were popular alliances in the colonial struggle compromised in some way? Has the postcolonial order somehow diluted class identities? These are the questions that might shed light on the persistence of popular subordination. But such questions rarely appear in Guha's work. They *do not* because they *cannot*. Guha cannot pose the questions because he mistakenly identifies the bourgeoisie as the pivotal actor in the emergence of "bourgeois" political culture. So, in the central essays that comprise *Dominance without Hegemony*, the analytical focus is trained single-mindedly on the shortcomings of, and mistakes by, the bourgeoisie and its political representatives. The factors that inhibited the accretion of subaltern power never move beyond the margins. When workers and peasants do appear, it is simply to establish the claim that they remained outside the reach of bourgeois hegemony.

Whatever the failings of the Indian National Congress, they only raise the more important question of why the popular classes were unable to push through a more radical agenda, based on a different political configuration, before or after Independence. In his opening essay in *Subaltern Studies 1*, Guha did pose the possibility of an alternative political alliance as an historical question, but this was quickly abandoned in favor of an exclusive focus on the bourgeoisie.[41] In the larger body of work by the collective's members, there was, much as with Guha, an initial impulse in the direction of such questions. In some of the earlier work—by Gyanendra Pandey and David Hardiman, for example—the focus on popular mobilization opened up the possibility of analyzing the relative strengths and weaknesses of Indian popular movements in relation to those of other colonies and the earlier movements of the West. But by the 1990s, such questions had rapidly receded to the background.[42] Interest in the subaltern classes during colonialism did not move much beyond the

---

41   See Ranajit Guha, "On Some Aspects of the Historiography of Colonial India," in Guha, ed., *Subaltern Studies I: Writings on South Asian History and Society* (Delhi: Oxford University Press, 1982), 6–7.

42   Of course, historians working outside the universe of *Subaltern Studies* have posed these questions and generated a fine body of work. A brilliant example of asking just the sort of questions I have urged here is John Roosa's study of the peasant movement in Telengana during the 1940s. See his "Passive Revolution Meets Peasant Revolution: Indian Nationalism and the Telangana Revolt," *Journal of Peasant Studies* 28:4 (2001), 57–94. One hopes that Roosa will publish the full study sometime in the future. Work of this kind, to the extent that it has been pursued, has largely occurred outside the Subaltern Studies collective. The leading members of the collective turned away from pursuing it by the 1990s. A summation of this early trend was Sumit Sarkar's excellent *Modern India: 1885–1947* (Delhi: Macmillan, 1983). But what ought to have been a catalyst for new research by the collective's leading members turned out to be its swan song.

exploration of their consciousness, its independence from Congress hegemony, its internal structure, and so forth.[43]

As for Guha's later work, the question never again commanded analytical focus. This was not just a reflection of the Subalternist collective's being swept up by cultural theory, though that was no doubt relevant.[44] The turning away from an analysis of subaltern groups was at least partly the consequence of their theoretical framework, which pointed firmly in the direction of the bourgeoisie and its allies as the key to understanding Indian political modernization. In making this mistake—attributing the emergence of bourgeois-democratic political formations to the practice of the capitalist class, and insisting that only one form of power can be regarded as capitalist—Guha not only made a colossal scholarly and analytical blunder; he also foreclosed the possibility of a genuine comparative study of the postcolonial world's path to modernity, based on real comparisons instead of the imaginary ones that populate the pages of Subalternist scholarship.

6.7 CONCLUSION

The central determination of this chapter is that postcolonial theorists are wrong to maintain that abstract theories cannot apprehend the production of, and persistence of, social differences. Their position seems to rest on a conceptual slip: that universalizing categories presume a homogeneous social landscape. *Universal* is thus equated with *homogeneous*. It is remarkable how often these terms can be found together in the literature. But the coupling of the two is a mistake. As I have shown here, the abstract logic of capitalism, elements of which Marx tried to capture through the concept of abstract labor, can sustain and even create tremendous diversity in social identities. Here we have examined only the problem of social hierarchies in the labor market; a similar case could be made for the connection between capitalism's abstract logic and diversity in other domains as well.

This argument has far-reaching implications for postcolonial theory. It means that as capitalism spreads across the globe, it does not inevitably turn every culture into a replica of what has been observed in the West. The universalization of capital is perfectly compatible with the persistence of social, cultural, and political differentiation between East and West. Capital does not have to obliterate social difference in order to universalize itself. It merely has to

---

43   Partha Chatterjee's later essays highlight this as the central finding of Subalternist historiography. See "The Nation and Its Peasants," in Chatterjee, *The Nation and Its Fragments: Colonial and Postcolonial Histories* (Princeton: Princeton University Press, 1993).

44   See Ramachandra Guha, "Subaltern and Bhadralok Studies," *Economic and Political Weekly* 30 (Aug. 19, 1995), 2056–58; Sumit Sarkar "The Decline of the Subaltern in Subaltern Studies," in Sarkar, *Writing Social History* (Delhi: Oxford University Press, 1997), 82–108.

subordinate those dimensions of social reproduction that are essential to its own functioning. These dimensions are the ones directly involved in the production and distribution of use-values.

Doubtless this will necessitate attendant transformations in certain aspects of social and political institutions in order to stabilize the changes in production activities. But the scope of these second-order changes—which aspects of the received institutions are transformed and which are not—cannot be prejudged. To make inferences about the degree of capital's universalization from the mere fact of social diversity is therefore a risky venture. It presumes we have a fixed and confirmed menu of identities that can be labeled "bourgeois" and those that cannot. What makes this risky is that we are still in the process of learning how traditional institutions and identities can find new life within capitalism. Further along, in chapter 9, we will see that this argument has some very damaging consequences for Dipesh Chakrabarty's analysis of social difference, as well as for his call to "provincialize" Europe.

Capitalism can sustain a broad gamut of power relations and social identities. Why, then, did the *actual* evolution of political power in Europe turn toward democratization? For members of the *Subaltern Studies* collective, it was because of the bourgeoisie. We have established that this view is unsustainable. In its place, I have proposed that the democratization of Western culture can be attributed largely to the political campaigns of subaltern groups, especially those of labor. It is an irony of modern history that the institutions most responsible for deepening the ideological hegemony of the bourgeoisie were implanted by the lower orders. But insofar as this is true, it does carry an important implication for the study of postcolonial formations. It suggests that, as capital universalizes, the emergence of what Subalternist theorists call "bourgeois forms of power," revolving around rights, citizenship, equality, and so on, cannot be presumed to follow in train. If they do insinuate themselves into the political culture, it will most likely be because they have been pushed by subaltern groups, much as took place in Europe. For this to be the case, however, we have to assume that subaltern groups in the East share certain psychological characteristics with their counterparts in the West—certain needs and interests. We have to entertain the proposition that they partake of a common human nature. Yet members of the *Subaltern Studies* collective have gone to some lengths to deny this possibility. They press, instead, for the view that agents in the East are driven by a very different set of dispositions than in the West. How they develop this view, and whether it is defensible, is the subject of the next chapter.

CHAPTER SEVEN

Culture, Interests, and Agency

In the course of the preceding chapters, two points have been established that set up the discussion in this one. The first is that *Subaltern Studies* wrongly attributes to the bourgeoisie achievements that were in fact the product of popular struggles. The phenomena that Subalternist theorists include under the rubric of *bourgeois* forms of power, hegemony, and culture were, to the contrary, brought about by challenges from below. They were not part of the design, or the preferences, of the capitalist class as it rose to power in Western Europe. Hence, the fact that capitalists sought to establish despotic forms in the East is not a sign that capital abandoned its universalizing drive—it was actually a natural expression of its universalizing drive. In other words, capital has always striven not just for economic domination but also for political domination, inasmuch as the latter helps secure the viability of the former.

The second point is that the forms of political power generated by capitalism are many and varied; they extend from highly coercive interpersonal domination to a reliance on impersonal structural forces. Chakrabarty and others within the Subalternist collective erroneously identify "bourgeois forms of power" with just one *particular* form, and then mistakenly conclude that the persistence of *other* power constellations in capitalism demands a fundamental reworking of received theory. They make this mistake because they build one specific form of domination into the very definition of capital—a somewhat ironic turn for a theory that claims the mantle of radical critique, since it amounts to a romanticized conception of the bourgeoisie and its strategies of domination and augments the ideological effect of Ranajit Guha's historical analysis, itself a rather loving portrait of capital in its early years.

If it is the case that capital has a natural preference for narrow and exclusionary political systems, we are forced to wonder what social agent could serve as a force for more egalitarian social relations. In Europe during its modernization, that agent was the labor movement, in alliance with other non-elite groupings. It seems reasonable to infer from the Western experience that in the East, too, subaltern groups might figure prominently as agents for democratic change. Certainly, for the vast majority of progressives over the past century, it was taken for granted that the push for democratization would feature laboring groups at its center. This expectation has not been mere fantasy. For much of the twentieth century, trade union and peasant-farmer groups did in fact figure prominently in struggles for democratization. If we examine the broad sweep of modern political history in the Global South, there is ample evidence that—in

nationalist movements during the colonial era, and continuing into the postcolonial era—organizations of the popular classes have pushed in much the same
direction as did their counterparts in Europe.

This view of subaltern groups has been virtual orthodoxy within progressive circles since the French Revolution. But it has not just been drawn
inductively from the empirical record. It is based on the conviction that social
actors in the East share the same *interest* in self-determination as do their counterparts in the West. The expectation that they will fight for greater respect, for
political enfranchisement, stems from the belief that they have the same basic
interests in these ends as did the British or French revolutionary agents. Postcolonial theorists rightly characterize this as a central element of the Enlightenment
tradition. But it has also been the view of virtually every important leader in the
anticolonial tradition through the twentieth century, from Sun Yat-sen and Ho
Chi Minh to Frantz Fanon and Che Guevara.

It is remarkable, therefore, that the Subalternist collective issues a firm
injunction against such universalistic ideas. They deny that agents share a
common set of needs or interests across cultural boundaries, arguing instead
that the peasants and industrial workers in the East have a wholly different
psychology from those in the West. In the West, we are told, political psychology revolves around secular conceptions of the individual and his rights;
whereas in the East, agency is motivated by the concept of duty, or obligation,
making the actor's basic orientation religious, not secular. To expect that political modernization in the postcolonial world will follow a course similar to that
of the West is therefore mistaken. As we know by now, for the Subalternists the
source of this mistake can be traced back to capital's nonuniversalization. In
Europe, part of the cultural mélange produced by capitalism was the creation of
secular identities. But because it forswore its mission as it ventured eastward,
capitalism settled for reproducing, and even reinforcing, religious identities.
Modern capitalism therefore produced two distinct cultural forms in East and
West. The fact that laboring groups in the East are not motivated by the same
commitments as those in the West is symptomatic of the distinctive modernity
that capital wrought as it left European shores. It was a modernity that witnessed
the implantation of modern political institutions, and even the language of
modern politics, but these, say the Subalternists, were foisted atop a culture in
which the basic elements of political identity remained unchanged. Western
theories fail to comprehend its distinctiveness, because they assume that capital
did in fact carry out its universalizing mission.

The main proponents of the argument from cultural specificity are Partha
Chatterjee and Dipesh Chakrabarty, and they deploy two distinct strategies to
make their case. The first is to use Ranajit Guha's highly influential book *Elementary Aspects of Peasant Insurgency in Colonial India* as a reference point,
inasmuch as they take it to have demonstrated the distinctiveness of Indian

peasants' consciousness. This is particularly true of Chatterjee, who clearly enumerates what he regards as Guha's findings. But neither Chatterjee nor Chakrabarty rests his case on the authority of *Elementary Aspects*. They also offer arguments of their own, both empirical and theoretical, to defend the notion that the psychology behind subaltern agency was sui generis. Chatterjee bases his endorsement of Guha's argument on his own empirical work on peasant movements in late colonial Bengal, which, he argues, shows that peasant political agency was not motivated by the pursuit of individual interests. Chakrabarty draws his conclusions from his study of jute workers, also located in Bengal, during the late colonial era. Both strategies demand close examination here.

The present chapter focuses on Chatterjee, who has argued that Western theories cannot comprehend the political psychology of Indian peasants. They fail in this endeavor because they assume that the peasantry's political agency was structured by its interests, whereas peasants actually had no conception of individual interests. They were driven, instead, he maintains, by internalized norms and, in particular, by their sense of obligation to their community. Communal norms, not individual interests, were the fount of rural politics. Chatterjee draws on Ranajit Guha's work in support of this argument, but he also bases his conclusions on his own research about Bengal peasant struggles in the late colonial era.

I will show that in fact, neither Guha's book nor Chatterjee's research supports the view that Chatterjee wishes to promote. Guha's presentation actually shows Indian peasants to be acutely sensitive to, and motivated by, their individual interests. But it is not just Guha's evidence that undermines Chatterjee's conclusions. Chatterjee's own description of peasant politics goes against his general characterization of peasant psychology. In other words, I will show that Chatterjee misrepresents the evidence, both his own and Guha's. What emerges from their findings is that the Indian peasantry was motivated by much the same concerns as was its counterpart in Europe. Indeed, I will argue that on this score, Guha's analysis not only undermines Chatterjee's ambitions but that Guha seems never to have intended anything else. The actual content of *Elementary Aspects* suggests that he wished to emphasize the commonality of Indian peasants with European peasants, and the book's reputation as a founding text for indigenist or nativist histories of the East is ill-deserved.

In the next chapter, I will turn to Dipesh Chakrabarty's attempt to mobilize broadly similar arguments for the Indian working class. These two chapters, which thus encompass the two classes that populate the universe of the subaltern in *Subaltern Studies*, seek to rebut the notion that an unbridgeable divide separates laboring classes in the East and the West. My intention, as I have stressed, is to sustain the idea, central to the Enlightenment tradition, that they are bound together by common interests. In other words, there are *two* universalisms we can defend, not just one. So far, I have argued that it is perfectly legitimate to refer to capital as having universalized its influence in India, *pace* the Subalternists. By the end of chapter 8, I will have shown that the universal drive of capitalism finds its complement in the universal interests of laboring groups to resist, both in the West and in the East.

7.1 *ELEMENTARY ASPECTS* AS HISTORY FROM BELOW

Since its publication in 1983, Ranajit Guha's *Elementary Aspects of Peasant Insurgency in Colonial India* has achieved something akin to iconic status within the Subalternist oeuvre. The 1999 edition by Duke University Press is accompanied by a blurb from Jose Rabasa hailing it as a "classic . . . in postcolonial studies" and another from John Beverly praising it as "the most significant—and potentially the most influential—work of social theory since Michel Foucault's *Discipline and Punish*."[1] It is hard to find any commentary on postcolonial theory that fails to recognize the book's significance. It is of some relevance, therefore, to examine what its claims actually entail.

Like *Dominance without Hegemony*, it is linked organically to the opening essay in the inaugural volume of *Subaltern Studies*, in which Guha unveiled his basic research agenda. A central element of his argument in that essay was that the subaltern domain was not only distinct from that of the elites, but was characterized by its own forms of domination, mobilizational patterns, and cultural idioms.[2] Because subaltern politics differed from mainstream political culture, many liberal and even Marxist historians dismissed peasant movements as apolitical or immature. But the lacuna was in the assumptions of these historians, not in the culture of the subalterns. Unable to comprehend the particularities of peasant culture or the forms of power peculiar to the subaltern domain, they either dismissed rural uprisings as not yet fully political or simply imputed to peasants the strategic priorities of elite leaders. We have already examined what Guha and other Subalternists regard as the quintessential forms of power in the subaltern domain—caste and ethnic hierarchies, interpersonal domination, and the like. As for the resources that peasants deployed in their struggles, Guha cited the importance of informal, kin-based and territorial networks, as against the formal mechanisms typically utilized in elite politics. The subaltern domain of politics was identifiable and distinct, left intact because capital abandoned its universalizing mission once having arrived on Indian shores.

---

1   Ranajit Guha, *Elementary Aspects of Peasant Insurgency in Colonial India* (Durham: Duke University Press, 1999).

2   Ranajit Guha, "On Some Aspects of the Historiography of Colonial India," in Guha, ed., *Subaltern Studies I: Writings on South Asian History and Society* (Delhi: Oxford University Press, 1982). See above, 31–33.

The inaugural essay of *Subaltern Studies 1* announced in programmatic fashion the existence of an identifiable subaltern domain. The ambition of *Elementary Aspects* is to show, through an analysis of peasant insurgencies in the nineteenth century, how this sphere of politics functioned. Since *Elementary Aspects* carries out part of the research program declared in *Subaltern Studies*, the core argument of the book is entirely in keeping with the essay.

Guha's main concern is to establish two facts: that the peasantry drew on its own discursive and institutional resources when it launched its campaigns against dominant classes over the course of the century; and that, whatever the distinctiveness of these resources, however different they might have been from the formal instruments of modern politics, they were nonetheless put to the service of a *politics*. Here Guha is reacting against what he sees as some historians' overly hasty dismissal of peasant insurgencies as somehow lacking in substance, as inferior to modern politics in certain ways—in sum, as *prepolitical*. His chief target is Eric Hobsbawm, though the latter is only a stand-in for the wider community of historians who refuse to recognize peasant movements as fully political.[3] The mistake of modern historiography is that it projects the particular political idiom and practices of the elite sphere onto the political dynamics of the subaltern sphere. In so doing, it fails to appreciate the ways in which subaltern political culture departs from that of the elites. Further, it cannot apprehend that the contestation peculiar to the subaltern domain is no less an instance of political engagement than is, say, electoral competition. Thus, Guha's ambition is to show that what these peasants were engaged in was no less a form of political engagement, even if expressed in codes and drawing on resources that are not easily assimilable into the language of modern, organized politics.

This is an entirely laudable project. Taken at face value, it fits comfortably with the call, heard during the 1960s and thereafter, for a "history from below." The turn to popular history was motivated by many ambitions. One of these, surely, was to understand the participation of working people in political culture, not just as dupes of elite designs, or as unthinking mobs, or as the passive recipients of structural pressures, but as active and thinking agents. One element of this project was to insist that the periodic explosions of popular protest in modern Europe, which seemed to come out of nowhere, were the product of long-simmering tensions and drew on resources internal

---

3   Guha focuses on Hobsbawm's pioneering study of rural rebellion in modern Europe, *Primitive Rebels: Studies in Archaic Forms of Social Movement in the 19th and 20th Centuries* (New York: Norton Library, 1959). I had intended to show here that even though Guha presents his analysis as a critique of Hobsbawm, in fact *Elementary Aspects* fully supports Hobsbawm's argument. Considerations of space made it necessary to forswear the inclusion of such a critique here. I should warn readers, however, that Guha bases his criticism on a rather serious misconstrual of the argument in *Primitive Rebels*.

to subaltern groups. Another was to recover the goals and aspirations of the popular groupings, to show that they had real goals and were often pursuing identifiable interests.

This sounds a lot like the project Guha announced in *Subaltern Studies* and then exemplified in *Elementary Aspects*. But members of the Subaltern Studies collective have claimed that its implications ran far deeper, to the point of forcing a rethinking of some foundational concepts. Some of the putative implications we have already explored; in chapters 5 and 6, for instance, we addressed Dipesh Chakrabarty's insistence that Guha's analysis in *Elementary Aspects* forces a rethinking of the relation between power and capital. Now we take up another proposal, this time from Partha Chatterjee, who argues that *Elementary Aspects* departs from the popular history tradition exemplified by Hobsbawm and others in that it urges us to rethink the nature of mobilization in peasant societies. It does not, claims Chatterjee, simply urge us to recognize and respect the political content of insurgencies; it calls for a displacement of the foundational concepts for political analysis. Naturally, the target here is Western theories.

7.2 THE PECULIARITIES OF THE INDIAN PEASANTRY

Guha's ambition in *Elementary Aspects* was to treat the history of agrarian uprisings in colonial India as a window into the nature of peasant consciousness. In six substantive chapters, he provides a brilliant analysis of themes that recur across the peasant uprisings—their typical forms of consciousness, patterns of mobilization, geographical scope, internal structure, and so on.[4] Partha Chatterjee argues that, in addition to these commonalities, Guha discovered a deeper element, fundamental to peasant consciousness in colonial India—the role of *community*. What is noteworthy about community, to Chatterjee, is not its sociological role as a social institution or material resource but its foundational status in peasant psychology. In this capacity, it makes peasant consciousness fundamentally different from other forms. This is how Chatterjee characterizes the role of community in constituting peasants as political agents:

> [W]hat the principle of community does as the characteristic unifying feature of peasant consciousness is directly place it at the opposite pole of a bourgeois consciousness. The latter operates from the premise of the individual and a notion of his interests (or, in more fashionable vocabulary, his preferences). Solidarities in

---

4   The best summary of Guha's book is in fact provided by Partha Chatterjee in "The Nation and Its Peasants," in Chatterjee, *The Nation and Its Fragments: Colonial and Postcolonial Histories* (Princeton: Princeton University Press, 1993), chap. 8, 162–3. Henceforth *NF*.

bourgeois politics are built up through an aggregative process by which individuals come together into alliances on the basis of common interests (or shared preferences). The process is quite opposite in the consciousness of a rebellious peasantry. There [sic] solidarities do not grow because individuals feel they can come together with others on the basis of their common individual interests: on the contrary, individuals are enjoined to act within a collectivity because, it is believed, bonds of solidarity that tie them together already exist. Collective action does not flow from a contract among individuals; rather, individual identities themselves are derived from membership in a community.[5]

Note the key to this passage—that Chatterjee *counterposes* community consciousness to individual interests. Most students of agrarian history would recognize that peasants typically evince a strong attachment to local community and take seriously their obligations to these structures.[6] But this disposition is assumed to rest on the individual peasant's actual interest in the community's survival, and his dependence upon it. Rural reproduction depends on cooperation and reciprocity between individual producers; peasants learn from hard experience that their well-being depends on a robust set of interrelations with neighboring households—for labor, material inputs, social insurance, marriage partners, and so on. All this is taken to generate strong norms of community attachment, or obligation, around village life. Community is seen, in the literature, as being coextensive with individual interests, not counterposed to it. But Chatterjee explicitly rejects this analysis. In his presentation, bonds of solidarity are pre-given—they "already exist." Peasants' sense of community obligation is not built up around the vicissitudes of rural life, as most scholars would have it. Rather, rural life and community norms are an *expression* of this basic element of peasant consciousness.

It might be tempting to forgive this passage as a rhetorical flourish or perhaps a momentary lapse in judgment. But Chatterjee makes the claim on several occasions. In his monograph on colonial Bengal, he describes peasants as articulating their demands "not in terms of a shared aggregate of interests but as the demands of a community united by pre-existing bonds of solidarity, whether real or imaginary."[7] He repeats this claim verbatim two years later, in an article on rural mobilizations in Bengal.[8] The sense that he is quite serious about the distinctiveness of peasant consciousness, of its immunity to the concern for individual interests, is deepened when we turn to the

---

5   *NF* 163.

6   I thank Jeff Goodwin for urging me to make this point clear.

7   Partha Chatterjee, *Bengal, 1920–1947: The Land Question* (Calcutta: K. P. Bagchi, 1984), 208–9.

8   Partha Chatterjee, "The Colonial State and Peasant Resistance in Bengal, 1920–1947," *Past and Present* 110 (Feb. 1986), 201–2.

theoretical conclusions he derives from this claim. Chatterjee insists that virtually all existing theoretical frameworks—all of which hail from the West, but span the ideological spectrum—have misunderstood the basic facts about peasant identity:

> The implication is that peasant consciousness cannot be understood in its own constitutive aspects if we continue to reduce it to the paradigm of bourgeois rationality. We must grant that peasant consciousness has its own paradigmatic form, which is not only different from that of bourgeois consciousness but in fact its very other. This central proposition is brought out by Guha's book, and it poses a basic challenge to the methodological procedures followed not only by bourgeois economists and sociologists (including those of the Chayanovian and "moral economy" varieties) searching for the "rational peasant" (however defined) but also many Marxist scholars writing on the agrarian question.[9]

Once again, Chatterjee sets peasant consciousness against "bourgeois rationality," by which he means a sense of individual interests. He does not explain why it is "bourgeois" to be concerned about one's interests. One might suppose that he takes the possibility of interest-based action to be impossible unless capitalism has torn apart precapitalist communities. In peasant collectivities, he implies, such an orientation cannot emerge among social agents because of the strength of community ties. Of course, this is quite a contentious assertion—that community ties obviate the possibility of self-interested motivations.[10] But let us set that aside for now. Let us take him at his word and follow the argument.

Here is what he urges us to consider. Peasants have their own "paradigmatic form" of consciousness, which is different from something called "bourgeois" consciousness. What sets the former apart from the latter is that bourgeois consciousness—at least when it comes to political participation—rests on the notion of individual rationality and interest. Peasant consciousness, on the other hand, does not: it is hard-wired for collective values. Hence,

---

9   Ibid., 163–4.

10   For evidence that self-regarding motivations are in fact endemic to societies with strong community ties, see Melford Spiro, "Is the Western Conception of the Self 'Peculiar' within the Context of the World Cultures?" *Ethos* 21:2 (June 1993), 107–53. For more recent evidence from social psychology and anthropology, see Michael E. Price, "Pro-community Altruism and Social Status in a Shuar Village," *Human Nature* 14:2 (2003), 191–208; Polly Wiessner, "Norm Enforcement among the Ju/'hoansi Bushman: A Case of Strong Reciprocity?" *Human Nature* 16:2 (Summer 2005), 115–45. The evidence from these studies shows that the strong case for self-interest understood as maximizing behavior, cannot be sustained. Agents are motivated by some notional understanding of fairness. But this understanding still has an important component of self-interest; agents are willing to cooperate with others as long as they do not feel cheated by them. Obligations are accepted as long as they do not entail undue hardship or being taken advantage of.

when peasants engage in political action, they do so as a preformed community, not as individual agents motivated by interests. This carries an important implication, namely that peasants do not have to engage in the hard work of *building* solidarity by persuading individual members of their community that a particular campaign is in their interest. Solidarity would be an elemental principle of peasant consciousness itself—pre-given. It does not have to be built, because it is already present. As Chatterjee explains in another passage, to Indian peasants "alliances are not seen as the result of contracts based on common interests; rather, they are believed to be the necessary duty of groups bound together by mutual bonds of kinship."[11] So, in cases of peasant action, interests are replaced by duty and obligation. All this flows from the fact that peasants are not like other agents. They think differently—they have their own "paradigmatic form" of consciousness. As a result, in terms of Western theories, the politics of colonial India necessarily appear somewhat mysterious. Western theories take the sovereign individual as the wellspring of politics, but for Indian peasants, it was the *community* that constituted the foundation for political identity and mobilization.

Finally, Chatterjee warns that the arguments he and his colleagues have developed should not be assimilated into a general theory of peasant consciousness. It is a theory of the *Indian* peasantry. As such, it will generate "a project to write an *Indian history* of peasant struggles," not a "history of peasant struggles *in India*."[12] The latter presumes the validity of a general theory of the peasantry, a set of categories that is universal in scope and is able therefore to abstract from the paradigmatic features of Indian agrarian culture. It would arrange "the historical material on peasant struggles in India according to a framework in which the fundamental concepts and analytical relations are taken as given, established in their generality by the forms of a universal history." Chatterjee's objection is that this approach would ignore the specificity of Indian history, and in particular the type of political consciousness generated by the colonial experience in India. It would assume that the cultural context of Indian revolts was the same as in Europe. By contrast, if we conceptualize the issue as an "Indian history of peasant struggles," it will call for "the relegation of the universal categories of social formations into a temporary state of suspension, or rather of unresolved tension."[13] Chatterjee thus makes clear that his description of peasant political psychology is not a general theory of rural consciousness: it describes only the psychology of *Indian* peasants.

This is a remarkable series of claims. Chatterjee seems unaware that he is reviving a well-established Orientalist notion of the East as a culture in which

---

11   "The Nation and its Peasants", *The Nation and its Fragments*, 165.
12   *NF* 167. Emphasis added.
13   *NF* 167–8.

actors are essentially other-oriented, lacking any notion of individuality, unmoved by their material interests. The West is the site of the bounded individual, while the East is the repository of Community. Chatterjee explicitly warns against assimilating an analysis of Indian peasants into a general theory of peasant action—Indians require their own theory, he asserts, because they do not *think* like other agents, especially those in the West. They need a theory of their own, sensitive to their peculiar psychology. All this has a drearily familiar ring to it, even if dressed in radical language, for it harks back directly to nineteenth-century colonial ideology, not to mention contemporary reifications of the unchanging East.

Still, the mere fact that Chatterjee's argument has a distinctly Orientalist whiff does not, by itself, count as evidence against it. He quite clearly bases his view on what he regards as compelling empirical evidence. The distinct political psychology of the Indian peasantry is what explains certain otherwise puzzling aspects of agrarian movements in late-colonial Bengal.[14] Chief among these is that, despite considerable peasant differentiation over the course of three decades, during which a class of substantial peasants emerged from within the smallholder population, rural mobilization continued to be organized around the axis of the local community.[15] Chatterjee sees peasants' communitarian identity as the key to unlocking the secret of rural politics, and also as posing the central theoretical problem for colonial historiography. With regard to politics, it explains why political strategies based on notions of individual, sectional, or class interests supposedly met with such uneven success in colonial Bengal. These strategies remained outside the discursive universe of the peasantry, whose identities remained wrapped up in community.[16] With regard to theory, these facts about peasant identity pose a challenge because, until mainstream historiography abandons its assumption that politics springs forth from the sovereign individual, it cannot apprehend the true wellspring of late-colonial politics in India.[17]

The specificity of peasant politics in Bengal is taken by Chatterjee as confirmation of two central arguments advanced by Guha: that the subaltern domain had its own political culture and forms of agency, and that a pillar of this distinctive culture was the group-oriented psychology of Indian peasants. Guha found evidence for it in the nineteenth century, and Chatterjee uncovered yet more

14   Chatterjee analyses Bengali rural politics in several publications, most centrally "Agrarian Relations and Communalism in Bengal, 1926–1935," in Guha, ed., *Subaltern Studies I*, 9–38; *Bengal, 1920–1947*; and "The Colonial State and Peasant Resistance," 169–204.

15   Chatterjee, "The Colonial State and Peasant Resistance," 201; Chatterjee, "Agrarian Relations and Communalism," 35–6.

16   Chatterjee, "Agrarian Relations and Communalism," 37–8; Chatterjee, "The Colonial State and Peasant Resistance," 196–7.

17   Chatterjee, "The Nation and Its Peasants," in *NF* 160–7.

evidence for the late colonial era.[18] Together, it is contended, the two projects—Guha's *Elementary Aspects* and Chatterjee's publications on Bengal—demonstrate the proposition that subaltern political agency in the East, during the colonial era, was organized around its own sui generis principles, altogether different from those characteristic of bourgeois politics. For that reason, they cannot but be mystifying to mainstream political theories, which universalize the political culture of the bourgeois West.

7.3 PEASANT PSYCHOLOGY IN *ELEMENTARY ASPECTS*

Turning to Guha's argument in *Elementary Aspects*, we must now ask whether the book supports the contention that Indian peasants were motivated purely by their perceived duty to the group, with little or no consideration of their individual self-interests.

In fact, there is little in *Elementary Aspects* to warrant Chatterjee's characterization. Whatever the book's flaws, it does not give the impression that Indian peasants functioned with a political psychology all their own, differentiable from "bourgeois consciousness," in which their individual interest played little or no role. What seems central to peasant psychology is not the sense of duty or obligation, but the appreciation of *risk*, the regard for their *interests*, and the *hesitation* to bear the costs of collective action. These aspects are brought out clearly in the book's introductory chapter, where Guha seeks to encapsulate his main findings. He observes that colonial rule tended to fuse the power of the landlord, the moneylender, and the state official into one powerful apparatus of exploitation. This was the fulcrum for political stability in the countryside, comprising a concentration of power that the peasantry had never before seen. When contemplating an uprising against a force such as this, Guha argues,

> There was no way for the peasant to launch into such a project in a fit of absent-mindedness. For this relationship was so fortified by the power of those who had the most to benefit from it . . . that *he risked all by trying to subvert or destroy it* by rebellion.[19]

The leaders of the community, Guha observes, were aware of the risks involved as well as families' worries about the consequences. This made for two responses on their part. The first was that they "took up arms only as a last resort when all other means had failed."[20] To the greatest extent possible, they avoided upris-

---

18   Chatterjee, *Bengal, 1920–1947*, xl–xlviii.
19   *EA* 9. Emphasis added.
20   Ibid.

ings—the preferred course of action being appeals to the authorities, petitions, or peaceful demonstrations.

When all such means failed, however, and peasant leaders turned to more direct and confrontational strategies, they had to find some way of overcoming the hesitation of many of their peers. This was the second kind of response. But to carry it out, community leaders had to take account of villagers' worries about their interests, because so many peasants threatened to withhold their participation in the insurgency. Leaders found they could not take for granted the solidarity that Chatterjee imputes to Indian peasants. Instead, they had to *build* it through a combination of persuasion and exhortation. As Guha notes,

> the preparation of an uprising was almost invariably marked by *much temporization and weighing of pros and cons on the part of its protagonists . . .* There were meetings of clan elders and caste panchayats, neighborhood conventions, larger mass gatherings, and so on. These consultative processes were often fairly protracted and it could take weeks or even months to *build up the necessary consensus* at various levels until *most* of an entire community was mobilized for action by the systematic use of primordial networks and many different means of verbal and non-verbal communication.[21]

This is not a description of insurgent leaders capitalizing on their community members' pre-given sense of obligation. What Guha is describing here is a process in which peasant families are being urged, both by their local leaders and by their peers, to overcome their *reluctance* to join in. No doubt the leaders remind them of their moral obligations to the community. But the important point is that they *have to be* reminded. The individual families were taking account of the risks, weighing up the pros and cons, and hesitating. They were urged to overcome their hesitation through a combination of persuasion and exhortation. The whole process would take weeks, presumably because it was not easy to convince everyone. Even then, not all of the families threw in their lot with the insurgents, meaning that many of them found the risk unacceptably high.

What this tells us is that there was a powerful, perhaps even pervasive, impulse among the peasants to shirk, to avoid the risks and costs of collective action, to hope these liabilities would be borne by their peers. The tactics Guha describes, which village leaders employed in the face of such reactions, are classic examples of sanctions and incentives.[22] But why would these measures be

---

21   Ibid. Emphasis added.

22   Readers familiar with rational choice theory will recognize that Guha's argument is not only consistent with a rational choice account of movements, but almost seems derived from it. The theory predicts that in the presence of public goods, rational actors will find a powerful inducement to shirk or to hold back their contribution to a social mobilization. The reason is, since the gains from the movement's success are nonexcludable—owing to their status as public

needed if mutual solidarity was an inbuilt, foundational element of peasant psychology? Guha is portraying a dynamic in which leaders must consciously forge a sense of mutuality through the deployment of considerable resources—they are unable to take it for granted. At the very least, they realize there is constant threat of peasant defection, which can be averted only through active intervention. And the possibility of defection is brought about because many families are reluctant to risk losing what little they have.

Guha's analysis of peasant unity is not confined to this summary statement. He devotes an entire chapter of *Elementary Aspects* to it, under the heading, appropriately, of "Solidarity." In this chapter, he points to two kinds of solidarities relevant to rural insurgencies in the nineteenth century: those forged *between* peasant communities, and those that obtained *within* them. Both, he shows, had to be built up through a combination of sanctions and exhortations. They could not be taken as pre-given. Guha devotes the first twenty pages of the chapter to showing the importance of solidarity as a condition for successful struggle, though his main concern here is to show that what many commentators have missed is that the solidarity was built along the lines of class, not of ethnicity or caste.[23] Having shown that peasant solidarity was critical to the launch of rural insurgencies, Guha then turns to an analysis of its constitution. Here he returns to the mechanisms described in his introductory chapter, which I presented above. He observes:

> Unity such as this *depended* for its strength on two types of *communal sanctions*—cultural and physical. The first of these was imposed usually as a *threat* to one's status within the community either by defilement or by social boycott...

goods—everyone is assured of enjoying their share of it. Each individual therefore has an incentive to reduce the cost to themselves that arise from participation, on the expectation that if the movement fails, they are not much worse off, but if it succeeds they will benefit from it as much as their peers, even though their own contribution was minimal. This is a dilemma, since if everyone reasons in this fashion, everyone will also shirk, and the movement will likely fail. How, then, can participation ever occur? It does so through a careful application of *sanctions and incentives* by the leadership on the movement's participants. The sanctions can be the use of violence, ostracism, subtle forms of coercion, etc.; the incentives can be the bestowal of fame, greater status, public recognition, and most important, the assurance of reduced risk by the promise of collective sharing of costs. Note that *this is exactly what Guha describes* as happening in Indian peasant movements. Far from overturning mainstream approaches, his argument is a ringing endorsement of the most "bourgeois" theory of all! The two classic statements of rational choice theory are Mancur Olson, *The Logic of Collective Action: Public Goods and the Theory of Groups* (Cambridge: Harvard University Press, 1965); and Russell Hardin, *Collective Action* (Baltimore: Johns Hopkins University Press, 1982). Another excellent text that specifically relates the theory to the problem of solidarity is Michael Hechter, *Principles of Group Solidarity* (Berkeley: University of California Press, 1987).

23   See *EA* 168–88; see esp. 169–70, 172–3, 176–7, 181, 188. Guha is careful to stress that the consciousness of class identity was often expressed in the language of ethnicity or caste, which commentators have used as a justification for denying the relevance of class in these movements. See *EA* 170, 173, 177.

More often, however, the price of dissidence from common action would *be denial of cooperation* by fellow villagers. *This could ruin a peasant economically as well as socially.*[24]

In other words, solidarity depended critically on sanctions, and what made sanctions work was most often their effect on the peasants' material well-being—the fact that they could be economically and socially ruined if their peers decided to punish them for shirking. Added to these sanctions was the mundane threat of violence against those who refused to participate.[25] "Rarely," Guha asserts, "would sanctions against breach of solidarity remain confined to a purely non-violent exercise in social boycott. It was common for the latter to be accompanied by threats of physical violence too."[26] He then devotes four pages to describing the various forms of violence visited upon recalcitrant community members who were found to be shirking. It is passages such as these that entirely overturn the analysis that Chatterjee imputes to Guha.

But sanctions and intimidation could not have been the only instruments for inducing local participation. Given the level of sacrifice involved, families surely had to see some beneficial results from their endeavors. After describing the various negative sanctions, Guha turns to more positive measures utilized by community leaders to elicit cooperation. The one he focuses on was known as "pressing," and it was designed not to intimidate or threaten, but to *exhort*. Exhort on what basis? Guha's answer is interesting, and deeply damaging to Chatterjee's case: the "purpose is to win support by appealing to the *mutuality of interest* between those who have already taken up arms and others who are yet to do so."[27] Reluctant peasants were urged to participate because it was in their individual interest to do so—they would benefit from it. It was not enough to remind them of their obligation to the collective; they had to be assured that it would be conducive to their well-being. Once again, Guha shows in detail that significant sections of the community did not regard their obligations to be so binding as to displace their concern for their individual interests. Insurgent leaders found they had to resort in many different ways to inducements, exhortations, sanctions, and even threats. Hence, there is little evidence that Guha regards solidarity as an elemental, pre-given datum of peasant consciousness, or that he sees individual interests as irrelevant to it.

Seemingly, then, Guha's depiction of peasant movements in colonial India is the very opposite of Chatterjee's characterization of it. There is no support in *Elementary Aspects* for the claim that Indian peasants have a unique political psychology. Rationality and individual interests appear to lie at the very heart of

24 *EA* 190. Emphasis added.
25 *EA* 191–94.
26 *EA* 190–1.
27 *EA* 194–5. Emphasis added.

peasant consciousness. The fact that Guha discovers these facts about peasant political culture should not surprise students of the subject. As Chatterjee notes, most of the reigning theories of agrarian society recognize rural agents' sensitivity to their interests. This is no less true of "moral economy" arguments, such as James Scott's, than it is of Marxist efforts.[28] Guha's analysis in *Elementary Aspects* simply joins the pantheon of classics in agrarian studies that confirm the importance of material interests in peasant psychology, both East and West.

7.4 INDIVIDUAL AND COMMUNITY IN LATE COLONIAL BENGAL

We now turn to Chatterjee's own work on peasant movements during the last years of colonial rule in India. In a book-length monograph and several articles, he provides an illuminating analysis of the patterns of rural mobilization in the 1920s and 1930s.[29] On the surface, it is unclear how his account supports the conclusions he wishes to derive from it, inasmuch as the actual story that Chatterjee tells is a thoroughly materialist one. At its core is the relation between the evolving class structure in rural Bengal and the forms of agitation that swept across the region in the final decades of British rule. Chatterjee shows, lucidly at times, the existence of a strong connection between the regional social structures and the demands taken up by the peasant movements. Time and again, he shows that the demands expressed particular interests, and that those interests could be derived from the alignment of classes in the regional economy. The question to be addressed now is how and why he thinks his evidence, which, much as Guha's does, seems to push in a materialist direction, can sustain his argument for the irrelevance of interests to Indian peasant consciousness.

THE CONTOURS OF RURAL MOVEMENTS IN LATE COLONIAL BENGAL

The agrarian structure of late colonial Bengal consisted primarily of a smallholding peasantry on one side and a traditional class of landlords on the other. These landlords, known as zamindars, had been the regional ruling class for centuries, and had maintained a dominant position under colonial rule. Colonialism incorporated zamindars into the state structure as an arm of British authority in the countryside. But peasants also felt the state's grasping hand more directly, through the burden of taxation. Hence, in the late colonial era, Bengal's smallholder population faced two great antagonists, who often worked in tandem—the zamindars and the colonial state. In the final decades of British

---

28   The assumption of rationality in the moral economy approach is evident in James C. Scott's classic argument, even though he seems to deny it. See Scott, *The Moral Economy of the Peasant: Rebellion and Subsistence in Southeast Asia* (New Haven: Yale University Press, 1976), chaps. 1–2.

29   The main texts are Chatterjee, "Agrarian Relations and Communalism"; Chatterjee, "The Colonial State and Peasant Resistance"; and Chatterjee, *Bengal, 1920–1947.*

rule, peasant agitations were primarily directed against one or both of these agents, sometimes in the form of anti-rent campaigns, at other times as mobilization against state fiscal demands.

But by the closing decades of British rule, another actor emerged on the rural scene, from within the smallholder community. This was a class of wealthier peasants, known as jotedars, who had accumulated more land for themselves and who often hired in additional labor or rented out their land, or even served as moneylenders to their less fortunate peers. Jotedars did not supplant the traditional landlord class. The latter continued to be a powerful presence, though they were physically more remote, often located in nearby towns or cities. The newer class of rich peasants merely inserted itself as an additional, albeit smaller, claimant on the peasants' surplus—though located closer to home, often in the same village, and always more familiar. They were not equally visible throughout the region. Chatterjee argues, through an impressive and quite careful examination of Bengal's regional economies, that jotedars had more of a presence in the southwestern districts and less in the eastern. Eastern districts were thus split more along traditional class lines of landlord and peasant, while in the southwest, peasants had also to contend with this new stratum from within their ranks. Jotedars exerted some influence across both regions, but not evenly, and in neither case did they push aside the traditional landlords.

The structure of politics that Chatterjee describes consists of the basic duo of peasants and landlords, modulated by the entrance of a class of rich peasants, and overseen by the colonial state.[30] Out of this alignment of forces emerged a wave of peasant agitations—stretching from the Great Depression to the Second World War—that, he contends, support his case for the specificity of Indian peasant consciousness. Yet the basic facts of peasant campaigns in those decades do not seem especially friendly to Chatterjee's theory. The lines of cleavage are more or less what one would expect: the main protagonists were the smallholding peasants, and they directed their campaigns against the two main actors that laid claim to their income, the traditional landlords and/or the colonial state. This seems consistent with an interest-based account of peasant politics and is reminiscent of what Guha found in the nineteenth century.

The entrance of the jotedars, however, complicates the story a bit. Jotedars affected rural political mobilizations in two ways. First, as Chatterjee himself shows, in both the southwest and the east they played an important role, often

---

30   In order to make Chatterjee's argument as strong as possible, I will assume that its empirical basis is sound. For an analysis of Bengal agrarian politics in the late colonial years that diverges from Chatterjee's, see Sugata Bose, *Agrarian Bengal: Economy, Social Structure, and Politics, 1919–1947* (Cambridge: Cambridge University Press, 1985). Bose explicitly suggests that Chatterjee overstates the importance of community consciousness within the Bengali peasantry. See chaps. 6 and 7, and his conclusion on 279–80. The point I wish to make in this chapter, however, is that Chatterjee's argument fails even if we accept his empirical account.

as leaders or organizers, taking up key positions, articulating peasant demands, effectuating strategy, and so on. But there was a difference. In the southwest, where peasant differentiation was greater and where jotedars were more powerful and had emerged as the exploiting class, deep antagonisms also emerged *between* peasants and jotedars.[31] While rich peasants and smallholders launched joint campaigns against the colonial state during these years, these alliances came apart time and again as smallholders turned against jotedars. A sort of seesawing rhythm ensued, with rich peasants leading mass campaigns against the colonial state, and then, as these campaigns subsided, the middling and poorer peasants breaking away and turning their wrath against the jotedars themselves.[32] The anti-jotedar campaigns did not greatly damage the class; indeed, the campaigns tended to peter out after an initial flurry, as peasants were unable to find an independent political identity. Nevertheless, the peasants in the southwest refused to accommodate to jotedar dominance.

Matters were a little different in the east. In these districts, rural differentiation was less advanced, and peasant-jotedar friction did not reach the same level as in the southwest. Eastern jotedars were able to attain a more secure position as political leaders of the peasant mobilizations. Here the main target of the campaigns was the landlord class—the zamindars—rather than the state. The political alignment in the east was therefore more consistent—the peasant-jotedar alliance against traditional zamindars.

Jotedars also figure in Chatterjee's argument in a second respect, with regard specifically to the eastern districts. In both the southwest and the east, the peasants launched their movements against external authorities, but in East Bengal the campaign took on a distinctly communal hue—it was not only anti-landlord but anti-*Hindu*. Once again, Chatterjee's own evidence seems to provide a straightforward materialist explanation. The peasant population in the east was overwhelmingly Muslim, while the zamindars were predominantly Hindu.[33] This was reinforced by the fact that in the eastern districts, the actors who ensnared the Muslim peasants in debt were also Hindus, living in the surrounding urban centers. On the other hand, the jotedars in the east, who figured prominently in the agitations, were Muslim. So it does not seem surprising that the anti-zamindar campaigns assumed a communal tint. On one side were Muslim peasants, and on the other, Hindu zamindars and moneylenders. By contrast, this overlap of economic identity and religious identity was not so clean in the southwest, and as it happens, the mobilization there did not assume the communal form that it did in East Bengal.

---

31   Chatterjee, "The Colonial State and Peasant Resistance," 192; Chatterjee, *Bengal, 1920–1947*, 195–6.

32   Chatterjee, "The Colonial State and Peasant Resistance," 110–14.

33   Chatterjee, "Agrarian Relations and Communalism in Bengal," 9–11; Chatterjee, *Bengal, 1920–1947*, 126.

The emergence of jotedars, then, cast its shadow on peasant politics during the late colonial era. It did not overturn the traditional political alignments, which continued to revolve around the basic conflict between peasants and the state/zamindar nexus. But the jotedars added an inflection to this traditional antagonism. For our purposes, the relevant question is how Chatterjee utilizes this dynamic as evidence for the unique political consciousness of the Indian peasantry, when, as we already observed, the story seems to fit quite neatly into a materialist explanatory framework.

THE ROLE OF COMMUNITY

Chatterjee rests his case—his confidence that Indian peasants were indifferent to their individual interests—on the fundamental place of the *local community* in Bengal's peasant mobilizations. His argument proceeds in two steps. First, he insists that it played an autonomous role in peasant politics. Even though the districts in the southwest and the east produced different kinds of demands, and even though the self-identity of one (the southwest) was less communal than that of the other (the east), what they had in common was their ability to gain momentum, and at times even exceed the boundaries set by their leaders, because they mobilized the peasantry as a pre-given community. Thus, community served as the common substratum on which the various mobilizations supervened.[34] The function of political organizations was not to *create* a political community through its agitations or its leadership, but merely to *activate* already formed collectivities—already in existence as *latent* political formations—and to give them a particular direction.[35] In so doing, the organizations created a link between the world of formal, organized politics and the autonomous subaltern domain—with its own identity and own political resources.[36] It is in this context that Chatterjee makes his assertion, which we encountered in his description of Guha's work: that when the peasantry participates in movements, it is not through the aggregation of interests, but as a pre-given community, in which members accept the authority of the collective because they already identify with it and have internalized a sense of obligation to its demands.

Establishing the foundational role of the peasant community is the first step in Chatterjee's argument. His second step is to argue that the place of community was so strong in peasants' consciousness that it suffocated their ability to appreciate their own material interests. Because of their identification with their peers, peasants were unable to de-link their own identities from the larger group identity; as a result, they could not recognize situations in which

---

34   Chatterjee, *Bengal, 1920–1947*, 110.
35   Chatterjee uses the language of "latent" structures being "activated" at least twice in his monograph. See *Bengal, 1920-1947*, 105, 115.
36   Chatterjee, "Agrarian Relations and Communalism," 35–6.

their material interests clashed with those of other members of the community. In short, their communitarian identity prevented them from recognizing class enemies when the latter were also community "insiders". And who might such "insiders" have been? The emergent class of jotedars, who, as I mentioned earlier, were increasingly laying claim to part of the peasants' surplus. Chatterjee observes that despite the emergence of this exploiting class in these districts, peasant agitations against them remained limited. The focus of their movements remained fixed on ostensible "outsiders"—the traditional class of zamindars or the colonial state. The reason "outsiders" were targeted instead of "insiders" was because the latter were regarded part of the community, in spite of their extraction of peasant surplus. So, the "paradigmatic form of peasant consciousness", as Chatterjee describes it, overrode the material antagonism of class interests.

In the Southwest, the hold of community consciousness was evidenced by the peasants' failure to break free of jotedar leadership and to locate them as class enemies, much like the zamindars. For Chatterjee, the key point is that, notwithstanding their periodic agitations against the emergent class of rich peasants, the smallholders remained under the jotedars' sway politically. The jotedars were able to leverage their leadership of the anti-tax mobilizations and assume powerful positions within the state structure, replacing the rule by colonial authorities with their own rule as Bengal entered the postcolonial era. The inability of the peasants to launch a full-blown attack on the rich peasants is explained by the obduracy of their communitarian identity.[37]

In the east, the key was the peasants' willingness to forgive jotedar malfeasance and to accept them as fellow Muslims in the struggle against Hindu landlords:

> [T]he available evidence seems to suggest that the crucial element which deflected peasant agitations into anti-Hindu movements was not that most zamindars were Hindu and that the grievances of the predominantly Muslim tenantry consequently took on anti-Hindu overtones, *but the fact that Muslim rent-receivers, where they did exist, were considered part of the community, whereas Hindu zamindars and talukdars were not.*[38]

Chatterjee seems to take the East Bengali peasants as a particularly striking example of community consciousness. Their experience shows how identity overrides interests, in that the peasantry seems to ignore the exploitative activities of community insiders while attacking those who are considered outsiders. But Chatterjee goes even further. It is not that peasants give insufficient weight

---

37   Chatterjee, "The Colonial State and Peasant Resistance," 194, 196–7.
38   Chatterjee, "Agrarian Relations and Communalism," 11. Emphasis added. See also ibid., 18.

to the divergence between their interests and those of the rich peasants, he says. It is that they cannot even recognize that their interests diverge from those of the exploiters within the village. The force of the community-oriented norms is so strong, its shroud over peasant cognitive abilities so thick, that it blocks the ability to recognize who is an exploiter and who is not:

> [T]he point which is crucial here is the inadequacy of the peasant-communal ideology to provide an adequate perceptual guide for the identification of friends and enemies in a situation of rapid agrarian change: the peasant-communal ideology *is incapable* of identifying "inside" exploiters or identifying the linkages between the "external" bureaucratic state apparatus and its agents within the putative community. Such an awareness can only be provided by alternative ideological systems, brought to the *peasantry from the outside,* from the organized world of politics.[39]

We should note, in passing, the hypervanguardism that Chatterjee ends up promoting here, which starkly contrasts to his programmatic call to recognize and respect subaltern agency. He does not deny the existence of individual interests—he simply denies that Indian peasants can apprehend them. He takes rural agents to be so handicapped by perceptual blinders that the very possibility of recognizing the reality of their situation is occluded; such capacities must therefore be developed by outside political forces. Peasants have to be *taught* to recognize when community members are harming them—a most curious turn for a project calling for the recognition of subaltern agency.

Yet there is an obvious, tautological sense in which Chatterjee is correct: insofar as peasant-communal ideology *defines* all members of the community as nonexploiters, it will be incapable of identifying "insiders" as members of a different class. Chatterjee has built this property into his definition of peasant ideology, so the prediction is not a surprise. But he is subtly obscuring the real issue here. The point is not whether *the ideology* has the resources to distinguish between exploiters and nonexploiters within the community. It is, rather, whether the force of the ideology is so strong as to prevent *the peasants* from recognizing a disjuncture between the ideology's claims and the reality that they experience. When they hand over their rent, when they labor on the jotedar's land, when the jotedar eats into their meager income, is the ideology so powerful that, on the basis of its influence alone, they continue to see these rich peasants as no different from the village smallholders? This is what Chatterjee would have us believe.

Perhaps there are other reasons why smallholding peasants do not identify jotedars as antagonists—material reasons, reflecting actual interdependencies in their social relations. But these would not help Chatterjee's case, because to

---

39   Ibid., 37. Emphasis added.

refer to such factors would be to invoke individual interests—a matter to which we will return shortly. For the moment, let us underline the implications of what Chatterjee is saying: that the peasants' inability to perceive the jotedars' actual role, and the resulting lack of hostility on the part of the peasants, was a consequence of their basic psychology, not of the alignment of interests between jotedar and smallholder. And that is why the cognitive resources to make such distinctions must be brought in from the outside by more enlightened agents.

7.5 CHATTERJEE'S CONTRADICTIONS

Does the willingness of Bengal smallholders to accept jotedar dominance show that Indian peasants functioned with a uniquely communitarian psychology, unburdened by considerations of individual interest? To answer this question, let us start with the character of the peasant movements.

Despite Chatterjee's confidence in the strong community orientation of peasant consciousness, his evidence in support of it is surprisingly thin. For the southwestern districts of Bengal, he bases his argument on smallholders' inability to wrest free of jotedar dominance, which made their mobilizations oscillate between an anti-zamindar pole and an anti-jotedar pole. But is it not significant that there was an anti-jotedar pole *at all*? Chatterjee rests his case on the argument that the smallholders did not undertake a decisive break with rich peasants. This is true, but it is also an insufficient basis for asserting that communitarian ideology had a viselike grip on peasant action. Chatterjee needs to explain why the peasants' willingness to renew their ties with the jotedars carries more weight than their decision to launch anti-jotedar campaigns. Recall Chatterjee's claim that the communitarian peasant ideology renders them "*incapable* of identifying 'inside' exploiters." Yet that claim is undermined by the very *appearance* of anti-jotedar movements again and again in the same region. The eruption of such mobilizations shows that the peasantry was in fact perfectly capable of identifying exploitation from within. We must contemplate the possibility that the reason these campaigns subsided was not due to the peasants' ideological limitations, for these limitations had *already* been transcended. The movement's ebb may have been due to organizational, political, or even economic factors.

Chatterjee appears to stand on stronger ground with respect to the eastern districts. Whereas the southwestern peasants in his narrative could boast of at least having launched some anti-jotedar agitations, in the east they remained glued more firmly to jotedar leadership. Chatterjee attributes this to their inability to identify insider exploitation. To counter this, we could simply insist that the southwestern peasants' ability to positively identify exploiters in their districts has already settled the matter, and indeed, if the argument is about the very possibility of interest-awareness among Indian peasants, it has—unless

Chatterjee wishes to insist that there is something about the peasants of eastern Bengal that forces us to assign their experience greater theoretical significance than we assign to those of western Bengal. But let us grant him that possibility as well. Let us suppose that, as goes the eastern Bengal peasantry, so goes our theory of peasant consciousness. The problem for Chatterjee is that here, too, the facts seem to undermine his case.

Let us recall that peasant differentiation in the east had not proceeded as far as it had in the west. The rich peasants in the east had smaller holdings, and received less rent, than did their counterparts in the west. They often continued to use their own family's labor on their holdings, making their actual class practice closer in substance to that of the less wealthy smallholders.[40] Another characteristic of the jotedars in the east, which Chatterjee mentions and then passes over in his broader discussions about the role of consciousness, is the fact that they did not engage in moneylending to any great extent, whereas this was widespread in the west. Hence, in the east, the vicious cycle of debt and destitution could not be laid at the feet of the local jotedar; instead, it was the zamindar and the professional moneylender, both "outsiders," who were identified with this practice.[41] Thus, in western Bengal the rich peasants were more fully an exploiting class, who augmented their rental exactions with usurious lending, while their counterparts in eastern Bengal were smaller, more similar to other peasants, and far less engaged as rapacious creditors. If jotedars in the east continued to be taken as part of the community, is it not possible that this was because they were *in fact* a part of the community, far more so than in the west? Furthermore, if they were in fact more like peasants, and less consistently like genuine exploiters, then it would make eminently good sense to bring them into the movement, precisely because of their greater material resources, more ramified social networks, better political connections, and so forth—all of which would increase the likelihood of the movement's success. Thus there seem to be sound reasons of material interest for eastern smallholders to include jotedars in the political mobilizations.

What we see, then, if we step back for a moment in our comparison of the southwest with the east, is that in districts where peasant differentiation was more pronounced and the class of rich peasants more exploitative, peasant movements often turned against them. But in districts where differentiation was less pronounced and rich peasants not very exploitative, smallholders allied with them against a common enemy, who also *happened to be* of a different religion. This is exactly what an interest-based theory of politics would predict.

But even while these facts about the movements are damaging to Chatterjee's case, there is another aspect that undermines it even more. The truly

---

40 Chatterjee, *Bengal, 1920–1947*, 186–8.
41 Ibid., 188.

devastating evidence is something that Chatterjee passes over in silence: the fact that peasant differentiation occurred *at all*.

Chatterjee maintains that the defining element of Indian peasants' agency is their insulation from "bourgeois consciousness," from strategies that prioritize individual interests. Their self-identities issue from their membership in the community, and their basic motivations derive from their sense of obligation to this community. If this is true, however, surely it should also mitigate the internal class differentiation of the peasantry? If peasants do not pursue their individual interests, it is unclear why they choose to encroach upon, and accumulate, resources that formerly belonged to their neighbors. Consider the actions entailed, and the psychological orientation presupposed, if certain peasants position themselves as a nascent class of jotedars. If they emerge through a process of internal differentiation, it can only mean that they have amassed land once owned or possessed by other members of their community. The emerging rich peasants acquired the land because their peers fell on hard times—perhaps taking out a loan they could not repay, or having to make a distress sale after a personal calamity. Whatever the particulars of each case, the wealthier peasants had a choice: they could assist their fellow villagers out of a sense of duty, as members of the community, without seeking personal gain; or they could take advantage of their peers' misfortune and usurp their land, their most precious resource, and condemn these poor unfortunates to their fate. For the class of jotedars to have emerged, it must be the case that a section of the smallholder community chose the latter course of action. They chose to pursue their *individual interests*. In other words, these smallholders acted on precisely the "bourgeois consciousness" that Chatterjee insists they lacked.[42]

His own evidence shows that the rise of the jotedars, the rich peasants, came about through just this process—through individual peasants' conscious pursuit of their community members' lands.[43] The main mechanism was through debt obligations. As Bengal's economy got pulled into the vortex of

---

42   In his theoretical essay on the peasantry, the same one in which he insists that Indian peasants were unmotivated by individual interests, Chatterjee does seem to allow for the possibility of peasant differentiation. See Chatterjee, "The Nation and Its Peasants," in *NF* 166–7. But two qualifications are immediately offered. First, whatever differentiation there is comes shrouded in a culture of "differential duties and privileges," i.e., within the discourse of obligation; second, the differentiation only modulates the organic unity of the community, rather than calling it into question. All this means is that the peasant community is a "differentiated unity" (167). The basic point—of community being the operative unit of action and analysis—still stands. But for the sake of argument, suppose that Chatterjee is suggesting here that differentiation can come from individual peasants acting in their own interest. If he were to admit of such a possibility, it would make his preceding argument for the priority of community, and of the irrelevance of "interests," collapse. So, either Chatterjee must keep the theoretical significance of differentiation tightly contained—making it only a slight amendment to the claim for the community's organic unity—or he must admit that his argument is internally contradictory.

43   Chatterjee, *Bengal, 1920–1947*, 142–57.

commercial agriculture, smallholders' need for short-term loans became virtually inescapable.[44] While external agents such as the lordly class of zamindars or
the moneylenders (mahajans) were traditional sources of credit, cultivators
could also turn to the more prosperous smallholders in times of need. In the
early decades of the twentieth century, peasants in distress often resorted to
these members of the local community.[45] The key point to note here is that,
when the wealthier peasants made these loans to their peers, they often did so
with the *intention* of leveraging more land out of them. Chatterjee himself
quotes one witness as saying that the wealthier smallholders often "had their
eyes upon the landed property of the loanees."[46] He quotes another authority as
reporting that there were "occasions when shrewd and wealthy jotedars
purposely advance money to certain agriculturalists on rather easy terms . . . in
order to secure from the debtor certain choice and fertile plots of land."[47] While
wealthier peasants amassed greater quantities of land in this fashion, their debt-
ridden peers were reduced to tenants, or laborers, or had to turn over some of
their best lands in lien.

Chatterjee glibly reports these phenomena, apparently unaware of how
damaging they are to his argument. The instances of land acquisition were not
just fortuitous accidents; they were often engineered by certain members of the
community with the intention of depriving others of their most precious
resource. And even when these situations were not intentionally crafted, the
abiding fact is that wealthier peasants took advantage of opportunities for
acquiring land with great alacrity. It is hard to see this as anything other than a
strategic pursuit of individual interests.

Let us pull together the various strands of our critique. I have argued that
the very fact of internal differentiation belies Chatterjee's claims about the
"paradigmatic form" of peasant consciousness in India. If individual interests
played little role in peasant agency, then peasants' acquisition of land, their
pursuit of a strategy to snatch away their peers' resources, is simply incompre-
hensible. These actions make sense only on the premise that peasants were
aware of, and acted upon, their material interests. Why, then, did the mass of
smallholders not mobilize against the rich peasants? In fact, as Chatterjee
shows, in the districts where the jotedars were more conspicuous and more
exploitative—the southwestern districts—peasants' hostility against them was
more pronounced. In contrast, we can reasonably surmise that if jotedars in the
eastern districts escaped the smallholders' ire, this might have been because
they did not pose the same danger to the latter's well-being as did the zamindars

---

44   The importance of the local credit market is emphasized by Sugata Bose in his *Agrarian
Bengal*, Chap. 4.

45   Chatterjee, *Bengal, 1920–1947*, 149–54.

46   Ibid., 149.

47   Ibid., 151.

and moneylenders. Furthermore, there were multiple sound reasons for the smallholders in the east to ally with these wealthier peasants, whose resources were more ample. The greater wealth and connections of the rich peasants—their networks, their contacts with the outside community, their political access—made them attractive as members of the anti-zaminadar mobilization. Their greater wealth had not yet become an obvious source of exploitation; even to the extent that it had, it paled in comparison to the zamindars'. Peasants could therefore see jotedars as a potential asset in the movement, something to be used against the greater threat of their traditional exploiters.

Given Chatterjee's own evidence, we have no basis for concluding that Indian peasants were motivated by a unique psychology, one that abjured individual interests or was incapable of understanding organized politics. Indeed, if we place his narrative alongside Guha's we have two sets of arguments showing in great detail that Bengali peasants were remarkably sensitive to their individual interests. Chatterjee insists that these two analyses lay the groundwork for an *Indian* history of the peasantry, as opposed to a history of the Indian peasantry—the former being a historiography that would emancipate Indian rural agents from a universal history of peasant struggles. But upon examination, we find that Guha and Chatterjee actually furnish us with a story in which Indian peasants look very much like peasants everywhere else. It is entirely possible to assimilate the history of Indian peasants into a universal history of the peasantry. The participants in the insurgencies of the nineteenth century, and in the mobilizations of interwar Bengal, were motivated by some sense of community, to be sure; but it was not qualitatively different from what we know to have been an aspect of the sensibilities of peasantries in Europe, China, the Middle East, or anywhere else.

7.6 CONCLUSION

We are now partway toward overturning the revived Orientalism promoted by Chatterjee and so much of the Subaltern Studies oeuvre. Postcolonial theorists commonly take the stance that political psychology is culturally constructed, all the way down. Even more to the point, they take one form of consciousness to be peculiar to the West—the capacity to separate one's own identity and interests from those of the social group to which one belongs. Chatterjee perpetuates the canard that this capacity is strictly Western. So incapable are Indian peasants of appreciating their own interests, he proposes, that they cannot even recognize when they are being exploited by members of their own village.

Even though such arguments are a striking revival of nineteenth-century colonial ideology, and have been rejected roundly by most critical scholars, they have been seized on enthusiastically within North American academia—so much so that they are, at present, widely accepted as banalities. Few theorists even feel compelled to defend them. What distinguishes the Subaltern Studies project is that its leading lights have tried to defend such notions both empirically and theoretically. We are thus able to weigh their conclusions against their own evidence. And what we find is a considerable gap between the two.

Neither Guha nor Chatterjee shows that Indian peasants functioned with a psychology all of their own. Nevertheless, we should resist casting the two sets of analyses in the same light. Unlike Chatterjee, Guha evinces no significant commitment to the thesis that Indian peasants were essentially different from their counterparts elsewhere. Indeed, *Elementary Aspects* swims with references to the commonality of the Indian peasantry's experience with that of its counterparts elsewhere. Time and again, Guha pauses in his narrative in order to highlight how the tactics or the instruments used by rural insurgents in India evoked those employed by the French, or the Chinese, or the British peasants.[48] If we take *Elementary Aspects* at its word, the struggles of the rural poor in India were motivated by concerns very much like those of the peasantry elsewhere—against rapacious exploitation and domination, for dignity, for self-determination. This does not in any way deny the salience of community consciousness in Guha's analysis. What I do contest, however, is the notion that Guha endows community consciousness with the power to overwhelm peasants' ability to reflect on their situation, to think about risks, to compare the weight of their obligations against the hazards of political conflict. His peasants are every bit as likely to be sensitive to their individual interests as are their counterparts in Germany or France. The difference between his analysis and Chatterjee's is that Guha's conclusions are in line with his evidence, while Chatterjee's are entirely out of synch with his.

---

48   See *EA* 37, 50, 64, 73, 91, 93, 115, 123, 137, 162, 195, 198–9—and this is just a smattering of the repeated parallels that Guha draws between Indian peasant uprisings and the Western experience.

CHAPTER EIGHT

Interests and the Other Universalism

Partha Chatterjee's claims regarding the Indian peasantry were intended to establish the deep significance of culture and consciousness. A similar set of claims about the unique psychological disposition of Indians is made by Dipesh Chakrabarty in his study of Bengal jute mills in the early twentieth century. The subject there, however, is not the province's peasantry but rather the industrial working class employed in these mills. Like Chatterjee, Chakrabarty looks to political agency as a window into subaltern consciousness. And, like Chatterjee, he purports to have discovered that subordinate groups are not motivated by a defense of their interests; instead, they are driven by their valuation of community, honor, religion, and other normative ends. Chakrabarty thus follows his Subaltern Studies colleague in counterposing norms to interests. Interestingly, Chakrabarty uses some of the same language as Chatterjee when he contrasts Bengali labor's psychological orientation with "bourgeois consciousness." We fare no better this time in learning exactly what is meant by this mysterious concept—like Chatterjee, Chakrabarty never directly reveals its content. Roughly, though, it appears to mean a consciousness attuned to the pursuit of material interests. Whatever it may be, Indian workers are not burdened by it. So, just like Chatterjee, Chakrabarty concludes that universalizing theories of class or class conflict must collapse as they travel eastward into the colonial world. The Indians employed in jute mills might be workers in a technical sense, but their political agency cannot be folded into the theories of class handed down by the Enlightenment tradition.

As in previous chapters, I will show that these claims cannot withstand scrutiny. It turns out that, even in Chakrabarty's own account, Indian workers are sensitive to their material interests, much as the peasantry was in Chatterjee's story, despite his denials. As I did with Chatterjee, I will make this case through data provided by Chakrabarty himself. Having shown that workers are no less cognizant of their interests than are peasants, I will then turn to the general criticisms often leveled at materialist theories of agency, criticisms which I believe feed the popularity of arguments such as Chatterjee's and Chakrabarty's. The main such worry is that reference to material interests or rationality ignores the cultural embeddedness of social agents—that it treats agents as asocial or even hedonist. I show that these concerns are unfounded. Recognizing the structuring role of interests does not require that we ignore the importance of culture and the abiding role of norms or ideology in shaping agency. It is just that such a theory refuses to allow that agents' socialization *entirely constitutes* their practical reasoning. Agents have the ability to reflect upon their norms and, when these norms threaten or undermine their well-being, to reject them. So the appreciation of certain universal interests among social actors does not require that we deny them their culture, but it does demand that we not treat them as cultural automata.

The first two parts of the chapter show that Indian workers were aware of their interests and that a historiography that recognizes this attribute of workers need not denigrate their location within a specific culture. In so doing, this chapter seeks to overturn the cultural essentialism of the Subalternists and thereby resurrects the very Enlightenment notion of universal interests that Chatterjee and Chakrabarty have sought to bury. Finally, I demonstrate that there is a distinct and quite generous payoff from defending the Enlightenment view. It enables us to anchor the rise of liberal democracy in a theory of human agency that is neither question-begging nor Orientalist. And it allows us to surmise that the same interests that drove the struggles for the deepening of democracy in the West have been and will be operative in the non-West. It allows us, in short, to anchor democratic politics in the bedrock of certain universal human interests, much as the post-Enlightenment theorists did, making it possible for us to dispose of the abiding Orientalism of the Subalternists.

8.1 THE CONVENTIONAL ANALYSIS OF WORKER CONSCIOUSNESS

Chakrabarty starts with a concrete question, from which, in the course of answering it, he derives some far-reaching conclusions concerning the consciousness of Indian labor. He notes that by the 1920s, many workers in jute mills around Calcutta had developed a strong class consciousness. As the industry experienced the shock of the Great Depression, management unleashed an economic offensive against jute workers, in an effort to hold the line on profits.[1] Labor responded with a flurry of job actions, which displayed not only enormous courage but also an emergent class identity.[2] This common identity was exhibited in the rise of militant trade unionism, which often crossed religious, regional, and linguistic lines.[3] All this sounds very much like a traditional class consciousness, and indeed, Chakrabarty agrees that the strikes of the 1930s amounted to "impressive demonstrations of working class solidarity."[4]

---

1   Chakrabarty's discussion of the managerial offensive is patchy. For more on this, see Subho Basu, *Does Class Matter? Colonial Capital and Workers' Resistance in Bengal, 1890–1937* (Delhi: Oxford University Press, 2004), 238–62.

2   Dipesh Chakrabarty, *Rethinking Working-Class History: Bengal 1890–1940* (Princeton: Princeton University Press, 1989), 186–7.

3   See ibid., 187, where he observes that in the working-class districts of Calcutta, workers had developed a variant of spoken Hindi that could not be found anywhere else in the country.

4   Ibid., 186. For more evidence on class consciousness among the jute workers, see Basu, *Does Class Matter?* 238–51; Ranajit Das Gupta, *Labour and Working Class in Eastern India: Studies in Colonial History* (Calcutta: K. P. Bagchi, 1994), 442–3, 477–8.

The problem was that these displays of class consciousness coexisted with an obdurate attachment to religious and cultural identities. Muslim workers continued to view themselves as Muslims, and Hindu workers as Hindus. More important, these identities were strong enough to stretch across class lines, uniting workers with wealthy Bengalis of the same religious background.[5] Jute workers were thus pulled in two different directions, identifying with their class but also placing great value on their religious community.[6] So intertwined were these attachments that an agitation on ostensibly economic grounds, organized by the poor, could spontaneously break into a communal riot.[7] Jute workers thus labored with a dual identity, rooted in two different conceptions of community, one economic and the other religious.

Chakrabarty then proceeds to examine why workers assigned such value to their membership in a religious community. He immediately sets his sights on the follies of conventional materialist explanations of the phenomenon: he warns that "none of these explanations . . . offer us any clues to the nature of the consciousness that was expressed through the 'duality' in question"—that is, the duality of class and communal identities.[8] He notes three mechanisms that figure prominently for materialists. The first is employers' promotion of workers' religious identities as part of a divide-and-conquer strategy. Though embarrassed at having to introduce a "crude theory of manipulation and conspiracy," he admits that employers did commonly, and often actively, resort to such devices.[9] Chakrabarty then observes, correctly, that employers' promotion of religious identities could not, by itself, have sufficed to implant these identities so firmly in workers' consciousness. Why did the workers not reject the traditional attachments and values that were being fostered in this fashion? The typical materialist answer, suggests Chakrabarty, is that other facts about workers' conditions made them easy targets for the employers' promotion of religion. Two such factors, which were closely intertwined, were the condition of the labor market and the importance of kinship networks for workers' material well-being.

The salient fact about the labor market was the oversupply of laborers. Jute workers were mostly unskilled and easily expendable. This made their work low-paid and their subsistence precarious. Workers therefore used whatever ties they had available to increase the likelihood of secure employment, to hold on to their jobs, and to eke out a living in spite of the pitiful wages. For the securing of employment, ties of region and kin proved very important. By the 1920s, most workers in the jute mills were migrant laborers who came to Calcutta from other districts or from the neighboring states of Bihar and the

---

5   Chakrabarty, *Rethinking Working-Class History*, 193.
6   Ibid., 194.
7   Ibid., 196–8.
8   Ibid., 198.
9   Ibid., 198–200.

United Provinces. But in making their journey, they did not treat it as a leap into the dark, because in order to reduce the uncertainty involved in seeking employment in a distant city, migrants relied on family members or on community members employed as labor recruiters for the jute mills. These recruiters, known as sardars, spoke their language and were typically of the same religion.[10] Sardars used their religious and regional links to provide cheap labor to the jute mills, and workers relied on their ties to the sardars to gain some sort of livelihood in a cutthroat labor market. Help from the sardars complemented the more common instrument for finding employment: the migrants' village and kinship networks. As has been the case everywhere else in the world, migrants in eastern India relied first and foremost on friends and family to find gainful employment in their new city.

The precariousness of employment meant that the ties of kin and community figured importantly not merely for finding jobs but for everyday survival beyond the workplace. Workers depended on temples and mosques, on their charity and their utility for expanding the workers' own social networks. In addition to their primary reliance on family and community, workers relied on the sardars for many necessities besides just a job. Sardars were a source for emergency loans and cheap housing, as well as for employment stability and for organizing the defense of their jobs against rival communities—sometimes through violent clashes with other workers. Indeed, sardars often built temples and mosques to serve the migrants of their communities, which in turn became sources for the supply of so many of the necessities described above.[11] Thus, the structure of the labor market—its oversupply, low remuneration, and high turnover—elevated the importance of kin and community for the worker. Cultural ties were reinforced in the looming presence of the sardar and in the temple/mosque complex, both of which became a crucial site of social support.

The importance of these traditional *ties*—of kin, language, and religion—is taken by many historians as a critical source of workers' attachment to traditional *identities*. This is what explains, to them, why workers were vulnerable to employers' divide-and-conquer strategies and to communal violence more generally.

8.2 chakrabarty's alternative to the conventional analysis

Chakrabarty acknowledges that workers relied on ethnic and religious networks for their material well-being. In other words, he fully endorses the view that workers depended on their traditional social ties for their reproduction. Yet he insists that this reliance on traditional ties cannot *explain* why workers remained

---

10   Ibid., 96–7, 111.
11   Ibid., 111–12

attached to their religious identities. His reservations do not rest on an empirical disagreement; he has no quibble with the description of traditional ties or of their role in workers' reproduction. His rejection stems from a metatheoretical injunction: that the explanation based on workers' material well-being is inadequate because any acceptable explanation must be couched in terms of the agents' culture. Any explanation that refers to workers' well-being or to their material interests, Chakrabarty insists, "empties 'culture' of all specific content." He continues:

> Serving the "needs of survival" is a function universal to all cultures in all historical settings. This functionalist logic can never be a guide to the internal logic of a culture, the way it constructs and uses its "reason" . . . The ties of kinship, religion, language, or race were of course of much economic and material utility to the jute worker. But to see in this "utility" the workers' *reason* for valuing and retaining these bonds is to invest the jute worker with a *bourgeois rationality*, since it is only in such a system of rationality that the "economic utility" of an action . . . defines its reasonableness.[12]

This is a challenging passage. Chakrabarty does not explicate why the utility of a certain set of ties cannot constitute a motivation for reproducing them. But he clearly suggests it cannot. What is more, his doubts stem from having taken a metatheoretical position on the relationship between culture and action, and this position inclines Chakrabarty to discount the possibility that workers' material interests, or their needs, could have served as reasons for their choices. To make headway, we will have to reconstruct what his underlying theory of action might be.

This is what Chakrabarty seems to be saying: Explanations of social action are obliged to reconstruct agents' reasons for their actions. These reasons are based on agential beliefs, both descriptive and normative, about their social world—their conception of their social surroundings, about what is good, what is bad, what is desirable, what ought to be avoided. But such beliefs are centrally shaped by the agents' socialization into a particular culture.[13] The grounds on which choices are made are, in this sense, *internal* to the culture into which they have been socialized. Hence, if historians are to seek out the reasons for agents' choices, they have no alternative but to decode the "internal logic of a culture," since it is this logic that shapes agential reasoning. Consequently, arguments that appeal to "utility" are problematic. They rely on the notion that agents make choices based on the likely effect of these choices on their material

---

12   Ibid., 211–12. Emphasis added.
13   For an analysis of ideology in this vein, see Göran Therborn, *The Ideology of Power and the Power of Ideology* (London: Verso, 1980).

well-being.[14] To Chakrabarty, the problem is that such an approach has to *impute* reasons to them rather than explore how a culture "constructs and uses its 'reason.'" Materialist explanations thus force agency into a universalist logic, instead of respecting the fact that it is locally situated understandings that motivate action. Call this the argument from *internalism*.[15]

We now seem to have an idea why Chakrabarty dismisses materialist or structural explanations for the jute workers' choices. This raises the next question: if considerations of physical well-being have no relevance to workers' attachment to their traditional social ties, what does? Based on the preceding discussion, the answer will have to be aspects of their culture—since it is their culture that generates their reasons. Unfortunately, here too Chakrabarty offers an exceedingly cryptic defense of his view. His basic proposition is that workers clung to their religious filiations because

> [they] acted out of an understanding *that was pre-bourgeois in its elements.* It was not that they did not value things economic: poverty itself would have often brought home to the worker the value of money. Yet the "economic utility" and the "reasonableness" of an action were different categories, the former often subsumed under the latter.[16]

The central point of this passage is that the workers' choices were motivated by a certain kind of normative orientation—what Chakrabarty calls their prebourgeois consciousness. This prebourgeois consciousness gave primacy to particular values and, as a result, drove workers to support whichever social institutions were most closely aligned with these values. The two that Chakrabarty sees as central are notions of *community* and *honor.*[17] For the Indians working in the jute mills, what mattered above all was to defend their conceptions of honor and dignity and to reproduce their ties of community. The high valuation of these norms had two important ramifications. First, it meant that

---

14   Utility does not, of course, have to refer to the effect of a choice on material well-being. Formally, utility maximization just refers to the condition that agents pursue things that they value—which can just as likely be nonmaterial ends. They can relate to welfare enhancement or to the pursuit of normatively sanctioned desires of the kind Chakrabarty has in mind. Since he clearly refers to utility in a pejorative sense, he must have the narrower, welfare-enhancing definition in mind, not the formal one.

15   Although I refer to Chakrabarty's position as "internalist," it should not be confused with the well-known defense of internal reasons proposed by Bernard Williams. There are some surface resemblances, to be sure, insofar as Williams, like Chakrabarty, does suppose that a reason for action must be consistent with the agents' own set of subjective preferences. But Williams's position does not rule out needs as potential reasons for action, as does Chakrabarty's. See Bernard Williams, "Internal and External Reasons," in Williams, *Moral Luck* (Cambridge: Cambridge University Press, 1981), 101–13.

16   Chakrabarty, *Rethinking Working-Class History*, 212.

17   Ibid., 212–14.

"distinctions based on birth—religion, language, kinship—were central to the jute-mill workers' sense of identity."[18] This is another way of saying that they were *naturally disposed* to value their traditional social ties. Second, of all the conventions that appealed to these groups, "religion was . . . *perhaps the strongest* source of a notion of 'community' and, therefore, of a sense of identity and honor as well."[19] The argument here is very much in line with the one espoused by Partha Chatterjee: workers' politics could not have been governed by their interests because their normative orientation precluded that possibility. A prebourgeois consciousness revolved around the notion of community and *obligations* to that community. This is how the "internal logic of a culture" explains the choices that workers make.

Contrast this orientation with one that is typical of a "bourgeois consciousness." For workers imbued with this second kind of orientation, it is possible to act in accordance with their individual interests. What makes it possible is that bourgeois culture is centered around concepts of equality and citizenship. The emergence of these norms is accompanied by the creation of a distinct public sphere, and the relegation of religion to the domain of the private. Politics thus becomes anchored to the public sphere, in which individuals interact as juridical equals and are therefore able to conceptualize themselves as distinct entities, separate from the community and with interests of their own. Correspondingly, the traditional norms associated with religion are reproduced in a distinct plane of social interaction—the private. That is the process by which bourgeois consciousness enables workers to recognize, and appreciate, their material interests. The Indian worker, by contrast, lacked these cultural resources:

> Unlike in the case of the "citizen," the jute worker's political culture, *lacking any bourgeois notions of equality of the individual*, had not split him into his "public" and "private" selves; and he had not, unlike the citizen, relegated all "the distinctions based on birth" to the sphere of the "private" . . . In this sense, *the jute-mill worker had never been "politically" emancipated from religion*. Religion, therefore— or we could say, ethnicity, or language or other similar loyalties—formed the stuff of his politics.[20]

So long as he was not politically emancipated from religion, the worker could not be expected to act on his interests, because to do so presumed a capacity to prioritize interests over commitments—which the workers in India lacked.

It follows that, until Indian workers were politically emancipated from religion—until, that is, they were schooled in a properly bourgeois culture—they

---

18   Ibid., 217.
19   Ibid., 213. Emphasis added.
20   Ibid., 217.

would not have the psychological resources to translate their interests into reasons for action. Notice that this raises an interesting puzzle for Chakrabarty: Whence would this culture come? It seems unlikely that it would emerge from the workers' own consciousness, since that consciousness actively reproduced the very ties that precluded the emergence of interest-based action. This is why, claims Chakrabarty, even after a decades-long process of industrialization in the environs of Calcutta, working-class culture revolved around communal and ethnic ties. Chakrabarty makes this argument in his concluding statement about the jute mill workers' consciousness. So, even though jute mill workers showed signs of being aware of their commonalities with other workers, and even though they sometimes acted on their common interests,

> in the jute worker's mind itself, the incipient awareness of belonging to a class remained a *prisoner of his precapitalist culture*; the class identity *could never be distilled out of* the precapitalist identities that arose from the relationship that he had been *born into*."[21]

As depicted by Chakrabarty, this was not a situation in which the workers' experience in the mills gradually imbued them with a sense of their interests and hence the ability to act on their needs. To the contrary, their prebourgeois consciousness set limits on the lessons they could take away from their experience. The language here is striking—workers were *prisoners* of their precapitalist identities; newer identities would be nothing more than *distillations* of the earlier ones. Hence, a prior transformation of their culture would be required before workers could become politically emancipated from religion, and for their needs and interests to become part of their motivational set.

On the basis of this argument, Chakrabarty permits himself a series of observations reminiscent of Chatterjee's highly Orientalist description of Indian peasants. Workers elevated community over individual interests; they "underplayed any idea of the individuality of the person";[22] they were "lacking any bourgeois notions of the equality of the [sic] individual";[23] "religion . . . —or we could say, ethnicity, language or other similar loyalties—formed the stuff of [their] politics."[24] So imbued with this religiosity were they that "events that historians often regard as 'trivial' " could spark violent religious conflicts.[25] Indians are thus trapped within their religiosity. They lack any concept of individuality, are inured to hierarchy, and remain unmoved by calls for equality. They can erupt into orgies of violence at the slightest provocation. Their

---

21   Ibid., 218. Emphasis added.
22   Ibid., 216.
23   Ibid., 217.
24   Ibid.
25   Ibid., 215.

consciousness is "split" between the modern and the traditional. And so on.[26] Chakrabarty unloads these bromides without even a hint of self-consciousness, without any recognition of their affiliation with traditional colonial ideology. But let us set aside these concerns for now. The dubious lineage of Chakrabarty's views does not, in itself, make them wrong; furthermore, we must acknowledge that they have found an incredibly friendly audience in American academia. We therefore need to address them on their empirical and theoretical merits.

According to Chakrabarty, Calcutta workers' entrapment within a religious and communal orientation would not change until they were schooled in a properly bourgeois culture. So whence came this culture? What is the source of its emergence? Surprisingly, after arguing that workers' consciousness could not break out of its prison-house, Chakrabarty simply puts down his pen. He never tells the reader what might be the source of the new culture of rights and equality. The reason, I believe, is that he thinks the answer is obvious: indeed, it is the foundational premise of the entire Subaltern Studies project—that it is the *bourgeoisie* which forges the new culture of equality and citizenship. Once we accept this premise, his argument becomes plausible, and takes on an appealing symmetry. In the West, the bourgeoisie led the struggle against feudalism and forged a new culture of rights, equality and citizenship. The working class was the happy beneficiary of this transformation, and in the process, was "politically emancipated from religion." Having been socialized into a culture of equality and citizenship, it was able to acquire the psychological resources needed for a politics based on interests. In the East, however, because capital had abandoned its universalizing mission, the bourgeoisie failed to bring about the cultural revolution experienced in the West. Workers were deprived of a proper bourgeois culture and were thus unable to consign distinctions based on birth to the private sphere. They remained prisoners of their prebourgeois consciousness, which therefore set limits on their ability to engage in the new politics of class and party.

The problem, of course, is that the foundational premise is gravely mistaken. As I showed in preceding chapters, it was not the bourgeoisie that brought about the culture of equality and citizenship. For those tropes to become part of the national cultures of Europe took more than two centuries of struggle by the

---

26   Four excellent critiques of Chakrabarty on this matter are worth mentioning. Sumit Sarkar, "Orientalism Revisited: Saidian Frameworks in the Writing of Modern Indian History," *Oxford Literary Review* 16:1–2 (1994), 205–24, is a wide-ranging essay on the Subaltern project more widely, in which he places some emphasis on their repackaged Orientalism. A less well-known, but very effective, demonstration and rebuttal of Chakrabarty's Orientalism is by the late Rajnarayan Chandavarkar, " 'The Making of the Working Class': E. P. Thompson and Indian History," *History Workshop* 43 (Spring 1997), 177–96. See also Amiya Kumar Bagchi's superb review essay on *Rethinking Working-Class History*, "Working-Class Consciousness," in *Economic and Political Weekly* 25:30 (Jul. 28, 1990), PE54–60; and Nandini Gooptu's excellent *The Politics of the Urban Poor in Early Twentieth-Century India* (Cambridge: Cambridge University Press, 2001), 185–91.

very groups that, on Chakrabarty's logic, ought to have been mired in a "pre-bourgeois consciousness," and hence incapable of fighting for their interests—workers, artisans, and peasants.

So now we face a difficulty. If workers led the movements that brought about modern democratic culture, how could they do so if they lacked the appropriate psychological resources? The long-standing demands for political equality and individual rights, central to labor struggles since the seventeenth century, now appear to be rather mysterious. The alternative, however unnerving it may be, is that Chakrabarty's entire argument about the relation between interests and reasons is flawed. Perhaps workers in the West were indeed capable of recognizing and acting upon their interests, even while being steeped in a traditional culture. If that is true, we might expect that Indian workers, too, might be similarly capable. And if they do have such a capacity, then Chakrabarty cannot rule out the possibility that when they clung to their traditional networks, they did so *because* of those networks' importance to their well-being.

The rest of this chapter shows that Chakrabarty is indeed mistaken in his rejection of materialism. I will show that actors are quite capable of appreciating their interests, even while imbued with their traditional culture. In so doing, I will, as in the previous chapter, draw on Chakrabarty's own evidence. But my defense of the materialist explanation will not presume a rejection of internalism. Instead, I will argue that a defense of the role of objective needs and interests can be made even if we insist that such needs have to be perceived as culturally mediated desires. Chakrabarty can therefore maintain his internalist credentials, even while recognizing the motivational force of workers' objective needs. The problem is that his view about the relation between interests, culture, and agency is based on a series of quite severe misconceptions.

8.3 REASONS AND INTERESTS

Chakrabarty's argument rests on a contrast between interests and reasons. His view is that agency must be motivated by reasons, and interests cannot be reasons. This is because reasons have to be based on beliefs, wants, values, and so on, all of which are culturally constructed. They are, therefore, *internal* to a culture. Interests, on the other hand, derive their explanatory power from their connection to agents' supposed *needs*. Chakrabarty takes needs to refer to baseline necessities for physical well-being—the need for physical safety, for food and water, for shelter. His view is that whereas beliefs and desires are internal to a culture, needs are not.

The idea that needs are *not* internal to *a* culture can be understood in two ways: first, it can be taken to mean that they are universal in scope, being common to many cultures; second, it can mean that they are not culturally constructed at all—they operate independently of culture. So, needs could be ruled out as reasons either because they are culturally constructed but not unique to a given culture, or because they are not cultural constructions at all.

The ambiguity of Chakrabarty's language leaves open the possibility that he objects on both counts to needs being cited as an explanatory mechanism. On the one hand, he says they are "common to all cultures" and immediately counter-poses this to *genuine* reasons, which emanate from the "internal logic" of *a* culture. He seems to be contrasting reasons that arise across cultures with reasons that arise from dynamics internal to a particular culture. This suggests that for reasons to be operative as needs, they have to be culturally *specific*. But Chakra-barty also appears to maintain that needs are not cultural *at all*. The idea here seems to be that if reasons must be based on culturally constructed beliefs and desires, then to say that needs *as such* are reasons is illegitimate, because reasons cannot be described independently of culture. What motivates agents is not needs per se, but needs as encoded through their culture. So, at best, needs-based expla-nations are incomplete and, at worst, deeply misleading, because unless we know in what culturally constructed manner agents experience them as genuine desires, we cannot be certain that needs are capable of motivating actions. Since it is unclear which version Chakrabarty believes, we will have to examine both.

MUST INTERNAL REASONS BE CULTURALLY SPECIFIC?

First objections first: let us consider the notion that a motivation—any moti-vation—cannot count as a reason if it is common to many cultures. It is hard to believe that anyone could seriously raise this as an objection, but since Chakrabarty is so obscure, we are forced to raise it as a possibility. The basic problem with this argument is that it equates a reason's being *internal* to a culture with its being *specific* to that culture. Surely this is unwarranted. When agents are motivated to undertake a particular action—say, to leave their village and look for employment in a nearby city—they do so because they think there are good reasons for doing so. These reasons are causally relevant insofar as they impel the agents to undertake the action. When an agent considers her reason for an action, she judges its motivational force on how closely it aligns her goals with the strategy that the reason recommends. She says, "Living here in my village will not provide me with the resources I need to survive, whereas finding a job in Calcutta probably will. This seems like a good reason to pack up and leave for Calcutta, and try to find employment in the mills there." But Chakrabarty seems to be urging that we hold off accept-ing such a motivation—acquiring the resources needed for survival—as a genuine reason. For him to permit it to count as a reason, we would also have to show that such a motive is *uniquely Bihari*. So, if workers in France were confronted with similar circumstances, their reasoning would have to be different. Now we begin to see how bizarre this demand from Chakrabarty is. Surely all we can reasonably require is that reasons we impute to the agent be described in in a manner recognizable by them. To demand that reasons also be unique to an individual's culture seems outlandish.

So a reason can be internal to a particular culture while also being common to other cultures. This means we can accept the argument from internalism but deny Chakrabarty's conclusion. In other words, we can agree that reasons should be sought in agents' desires but deny that the desires must be unique to their culture. Those same basic desires might be internal to other cultures as well, and in that respect could be more universally operative, but that does not make them any less internal to *this particular* culture. Thus, the grounds on which Chakrabarty rejected structural explanations for workers' attachment to their religious or ethnic ties may now themselves be rejected. We can therefore be internalists about reasons but also accept the structural explanation.

CAN NEEDS FUNCTION AS REASONS AT ALL?

It is unlikely that Chakrabarty really adheres to the objection I examined above. So let us turn to the second objection, which rules out interest-based explanations on the grounds that agents' needs are being defined *independent* of culture. Can needs, defined in some culturally neutral way, stand in as reasons at all? Chakrabarty says we have no grounds to believe that they can, unless and until we understand how they are filtered through the local culture.

Two concerns are at work here. The first is that even if needs exist, they cannot motivate action until actors consciously perceive them as desires—and all desires must be perceived through the local cultural codes, as part of the norms or values that actors find meaningful. Second, there is a concern that the reasons ascribed to the actors might simply reflect the prejudices of the analyst—she might be imputing to the actors reasons that they could never have held. When we impute to workers a certain motivation, which we explain by reference to their circumstances, Chakrabarty enjoins us to ask, "is the consciousness that informs this observation the same as the jute worker's consciousness?"[27] I take Chakrabarty's challenge here to be an expression of the concern that the analyst is imputing a set of motives to the worker that the latter might not have had. To guard against this possibility, we are urged to uncover the desires and beliefs that the worker actually had when she made her choices. The anxiety about needs-based explanations thus issues from two distinct but related sources.

The first question to tackle is whether Chakrabarty agrees that there are any basic needs at all. To his credit, Chakrabarty does not join the chorus of

---

27 Dipesh Chakrabarty, "Rethinking Working-Class History," *Economic and Political Weekly* 26:17 (Apr. 27, 1991), 1118. This piece is his response to Amiya Kumar Bagchi's criticisms in his review cited above (186 n26), which are for the most part correct. Unfortunately, Chakrabarty evades most of the points Bagchi raises. It is doubly unfortunate because this is one of the few occasions when Chakrabarty even tries to respond to criticisms from outside the postcolonial camp.

theorists who deny their very existence. We do find hints that he is uneasy about it—he expresses some reservations about the "essentialist presuppositions regarding 'human nature' " that seem to underlie a commitment to needs.[28] But he is quite clear that when workers went to the city in order to find employment, they did so because they were driven by a basic concern for their well-being. As he observes, "in a life characterized by poverty and insecurity of work, a laborer's *need for economic and physical support* from kin (real or putative) and linguistic or religious community extended far beyond the stage of obtaining employment."[29] Or again: "The ties of language, religion, or village thus served the worker well in regard to *his need* for accommodation and shelter."[30] And "the structure of the labor market was such that the ties of language, religion, or kinship . . . *had a practical and economic utility* to the worker in his struggle for survival in the face of poverty and insecurity."[31] He gives the example of a female migrant named Mia, "whose *existence depended* to a large extent on the material assistance she received from her coreligionists."[32] In all these passages, Chakrabarty recognizes that workers had real needs, and he describes them in culturally neutral language. The needs—for physical support, for accommodation and shelter—do not emanate from peculiarities of Indian culture. These are not culturally constructed drives, and Chakrabarty clearly sees them as independent of the culture.

Chakrabarty, then, does not believe that all needs are purely cultural constructions. [33] He takes seriously social agents' objective need to protect their physical well-being. The next question to arise is whether these needs can serve as sources of motivation for the agents. The difficulty for Chakrabarty here is that once we admit to the *reality* of basic needs, the grounds on which to *deny* their motivational power become shaky. Our confidence that agents will be sensitive to their basic physical needs requires no heroic assumptions about their cognitive abilities, nor does it involve imputing to them a "bourgeois consciousness." It is a precondition to any culture that the social actors who comprise it have found means of sustaining themselves. If agents do not perceive the need to find subsistence, then the elementary precondition for the culture's existence has not been met. Hence, every culture must have codes through which agents can recognize their basic needs as desires—for it to fail in this regard would consign the culture itself to oblivion. It follows that basic needs not only *can* become reasons, but they *must* become reasons. This means, in

28 Chakrabarty, *Rethinking Working-Class History*, 211.
29 Ibid., 208. Emphasis added.
30 Ibid., 210. Emphasis added.
31 Ibid., 211. Emphasis added.
32 Ibid. Emphasis added.
33 See also Chakrabarty's response to Bagchi, "Working-Class Consciousness," where he affirms the reality of "economic factors," by which he means basic needs.

turn, that there is nothing particularly "bourgeois" about the mental state that orients human beings toward their basic well-being.

The upshot of the preceding argument is that at least some basic needs *can* be assumed to generate codes appropriate to their protection. If so, we can also assume that the needs can serve as a motive for action, even if we insist that all motives have to be perceived through the lens of culture. Agents will understand their needs as reasons for action, since they will recognize the needs through whatever discursive scheme is available to them. *Pace* Chakrabarty, in order to cite needs as reasons for action, we do not have to know *how* a culture turns these needs into reasons. We will be justified in *imputing* to the agents the codes in which they probably felt their needs as real desires. When social actors are observed to be in situations where their basic well-being is threatened, and if we observe that they resort to a particular strategy that has the effect of increasing their chances of survival, then we can justifiably ascribe to them a mental state—of having a *reason*—that would have motivated them to adopt this survival strategy. We can, in other words, infer that they undertook that action because they had *good reason* to do so.

Take the example of Mia, the jute worker "whose existence depended to a large extent on the material assistance she received from her coreligionists."[34] Suppose it was learned that Mia placed great value on her ties to her coreligionists and sustained her ties with them during her tenure in the jute mills. We would have to impute to her a mental state—some complex of reasons—that we think would connect the material importance of these ties to her decision to sustain them. Chakrabarty's worry is that the desires she actually perceived may not have been the ones we ascribe to her, and in ascribing them to her, we might be projecting our own preferences onto her consciousness. Now, this is *formally* true—but is it likely? More important, would it be typical? The motive we ascribe to her is something like, "My ties with these people are my lifeline while I work in the jute mills. If I break these ties, I lose my most important source of material support. It makes sense, therefore, for me to maintain my relations with them." Is it unreasonable to assume that Mia might have had reasons of this kind, given what we know about her? Merely posing the question shows how strange it is. Mia has a choice between turning away from social ties that, by Chakrabarty's own description, are the key to her very survival, and accepting those ties as valuable to her. If she did *not* agree that there was good reason to attach value to these ties, we would have grounds to think that there was something terribly wrong with her—that she was suffering from some kind of cognitive failure.

Hence, even when we do not know the particular codes in which needs translate into desires, we can infer that some such translation took place. We only have to be confident that the actors would recognize and comprehend the

34   Chakrabarty, *Rethinking Working-Class History*, 210.

reasons we impute to them, and would, if they had the opportunity, validate those reasons as more or less accurate.[35] Even though Mia may not have thought about her decision in exactly the terms I have described, I just need to be confident that, were she to come upon my description, she would take it as a legitimate construal of her reasoning. She would deem it so even though we are separated by a century of historical development, because the reasons that I ascribe to her are not especially complex, nor are they particular to her local culture. Precisely because they relate to some very basic needs, they belong to a family of reasons that could be understood across every culture. The reasons will therefore be internal to every culture.

We must conclude, then, that a structural or materialist explanation for workers' attachment to their traditional ties can be accepted by anyone who hews to internalist principles. Thus, Chakrabarty is entirely justified in observing that an agent's reasons have to be perceived in codes that are internal to his culture; his error is that he thinks the codes required by the structural explanation would be alien to Calcutta's jute workers. Quite the contrary: the reasons that his interlocutors impute to the workers would be as recognizable to them as they are to us.

8.4 INTERESTS AND CULTURE

We have now seen that there is every reason to believe that members of the laboring classes in India were capable of recognizing and acting upon their individual interests; and that despite Subaltern theorists' endorsement of cultural essentialism, their own evidence shows this to have been the case. This leaves us with a sense that interests do count as causal and as explanatory factors in social agency, whatever the cultural background of the agents might be. For many students of the East, this sort of assertion generates considerable anxiety. It seems to veer toward the image of the asocial individual, hovering above his

---

35   This is an important point. In historical research, the analyst is never in a position to know the conscious mental state of any actor whom she is studying. It is hard enough to discover in ethnographic work and interviews, and far more so when the only sources available are stray letters or second-party reports. This means that recovering the meaning orientation of any action cannot be a simple inductive enterprise. The meaning of the action—and its motivation—must be imputed to the agent by the analyst, based on the information available to her. It is, and has to be, an inference. This constraint has been recognized by the central theorists of the *Verstehen* tradition in sociology, as well as by many proponents of hermeneutics. Their proposed solution is that the reasons must be ones that the actor *would have recognized* as valid, given her cultural conditioning and the information available to her. Hence, even if the language in which we reconstruct her reasoning is not the precise one that she used, it ought to be one that she would have validated or would have recognized as legitimate. Alfred Schutz refers to this principle as the *postulate of adequacy*; see Schutz, *Collected Papers I: The Problem of Social Reality* (London: Kluwer/Springer, 1974), 43–4, and *Collected Papers II: Studies in Social Theory* (London: Kluwer/Springer, 1976), 85–6.

culture, ranking his preferences, and remorselessly disposing of social relations as they lose value on his utility meter. Arguments like those made by Chatterjee and Chakrabarty, which reject the relevance of interests, casting them as instances of "bourgeois consciousness," fit with a widespread suspicion that interest-based explanations abide by an impoverished conception of social agency. I have already shown that reference to needs or rationality need not efface agents' cultural commitments, but it is likely that the arguments offered thus far will be deemed insufficient unless they are backed up by a more general account of culture and rationality. So, in this section, I will try to allay such concerns by offering a summary of the underlying conception of agency that is at work in my argument, in hopes of showing that the recognition of interests does not amount to a rejection of culture. It does, however, require that we accept the *limits* of culture as a source of agency.

Two objections often figure prominently in criticisms of materialist explanations. The first has to do with how agents make their choices, the second with the goals they pursue. On the first issue, critics charge that the assumption of rationality seems to treat agents as *asocial*. Treating agents as rational seems to imply that they can step out of their cultures and make decisions based on a neutral, unchanging algorithm. Both Chatterjee and Chakrabarty were, at least in part, motivated by this concern. Both of them placed great stress on the cultural subjectivity of their agents, contrasting it with the asocial rationality imputed by materialist theories. The second objection is that ascribing material interests to non-Western people unduly universalizes a Western conception of the self and of social interaction, making the assumption a carrier of parochialism, even of cultural imperialism. Chatterjee and Chakrabarty offer the heavily socialized, culturally constructed agent as an antidote to the parochialism of Western theories. As I will show, both objections are unfounded.

ASOCIAL INDIVIDUALS

Let us start with the notion that the assumption of rationality requires agents to be placed outside their cultures or belief systems. Imputing rationality to actors requires, so the argument goes, that we treat them as largely asocial, responding to every situation by taking out their utility calculator, tallying up the cost-benefit ratio of every available option, and then picking out the one with the highest payoff. Preference-enhancing relations and institutions are maintained, while preference-blocking ones, or even those that are suboptimal for the realization of preferences, are rejected. However, argue the critics who dispute rationality, individual agents do not go through their day as choice-making machines. They do not pick and choose their norms, nor do they assess their social relations on a utility scale.

There are two related but distinct points that critics make in this regard. The first is that people's identities are not the product of their choices; rather, having an identity, a set of cultural dispositions, is the precondition to exercising any choices at all.[36] The second point is that materialist theories vastly overstate the role of choice in social reproduction. Most people live their lives as a series of routines, which they practice as a matter of habit, on norms that they have internalized.[37]

There is considerable merit in this criticism of rationality. As a behavioral fact, it is certainly true that people do not stop and ponder the cost-benefit ratio of every interaction they undertake. Habit and routine govern most people's daily lives, in which their beliefs, values, and obligations are treated as givens, as parameters, not variables. Yet it is possible to overstate the weight of values and routine. Part of being a social agent is to have the capacity for reflection and introspection, and this capacity incorporates the beliefs and values we have internalized, as well as the demands made on us by our social arrangements. As the ethnomethodological tradition in sociology has stressed, while actors do go through daily life mostly following conventions and habits, even this somewhat routinized process takes considerable imagination.[38] Roles must be interpreted, minute variations in routines necessitate adjustments, and every now and then, the very grounds on which norms are accepted might come under scrutiny. At the very least, agents practice a reflexive monitoring of their daily interactions;[39] at other times, they initiate what Margaret Archer refers to as an "inner conversation" about their received roles and beliefs—a more active, conscious rumination on the reasons behind their actions, their legitimacy, possible alternatives, and so on.[40] This kind of active reflection is especially likely when agents feel pulled in different directions, as when they are

---

36 See Michael Taylor, *Rationality and the Ideology of Disconnection* (Cambridge: Cambridge University Press, 2006).

37 The strongest version of this argument, developed by Talcott Parsons, has very few defenders today. But the role of habit is also prominent in John Dewey's theory of action. See his discussion in *Human Nature and Conduct: An Introduction to Social Psychology* (New York: Henry Holt, 1922), pt. 1 *passim*.

38 The central figure in American ethnomethodology, stressing the interpretive vigor of social reproduction, is Harold Garfinkel. See Garfinkel, *Studies in Ethnomethodology* (New York: Prentice Hall, 1967). The active, problem-solving component of agency also figures prominently in recent sociological theories of a more pragmatic bent, such as Mustafa Emirbayer and Anne Mische, "What is Agency?" *American Journal of Sociology* 103:4 (Jan. 1998), 962–1023.

39 The phrase was introduced into social theory by Anthony Giddens in his *Central Problems in Social Theory: Action, Structure and Contradiction in Social Analysis* (Cambridge: Cambridge University Press, 1979).

40 See Margaret S. Archer, *Being Human: The Problem of Agency* (Cambridge: Cambridge University Press, 2000), 222–49. In her more recent work, she grounds the argument for an inner conversation in an empirical research design. See Archer, *Structure, Agency, and the Internal Conversation* (Cambridge: Cambridge University Press, 2003). Archer has been influenced by Roy Bhaskar's philosophical work on critical realism, and it bears mention that her books, like Bhaskar's, are not for the faint of heart. Both theorists indulge in a turgid expository style, with a seemingly endless stream of neologisms. But underneath it all are some interesting arguments.

subject to conflicting demands or when the demands on them run up against their own perceived needs and desires.

To engage in an inner dialogue of this kind is to seek a rationale for one's actions. It is an attempt to extract justifiable *reasons* for the kinds of interactions we engage in or the demands being placed on us. But doing so opens up the possibility that whatever reasons the agent discovers might not be deemed sufficient. The very act of reflection presupposes that the agent can distinguish between good and bad reasons for action. And if the reasons are deemed insufficient, she could very well decide not to accept them, even though they have the sanctity of tradition or the backing of political authority. So while we can acknowledge the importance of norms and habit, it is important to resist the notion that human agents are nothing other than bearers of social relations, or *Träger*, as Althusser famously insisted.[41] They do reproduce their social relations, but they also have the capacity to resist the roles assigned to them and even, on some occasions, to change them. Cultures, after all, are not only reproduced, but are also transformed.

I have tried to show that this sort of agential reflexivity is no less operative in the East than it is in the West. For evidence, we need look no further than the Subalternist collective's own findings. In Guha's history of peasant insurgency, which we examined in the previous chapter, he does not in the least deny that peasants were immersed in a distinct assemblage of roles and normative entanglements. Indeed, he affirms that they were powerfully shaped by their culture, and that this culture imbued them with deep-seated mutuality. But Guha does not take this as a preconstructed, unalterable datum about peasant psychology. In his account, peasants reproduced their roles, but not passively. They were capable of reflecting on the demands being made by their community—the appeals to their sense of obligation—and distinguishing between reasonable and unreasonable demands. The call to rebellion against massive power centers, which would involve great risk, was deemed by many peasants to be an unreasonable demand. The weeks-long deliberation that ensued was nothing other than their leaders working to persuade them to abide by their duties. It was a plea to extend their sense of communal obligation to this new and highly dangerous group endeavor. And in many cases, even after considerable effort by the community leaders, families remained unconvinced. When peasants called

---

41   Althusser's highly influential characterization drew on Marx's preface to vol. I of *Capital*, in which Marx announced that he would treat capitalists only as personifications of the function of capital—not as real agents with real needs. What Marx used as an expository device, Althusser turned into an ontological orthodoxy. It was very effectively subjected to critique by Norman Geras, in his *Marx and Human Nature: Refutation of a Legend* (London: Verso, 1984). But the branch of Althusserianism that later morphed into poststructuralism never got the message. The continuing influence of Althusser on *Subaltern Studies* is palpable, both in their substantive commitments and in their style of theorizing.

for more deliberation and a stronger justification for the risks they were being asked to undertake, and when they contemplated refusal, they were making choices *about* their culture, even while being immersed *within* the culture.

Similarly, in Chatterjee's analysis, when peasants decided to usurp lands belonging to their neighbors and enrich themselves, they were doing so in spite of the general norms endorsing mutual sacrifice and solidarity. They could not accumulate more land for themselves without *rejecting* some of the norms into which they had been socialized. In so doing, they were making choices about their culture. And in Chakrabarty's analysis, when migrants came to the city, they constructed new communities when they became involved in trade unions or forged new social solidarities with migrants from other parts of the country. They showed themselves capable of forming a different cultural sensibility—organized around a more secular and economic axis—than the one into which they had been socialized. It is because they exhibited this capacity for adopting new identities that many historians see their attachment to regional or religious networks as a choice they made, a choice that must be explained—and it is a choice precisely because they showed that they were capable of opting for social networks of a quite different kind.

What all of these examples show is that agents have the capacity to reflect on, and even reject, aspects of their culture. At the very least, they show that we need not assume asocial individuals in order to allow for social choices. But the examples also show something more. In all of them, actors are not simply making choices about their norms, but are doing so on broadly similar grounds: they are choosing in a manner consistent with their material interests. To return to Guha's account, it is not just that peasants airily demand public deliberation as an end in itself. They call for a discussion because they are worried about what the call to arms will mean for their well-being. They make their choices after some discussion and reflection on how taking up arms will affect their individual interests. Similarly, Chakrabarty's migrant workers are aware that their attachment to their religious networks makes sense because it is crucial to their economic survival. Choices are, in these examples, made on clearly identifiable grounds—they seem to serve actors' material interests. And since many historians of the East are unnerved by this kind of talk, we must now turn our attention from the actors' capacity for choosing to the *ends* served by their choices.

THE PROBLEM OF INTERESTS

Are the grounds on which agents make their choices entirely constituted by the agent's culture, or are some goals independent of culture? If the former, then the mere fact that actors can make choices, as argued in the preceding section, does not get us very far from the kind of culturalism espoused by the Subalternists. Choices will be in pursuit of goals that are themselves generated by the culture; agents will thus reflect upon certain norms, as described above, but only by drawing on other elements of their normative ensemble. However, if there are some goals, some needs or interests, that are independent of culture, then we have the basis of a different and more materialist accounting of agency. In this case, agents will have the capacity to recognize instances in which their roles or norms are causing real harm—when their obligations are undermining their well-being. All the cases examined thus far seem to point toward Indian workers and peasants having just this sort of capacity, even though Chatterjee and Chakrabarty deny it. How demanding must our assumptions about rationality be, then, in order to make sense of these examples?

Arguments in defense of objective needs tend to enumerate those regarded as fundamental.[42] They describe the various needs that agents are presumed to have and then explain why we should accept those particular candidates. Here I will instead take a more conservative approach and simply defend *one* need, which seems operative in all the cases we have discussed in this chapter and the preceding one. I wish only to make the case that the thoroughgoing hostility evinced by Chatterjee and Chakrabarty to any talk of interests is unsustainable. In other words, I want only to demonstrate that *some* objective needs, and hence interests, do exist, and that agents can act in accordance with these interests. Just how *many* such interests, or needs, there is is of secondary importance. Enumerating them would add to my argument but would not change its basic thrust. I defend only one such need here because it is the one for which there is the most copious evidence in our case studies, and so it is the easiest to defend. Moreover, acknowledging the existence of even this one particular need has a rather remarkable payoff. It explains much of the political history we have covered throughout this book, and it enables us to tie together the political struggles of laboring classes in East and West as part of one—dare I say it—universal history.

The single objective need I wish to defend is the same one I have already examined: the simple need for physical well-being. By this I mean the need to ward off direct bodily harm by others and the need for a livelihood. That agents do have this interest, and that they typically act to defend it, is not only acknowledged by every theory of need; it is also at work in the Subalternists' own findings, even if they refuse to acknowledge it. It is the rationale for Guha's peasants' refusal to fall into line when their leaders issue the call for rebellion; it is the reason Chakrabarty's migrants leave the familiar setting of their village to seek employment in faraway Calcutta; it is why they try to minimize risk by relying on their kinship circles in the city; it is why Chatterjee's peasants accumulate land for

---

42   The most well-known such list is probably developed by Martha Nussbaum. See her "Human Functioning and Social Justice: In Defense of Aristotelian Essentialism," *Political Theory*, Vol. 20, No. 2 (May, 1992), 202–46. See also David Braybrooke, *Meeting Needs* (Princeton: Princeton University Press, 1987); Len Doyal and Ian Gough, *A Theory of Human Need* (New York: Guilford Press, 1991); Lawrence A. Hamilton, *The Political Philosophy of Needs* (Cambridge: Cambridge University of Press, 2003). For a defense, see Bernard Gert, "Rationality, Human Nature, and Lists," *Ethics* 100:2 (Jan., 1990), 279–300.

themselves when given the opportunity, since more land means greater security of their well-being;[43] it is why they resist rental demands from their landlords in times of dearth. In all these instances, Indian peasants and workers exhibited the capacity to think about their socialization and to reject certain of their cultural codes. We can now add this clarification: they rejected their codes when these codes undermined the conditions for their physical well-being. Agents made choices, to be sure, but what all of these choices had in common was that they were in defense of their physical security. The concern for basic well-being thus constituted the grounds on which the choices were made.[44]

The concern for well-being, we should note, does not amount to a maximizing strategy. To assume that agents are cognizant of, and defend, their physical well-being does not entail that they maximally advance their economic interests. When Chatterjee and Chakrabarty invoke the specter of a bourgeois consciousness to dispel any talk of interests, they trade on this elision. They suggest that if actors are allowed to be interest-sensitive, then they must also be relentlessly self-oriented. The former, however, does not entail the latter. It is certainly true that one particular version of interest-based theories, developed by neoclassical economists, takes actors to be maximizers of the kind that Chatterjee and others have in mind.[45] But this is a conception that is now widely rejected, even within

---

43   There are some grounds for arguing that the accumulation of property by the jotedars in Chatterjee's analysis can accommodate an even more stringent assumption: that actors are actually welfare maximizers. They usurp other peasants' land because they see it as an opportunity to advance their welfare, not out of a need to defend their basic security. I believe that this might be a mistaken inference. But even if it is true, it only strengthens the case for an interest-based explanation, since it accommodates a more stringent assumption. If agents can be welfare maximizers, then it already presumes they can be need-sensitive.

44   There is a subtlety here that bears mentioning. While all agents have an interest in their well-being, not all needs attached to their well-being can serve as motivators. Some needs are easily perceived, such as the need for food or the avoidance of pain. But there are needs which, though vital, do not manifest as urges. Lawrence Hamilton points to the need for exercise as an example. This is most certainly a real precondition for physical well-being, but agents do not perceive it as an urge, as a motivation to act. It is achieved as a side product of the pursuit of other interests. But there are times when it is not acquired at the needed levels, because agents do not feel compelled to respect its importance. Hence, not all basic needs can serve as reasons for action. But while this does force us to modulate our endorsement of basic needs as motivating agents, it does not change the basic argument. As long as there are *some* basic needs of the kind I have described, and these are perceived by agents as real, then they can serve as reasons. In the discussion that follows, readers should assume that when I refer to basic needs, it is this latter sort that I have in mind. For Hamilton's perceptive discussion of this matter, see his *Political Philosophy of Needs*, 27–31.

45   For a quick introduction to rational choice, two good places to start are Jon Elster, *Explaining Technical Change: A Case Study in the Philosophy of Science* (Cambridge: Cambridge University Press, 1983), chaps. 3, 4; and Elster, *Explaining Social Behavior: More Nuts and Bolts for the Social Sciences* (Cambridge: Cambridge University Press, 2007), chaps. 11, 12. Another excellent examination of rational choice theory, which also places it in the broader context of moral philosophy, is Daniel M. Hausman and Michael S. McPherson, *Economic Analysis, Moral Philosophy, and Public Policy* (Cambridge: Cambridge University Press, 2006). See especially chaps. 4, 5, 8, 9.

economics and certainly outside it. One prominent alternative has been to treat actors not as maximizers but as *satisficers*; in this view, actors do not choose strategies because they maximally advance their interests but because they are simply *consistent* with those interests. Choices are made not because they are the best possible ones but because they are good enough.[46] Hence, if, as satisficers, agents are taken to have an interest in their well-being, it does not imply that they seek out personal gain from every interaction, nor does it suggest that culture is just a cover for welfare maximization. It merely suggests that culture cannot extinguish people's regard for their basic survival needs.

In sum, for agents to be rational does not require that they be asocial automata, nor does it take them to be unrelenting hedonists. What I have defended is a stripped-down, minimal account of rationality, just enough to accommodate the empirical cases we have examined in the past two chapters. I have stayed close to the Subalternists' own historiography, since they believe that their findings cannot be accommodated within a conventional materialist framework. It is around these case studies that they build their theoretical arguments for the specificity of the East, for its peculiar modernity. They believe that the political culture they have uncovered is the product of a very different kind of psychology than the one assumed by Western theories. They also seem to believe that it is in fact different from the psychology of subaltern classes in the West.

One point in the Subalternists' favor, as theorists, is that they at least try to base their arguments on real evidence, unlike so many postcolonial theorists, for whom avoidance of evidence is something of a first principle. I have examined Guha's, Chatterjee's, and Chakrabarty's evidence with some care because it deserves to be taken seriously. What emerges is that their own historiography undermines their argument for Eastern uniqueness. There is simply no evidence that Indians were indifferent to their individual interests. What we have seen is that the laboring classes were no less capable of recognizing when their basic needs were threatened, and that they made choices intended to protect those needs. In other words, they took the protection of their needs as a reason for action. I have offered a theoretical framework intended to accommodate this fact about agency—its interest-sensitivity— while also recognizing that social agency is immersed in local cultures. Where my account differs from the Subalternists' is that it does not allow culture to extinguish a regard for one fundamental interest: the concern for physical well-being.

What remains is to assess the payoff from this minimalist version of rationality. Some materialists may well object that my having stripped down the

---

46 The classic work here is by Herbert A. Simon, who developed this conception while working on a theory of administration. See Simon, *Administrative Behavior* (New York: Free Press, 1976). For more up-to-date treatments, see Martin Hollis, *The Cunning of Reason* (Cambridge: Cambridge University Press, 1987); and Elster, *Explaining Social Behavior*.

content of agential interests to just one is far too concessive to culturalists. Surely the list of basic interests is longer than this, they may insist. I cannot disagree, but as I admitted earlier, my defense of well-being as a basic need is not intended to be a full theory of interests. Its purpose is simply to show that culture does not go "all the way down." Actors, even those in the Orient, are capable of judging their norms against at least *this* basic interest.

Now, once we establish that basic interests can cut into culture in this fashion, then of course we open the door to examinations of what other elements might be in the list. Such an examination is beyond the purview of this chapter. However, I do intend to show how far-reaching are the implications of the existence of even this *one* interest in physical well-being. Not only does it offer a basis for assimilating the struggles of popular classes in the East and in the West under the same rubric—the same Grand Narrative, as the Subalternists might say—but it can also account for many aspects of what they call bourgeois culture. In other words, the advent of a liberal, rights-based culture can be linked to popular struggles around the defense of basic needs, both East and West. And this makes it possible for us to explain what, in Chakrabarty's version of internalism, had emerged as so mysterious at the end of Section 8.2—the fact that Western workers fought for their "interests" even when they were immersed in a prebourgeois consciousness.

8.5 THE UNIVERSAL HISTORY OF CLASS STRUGGLE

Using the Subalternists' own evidence, we have arrived at the point of being able to cite at least one interest that seems valid even for supposedly otherworldly Indians—an interest in physical well-being. But does the existence of this interest motivate agents to democratize their social relations? One can see how an interest in physical well-being might induce labor to pursue greater *economic* gains for itself, but it is not so obvious how it can motivate the pursuit of more *political* rights. That would seem to require other interests—such as the need for autonomy or self-direction. So I have yet to demonstrate that agents in the East and West share a motivation to lessen their subjugation. What I need to show, then, is that having an interest in their physical well-being can also motivate agents toward political liberties. If I can do so, this will be a significant inroad into the Subalternist argument.

In chapters 5 and 6, I showed that, in their drive to maximize profits, employers across Europe resorted to political domination over their labor force. Market conditions demanded a certain intensity and duration of work for firms to remain viable; workers, on the other hand, offered a level of effort that they deemed consistent with their preferences, which typically fell short of what employers demanded. Employers therefore resorted to all forms of coercion, both institutional and interpersonal, to *induce* compliance from workers. All across the capitalist world, firms' profit-maximizing strategies relied critically on mechanisms of *political* control, both institutional and interpersonal—hence the promotion of contract labor, company towns, private militias, indentured labor, and so on at the micro level, and the disenfranchisement of labor at the macro level. All these measures were taken in order to further dominate workers, because the "dull compulsion of economic relations" was evidently insufficient to induce compliance with the desired intensity of work. The lesson here is that even though capital*ism* does not depend on extra-economic coercion for its reproduction, capital*ists* are happy to turn to it when and where they can.

The domination that workers experienced on the shop floor and beyond was not just an affront to their autonomy. It amounted to a direct assault on their well-being—long hours, brutal discipline, unsanitary work conditions, and crowded lodgings, all of which culminated in a tragically short life expectancy.[47] Workers thus had a direct interest in challenging managerial authority in the workplace. But because of the fusion between economic and political power outside the factory, they could not undertake an *economic* campaign without also confronting their own *political* disenfranchisement. What we take to be political rights—the legalization of trade unions, rights against police brutality, the banning of child labor, the ban on property qualifications for the franchise, the reform of master-servant laws—were rights demanded, in part, to enable workers to defend their basic physical well-being. As long as employers sought to tighten their economic control by relying on political mechanisms, labor had to embed its economic struggles within a series of far-reaching *political* campaigns.

The structural imperatives of capitalism make this no less true in the twentieth and twenty-first centuries than it was in the eighteenth and nineteenth. The fight for economic security has continued to require that attention be paid to political liberties as well, only because employers still seek to cement their economic domination with political control. This is most evident in the fast-growing "special economic zones" of the Global South, which are often "rights-free zones" for labor. But it is also the defining element of the political culture of entire geographical regions—northern Mexico, dominated by the maquiladoras; the export processing zones in China; the sweatshops of

---

47 Frederick Engels' *The Condition of the Working Class in England* (Oxford: Oxford University Press, 2003) chapters 5 and 6 remain still the classic account of the unbearable conditions of work. But this should be complemented with Marx's analysis in *Capital, Volume 1* (London: Pelican Books, 1978), Chapter 10. For superb recent scholarship on the consequences of employer domination on workers' well-being, see Anthony S. Wohl, *Endangered Lives: Public Health in Victorian Britain*, (Cambridge: Harvard University Press, 1983) and William Coleman, *Death Is a Social Disease: Public Health and Political Economy in Early Industrial France* (Madison: The University of Wisconsin Press, 1982).

Southeast Asia; the mining districts of India. In these and other such regions, the economic exploitation of labor has been effectuated by a despotic political culture. Even in the West, the economic crisis of 2007–8 opened a new campaign against labor, in which the decades-old attack on wages and benefits has been complemented by an attack on collective bargaining itself. In all these instances, labor has found that if it is to pursue its economic interests, it cannot avoid also engaging employers on the political front.[48]

We have seen that Indian subaltern classes are motivated to defend their physical well-being, just as their counterparts in the West are. We have also seen that employers in the East are no less inclined to resort to political control than are employers in the West. This means that, *insofar* as laborers in the East mobilize to defend their physical well-being, they have the same interest in demanding political liberties as did workers in the West. They cannot avoid fighting for their political enfranchisement and for the broadening of their basic freedoms, as preconditions to securing their economic and physical necessities. Hence, when the political culture is transformed so that "bourgeois forms of power" displace and supplant the various forms of traditional, interpersonal coercion, the route to that transformation may very much resemble the one taken in Europe—with the subaltern classes at the front of the campaign. All this follows from the defense of a single basic need: to defend one's physical well-being.

8.6 THE OTHER UNIVERSALISM

Having demonstrated that subaltern classes have at least one basic need, and that this need generates a universal interest in resisting the harms caused by capitalist employment relations, we may draw from this a quite important conclusion—that there are *two universalisms* that can be held up as real, not just one. The first is the *universalizing drive* of capital, which has operated in

---

48 My argument seems to run counter to the idea that the structure of capitalism inclines workers to insulate economic demands from political ones. This has come to be known as "economism." But there is a subtle difference between the argument from economism and my point here. When analysts charge trade unionists with embracing economism, and thereby ignoring politics, they mean that unions are pursuing purely economic gains instead of focusing on the structural situation of the workers—the fact that they are still bound to the rules of capitalism, and hence those of wage labor. Unions are thus negotiating over the terms of the wage relation while failing to challenge the wage relation itself. My argument is actually consistent with this view. I do not claim that, when they push back against their domination, workers are necessarily driven to question their employers' class dominance. My claim is that workers may well be inclined to pursue economic interests alone, but, insofar as this pursuit calls for a certain broadening of political liberties, they will be forced also to pursue these liberties. The liberties they pursue are those that must be secured *in order* to pursue their economic interests *as wage laborers*. There is no spontaneous tendency to push beyond, to the point of questioning the structural basis of wage labor itself. Indeed, one of the perverse results of labor rights is to normalize the fact of wage labor.

the East as well as in the West, albeit at different tempos and unevenly. The second is the *universal interest* of the subaltern classes to defend their well-being against capital's domination, inasmuch as the need for physical well-being is not merely specific to a particular culture or region. It now follows that if capital is driven to dominate labor wherever it takes root, and if this domination generates palpable harm to workers' physical integrity—through dangerous work conditions, poverty-level wages, high mortality, ill health, environmental hazards, and so on—then workers will be motivated to undertake steps to defend their basic interest in their welfare. I argued above that agents' ability to perceive this need as a motivation to act will be universal, regardless of culture.[49] It is reasonable to assume that social agents typically have the capacity to discern when their basic well-being is being undermined by the authority relations under which they toil. If this is so, then the centuries-old anchor for the labor movement—that workers everywhere are bound by certain fundamental interests—stands affirmed.[50]

The interest in their own well-being is what subaltern classes draw on when they pursue the dismantling of the various forms of political domination imposed upon them. Were it not for this interest, the ubiquity of subaltern resistance would be an utter mystery. Members of the Subaltern Studies collective insist that the prebourgeois consciousness of postcolonial social agents does not allow for interests to act as reasons for action. For interests to figure in this fashion is, for them, an attribute of "bourgeois consciousness." According to this view, agents steeped in a prebourgeois culture cannot be motivated by their individual interests, nor can they have any conception of rights. This is why Chakrabarty et al. describe them as *Western* notions, the product of a successful bourgeois revolution, something that is possible only where the bourgeoisie has lived up to its historic competence. But the difficulty of this whole line of reasoning is that, in actuality, the agents who really brought about the advent of bourgeois rights, even in the West, were the lower orders—who were steeped in the prebourgeois culture that the Subalternist theorists insist is *incapable* of generating *the very goals* that these agents pursued.

The laboring classes in the West who fought for, and attained, liberal political freedoms were immersed in a community consciousness, in religious doctrines, in traditional conceptions of hierarchy—exactly as is labor in the East. And how could it be otherwise? The American, French, German, and Italian workers who fought for their rights were often just one generation away from having worked the fields as peasants, or were recent migrants into the city or to a faraway land. They carried their traditional norms with them as they

---

49   See Chap. 8.

50   To say that workers have an interest against employer malfeasance is not to say that there is a natural process through which they will acquire a class consciousness. There is no presumption of teleology here. See above, 190–2.

made the transition to factory life, just as the migrants from Bihar did when they undertook the journey to Calcutta's jute mills. When they organized their unions, or fought for voting rights, or demanded more humane working conditions, they did these things while still being steeped in elements of their culture—the culture that Chakrabarty calls "pre-bourgeois".

If Chakrabarty and Chatterjee are correct that a prebourgeois consciousness will not countenance any notion of individual interests, then the struggle against the bourgeois despotisms in Europe, or slavery in the Americas, has to be a modern miracle. European workers were not born into the world holding a copy of *The Rights of Man* in one hand and *The Social Contract* in the other. They were every bit as enveloped in traditional ideology and primordial loyalties as were their Indian counterparts a couple of centuries later. They were no more the secular citizen-subject than were the jute workers in Calcutta. So, on what psychological resources did workers or slaves draw upon when they fought against their masters, if they could not understand that their well-being was undermined by their oppression?[51]

One explanation is in fact available to those who accept the Subalternists' framework—and it is not without irony. Suppose we accept, following Chatterjee and Chakrabarty, that social agents born into a prebourgeois culture cannot be motivated by their individual interests. This would have to be true of British and French workers in early modern Europe no less than it is of nineteenth-century Indians. If the workers who fought for their liberties in England could not conceive of their interests, if their consciousness was entirely shaped by their socialization—rendering them completely unable to shake that socialization's influence—then they must have drawn on some aspects of the *traditional* culture itself when they launched their campaigns. This would suggest that there must have been something in the European heritage that imbued its people with a love of freedom, with a basic respect for human dignity, with an appreciation of something like basic rights. These disparate cultural beliefs, handed down through the ages, must have endowed laboring classes in the West with the psychological resources to pursue what we now know as bourgeois liberties.

Perhaps it was something within Christianity? Maybe it reached further back into history, such as the inheritance of Greek philosophy or the particulars

---

51   For an argument that slaves' resistance in the United States was generated by their real interest in their well-being, see Joshua Cohen, "The Moral Arc of the Universe," *Philosophy and Public Affairs* 26:2 (Spring 1997), 91–134. For a broader defense of the link between social resistance and real interest, see Alan Gilbert, *Democratic Individuality* (Cambridge: Cambridge University Press, 1990); and William J. Talbott, *Which Rights Should Be Universal?* (Oxford, Oxford University Press, 2005). All of these authors support a set of interests that is wider than the one I have defended, especially an interest in autonomy. I agree entirely with this, even though I have restricted my defense to just one.

of Roman law? Or perhaps it was the particular cultural mélange produced by the Reformation? Whatever it might have been, the hunt is now on to locate those elements of Western culture that bred a love for liberty, autonomy, democracy, and other universals. If this sounds familiar, it should do. It is part of the centuries-old canard about the uniqueness of Western Civilization, or the genius of the Western Mind. It formed the basis for the view, still held by many historians, that there is something peculiar to Western culture that generates a desire for basic liberties. These are a Western invention, according to this view, because it was the West that produced the moral resources to craft them. And, of course, this prejudice about the West was also the foundation on which the defense of imperialism was constructed.

Here, then, is the irony: the promotion of a view such as this, which attributes the growth of basic freedoms to the genius of Western culture, is probably not what the Subalternist theorists had in mind when they put out their call to provincialize Europe. Yet if we accept Chakrabarty's premise that the basic preconditions for the pursuit of liberal freedoms are *cultural*, it seems hard to find any other explanation for the achievement of those freedoms.

The way out of this rather embarrassing cul-de-sac is to accept another premise, one that Chakrabarty rejects—that social agents have basic needs, and that the capacity to recognize at least some of these needs is generally available to them regardless of their cultural location. On this premise, it is no longer a mystery that European workers were able to appreciate the importance of basic liberties, even though they were mired in prebourgeois ideologies. They did so because they recognized that such liberties would enable them to defend their well-being, which was under constant threat by the profit-maximizing strategies of employers. The psychological resource on which they drew was not the genius of European culture, but the universal interest in advancing their basic needs. Since this is a universal interest, and since the capacity to perceive it as an interest is common to agents across cultures, we can affirm that Indian and Egyptian workers are every bit as capable of mobilizing to attain liberal freedoms as were their British forebears. The importance of political freedoms, then, is not something they have to be *taught*. These groups strive to defend their individual freedoms because these freedoms are naturally attractive to them, just as they were for their European predecessors. Hence, there is nothing intrinsically Western about the valuing of democratic liberties.[52] True, the institutions of

---

52 Among contemporary political philosophers, Amartya Kumar Sen has been perhaps the most eloquent and consistent defender of the universal validity of some core values. For a brief statement, see Sen, *Reason before Identity* (Oxford: Oxford University Press, 1999). For a collection of some shorter essays on culture and universalism, see his *The Argumentative Indian: Writings on Indian History, Culture and Identity* (New York: Picador, 2005) esp. chap. 13. A more sustained presentation is in his magnum opus, *The Idea of Justice* (Cambridge: Harvard University Press, 2009), where he presents specific examples from Indian and other non-Western history that

democracy largely originated in the West, but the aspirations that motivate its pursuit are no more Western in their *essence* than is capitalism.[53]

How could the Subalternist theorists not see the deeply conservative implications of their view? I believe it is because they never had to ask why a prebourgeois consciousness did not prevent Western workers from appreciating their interests, if it so successfully blocked Eastern workers from doing so. They simply never posed the counterfactual and they never posed it because their framework allowed them to side-step the issue. Every member of the collective accepts that the implantation of "bourgeois forms of power" was an *achievement of the bourgeoisie*—that workers were simply handed a bourgeois culture as a consequence of the bourgeois revolutions, and did not have to mobilize themselves in order to attain it. This allows Chakrabarty, Chatterjee, and others to *assume* the existence of a bourgeois consciousness among Western workers as part of European modernity at its inception, whereas modernity in the East is handed a working class mired in a prebourgeois consciousness. The Subalternists never considered the possibility that modernity on both sides of the world was brought into being by agents still immersed in premodern cultures. As a result, they never asked how it was that workers in the West were able escape *their* prebourgeois consciousness, if workers in the East were shackled so tightly to theirs.

Had Chakrabarty et al. just posed the question, they might have seen that their arguments about the debilitating effects of culture are very hard to sustain. But it seems that they never posed it, and the cost of not having done so was high. Not only have they ended up with conclusions that their own evidence undermines, but they promote some of the most objectionable canards that Orientalism ever produced—all in the guise of "High Theory."

8.7 CONCLUSION

Let us return to Chakrabarty's assertion, which we encountered early in chapter 5, that the structure of colonial modernity demands a thorough overhauling of

---

directly undermine Subalternist claims for the "Western" provenance of reason and democratic values; see 37–9, 149–51, 329–35. To my knowledge, there has not been any serious engagement with his views by the Subalternists.

53 Hence, we should firmly reject the rhetorical ploy that Subalternist theorists often use, whereby they preface concepts such as rights or agency or liberty with the qualifier "Western concepts of." They thus imply that when scholars explain any action by Eastern agents as reasonable or rational, they are projecting Western values onto the agents. This is a favorite strategy of Chakrabarty's, but Chatterjee and others also resort to it. It draws on the arguments I have examined and rejected in chapters 7 and 8—that Western agents are secular while Eastern agents are religious, or communitarian, or the like. Its abiding Orientalism should be evident by now, as should the reasons for rejecting it. The assumption of rationality, in the sense defended in the present chapter, is no more parochial with respect to Indians than it is with respect to the British.

conventional theory. He made that claim with regard to the issue of power; we have added to it another claim he has made, in tandem with Chatterjee, regarding political psychology. Chakrabarty's view is that politics in the East is embedded in power relations, and motivated by a psychological orientation, quite alien to Western theory, by which he generally means Marxism. The idea is that Marxism uses certain highly abstract and universal categories which are stricken with two weaknesses: they project a specifically Western experience onto the social relations of other cultures, and, because of their highly abstract character, simply ignore all the particularities in Eastern social relations that depart from the general model. They miss how capitalism has created and sustained power relations in the East that are fundamentally different from those in the West—so different that they cannot be viewed as "bourgeois forms of power" at all. Moreover, they ignore how political consciousness in the East rests on mutuality and obligation, not on needs and interest. This is why we must overhaul Marxist theory in particular, and post-Enlightenment frameworks in general—not just because of their universalisms but also because of their Eurocentrism, which cause them systematically to obscure the specificity of the East.

In the past four chapters, I have shown that both these arguments are without merit. There is nothing especially novel or anomalous about the persistence of interpersonal coercion or social hierarchy in postcolonial countries. True, many of these are nonbourgeois forms of power, and they persist because noncapitalist forms of production persist in many parts of the world. But interpersonal coercion is not *necessarily* a departure from capitalist power relations.

As shown in chapters 5 and 6, all manner of hierarchy, coercion, domination, and so on is consistent with capitalist forms of production. This holds not only in the case of backward agriculture, labor-intensive manufacture, or what Marx more generally called "the formal subsumption of labor." Interpersonal coercion is also fully compatible with advanced industrial manufacturing. The mere fact that such forms of domination exist is no evidence that capitalism in the East differs in some fundamental way from that in the West. Furthermore, if these forms of power are indeed a direct product of capitalism, then they can be analyzed and explained by those very universalizing categories that Chakrabarty urges us to reject. This is what we explored in some detail in chapter 6, with regard to social domination and abstract labor—which was intended to serve as a demonstration of exactly how a highly abstract theory can produce an analysis of the variability in forms of social domination.

In chapters 7 and 8, we have seen that Chakrabarty and Chatterjee are mistaken as well in their view of social agency. They insist that political psychology in the East is fundamentally different from that of the West. And they counsel, on the basis of this assertion, that we launch an overhaul of political theory, in order to better theorize the politics that flows from this psychological orientation. Yet their own evidence, as we have shown here, undermines their claims. Their own historical work demonstrates that members of Indian subaltern classes were as motivated by their individual interests as were their peers in the West—as does the empirical analysis by Ranajit Guha, as exemplified in his *Elementary Aspects of Peasant Insurgency in Colonial India*. Furthermore, I argued that the imputation of interests by no means effaces the role of culture in social agency—unless we are to insist that anything short of cultural essentialism amounts to a denial of culture. An interest-based theory is perfectly capable of appreciating that agents are rooted in their cultures; it resists only the claim that their socialization runs so deep as to blind them to their own physical well-being. These theories can, of course, make more ambitious claims as well, which link interests to more than physical well-being. But these more ambitious claims are not my concern. I wish only to defend the *possibility* of a materialist theory, not extend it to its most ambitiously developed form.

This chapter leaves us with an interesting conclusion—that non-Western agents are just as capable as are Western ones of appreciating their individual interests. We therefore have a defense of *two* universalisms, one pertaining to capital and the other to labor. Hence, we have reached much the same conclusion that progressive intellectuals have embraced ever since the French Revolution . . . that is, until postcolonial theory came along. It is the idea that the modern epoch is driven by the twin forces of, on the one side, capital's unrelenting drive to expand, to conquer new markets, and to impose its domination on laboring classes, and, on the other side, the unceasing struggle by these classes to defend themselves, their well-being, against this onslaught. This dual process encompasses both East and West, thereby binding both parts of the world together in the same global process—or, in the jargon of postcolonial theory, the same universal history.

But there is life in the Subalternist project yet. Thus far we have encountered one set of arguments insisting on the uniqueness of the East and rejecting the plausibility of abstract, post-Enlightenment theories. In the next chapter we assess an entirely new argument, which has gained much currency among cultural theorists, anthropologists, and historians. Like the others we have examined so far, it too is dedicated to emphasizing the inscrutability of the East to Western frameworks. But it does not base its claims on any particular facts about Eastern cultures. It relies instead on a novel defense of the idea that capital's universalization is never complete. The argument is advanced by Dipesh Chakrabarty in his most recent and certainly most influential book, *Provincializing Europe*. My intention is to show that while it tries to defend the uniqueness of the East in a new way, it is no more successful at doing so than the others we have encountered.

CHAPTER NINE

The (Non)Problem of Historicism

This chapter takes up the analysis of historical diversity again, but in a slightly different vein. Up to this point, the arguments examined have orbited around clearly identifiable historical phenomena—the forms of power in modern social formations, the heterogeneity of the working class, the forms of agency in colonial India. The basic challenge has been to show that Enlightenment theories, particularly Marxism, are capable of apprehending how these phenomena play out in both West and East. But now, rather than engage the problem of universalism and Eurocentrism through specific empirical or historical challenges, I tackle it at a conceptual level, by taking up the arguments developed by Dipesh Chakrabarty in his hugely influential recent book, *Provincializing Europe.* After Ranajit Guha's *Elementary Aspects,* this is perhaps the most prominent work in the Subalternist oeuvre, certainly the most important since their turn toward postmodern themes. It is in this book that Chakrabarty offers the most far-reaching objections of any postcolonial theorist to the abstract, universalizing categories of Enlightenment theories. As usual, it is Marxism that bears the brunt of his critique, but he clearly intends to question the broader European inheritance.

The main issues to be addressed in this chapter are Chakrabarty's analysis of the abstract categories of political economy, which he cashes out through his distinction between History 1 and History 2, and his critique of "historicism," which he presents as one of the two main contributions of *Provincializing Europe.*[1] I place the term in scare quotes because Chakrabarty's understanding of the concept of historicism is unconventional, and in fact, unravelling just what he means by it is no small challenge. The two issues—abstraction and historicism—are closely related in Chakrabarty's argument, and comprise the heart of his case against the Western canon. I will show that while the distinction he generates between the Two Histories is valid, the conclusions he tries to derive from it are not. I then show that once we reject his conclusions about historical difference and abstraction, his critique of historicism also collapses. Indeed, I will argue that there is no problem of "historicism" at all—as *he* defines the concept.

---

1 The other contribution of Dipesh Chakrabarty's *Provincializing Europe* (Princeton: Princeton University Press, 2000), according to the author himself, is the analysis of power, which I have examined in chap. 5 above. Henceforth, *Provincializing Europe* is cited as *PE.*

9.1 WHAT IS AT STAKE

In the arguments we have examined so far, Subalternist theorists have rejected universalizing theories on the grounds that capitalism outside the West has had a fundamentally different trajectory than it had in the West. Among the claims we encountered, and rebutted, have been that the Eastern bourgeoisie was not revolutionary, the way the Europeans had been; that it failed to implant liberal institutions; that it continued to rely on political coercion and hence failed to generate "bourgeois" forms of power; that peasants in the East are not motivated by material interests; that workers are innately religious; and so forth. Because of these deep fissures between East and West, the theories emerging from the Western experience are deemed problematic, inasmuch as they assume that the logic of social reproduction in the East is more or less akin to that in the West. But because it is not, assert the Subalternists, because the social and economic institutions rest on such different psychologies and power relations from those in the West, Western theories end up obscuring the real dynamics of Eastern modernity. With regard to the arguments encountered thus far, this is the source of Subalternists' rejection of the Enlightenment tradition in Western thought.

In *Provincializing Europe*, Chakrabarty introduces a second kind of objection.[2] Instead of invoking the distinctiveness of the East in order to raise doubts, he points to some fundamental problems with the process of abstraction itself. Whenever we try to categorize any local practice as a specific instance of a "grand narrative," he asserts, intractable dilemmas arise. This is nowhere more evident than in the Marxist analysis of capitalism. Marxist theory operates at a high level of generality. It is an abstract theory, built to travel, its relevance supposedly extending to any part of the globe where capitalism has taken root. As economic reproduction becomes subject to capitalist imperatives, its logic is supposed to be explicable through the universalizing categories of political economy, whether the location is Birmingham, Detroit, Bombay, or Shanghai. Local history, Chakrabarty avers, becomes *subsumed* into the history of capital. The local becomes a specific instance of a more general *kind* of process—Bombay textile mills are no less an instance of capitalist processes than are the mills of Lancashire. This is how the abstract theory is seen as relevant to capitalist processes, no matter where they occur.

Chakrabarty raises fundamental objections to this mode of theorizing.

---

2   Of course, he also relies on the putative divergence between Western and Eastern modernity, as we have seen. The argument from divergent modernity is evident in his critique of the Marxist theory of power, examined in chap. 5 above, and in his account of working-class identity, examined in chap. 8. Now, however, we are considering another line of argument developed by him.

Early in *Provincializing Europe*, he lays out the conventional understanding of capitalist development, as he sees it, along with his objections to it. The passage encapsulates well his motivation for developing an alternative. The dominant approaches to capitalist development, he says, share certain assumptions about its basic properties:

> They all share a tendency to think of capital in the image of a *unity* that arises in one part of the world at a particular period and then develops globally over time, encountering and negotiating historical differences in the process. Or even when "capital" is ascribed a "global," as distinct from a European, beginning, it is still seen in terms of the Hegelian idea of a *totalizing unity*—howsoever internally differentiated—that undergoes a process of *development* in historical time.[3]

Notice that Chakrabarty raises the issue of capital's geographical origins but does not see that as a central problem. The problem with conventional theories is not that they locate capitalism's birth in Europe.[4] Rather, the basic issue is how they understand its *spread*, or universalization, wherever it might have originated. Conventional views about capitalism's universalization have two components that disturb Chakrabarty: first, that capital itself is viewed as a unity, an organic whole whose various parts are bound together; and second, that it is viewed as developing over time through predetermined stages, toward a predicted end point. Both components of the dominant approaches, he says, end up *erasing historical difference*. To illustrate this point, he follows up the passage just quoted with a jab at the British historian E. P. Thompson. He recalls how Thompson famously predicted that capitalism would spread into the Third World, compelling workers, as it spread, to submit to the requirements of its labor process. Chakrabarty urges us to reject Thompson's view. The assumption that capitalism will spread into the world, forcing agents to submit to its logic, says Chakrabarty,

> sees capitalism as a force that encounters historical difference, but sees it as something external to its own structure. A struggle ensues in this encounter, in the course of which capital eventually *cancels out* or neutralizes *the contingent differences* between specific histories. Through however torturous a process, it converts those historical specificities into historically diverse *vehicles* for the spread of its own logic. This logic is seen not only as single and homogenous, but also as one that

---

3   *PE* 47. Emphasis added.
4   Chakrabarty is not insisting that it is Eurocentric to locate the origins of capitalism in Europe. In this regard, his argument diverges from those of other critics, such as James Blaut, who deny that capitalism was European in origin and thus insist that any theory claiming otherwise is Eurocentric. See J. M. Blaut, *The Colonizer's Model of the World: Geographic Diffusionism and Eurocentric History* (New York: Guilford Press, 1993).

unfolds over (historical) time, so that one can indeed produce a narrative of a puta-tively single capitalism in the familiar "history of" genre.[5]

This is a plea for recognizing the role of contingency and local particularities, and an accusation that universalizing theories become blind to the local, and to the myriad ways in which agents deviate from the logic of capitalism. What Chakrabarty sees as problematic about approaches such as Thompson's, which is to say Marxist approaches, is that while they recognize historical difference, they either view it as a temporary condition or dissolve its specificity into the unified logic of capital. Either way, capitalism is assumed, by Marxists, to have the power to subordinate other social practices to its own logic. This assump-tion makes Marxists view capitalism as an ineluctable force, which "cancels out" all differences between local histories as it subsumes them under its own logic.[6] They just become instances of a more global process, the universal history of capital. They are folded into the "history of" something or other—in this case, the global history of capitalism.

Chakrabarty seeks to defend the local against the universal story of capital. His complaint against Marxism is that it is insufficiently attentive to the particu-larities of the local. Marxists ignore the contingencies that such particularities import into historical development, the way they resist being incorporated into the "grand narrative." He wants the East to have a history of its own. Certainly this history will make reference to capitalism, for Chakrabarty does not wish to deny the latter's historical relevance. But it will not lose sight of the innumerable ways in which the local retains its specificity—and this is precisely what Marx-ism and other universalizing theories ignore.

Readers will notice that we find ourselves back at the topic of capital's universalization. Like Ranajit Guha, Chakrabarty wishes to defend the specifi-city of the East. Like Guha and Chatterjee, he does so by denying the applicability of Western theory's universalizing categories. And finally, like so many other postcolonial theorists, he does so by denying that capital success-fully universalizes. The present chapter will examine just how Chakrabarty goes about deploying his argument, which is different from any we have encountered thus far. In the next section, I present it in some detail. This is the longest and perhaps the most demanding chapter in this book. Chakrabarty's argument is a complicated one, and addressing it properly requires some space. So it might be useful to offer a brutally condensed summation of what is to come.

Chakrabarty's core argument is that the properties of capitalism that are regarded as having been universalized, and that the categories of political

---

5 *PE* 48. Emphasis added.
6 ˙ See Chakrabarty's comments about Marxism's treatment of "the local" in his new Preface to PE, 2007 edition, xvi–xvii.

economy are supposed to describe, are not *in fact* ever really universalized. If the underlying process of universalization is incomplete, then the abstract categories of political economy artificially impose an inaccurate, and hence misleading, description of local practices. Something that is in fact a hybrid social form, in which capitalist elements are forced into a compromise with noncapitalist forms, is illicitly turned into a pure, unalloyed instance of capitalism.

When abstract theories misdescribe local practices in this way, it is not just that the specificity of the local is obscured. The causal dynamics are also misrepresented, since certain practices are taken to have fully and successfully universalized, whereas in fact they failed to do so. This imparts to them a stability, and an internal coherence, which they actually lack. Because of this, the reliance on abstract political economy generates two kinds of errors. First, it views societies as driven by certain logics—of accumulation, of maturation through identifiable stages, of growth and then decline—that they do not in fact have. In so doing, it makes incorrect predictions about them, attributing to them a future that is false. Second, it imbues these societies with an internal coherence that is also misplaced. Social relations are assumed to be bound together by the same causal forces, in a kind of functionalist logic. Whereas the first of the two mistakes leads to a kind of developmental teleology, the second generates an unwarranted essentialism. What both mistakes have in common is that they impose an artificial closure on the contingencies of real history. As we will see, this worry about artificial closure is central to Chakrabarty's critique of historicism.

In the next section, I will offer a more detailed explication of Chakrabarty's worries. I will then show that they rest on some subtle but basic confusions about how abstraction works and how it is connected to historical analysis.

9.2 THE TWO HISTORIES OF CAPITAL

The core problem with which we have been grappling in this book is how the history of the non-West has been affected by the incursion of capitalism. Marxism is known for claiming that once capitalism becomes the organizing principle in a social formation, its historical development is centrally shaped by capitalist imperatives. The particulars of this argument vary. For some Marxists, the regulating principle becomes class struggle between labor and capital; for others, it becomes the "laws of motion" specific to accumulation; for still others, it becomes the global dynamic of the world economy. But what is common to all of them is the idea that local history becomes subject to the same forces as histories in other parts of the capitalist world. The history of modern India, or Nigeria, or Argentina, becomes part of "capitalist history." This is what it means for capitalism to have universalized. The analytical complement to this process is an increasing need for a conceptual frame adequate to its study. As the economic system spreads around the globe, bringing disparate regions under its sway, the categories that political economy generates to analyze its dynamics also become the lens through which we apprehend those regional histories. As Partha Chatterjee explains,

> If there is one great moment that turns the provincial thought of Europe to universal philosophy, the parochial history of Europe to universal history, it is the moment of capital—capital that is global in its territorial reach and universal in its conceptual domain. It is the narrative of capital that can turn the violence of mercantile trade, war, genocide, conquest and colonialism into a story of universal progress, development, modernization, and freedom.[7]

This notion of universal history is exactly what disturbs postcolonial theorists. They offer two objections to the universalizing mode of thinking described in the previous paragraph. One is that the basic idea of capitalism's having transformed regional dynamics along particular lines is mistaken; in the East, the putative transformation did not come about, because capitalism abandoned its universalizing mission once it reached Eastern shores. This is the argument I have examined, and rejected, in this book so far. I have shown that all the phenomena that Subalternist theorists adduce as symptoms of capitalism's *failure* are in fact quite consistent with its *success*. So there is every reason to believe that the capitalism of the East is basically the same as that of the West.

The second objection is the one that we will take up in this chapter, for it is what Dipesh Chakrabarty develops in *Provincializing Europe*. It is that the very idea of describing the dynamics of the East as "capitalist history" is deeply misleading, if not mistaken. To motivate this argument, Chakrabarty first makes a distinction between two different ways in which capitalism absorbs, and interacts with, existing institutions as it matures and extends its influence. He then draws out the implications of this differential absorption. This argument is somewhat more involved than others we have encountered in this book. I will therefore present it as distinct theses, and then address them seriatim.

HISTORY 1 AND HISTORY 2: INTRODUCING THE DISTINCTION

To understand how capital affects historical development, declares Chakrabarty, it is necessary to distinguish two different ways in which it absorbs existing institutions. Suppose that a region is, at some initial point, not yet capitalist. Then, whether through colonialism or some other conduit, it is gradually transformed along capitalist lines. This will result in the transformation of local

---

7   Partha Chatterjee, *The Nation and Its Fragments: Colonial and Postcolonial Histories* (Princeton: Princeton University Press, 1993), 235.

structures and local institutions to make them adequate to the demands of capital accumulation. These institutions now contribute to capitalist production, and are in turn reproduced by it. However, not all institutions contribute to the system's viability in the same way. Some contribute to capitalist stability in a way that is more determinative than others. Chakrabarty leans on some rather thick Hegelian terminology here, without defining what he intends for it to convey. But he is clearly pointing to the fact that some structures and institutions within capitalism occupy a central place in its reproduction. He refers to them as part of the "life process" of capitalism. He also describes them as being "posited" by capital, which suggests that they not only constitute part of the system's essential conditions of reproduction but are themselves constrained by its architecture in some way. The history of these institutions is thus absorbed into, and becomes part of, what is encompassed by "capitalist history." This Chakrabarty describes as *History 1*, observing that "[t]his is the universal and necessary history we associate with capital."[8] So, for Chakrabarty, it is not that the universalizing categories of political economy are irrelevant. Clearly they have some purchase. They reflect the social institutions that have become intrinsically connected to the reproduction of capitalism. These are the institutions that become part of capitalism's "life process."

He then distinguishes a second kind of history, which results from a very different pattern of institutional absorption. This he calls History 2. It, too, is a history associated with capitalism. The institutions, social practices and social relations particular to it have been incorporated into the orbit of the capitalist system, and thus it should not be understood as being external to capitalism. However, even though these social relations come under capitalism's sway, they do so "not as antecedents established by itself, not as forms of its own life-process."[9] So, while History 1 contributes to capital's life process, History 2 does not.

What does this mean? Chakrabarty explains that "to say that something does not belong to capital's life-process is to claim that it does not contribute to the self-reproduction of capital."[10] Again and again he returns to this characteristic of History 2: that it is independent of the reproductive logic of capital and thereby does not form part of its "life process." In his words, "nothing in it is automatically aligned with the logic of capital"; practices labeled History 2 "do not lend themselves to the logic of reproduction of capital."[11] What these formulations suggest is that the reproduction of the institutions in History 2 will certainly be affected in some way by capital, since they have been absorbed into the system, but their reproduction will not be subordinated to capitalism's

---

8   *PE* 63.
9   *PE* 63.
10   *PE* 63–4.
11   *PE* 67.

logic. So, while History 1 is part of the universal history of capital, History 2 will not be.

Clearly, one axis on which to differentiate the two Histories is their relation to the reproduction of capitalism. But Chakrabarty is also introducing a second difference between them. He often describes History 1 as encompassing not just capital and its universalizing drive, but other universalizing categories of Enlightenment thought. His list includes citizenship, nationalism, industrialization, and of course, Reason, all of which come under the rubric of History 1, inasmuch as they represent Enlightenment universals.[12] Conversely, History 2 is identified with the local, the particular—those elements that cannot be easily assimilated into the categories associated with History 1. Whereas the abstract categories associated with History 1 impose a uniform analytical grid on social topography, History 2 resists being assimilated into it. Hence, what slots a practice into History 2 is not just that it does not contribute to capital's life process but that it also cannot be seen as an instance of some abstract category typical of Western theories.

The distinction Chakrabarty makes is not new, even if his somewhat infelicitous terminology might be. He derives much of its substance from Marx, and it has been made by many other neo-Marxists in the twentieth century.[13] It is the simple observation that some kinds of practices are central to capitalism's reproduction (History 1), while others are not (History 2). If his argument went no deeper, it would not do much to puncture the universalizing ambitions of Marxist theory, for the distinction has been upheld, and even insisted upon, by some rather brazen universalizers. And I, too, will defend it in the course of this chapter, even while contesting the conclusions Chakrabarty derives from it. The twist in his argument comes not from the distinction itself, but from the particular role he attributes to History 2.

---

12   See *PE* 23, 67, 250.

13   That Marx makes this distinction is indisputable. But the particular passages from which Chakrabarty claims to have extracted it, from the Addenda to vol. III of the *Theories of Surplus Value*, do not much support the further points that Chakrabarty claims to derive from them. Marx's concern in these passages is simple—he wishes to argue that capitalism's development requires that practices which were preconditions for its emergence, and hence, by definition, had to be in place for it to take root, become subordinated to its logic as it consolidates itself. Hence, even though money and interest precede capitalism, they are subordinated to it once it has taken hold of their functions. Formerly its antecedents, now they are "posited" by it. The Hegelian language notwithstanding, it is a very simple argument, directed at a very basic point. The idea is that what was once independent of capital increasingly becomes subject to its logic. There is nothing in those passages about the obduracy of History 2, or its function being to disrupt the logic of History 1. All this is what Chakrabarty imports into the passages, in a rather tortured reading of them. Readers should especially compare Chakrabarty's reading of the passages on p. 468 of *Theories of Surplus Value*, vol. III (Moscow: Progress Publishers, 1971) with what Marx actually says.

HISTORY 2 DISRUPTS UNIVERSALIZATION

The practices included in History 2 have their own logic of reproduction, distinct from that of History 1. While History 1 represents the universal, abstract logic of capital, History 2 embodies the "diverse ways of being" rooted in the particular cultures of any given region of the globe. As capital spreads across the world, it faces the challenge of subordinating these various practices to its own dynamic. Chakrabarty describes this as "a question of transition/translation from many and possibly incommensurable temporalities to the homogenous time of abstract labor."[14] But this process of translation is never complete. Agents manage to retain aspects of their culture, their practical orientations, which are independent of capital. Hence, even while History 2 is dominated by capital, it retains its own integrity. As we observed in the preceding section, the two Histories are permanent features of capitalism's unfolding dynamic.

The fact that History 2 retains its autonomy gives it a special place in the modern era. It bears the distinction of being the "category charged with the function of constantly interrupting the totalizing thrust of History 1."[15] To interrupt the totalizing thrust of capitalism in this fashion is to undermine its *universalization*. Chakrabarty draws a portentous conclusion from this premise:

> No historic form of capital, however global in its reach, can ever be a universal. No global, or even local for that matter, capital can ever represent the universal logic of capital, for any historically available form of capital is a provisional compromise made up of History 1 modified by somebody's History 2.[16]

For Chakrabarty, this means that capital's *globalization* should not be confused with its *universalization*:

> [The] *globalization* of capital is not the same as capital's *universalization*. Globalization does not mean that History 1, the universal and necessary logic of capital so essential to Marx's critique, has been realized. What interrupts and defers capital's self-realization are the various History 2s that always modify History 1 and thus act as grounds for claiming historical difference.[17]

In other words, capital may spread to all corners of the world, but this does not mean that it manages to subordinate all social relations to its particular rules of reproduction. This, for Chakrabarty, means that it fails in its universalization. Notice that Chakrabarty has reached the same conclusion as Guha, which Chakrabarty has endorsed in other contexts—that capital in the modern era

---

14   *PE* 92, 95.
15   *PE* 66.
16   *PE* 70.
17   *PE* 71; emphasis added.

failed to universalize itself. But in this instance his reasoning is different. For Guha, what derailed the universalization process was that capital abandoned its mission when it reached the colonies: capital failed to universalize because it changed its own nature. Chakrabarty's argument in the preceding paragraph, on the other hand, proposes that what undermines universalization is not that capital transmutes into a different species but that it is never able to expunge History 2. Capital's internal drive remains the same—it is just that the *force* of this drive turns out to be limited.

THE ANTAGONISM BETWEEN HISTORY 1 AND HISTORY 2

The fact that History 2 retains its own logic of reproduction, that it does not conform to capital's dictates, carries another implication for Chakrabarty. If there exist practices that do not bend to capitalism's logic, they also carry the potential to *disrupt its reproduction*. With History 2,

> capital has to encounter in the reproduction of its own life process relationships that present it with double possibilities. These relations could be central to capital's self-reproduction, and yet it is also possible for them to be oriented to structures that do not contribute to such reproduction.[18]

If social relations are not guided by capitalist imperatives, agents embedded within them may have priorities that are inimical to the system. Work habits may not adjust to competitive demands; social priorities may not serve the requirements of accumulation; norms of comportment may not adjust to bourgeois authority relations. When social relations become absorbed into capital's self-reproduction, they become part of History 1 and thus functionally compatible with it. But if they remain in History 2, they are not only independent of capital but, *by being* independent of it, pose the threat of disruption. It is critical to register this component of Chakrabarty's argument: the very fact that History 2 is not aligned to the logic of capital makes it a threat to capital. And because of this threat, Chakrabarty concludes, "History 1 . . . has to subjugate or destroy the multiple possibilities that belong to History 2."[19]

One example of this is the factory, where the "disciplinary process . . . is in part meant to accomplish the subjugation/destruction of History 2."[20] Workers come to the factory with some inclination to accept capital's dictates. They have this inclination because submitting to capitalists is their only means of survival. In this respect, they become part of capital's universal history, History 1. But they also come immersed in their local culture, local work habits, their

18   *PE* 64.
19   *PE* 65.
20   *PE* 67.

individual preferences and proclivities. These have been formed independent of capital, and are what the latter sees as potentially disruptive. As a result, they have to be destroyed in order to turn the worker into a replaceable, abstract provider of labor power, into "sheer, living labor—muscular energy plus consciousness."[21] The labor process, for Chakrabarty, is an arena where History 1 wages its campaign for the "subjugation/destruction" of History 2. It is designed to obliterate all those particularities of local culture, all those ways of being that do not conform to the universal logic of capital and that obstruct the transformation of actual historical workers into "abstract labor."[22]

THE OBDURACY OF HISTORY 2

History 1 is forever striving to obliterate History 2. The problem is that, try as it might to bend all social relations to its own logic of reproduction, History 1—or capital, which is its agent—fails in its effort. Having said that History 1 must "subjugate or destroy" History 2, Chakrabarty follows it up immediately afterward by saying, "There is nothing, however, to guarantee that the subordination of History 2 to the logic of capital would ever be complete".[23] Capital has to learn to live with the incompleteness of its rule. It must coexist with History 2 and with the persistence of institutions and practices that do not align with its reproductive logic. History 2, in turn, is never able to break free of capital, because it comprises practices that have come under capital's domination. But even while they cannot wrest free of it, they are never fully absorbed by it either. Their fate is to remain under its shadow even while constantly frustrating its "totalizing" thrust.[24]

The dynamic between the two histories plays a central role in Chakrabarty's theory of global modernity and also forms the foundation for his critique of Enlightenment theories, especially the Marxist tradition. For him, the fatal flaw in the Enlightenment tradition is that, while it is alive to the role of History 1, it consistently fails to register the impact of History 2, especially in the non-West. This results in a universalizing discourse that ignores contingency and local particularities, downplays the role of agency, and imposes an unwarranted teleology on historical development. All these flaws come under the rubric of historicism. Chakrabarty views the critique of historicism as one of the two central contributions of *Provincializing Europe*, and it is to this concept that we now turn.

---

21 Ibid.

22 The practices associated with History 1 are not confined to the simple act of labor. They include other universalisms associated with modern capitalism. Two examples of this that Chakrabarty provides are unionization and citizenship. Workers who join the ranks of citizens and trade unionists become part of the narrative of capital (*PE* 67). Both institutions are products of the modern era, both part of the cultural transformation that came about with the rule of capital. They are accompaniments to the universalization of capital.

23 *PE* 65.

24 *PE* 254.

9.3 THE PROBLEM OF HISTORICISM

While Chakrabarty makes clear that historicism is a form of reasoning that ought to be avoided, just what the concept denotes precisely is not easy to glean. This is owing, in part, to Chakrabarty's self-indulgent style of theorizing, whereby the search for ever more abstruse formulations often overtakes any discernible interest in communication.[25] But it also is owing to some genuine confusion in Chakrabarty's presentation of the concept. In what follows, I have chosen to present the strongest, most defensible interpretation of the concept.

Let us begin by introducing Chakrabarty's own summary statement of it, which is also one of his less obscure renderings. He describes it as "a mode of thinking about history in which one assumed that any object under investigation retained *a unity of conception* throughout its existence and attained *full expression through a process of development* in secular, historical time."[26] Or again, "it tells us that in order to understand the nature of anything in this world we must see it as an *historically developing entity*, that is, first, as an *individual and unique whole—as some kind of unity* at least in potential—and second, as something that develops over time."[27] The italicized phrases encapsulate the two elements that comprise historicism's core. The first is an assumption that the parts that comprise a social whole are in a relation of functional interdependence. They cohere or hang together in such a way that their constituent parts develop in synchrony. This assumption rules out the possibility of ruptures, instability, or tensions between parts of a social whole.[28] The second element is the idea that social complexes develop ineluctably through time toward a predestined end—a notion that makes history seem to be something "merely waiting to become actual—like the possibility of ripening inherent in a fruit."[29]

What induces historicists to treat social complexes as if they were functionally integrated wholes, maturing through time like the ripening of a fruit, is that they are in the thrall of History 1. Once theorists forget about all the diverse

---

25   Consider, for example, the following passage, in which Chakrabarty explains the problems with historicism: "For a possibility to be neither that which is waiting to become actual nor that which is merely incomplete, the possible has to be thought of as that which already actually is, but is present only as the 'not yet' of the actual. *In other words*, it is what makes not-being-a-totality a constitutional characteristic of the 'now.' It is in this radical sense of not being a totality that the now is 'constantly fragmentary' and not-one" (*PE* 250; emphasis added). Is this passage meant to explain anything at all? I doubt it. The clause that follows "in other words" is even more impenetrable than the one preceding it. What is even more remarkable is that, in his response to criticisms, Chakrabarty often feigns outrage at having been misunderstood, as if the fault lies with his readers, and not in the mountain of indecipherable prose that he forces them to wade through. On the other hand, while his style prevents any straightforward interpretation of his argument, it does set up a very effective "that's not what I meant" defense in the face of criticism.

26   *PE* xiv, 2007. Emphasis added.

27   *PE* 23.

28   Ibid.

29   *PE* 249.

modes of interaction, all the different ways of being, that continue to persist within capitalism, then capitalism increasingly takes the appearance of an all-pervasive force. It becomes a unifying principle of social development, which erases any hint of a future that does not conform to capital's logic. The future increasingly becomes a knowable entity, drawing toward a determinable end. Chakrabarty calls this the future "that 'will be,'" by which he means a future that *has* to be, that has to take a predicted course. This is the future toward which we seem to be plummeting headlong, once we view society through the prism of History 1:

> This is a future of which we know at least the constitutive principles, even if we do not have a blueprint for it. Let us call this the future that "will be" . . . The future that "will be" aligns itself with what I called History 1 in my chapter on the "The Two Histories of Capital" [i.e., the preceding section]. This is the universal and necessary history posited by the logic of capital. In this history inhere the Enlightenment universals.[30]

So the slide into historicism comes when we substitute History 1 for the diversity and contingency of real history. Hence, "[to] critique historicism in all its varieties is to unlearn to think of history as a developmental process in which that which is possible becomes actual by tending to a future that is singular."[31] Here we see the connections between History 1, historicism, and what appears to be a historical teleology.[32] Once it is accepted that social wholes are subjected to the unifying force of capital, it erases any sense of a plural, open-ended future; the future becomes whittled down to a singular, determinable end point.

A second consequence of historicism, issuing from the same source, is that social institutions are assumed to be seamlessly woven into an organic whole. What Chakrabarty seems to mean by this is that historicists assume a kind of functional compatibility among all the diverse elements of society. They assume away contradiction, instability, incompatibility, and so on. It is easy to see how this, too, relates to the suffocating hold of History 1 on our imaginations. Recall that the function of History 2 is always to frustrate the "totalizing thrust" of History 1. This means that there are always some institutions, or practices, that remain stubbornly independent of capital, or of whatever universalizing principle the historicist happens to fix upon. Because these practices retain their independence, they exercise their own influence on social reproduction, at times even destabilizing it. Certain practices or norms of comportment resist

---

30   *PE* 250.
31   *PE* 249. Emphasis added.
32   Oddly, Chakrabarty denies that historicism implies teleology (*PE* 23). But his description of its basic elements, and his examples, create a strong impression that teleology is in fact what he has in mind.

the logic of capital, and thereby insert numerous "heterogeneities and incommensurabilities" into its homogenizing drive.[33] But the hold of History 1 makes historicists blind to these differences. And where they cannot ignore them, they simply affix an expiration date on them: historicism creates the illusion that the myriad social practices that escape the logic of capital, that do not reflect its basic properties, are bound to dissolve in due course. History 1 will subjugate/subordinate them as it proceeds toward its singular future.

Chakrabarty's abiding concern here seems to be how to best understand capitalism's spread. Chakrabarty worries that universalizing theories project the experience of Western modernity onto the postcolonial world. They assume that just because capitalism has globalized, it will trigger the same political and cultural transformation in the East as it did in the West. Historicists, he argues, are so convinced of capital's homogenizing effects that they treat the postcolonial world as if it is in a waiting room, biding its time as it waits for its own modernity to become a reflection of the European. Whatever differences there now are will be erased as capitalism attains full expression. And since they are destined to disappear, these differences are treated as mere anachronisms or holdovers, unworthy of serious analysis, precisely because their days are numbered. So historicists become incapable of appreciating the specificity of postcolonial modernity, because they are convinced that capitalism dissolves all social difference—you just have to give it time.

And which theories are likeliest to generate such a blindness to this sort of teleology? Theories stemming from the West, of course—the products of Enlightenment thinking:

> Ideas, old and new, about discontinuities, ruptures, and shifts in the historical process have from time to time challenged the dominance of historicism, but much written history still remains deeply historicist. That is to say, it still takes its object of investigation to be internally unified, and sees it as developing over time. This is particularly true—for all their differences with classical historicism—of historical narratives underpinned by *Marxist or liberal* views of the world, and is what underlies descriptions/explanations in the genre "history of"—capitalism, industrialization, nationalism, and so on.[34]

It is important that we see the close connection between Western theories' blindness to History 2 and their abiding Eurocentrism. As I observed above, within the terms of Chakrabarty's argument the existence of History 2 presents a problem for all abstract theorizing, whether of the West or of the East. But the problem does not affect the basic analytical frameworks symmetrically. It

33   *PE* 95.
34   *PE* 23. Emphasis added.

is far more damaging when Western theories travel to the East than it is when they train their lens on the West. For the West, we should remember, has been "blessed" with a genuinely revolutionary bourgeoisie, which has transformed its social space, integrated the subaltern domain, and brought a far greater range of social relations into conformity with capital's reproductive logic. The West conforms to History 1 far more than does the East, where capital abandoned its universalizing mission. When categories developed out of the Western experience travel eastward, they take for granted that a social transformation has occurred more or less in line with what transpired in Europe. In this sense, Chakrabarty argues, they carry an imprint, a marker of the conditions from which they arose. When it is mobilized in the analysis of non-Western social formations, this imprint becomes a *prejudice*—it becomes Eurocentrism. It refuses to recognize the numerous ways in which real history in the non-West fails to conform to the homogenizing assumptions of Western theory.[35] Or, owing to their historicist bias, when these theories do take notice of differences, they blithely assume that these are only temporary phenomena, because sooner or later History 1 will end up subjugating all the diverse History 2s and remake the East into the image of the West.[36] Hence, while the existence of History 2 is problematic for Enlightenment theories *tout court*, it becomes something more specific when they are brought to the East. It generates what we know as Eurocentrism.

This brings to a close our synopsis of Chakrabarty's arguments about the Two Histories, the special role of History 2, and the consequences of historians ignoring that role. It is worth noting that his analysis of historicism rides almost entirely on his understanding of the Two Histories. It is a mode of reasoning that fails to appreciate the *way* in which History 2 punctures and destabilizes both capital's universalizing drive and also its reproduction. All of this presupposes, of course, that capital's universalization is *in fact* disrupted in the manner described by Chakrabarty, that History 2 is the reason for its disruption, and that History 1 is committed to subordinating all elements of History 2 to its own functional requirements. If the dynamics of the Two Histories do not in fact have these properties, then we certainly cannot indict historians of being insensitive to their effects. What Chakrabarty calls historicism is a failing only if his theorization of the Two Histories has some purchase. I therefore turn our attention to an assessment of his argument about the two histories and then move on to his critique of historicism.

---

35   Cf. Chakrabarty's comments on the imprint left by a theory's origins, and its relation to prejudice; see "Preface to the 2007 Edition," at *PE* xiii–xiv, xvi.

36   See Chakrabarty's discussion of anachronisms at *PE* 238–9, 253–4.

9.4 ABSTRACT CATEGORIES AND THE REAL HISTORY OF CAPITAL

Chakrabarty is right to distinguish between those practices that are constitutive of capitalist reproduction—and are thereby "posited" by capital, or part of its "life process"—and those that are not. This is simply another way of recognizing that some practices are essential to capitalist reproduction, while others are not. Not every social relation is an expression of capitalism, even after that system has taken hold of a social formation. In a very broad way, then, I agree with his distinction between something akin to History 1 and History 2. As he observes, it was a distinction made by Marx and, we might add, defended by many analysts within the Marxian tradition over the course of the twentieth century. But despite my having agreed that such a distinction is warranted, I intend to argue that *none* of the conclusions Chakrabarty derives from it can be defended: the existence of History 2 does *not* mean that universalization is never complete; it does *not* follow that the source of instability for capital is History 2; it is *not* the case that there is an inbuilt antagonism between History and History 2; and finally, it is *not at all* the case that History 1, through the agency of capital, is committed to the subjugation or erasure of History 2. Hence, we find ourselves confronted with quite different implications concerning the viability of the abstract, universalizing categories of the Enlightenment tradition, and are led to the view that these frameworks are not only quite defensible but also a great deal more robust than Chakrabarty seems to think.

HISTORY 2 DOES NOT UNDERMINE CAPITAL'S UNIVERSALIZATION
Chakrabarty is quite clear that as long as there are social practices that remain outside the orbit of capital, the universalization process has to be regarded as incomplete. This is what it means to say that the presence of History 2 serves to block the universalization of capital. It should be evident that this is an astonishingly stringent test for capital's universalization. As I argued in chapter 5, Subalternist theorists work with an unduly expansive notion of what capitalism is supposed to universalize.[37] We saw that the most defensible case is for a narrower conception, in which capitalist globalization amounts to the universalization of practices relating to economic production. This is what most Marxists have understood by the term, as have many proponents of the scholarly traditions that Subalternist theorists traduce. Chakrabarty's argument amounts to the rather absurd view that universalization requires the subordination of *all practices* to the dictates of capitalism, to the "logic of capital." Yet I am · unaware of any theorist outside the domain of postcolonial studies who would defend this view, nor do I see any justification for it.

As it happens, Chakrabarty admits that *economic* practices *have* been so

---

37   See above, 101–2. 101–12.

transformed in many postcolonies. He agrees that the economic logic of capitalist production has established itself in the East; he even allows that it might have become dominant. But he insists that the fact of production having changed in this fashion is insufficient to warrant the conclusion that capitalism has universalized—because, for him, capitalism must do more than just change the logic of *economic* activity. As long as practices that fall under History 2 can maintain their independence, he insists that the universalization process is incomplete.

But why should we accept the notion that for capital to have universalized, it must have obliterated History 2? Why can we not say that as long as History 1 has established itself, is stable, and reproduces itself over time, then its universalization is a fact of life, even if the practices in History 2 continue to exist? Chakrabarty does not present a systematic argument to counter this objection. Based on scattered comments in the text, however, his justification seems to be the following: the reason we can deny that capital has universalized is that History 2 *modifies the operation* of History 1. Consequently, the pure logic of capital, which is what universalization is putatively importing into the East, never really takes hold. What does take hold is a logic *modified* by the influence of History 2. Chakrabarty variously refers to these effects of History 2 as "modifying," "disrupting," "interrupting," and the like, in regard to their relation to History 1. All these expressions push in the same direction, namely, that History 2 matters because it forces changes in the operations of History 1. A charitable interpretation of Chakrabarty's argument, then, is that History 2 forces a modification of what is being universalized. This being the case, he would suggest, we cannot assume that the story told through the logic of History 1 will ever be the story actually unfolding on the ground. It will be inflected through the workings of History 2.[38] This is the most favorable interpretation of Chakrabarty's argument. It constitutes the premise from which he draws his conclusion that capital never in fact universalizes, even as it globalizes.

But here is the problem: *even if we accept Chakrabarty's premise*—that History 2 modifies or interrupts the logic of History 1—*it does not justify his conclusion* that universalization cannot ever be complete. Consider what it means for such a modification to take place. We have certain expectations of agents as bearers of History 1—as workers, as capitalists, as landlords. Our expectations are that they will follow certain basic rules in order to reproduce themselves. These rules are what we describe as their "logic of reproduction." Now, suppose that under the influence of History 2, agents are forced to modify the pure logic of their position, as described in History 1. When practices depart in some way from the logic, or rules, of reproduction, as described at a general level, this departure can be of two kinds: one that maintains the integrity of the

---

38   See his discussion at *PE* 70.

rules, even if it modifies them somewhat; or one that forces a transformation of the rules' basic integrity.

In the context of Chakrabarty's argument, surely the question is whether the modification induced by History 2 preserves the basic integrity of the rules, even if it makes some modifications in their details. If the effects of History 2 leave intact the basic rules, then they do not change the *type* of practice that the rules are generating. The modification, in this case, would be considered *type-preserving*. On the other hand, if the changes wrought by History 2 are of a more significant order, such that they undermine the basic integrity of the rules that agents are following, then they would end up changing the very nature of the practice generated by the rules. If the change is of this kind, then the effect of History 2 would be *type-transforming*. Changes that are type-preserving do not justify the conclusion that Chakrabarty wishes to endorse. They would keep intact the basic structure of the rule, and hence of the practices it generates. Only changes that are type-transforming—those that change the basic goals or the strategies of the actors—would justify the conclusion that the practice no longer conforms to its abstract description.

The crucial point here is that Chakrabarty provides no evidence that the modifications caused by History 2 are type-*transforming*. All his descriptions of the effects of History 2 are instances of type-*preserving* modifications. Indeed, in much of his discussion, the effects of History 2 are even weaker. They simply change certain details of the practices that embody capital's basic reproductive logic, without making any discernible changes at all in the logic itself. Or they carry the *potential* of disrupting the logic of reproduction inscribed in History 1, but without any guarantee that they will in fact do so.[39] If History 2 merely manages to tweak the social relations or practices of History 1, but leaves intact their basic integrity, then Chakrabarty's argument loses its force. As a result, even if we accept his characterization of History 2 and his description of how it

---

39   See his discussion of festivals in which Bengali workers offer prayer to their machines, or of weavers who recite hymns while working on their looms (*PE*: 77–83). Chakrabarty apparently sees these as instances of History 2 having modified the universalizing logic of History 1—these workers and weavers are not embodiments of the "secular" logic of capital. To them, work and religion, the secular and the sacred, are inextricably fused, which means that the abstract description of their status as workers or weavers has been modified by the concrete elements of their worldview. But does this in any way succeed as an indictment of the abstract categories? On my argument, it does not. What those categories, and the framework in which they are embedded, predict is that laborers who are dependent on the market will have to produce at certain levels of efficiency—it simply makes no claims about their normative universe, except that it will have to accommodate a subjective orientation sensitive to the compulsions of market success. Whether that comes with a secular or a sacred conception of work is irrelevant, as long as the laborers are attuned to the compulsions of the market. No doubt, their practice has been modified in some way by their local beliefs or institutions—by History 2. But these modifications do not disturb the basic integrity of the rules to which they are now subject. Nothing in Chakrabarty's description leads us to think otherwise.

affects the operation of History 1, these are consistent with capital's universalization. That is, even if History 2 has the effect of modifying History 1, it does not alter the latter's fundamental logic. We are therefore justified in concluding that the basic rules of the agents' reproduction have not been disturbed, even if their workings, or the form in which they are instantiated, may have been affected to some degree.

The main principle at issue is this: no practice ever conforms in every detail to its abstract description. It is not an insight, therefore, to declare that this or that social fact has elements in it that are not present in its abstract delineation. The task of conceptual analysis is to decide whether its departure from the abstract description warrants an abandonment of the category attached to that description—such as the category "capitalist," or "accumulation"—or whether the departure can be accommodated by recognizing the modified practice as a variant or a subtype of the abstract category. If it is recognized as a variant or sub-type, then we preserve the abstract description, and the category to which it is attached. We agree that the category is real, that it has purchase on how social dynamics are actually unfolding. We simply recognize that the category can be instantiated in *variable forms*.

Chakrabarty argues that the universalization of capital is a myth, that it is forever incomplete because the actual practice of reproduction in the East does not conform to its abstract description as presented in the works of Marx or other Enlightenment thinkers. And the reason it does not conform to that description is that History 2 forces modifications in it. As demonstrated above, however, the mere fact that a practice fails to conform to its abstract description is not significant. What is significant is whether the departure changes the basic nature of the practice. In the context of our discussion here, the question becomes: When they impose modifications, do the various instances of History 2 force a type-transforming change in the logic of capitalist reproduction?

Since Chakrabarty repeatedly describes History 2 as modifying the *logic* of capitalist reproduction, he clearly agrees that capitalism does have an identifiable logic. Yet he offers no evidence that the modifications are of an order that would justify the conclusion that capitalists no longer follow the basic rules of accumulation, or that workers no longer reproduce themselves by selling their labor power. Yet this is exactly what it would mean for the *logic* of capital to be modified in a type-*transforming* way. Since he does not establish that the modifications are of the relevant kind, the simple fact that History 2 modifies or interrupts the reproduction of History 1 is inconsequential. We can accept his claim that it does—but still conclude that the universalization of capital is an accomplished fact.

THE SOURCE OF CAPITAL'S DESTABILIZATION IS NOT HISTORY 2

We have now established that capital's universalization does not require that each and every social practice abide by its logic of reproduction. The mere fact some social relations have their own particular rules, independent of the rules generally characteristic of capitalism, does not allow us to conclude that the universalizing process has been interrupted. It follows that capital can universalize its rule and establish its control over economic reproduction even while myriad components of social life maintain their autonomy. And even when History 2 interacts with and modifies capital's reproduction, what matters is whether the modification transforms the basic rules of reproduction essential to capitalism. The mere existence of History 2 does not undermine the claim that capital has universalized its rule over the course of the modern era.

If it is true, contrary to Chakrabarty's contention, that universalization can proceed even while History 2 maintains its integrity, then Chakrabarty is also wrong to insist that the basic *function* of History 2 is to undermine capital's universalization. The only way this conclusion could be justified would be if History 2 necessarily forced fundamental changes in the logic of History 1. But this characterization is impossible to derive from Chakrabarty's own argument. Remember that he defines History 2 simply as those practices that "do not lend themselves to the logic of reproduction of capital";[40] elsewhere he quotes Marx to define it as practices that capital influences in some way but "not as antecedents established by itself, not as forms of its own life-process."[41] Theses characterizations can only establish that History 2 retains its integrity inside capitalism and that it refuses to align itself with bourgeois rules of reproduction.

But the mere fact that some social relations retain their independence cannot possibly justify regarding them as practices that will *undermine* or *disrupt* capitalism. They might just as easily continue to reproduce themselves on a parallel track, abiding by their own internal logic, while capital pushes along in its own grooves. They will be a source of instability only if their conditions of reproduction *clash* in some way with the conditions that sustain capitalism. But is this a realistic assumption? Even while *some* relations associated with History 2 might be dysfunctional for capital, it is simply impossible to imagine that *every* such relation would have to be. Chakrabarty seems to equate the autonomy of a practice from the logic of capitalism with that practice being corrosive to capitalism. This amounts to the claim that unless a social practice is functional to capitalism's stability, it is *necessarily* dysfunctional. It is hard to imagine how such a claim could be supported. Chakrabarty is therefore quite mistaken to conclude that, just because History 2 might retain its own integrity, it has the effect of interrupting capital's universalization.

Of course, it is probably true that *some* practices internal to History 2 will indeed conflict with capitalist dynamics. But even though they may conflict with capitalism, it does not follow that they will disrupt its reproduction or its

---

40   *PE* 67.
41   *PE* 63.

universalization. The mere fact that a practice or norm conflicts with capitalism's logic says nothing at all about its capacity to successfully block capitalism. It could very well be that instances of History 2 will encounter capitalism, clash with it . . . and then find *themselves* transformed by it. In other words, it could be that, on those occasions where the logics of History 1 and History 2 clash, it will be History 1 that prevails. Workers might change their work habits to keep their jobs, capitalists might ignore their sectarian beliefs and hire workers from other religions, and so on. Hence, the mere fact of there being an incompatibility between the two will not suffice to resuscitate Chakrabarty's argument. In addition to their incompatibility, it must also be the case that the practices associated with History 2 have the social support—and its agents the capacity—to overturn the demands imposed by capitalism. Only if all these conditions are in place can we conclude that History 2 will have the effect of blocking the universalization of capital.

Since it is impossible to assume that the conditions enumerated here are in fact intrinsic to History 2, we are justified in rejecting the argument that it is the *function* of History 2 to destabilize History 1. At best, we can say that *certain instances* of History 2 *might*, in *some situations*, succeed in doing so. Whether or not they do depends upon some contingent facts about their content, their obduracy, the social strength of their practitioners, their capacity to defend themselves against the demands of capital, and so on. In other words, the best we can do for Chakrabarty is to break down History 2 into two categories, History 2_1, which encompasses practices that are independent of capital but in a benign way, such that they do *not* clash with it; and History 2_2, which encompasses practices that are independent of capital and *do* clash with it. Only the latter pose any threat to capital's universalization, and even here, only a further subset of these could be expected to hold up under the pressure of capital's formidable demands.

We have thus arrived at two conclusions. First, even given Chakrabarty's own definition of them, there is no *systematic conflict* between the Two Histories. The conflict involves only a small subset of History 2; moreover, the outcome of that conflict, when it does occur, cannot be prejudged. Second, it follows that History 2 poses no *systematic threat* to the integrity, or the outward thrust, of History 1. Again, it could do so under certain conditions, but those conditions cannot be assumed to be always in place. The broad conclusion that derives from this is that insofar as History 2 constitutes any threat to History 1, that threat is contingent and episodic.

THE MAIN SOURCE OF CAPITAL'S DESTABILIZATION IS HISTORY 1

If Chakrabarty overestimates the power of History 2 to destabilize History 1, he vastly *underestimates* the sources of instability within History 1 itself. It is hard to find many passages in *Provincializing Europe* where he discusses the sources of disruption to capital's reproduction that are located within Enlightenment universals—capital, freedom, democracy, citizenship, etc. But it should be clear that there exist *systematic contradictions* between capital's logic of reproduction and some of these universals—in other words, between capital's logic and various components of History 1. Furthermore, I propose that these conflicts are not only systematic, but are far more corrosive to the conditions of capital's reproduction than the practices associated with History 2. Let me now move to a defense of this proposition.

That Chakrabarty never seriously considers the possibility of capital being destabilized by elements internal to History 1 is a consequence, I believe, of his characterization of History 1 as those practices that are "posited" by capital itself and that "contribute to the life-process" of capitalism. Since they are implanted by capital, and since they are conditions of its reproduction, they are assumed to be univocal in their effects—benign, never corrosive. But this conclusion does not follow from the premise.

The fact that certain practices or institutions are critical to the survival of a system does not preclude the possibility of their becoming a source of breakdown. One way in which such breakdowns can occur is through what Jon Elster has called *counterfinality*: when actions or practices that might be individually beneficial aggregate into outcomes that are self-defeating.[42] For example, the universal drive for profits is certainly an essential practice within capitalism, but actions that benefit an employer individually can become self-defeating if carried out by everyone—such as when the higher profits that come from suppressing wages in one firm are undermined once all employers suppress wages, thereby contracting the market for their goods. The fact that key elements contribute to capitalism's reproduction does not guarantee that they will not also contribute to its breakdown. Indeed, it is precisely because of their being essential to its reproduction that they can act as a source of instability for the system itself.

From Smith to Keynes, every major theory of capitalism has located deep and abiding sources of instability within what Chakrabarty would call History 1—but not in History 2. Marx was, of course, the most obvious exemplar of this view. In his theory, capitalism's reproduction is interrupted, not by the obduracy of local cultures, norms, or practices, but by the very practices that are "posited" by capital. None is more central to this than accumulation itself. As Marx famously expressed it, "The *true barrier* to capitalist production is *capital itself*."[43] What he meant was that the rules by which capitalist accumulation takes place are self-defeating. They demand of each entrepreneur that she place

---

42   To my knowledge, Jon Elster introduced this concept in his *Logic and Society: Contradictions and Possible Worlds* (New York: Wiley, 1978), chap. 5.

43   Karl Marx, *Capital*, vol. III (New York: Vintage, 1981), 358.

the profit motive above all else, as a condition for surviving in the market. Yet, even though each individual capitalist has good reason to pursue success through cost-cutting innovations, the aggregate effect of these strategies is to weaken the underlying conditions of reproduction for capital, and eventually to plunge the economy into a crisis—thereby creating a rupture in the cycle of reproduction.[44] The crisis thus stems from the very core of the universal, abstractly defined rules of accumulation. But this is not just a fact about Marx's theory. It is also true of Smith, Ricardo, and Keynes. Each of these theorists developed an analysis of capitalism that located its fragility, its vulnerability to crisis, within the basic rules of the system itself. Furthermore, precisely because its source is the very practices essential to the system, the connection between these practices and breakdown is both deeper, and more explosive, than anything Chakrabarty establishes for History 2.

There is, however, a second source of disruption to capital's logic that is located within History 1. This is the universal interest that working people have to protect their well-being from capitalist authority and abuse. I have already defended the notion that some such interest exists, and indeed, that the Subalternist theorists themselves rely on the existence of this interest in their historical analyses. Recall that Guha pointedly defends this view in *Elementary Aspects of Peasant Insurgency in Colonial India*, as we witnessed in chapter 7; Chatterjee sneaks it into his account of Bengali peasant mobilizations, which we also examined in chapter 7; Chakrabarty admits to its existence in his labor history, examined in chapter 8. For our purposes, what deserves emphasis is that this interest—and others we might include, such as the interest in autonomy or self-determination—properly belong, on Chakrabarty's own definition, to History 1. What distinguishes History 1, remember, is that it encompasses the "Enlightenment universals." Capital and its cognates are central to this group of universals, of course, but so are such abstract concepts as freedom, democracy, and citizenship. On more than one occasion, Chakrabarty explicitly makes reference to these as belonging to History 1.[45]

The interest in well-being is a fundamental source of instability to capital, simply because of its ubiquity—it is built into the psychology of social agents, regardless of culture or location. The very fact that cultures exist at all presupposes that social agents have a drive to protect their basic needs. But precisely because this interest is a component of human nature, it necessarily brings workers into conflict with the logic of accumulation, wherever and whenever it

---

44   I have deliberately formulated this logic at a very abstract level, so that it does not depend on the viability of any particular Marxist crisis theory. My construal of the dilemmas of accumulation is intended to be agnostic toward, and consistent with, the three main crisis theories within the Marxian tradition—the rising organic composition of capital, underconsumption, and disproportionality.

45   See *PE* 67, 250.

unfolds. And thus, as explored above in chapters 6 and 8, it was only through subaltern mobilizations that capitalism was civilized. These nineteenth-century struggles were nothing other than a *modification of capital's logic*. As Marx showed in such graphic detail in the chapters on machinery and the working day in the first volume of *Capital*, the struggle for limiting the working day not only added to the well-being of British workers, it also forced capitalists to change their accumulation strategy, making them abandon a wholesale reliance on increasing surplus value by sweating labor—what he called absolute surplus value—and turn instead to productivity-enhancing means—what he called relative surplus value.[46] These specific struggles occurred in Victorian England, but they have been played out all over the globe, wherever capital has established its rule. They are, to use Chakrabarty's language, a part of the *universal and necessary history of capital*, and hence of History 1.

Even though both these sources of instability—capitalism's structural pathologies and labor's resistance—can disrupt capital's reproduction, they do not operate in the same way, nor do they have the same effects. Although Chakrabarty often uses the two phenomena interchangeably, it is important to maintain a distinction between the disruption of capital's *logic* and the disruption of its *universalization*. A pattern of reproduction can be disrupted, interrupted, or dislocated—all expressions used by Chakrabarty—and it can then resume anew, begin a new cycle, after the disruption. In other words, the mere disruption of its reproduction need not derail its ongoing universalization, because the disruption can simply be temporary, after which the universalization can continue apace, once the system has recuperated. But for the universalization of its logic to be undermined requires something beyond a mere interruption of its normal routine of reproduction. It requires a transformation of the rules of reproduction in a fundamental way, as argued above.

Both these sources of instability interrupt and destabilize capital's logic of reproduction, but only one truly undermines its universalization. Structurally generated crises—whether from falling profitability or from imbalances across sectors—do not, as far as I can glean, constitute a block to capital's universalization. If anything, they probably accelerate it. As David Harvey has noted, crises often trigger an outward expansion of capitalism, in search of new markets, new and cheaper inputs, as a "spatial fix."[47] In this manner, crises accelerate the outward expansion of capital, and the imposition of its own rules of reproduction on new territories. By contrast, labor struggles offer the promise of far more fundamental threats to capital's reproduction. True, in many cases, even in most cases, such struggles modify these rules, keeping their basic integrity unchanged. But when and where the rules themselves

---

46   See Karl Marx, *Capital*, vol. I (New York: Vintage, 1976), pts. 3, 4.
47   David Harvey, *The Limits to Capital* (New York: Verso, 2007).

have been transformed in some far-reaching way, it has been as a consequence of the universal struggle of working people to defend against capital's depredations and to improve their welfare.

Hence, if there is any genuine source of opposition to capital's universalizing drive, it is the equally universal struggle by subaltern classes to defend their basic humanity. That is the core motivation in all those thousands of campaigns for wages, land rights, basic health, and security, dignity, self-determination, autonomy, and so forth—all those Enlightenment concepts against which postcolonial theorists inveigh. The "heterogeneities and incommensurabilities" of History 2 pale in comparison.

THERE IS NO NECESSARY ANTAGONISM BETWEEN HISTORY 1 AND HISTORY 2

If it is not the function of History 2 to interrupt or derail capital's reproduction, then there is no reason for capital to "subjugate or destroy" History 2, as Chakrabarty insists it must do. There is no necessary antagonism between History 1 and History 2. I have suggested that we should disaggregate History 2 into two subcategories—History 2_1, which is independent of capital and does not clash with it in any way, and History 2_2, which is independent of capital and does clash with it. It should be evident that there is no question of any antagonism between History 1 and History 2_1. If there is any conflict at all, it is with History 2_2. So, at best, we can only allow that History 1 might have to destroy or subordinate elements of History 2_2. But this gives only limited succor to Chakrabarty's argument, because, crucially, we have no idea how extensive or powerful are the practices associated with History 2_2, compared with those of History 2_1. It could be that the vast majority of social practices in History 2 are in fact located in the 2_1 group, which is neutral toward History 1.

Indeed, this latter possibility would seem the more likely. Consider the implications if most practices that are independent of capital's rules are also inimical to its reproduction—in other words, that they belong to History 2_2. If this were the case, then capital would have to transform *entire cultures* as a precondition to its stable reproduction. On the other hand, if it were the case that most components of History 2 belonged to History 2_1, which is neutral toward capital, then the cultural preconditions for capitalism's stable reproduction would be far less demanding. It would now require the transformation of a far smaller set of practices, meaning that capitalism would face fewer cultural obstacles to its implantation in the far reaches of the globe. Surely, if we look back at the experience of the twentieth century, in which capitalism has spread to every corner of the world despite the enormous diversity of cultures, it is the second proposition that seems the more plausible. This is not to deny that globalization has brought with it some deep and lasting cultural changes. But it has not homogenized the cultural landscape. This suggests that capital can subsist, even flourish, without having to revolutionize entire cultures.[48]

The absence of antagonism between History 1 and History 2 is best illustrated through a consideration, once again, of abstract labor. We have already broached this issue in chapter 6, where I examined Lisa Lowe's mistaken view that the persistence of racial and cultural hierarchies in the labor force counted against the concept of abstract labor. I took up the issue because it exemplified the postcolonialists' suspiciousness toward abstract categories, and showed the mistakes that bedevil their analysis. Let us now turn to how Chakrabarty mobilizes the concept of abstract labor to prove his particular arguments, and I will show that, as with Lowe, his analysis is based on subtle but fundamental misconceptions about the concept.

Chakrabarty uses the example of abstract labor to illustrate his claim that History 1 must subjugate or destroy History 2.[49] He invites us to consider the example of a laborer who shows up at the factory gates at 8:00 AM, ready to put in a full day's work. In his capacity as a worker, as a person willing to sell his labor power for a wage, he embodies all the abstract categories of political economy. As he walks through the factory gates, he becomes part of the universal history of capital, hence a part of History 1. Chakrabarty observes that inasmuch as the worker comes prepared to offer his laboring activity, "Everything I have said about 'abstract labor' will apply to him or her."[50] But the worker is also a concrete person, steeped in his local culture and norms and shaped by his biographical peculiarities, none of which are part of History 1. This, Chakrabarty says, places some parts of his past experiences, and some of his current proclivities, in the category of History 2:

> While walking through the factory gate, however, my fictional person also embodies other kinds of pasts. These pasts, grouped together in my analysis of History 2, may be under the institutional domination of the logic of capital and exist in proximate relationship to it, but they do not belong to the "life-process" of capital. They

---

48   We need look to no other source than Chakrabarty and his fellow postcolonial theorists for support on this front. Remember that it is a premise of postcolonial theory that capital has not been able to homogenize the social landscape. This was the argument that Lisa Lowe advanced in her mistaken criticism of Marx's concept of abstract labor. It is also a foundation for Chakrabarty's insistence that universalization has failed. Both of them take the persistent heterogeneity of cultures as a datum, even while they admit that capital has spread across the world. It is just that they interpret the persistence of diversity as evidence for the failure of capital's universalization. The fact that they are mistaken in their conclusions is not really important here. The important point is that they admit the implantation of capitalism in enormously diverse cultural settings. What this shows is that capitalism does not *need* to homogenize the entire social landscape. The reason is that most of the landscape belongs to History 2_1, the part that is neutral to capitalism's basic rules.

49   PE 65, 67.

50   PE 66.

enable the human bearer of labor power to enact other ways of being in the world—other than, that is, being the bearer of labor power.[51]

So the worker embodies both kinds of possibilities within his own person. On the one hand, he is capable of being the abstract laborer, the repository of labor power that capital seeks in order to sustain the accumulation process. On the other hand, the worker also reflects the particularities of the local culture, which were not molded by capital and which reflect ways of being that do not conform to its functional requirements. This, Chakrabarty declares, represents a fundamental threat to capital, and it responds to the threat by trying to destroy History 2. The site where capital carries out its assault on History 2 is the labor process:

> The disciplinary process in the factory is in part meant to accomplish the subjuga-tion/destruction of History 2. Capital, Marx's abstract category, says to the laborer: "I want you to be reduced to sheer living labor—muscular energy plus conscious-ness—for the eight hours for which I have bought your capacity to labor. I want to effect a separation between your personality (that is, the personal and collective histories you embody) and your will (which is characteristic of sheer conscious-ness) . . ."[52]

Chakrabarty is building here on his analysis of abstract labor, which precedes this discussion of the labor process.[53] For him, capital *creates* abstract labor in the labor process by imposing work discipline on the laborers. What the capital-ist acquires as the worker enters the factory gate is not abstract labor, but what Chakrabarty calls "real labor."[54] The challenge for management is to turn this real, concrete labor into abstract labor. This transformation is what the labor process is meant to accomplish, through the imposition of factory discipline.[55] The disciplinary process is geared toward reducing the worker to sheer living energy, pure muscular activity, an appendage to the machine. In so doing, it erases his history, all the local norms and conventions that have produced him as a concrete person—"the personal and collective histories you embody"—so that he conforms to the needs of his employer. The motivation behind this assault on the worker comes from the threat posed by History 2. Notice that in the passages I have quoted, Chakrabarty locates the threat of the worker's noncompliance in those dimensions of his past that are located in History 2. It is History 2 that generates "ways of being in the world other than being the

51   Ibid.
52   *PE* 67.
53   See *PE* 51–6.
54   *PE* 92, 94–5.
55   *PE* 55–7, 95.

bearer of labor power." Hence, in order to establish its authority over the laborer, capital must turn him into the bearer of labor power pure and simple. It does this by destroying History 2.

This entire line of reasoning, however, rests on a basic misconception about what capital seeks. Chakrabarty treats capitalists' desire to mold their workers into "sheer living labor" as the main object of the labor process. But this is erroneous. While managers do design the organization of work in a way that enables them to dominate labor, this is a secondary aim, put to the service of another, more fundamental desideratum. Recall the core of my argument in chapter 6: what managers pursue when they hire labor is, in the first instance, the extraction of work effort at benchmark levels of intensity. This is what we might call the first-order commitment of every capitalist. All of their shop-floor strategies toward labor, upon which Chakrabarty focuses, are *derived* in pursuit of this basic goal, and are therefore to be regarded as second-order goals. The degree and kind of authority that are wielded in the labor process are thus useful only because they serve the purpose of extracting the needed level of work effort.

This being the case, we are compelled to ask whether the pursuit of socially necessary labor requires that managers try to eliminate all of the laborer's History 2. Does it demand that the worker lose all connection with "the personal and collective history" that shaped him? This would be the only justification for treating the labor process as if it were fundamentally geared toward these ends. It would have to be the case that, in order to secure the socially necessary labor effort, managers would have no choice but to obliterate every trace of each worker's particular normative universe. But it should be quite obvious that extracting the needed labor effort requires the subjugation of only those aspects of the worker's culture that *inhibit* his ability or his willingness to work as needed. Moreover, these recalcitrant elements of his culture will comprise only a part of the total. The only grounds on which we could accept Chakrabarty's argument—that capital requires an all-out assault on History 2 as a whole— would be if we presume that every component of local culture that deviates from the direct needs of capital is thereby, and necessarily, inimical to capitalist reproduction. Simply stating this premise reveals it as utterly bizarre.

A far more reasonable argument is that managers will initiate measures to "subjugate or destroy" elements of History 2 only in *those* instances where they *do* conflict with the extraction of socially necessary labor power. But, in those instances where the elements are *neutral* to the labor effort, managers will simply be indifferent to them. In other words, capital simply does not care about workers' local culture as long as it does not interfere with the accumulation process. Managers' attitude toward the manifold elements in History 2 will therefore be indifference, not hostility, *as long as they are able to acquire the labor effort they seek.* As long as capitalists are able to transform this particular dimension of the workers' culture, they are content to let the other dimensions persist in all their glory. Indeed, management may even patronize these other dimensions if they feel this will help inure workers to their authority. It has been a staple of human resource management for some time now to pay homage to local cultures as a way of reducing friction on the shop floor. Business schools often encourage and offer training in multiculturalism, not as a sign of resignation against the proud resistance of History 2 but as a savvy realization that the valorization of the neutral dimensions of local culture can help in the domestication of the problematic ones. Some of the more insidious mutations of this strategy were described in Chapter 6, where I discussed the possibility of managerial promotion of sectarian identities as a means of disciplining labor.

If it is true that capitalists can securely extract the socially necessary effort from labor without having to wipe out History 2, then we have established, once again, that there is no necessary antagonism between History 1 and History 2. We have also seen that such antagonism as can be expected will encompass only a subset of the worker's practical culture. A significant array of his practical orientations will be of little consequence to managers, and hence to capital. History 1 is therefore perfectly happy to coexist with many elements of History 2.

This conclusion is entirely consistent with my earlier analysis of abstract labor in chapter 6. I argued there that employers' pursuit of abstract labor should not be understood as a desire to render all labor the same. Abstract labor is not a distinct *kind* of labor. It refers to only one dimension of workers' productive activity, which is their ability to labor at the socially necessary level of efficiency. Capitalists try only to bring that dimension of their workers' activity into line with that achieved by their rivals; however, in striving to homogenize *this* dimension of labor, they may well *deepen* the heterogeneity in *other* dimensions, such as race, caste, culture or gender. Lisa Lowe and David Roediger make the error of equating the homogenization of *one dimension* of labor with the homogenization of labor *tout court*. It should now be evident that Chakrabarty is making the same mistake. For him, as for Roediger and Lowe, the pursuit of abstract labor can be understood only as its homogenization. In his insistence that capital must eradicate all History 2s, he is asserting that capital will not tolerate in its workers any vestige of local customs, practices, or expectations that do not conform to its functional requirements. Either capital homogenizes labor's practical orientation, making every worker a mere assemblage of nerves and muscle, or the universalizing process must be deemed a failure. The preceding discussion demonstrates that he is as mistaken in his view as are Lowe and Roediger.

A final point: Because of his mistaken view that it is by History 2 that the universalizing drive of capitalism is disrupted, Chakrabarty assigns a moral and political urgency to its study. If Enlightenment theorists efface historical difference because of their obsession with History 1, then a central task for critical historians is to defend the reality of difference by attending to the practices embodied in History 2—to treat them as instances of resistance to capital, not as relics or anachronisms. Now, the preceding sections should suffice to show that the idea of History 2s being special sites of resistance to capital is baseless. What, then, should be said of the celebration of what Chakrabarty calls, at various points, the East's heterogeneities, heterotemporalities, incommensurabilities, incommensurable temporalities, and so forth? Once the theoretical heavy breathing is allowed to slow, what it amounts to is just what it seems to be—*a license for exoticism*. Once we recognize that History 2 neither destabilizes capital's universalization nor poses any threat to its reproduction, then there is nothing to justify Subalternist historians' seemingly endless fascination with religion, ritual, spirits, indigeneity, and so on. We are free to criticize it for what it seems to be—a revival and celebration of Orientalist discourse.

9.5 HISTORICISM AS A NON-PROBLEM

Let us turn now to the problem of historicism. Chakrabarty's conceptualization of historicism, as we have seen, depends entirely on his prior theorization of the Two Histories. And, as just discussed, even though the basic distinction between the History 1 and History 2 can be justified, none of the consequences that Chakrabarty wishes to derive from them can withstand scrutiny. If this is so, it carries some rather severe implications for his critique of historicism.

Recall that Chakrabarty highlights two assumptions as being central to historicist analyses. One is that they tend to attribute an unwarranted coherence to social complexes, making their various elements seem functionally integrated. Social practices are assumed to fit into a single seamless whole, operating under the same logic and explicable by the same principles. Second, they treat history as if it were irrevocably driven toward a known future. For the future to be known is to assign to it a *telos*. It is the idea that even if we cannot predict the actual course of events in any given region, we can have a good idea of the basic principles that will govern its institutional development. Chakrabarty accuses historicists of embracing these fallacies because of their valorization of History 1 and their corresponding demotion of History 2. Both orientations lead to the same basic problem: they make it impossible to appreciate difference. Where practices fail to align with capital, and cannot therefore be explained by its properties, it is simply assumed that *if we just wait long enough* these practices will either disappear or be brought into conformity with capital's rules. He charges his target with the assumption that historical difference is taken as an aberration, a conceptual non-problem, for every instance of it must be temporary.

It is of course regrettable if theorists hew to a thick-headed functionalism about social wholes, and equally deplorable if they refuse to acknowledge historical diversity. The point is not to defend these mistakes, nor to deny that they exist. The issue here is whether theorists who affirm the universalization of capital are bound and committed to such views and, by extension, whether Enlightenment theories necessarily generate them.

Let us start with the problem of social coherence. Based on my earlier arguments, we can glean two flaws in Chakrabarty's criticism. First, a theory that affirms capitalism's universalization does *not* have to assume that capital will subordinate the entirety of social practices to its own logic. Such a theory— Marxism, for instance—can perfectly well recognize the enduring independence of all sorts of practices and institutions, as was established earlier in the present chapter, where I argued that capitalists have no interest in subordinating all practices to the logic of accumulation. If indeed they have no such interest, then they can continue to reproduce themselves as capitalists on whatever resources are available to them. There is ample elbow room for History 2 to persist, and for a happy coexistence between it and History 1. This means, in turn, that the social whole—the ensemble of social relations in any geographic region—need not be subsumed under one particular set of rules. The various practices that comprise the whole can be governed by very dissimilar internal logics, even as capital universalizes. The most we can say is that practices necessary to capital's reproduction will fall under its sway. Many of them will internalize its rules of reproduction. But there will continue to be practices that retain their integrity, and also remain stable. Hence, theories affirming capital's universalizing drive do not have to efface historical diversity.

Second, it is simply not the case that post-Enlightenment theories' emphasis on universals blinds them to the possibility of "discontinuities, ruptures, and shifts in the historical process," as Chakrabarty puts it.[56] As just discussed, the possibility of discontinuities and ruptures in capital's reproduction, as well as departures from its logic, was central to the Marxist framework, as also to several other theories in classical and modern political economy. Chakrabarty is in fact doubly mistaken: both in his view that Western theories cannot apprehend the discontinuities and ruptures in historical development, and in his belief that the main source of these ruptures is History 2. As shown above, the main source of instability and breakdown is not History 2 but rather the general, system-wide properties of capitalism itself, i.e., History 1. For Marxists—always the main target of Chakrabarty's criticism—the friction from the constituent elements of capitalism is amplified by another source of disruption, namely, the subaltern classes' universal drive to defend themselves against domination. Marx thought that the general drive to exploit was necessarily countered by a general resistance to it on the part of workers. This, too, is an instance of systemic friction coming from *within* History 1. Chakrabarty's insistence that the attention to universals occludes the appreciation of dislocation and

---

56   *PE* 23.

disruption is therefore baseless. If anything, we can insist on the opposite—it is simply impossible to understand the sources of disruption to capitalism's reproductive logic *except* through the categories of History 1.

So much for the first consequence that Chakrabarty attributes to historicism. Now to the second: that it leads theorists to deny the place of historical contingency. Does the affirmation of capital's universalization impose some kind of determinism, or teleology, on historical development? Marxists often respond to accusations of determinism by denying it, by jumping onto the contingency bandwagon—especially in the current intellectual climate, where any whiff of determinism is often viewed as the grossest folly. But it is important to resist this temptation. The fact is that the universalization of capital *does* impose limits on agents' choices, and if it imposes limits on their choices, it must, by definition, also impose limits on "possible futures." In other words, Chakrabarty is right that you cannot affirm the dominion of History 1 while also affirming that all futures are possible. So there is little doubt that the universalization of capital—by virtue of the fact that it is the universalization of a specific set of social structures and roles—does impart a degree of stability, and hence of determinism, to social outcomes. This is, to use Chakrabarty's language, a recognition that, once capitalism becomes dominant, at least some futures have been closed off. But should we take this as an *unwarranted* determinism? The only way it could be objectionable would be if it exaggerated the constraints imposed by capitalism. In other words, if capitalism really does close off some options, then Marxists can hardly be maligned for incorporating this into their theory. The only legitimate criticism would be if they are unduly deterministic—in other words, if their theory is more deterministic than reality.

How exactly, then, do Marxists fall into the trap of determinism? Chakrabarty neither accuses them of predicting the actual course of future events nor suggests that, for Marxists, all capitalisms are headed for a narrow institutional convergence. Determinism of that kind would certainly be objectionable, but it is not what Chakrabarty identifies with Marxist historicism.

What he identifies as the problem is their conviction that the future is "a future of which we know at least the *constitutive principles*, even if we do not have a *blueprint* for it."[57] Note the contrast between the italicized concepts. It is quite clear what it would mean for there to be a blueprint for the future. Blueprints describe how the various elements of a whole fit together. They tell us what the elements are, their size, their shape, their interconnections. If we utilize this as a metaphor for historical knowledge, it suggests that if we have a blueprint for the future, we have the ability to enumerate the actual institutions that will comprise future society—their internal structure, mutual interrelations, relative weight, and so on. This would amount to being able to predict the

---

57   *PE* 250. Emphasis added.

actual design of a particular society. Chakrabarty agrees that Marxist historicism *does not* make any such claim.

What Chakrabarty does identify as central to Marxist historicism, and finds objectionable, is its claim to have identified the constitutive principles that will define future development. As usual, though, Chakrabarty does not tell us what this expression is intended to convey. But the contrast with blueprints hints at what he has in mind. When we say that a process is governed by some principle, what we usually mean is that there is a set of *rules* in place whose function is to allow for certain kinds of properties while discouraging others. It is a selection mechanism. Therefore, even if we do not know the details of what is to come, we have an idea of certain formal properties that it will abide by, because these properties are what the rules select for.

Now, if we carry this intuition over to the problem of historical development, it acquires a clear implication. It means that capitalism establishes a set of parameters that select *in favor* of certain *sorts* of institutions while selecting *against* others. Hence, if Marxists argue that the future is governed by certain constitutive principles, this amounts to the claim that future social institutions will be powerfully constrained by pressures linked to capitalism—pressures like capital accumulation, the social power of the bourgeoisie, the demands of wage labor, and so on. The principles do not select for particular persons or any particular institutional layout. They would not mandate that the future nation-states take the design of David Cameron's United Kingdom, or that cultural production become exactly what Hollywood produces, or that labor processes look like mid-twentieth-century mass production. *That* would indeed amount to a blueprint. What they would impose is a set of parameters that social institutions would be constrained to respect. The main such parameter is that they not interfere with the accumulation of capital, and even that they encourage it. Social institutions could therefore be highly varied in their details, as long as they were consistent with the reproduction of capitalism. Marxists would predict that there will be pressure to commodify cultural production, but not to produce any *particular* product; pressure for states to favor capitalist interests, but not the interests of any *particular* capitalists; pressure for labor processes to conform to the demands of profitability, but not to hew to a *particular* model. Therein lies the difference between blueprints and principles.

I believe we now have an idea of what it might mean to have knowledge of certain constitutive principles governing historical development. But would those principles be equally binding on all social institutions? Does capitalism impose its imprint on every social practice or convention? The answer is already implicit in what has been explored in this chapter: that, in fact, capital's selectional pressures are not equally binding on all dimensions of social life. When capitalism takes root in a region, its transformative effects are felt, above all, in economic activities, while they are less powerful with respect to political and cultural practices. True, some aspects of the latter two will no doubt be pulled quite firmly into a supporting role for capitalist production. Legal norms will have to recognize and defend property, the state will have to encourage accumulation, and even some cultural norms will have to accommodate the profit drive if they do not do so already. But there will be large swaths of political and ideological conventions that will be left largely to their own devices. What this means, then, is that some practices will find capitalism's "constitutive principles" quite powerful, even binding. These will be the practices that are intimately connected to economic reproduction—the practices Chakrabarty files under "History 1." But on other practices, more distant from material production, the pressures will impinge in varying degrees of intensity—rather powerfully on certain ones, and on others not at all. This is what is entailed in the proposition that capitalism establishes the constitutive principles for historical development, and thereby closes off certain futures.

If this is what it means for the future to abide by certain constitutive principles, then we are justified in asking—is it really so outrageous a claim? Does Chakrabarty really wish to deny that capitalism imposes limits on institutional variation? Does he think that all social practices are possible once capitalism takes hold? That it does not impose any limits on their diversity? That would be an odd position for someone who sees himself as a critic of capital.

We know by this point, of course, that Chakrabarty's main worry is not about the existence of constraints per se, but with how tight they are taken to be. He seems to think that, for Marxists, the constraints are so binding that they lead to the subordination of all social practices to the logic of capital—and if this were what the Marxist position demanded, then his worries would be justified. But I have shown in some detail that the concern is a figment of Chakrabarty's imagination. Marxist arguments do not require that all social relations become subject to capitalism's logic. They certainly do require that *some* practices become directly subject to capitalism's rules, namely the practices that govern the production of goods and services. As for practices and institutions that are not intrinsically connected to economic production, the requirement is less binding; in most cases, the extent to which they will be sucked into capital's orbit cannot be prejudged. This is another way of saying that it will be a contingent outcome of social contestation. But then Marxists can readily believe that historical development will be guided by certain constitutive principles, while still allowing for indeterminacy in a wide array of social outcomes.

So much for the second dimension of historicism. But if neither of the two dimensions poses a genuine threat, then nothing remains of Chakrabarty's argument. In other words, *the problem of "historicism" vanishes*. It is not that Chakrabarty's critique of historicism is flawed—rather, he has invented a problem where none exists. He deems it a live issue only because he first misunderstands the implications of his distinction between History 1 and History 2, and then, on the basis of that misunderstanding, attributes to post-Enlightenment theories views that they do not hold. He thinks that if a theory is committed to the possibility of capital's universalization, it cannot allow for the enduring presence of the myriad practices in History 2. This incapacity supposedly flows from the idea that History 1 will necessarily subsume every social relation under its logic. But Chakrabarty's entire argument is based on a flawed premise—that for capital (History 1) to universalize, it must subjugate/subordinate the independence of History 2 – hence, every element of the social whole that does not conform to capital's logic. Once we reject this premise, the rest of the framework he builds in *Provincializing Europe* simply collapses. Since universalization does not require the extinction of History 2, there is no necessary antagonism between the Two Histories. History 1 has no need to extinguish History 2. And since there is no antagonism, History 2 can happily persist, in all its multifarious glory, alongside History 1. Since History 2 can persist in this manner, there is no presumption that, if only we wait long enough, History 2 will just dissolve away or lose its independence. To be sure, practices internal to economic reproduction will be transformed along capitalist lines—this is where the "waiting room" metaphor is apt, and entirely defensible. But this transformation will not entail a corresponding erasure of all the elements in History 2. They will face no similar pressures to conform to a universalizing logic. Hence, the Two Histories can retain their own dynamic properties even while continuing to intersect now and again. Theories committed to the reality of capital's universalization do not, therefore, have to be blind to historical diversity. They can affirm the former, while also recognizing the viability of all the relations and practices that Chakrabarty groups under History 2.

9.6 CAPITALISM AND DIVERSITY REVISITED

It is now time to draw together the argument about historical diversity and to show the multiple channels through which a universalizing capitalism generates a diversity of social forms.

Readers should take away two main points from the discussion below. The first is that capitalism is not only compatible with social difference, but systematically produces it. The second is that, insofar as a great deal of what we take to be social difference is in fact causally related to capitalist reproduction, it follows that the analysis of that diversity must, of necessity, draw on the universalizing categories of post-Enlightenment theories. So, while the first point undermines the frequently encountered postcolonialist argument that capitalism homogenizes the social, the second belies the claim that universalizing theories cannot apprehend heterogeneity.

THREE SOURCES OF DIVERSITY IN CAPITALISM

We have engaged with the Subalternist argument from diversity at several places in this book. It was central to chapter 5, on the matter of power; it was the focus of chapter 6 and its defense of abstract labor as a category; and of course, it was central to the discussion of historicism earlier in the present chapter. At all of these junctures, I have suggested both that capitalism can live with, and even generate, tremendous social heterogeneity, and that the abstract categories of Enlightenment thought can apprehend the connection between the two. Let me now bring together the arguments scattered across these four chapters and present them in consolidated form. The following are channels through which capitalism accommodates with, or generates, historical diversity. My list is by no means exhaustive, but I do believe these channels are the more important ones.

- *First channel: Reinforcing existing heterogeneity*

We have already encountered this dynamic in the discussion of abstract labor.[58] Capitalism does not have to dissolve social differences in order to reproduce itself; in fact, it can be in the interest of managers to rely on social distinctions as they find them, in order to more effectively extract labor effort from their workers. A second mechanism through which it can reinforce existing divisions is by making it rational for workers to cling to their kith and kin, thereby further cementing their existing identities and reinforcing social heterogeneity, as we saw in our discussion of Chakrabarty's labor history.[59] Both processes are endemic to capitalist reproduction. The former reinforces divisions from above, the latter from below.

- *Second channel: Producing new heterogeneity*

As we observed earlier,[60] the main sources of friction in capitalism's reproduction, as well as in its universalization, are elements internal to History 1. One of the main consequences of the resulting instability is that capitalist development is markedly uneven across space and time. On the one hand, as capital moves from one region to another in the course of seeking out profits, it creates waves of destruction in certain places while fueling the creation of entirely new zones of accumulation elsewhere. But this movement occurs at different speeds across regions, as profits fall rapidly in some but more slowly in others. The differential speeds of capital's movement generate highly diverse rates of economic growth, which means in turn that some regions decline and decay, while others rise—all at very different tempos. These difference-producing dynamics are amplified by the contestation between labor and capital—also internal to History 1—that

---

58   See Chap. 6 above.
59   See Chap. 8 above.
60   See Chap. 9 above, 229–33.

necessarily accompany the accumulation process, both as it winds down in a given region and as it takes off.

Thus, the diversity that comes from the unevenness of each cycle of accumulation, and from the rise and decline of economic regions, is heightened by the contingent effects of the capital-labor conflict. In some places, capital is able to impose its will with alacrity, while in others it is forced to accommodate labor's defense of its own well-being. Whatever the power balance happens to be in a given place, it produces its own institutional structure reflecting that balance. Thus, in postwar Europe, labor amassed enough power to build and sustain a powerful welfare state, trade unions, infrastructure, and so on, all of which in turn affected the pace of accumulation and the means of working-class reproduction. In the United States, on the other hand, a very different power balance between labor and capital led to a weaker social democracy, less powerful unions, highly privatized social provisions, and so on, producing a rather different set of accumulation strategies as well as quite distinct patterns of working-class reproduction. All this can be contrasted to the kinds of capitalism that were built up in the postcolonial world, with their own temporalities and their own accumulation patterns. And although all of these are variants within capitalism, they each exhibit their own temporal and spatial particularities. This is just another way of saying that capitalism promotes development—but that the development thus promoted is highly differentiated and uneven. Capitalism is anything but a purely homogenizing dynamic.

- *Third channel: Indifference to existing heterogeneity*
The third source of heterogeneity is capitalism's capacity for coexistence with all manner of social practices, so long as they do not clash with its logic of reproduction. Much of the current chapter has been devoted to this view.

Of the three channels just outlined, only one counts as being purely internal to History 1—the second channel, which concerns uneven development. The other two are either complete or partial cases of History 1's coexistence with History 2. If we consider the first of the three channels, whereby capitalism further promotes the inherited social diversity, this can certainly be accomplished through the destruction of History 2 or its subjugation to History 1. But this need not be so. It is not necessary to assume that the practices reinforced by capitalism will become absorbed into its reproductive logic; they can be strengthened without becoming dependent on it. To give but one example, in certain colonial settings, employers relied on traditional ruling classes to supply them with labor and to maintain political order. They did so not by destroying the basis of local authority, but by strengthening it. This was an example of capital's further solidification of practices that it did not control, and that did not follow the same reproductive rules as it did itself. No doubt, certain aspects of traditional life were dramatically changed, as producers who had formerly been peasants were now forced to work for colonial firms as wage labor or indentured labor, but this transformation went hand in hand with the reinforcement of other traditional practices, which retained their own integrity. Hence, even while History 1 and History 2 interacted with each other, the former did not destroy the latter. What this example demonstrates is that when capitalism reinforces existing forms of social heterogeneity, it can do so without destroying the basis of their independent reproduction. It is an example of History 1 *promoting* History 2—the very opposite of what Chakrabarty predicts. Finally, of course, the third channel exemplifies the happy coexistence between the two Histories.

WHAT IT MEANS FOR THEORY

What do these three channels imply for theory? To develop an analysis of cases in which the production of diversity is causally related to capitalism, it will most likely be necessary to employ the very framework that Chakrabarty denigrates. In other words, since the practices or social forms under scrutiny are causally linked to capitalism, their analysis will make reference to whichever properties of capitalism are implicated in their reproduction. These properties may be *internal to* History 1, as in cases that fall under the second channel, or they may be *interlocked with* History 1 through some network, as in the case of colonial labor recruitment in the discussion of the first channel. In these cases, social difference will be explained as a consequence of capitalism's universalizing drive, and will deploy the universalizing categories of post-Enlightenment thought.

But in cases that embody the third channel, the universalizing categories of post-Enlightenment thought could well have no relevance to the practices in question. This is because the diversity being examined will be an instance of History 2 to which capitalism is largely indifferent. Remember that the myriad social practices to which we are referring here are the ones that retain their independence from the rules of capitalism. The explanations as to how and why they persist will, as a result, likely make no reference to capitalism. Unlike the first two channels, therefore, histories of these practices will not have to draw on the universalizing categories of capital. They might turn out to be driven by highly localized institutional dynamics, or be tied to other cultural practices, or be highly contingent outcomes of social conflict not connected to capital. Consequently, the main issue will not be whether or not they are products of capitalism, since they are not. It will be whether they are products of material social practices or are produced by dynamics internal to discourse or culture. In other words, what will be at stake is not the relevance of a Marxian framework, but rather the relevance of a materialist framework.

This means there is no presumption that a universalizing capitalism must become the explanatory master key for every social phenomenon. It will be highly relevant for phenomena that are generated in channels one and two, but not in channel three. Where we find that a phenomenon falls into channel three, it is not in any way corrosive to the universalizing claims of the theory, for it is entirely consistent with the latter that a large range of practices will fall outside the theory's scope. These phenomena will have their own explanations, and what these are cannot be prejudged. As I suggested in the preceding paragraph, there is not even a presumption that the explanation must be a materialist one, at least not with respect to the proximate cause.

Chakrabarty is therefore quite wrong to maintain that practices that do not clearly fall in with prototypically "modern" ones must be a source of anxiety for universalizing theories. He holds that "modern historical consciousness"—that is to say, modes of thought influenced by "historicism"—feels a need to "construct a single historical context for everything" in order to explain it.[61] Everything must be seen either as a direct result of some universalizing principle or as a holdover, an anachronism, that will sooner or later disappear. But it should be clear by now that Chakrabarty is mistaken. It is entirely consistent to affirm capital's universalization and also to accept the potential viability of traditional practices. In some cases, they might be reproduced because of their connection to capitalism, as in the case of workers who hold to their communal identities, examined in Chapters 6 and 8. In other cases, they will be independent of capital and have sources of their own, as with Chakrabarty's History 2. Even though both kinds of practices will be based on different foundations, in *neither* case must they be treated as anachronisms. A universalizing theory will be quite capable of accommodating these phenomena with its core commitments.

9.7 CONCLUSION

One of the central motivations of postcolonial studies is to analyze how the globalization of capital in the modern epoch has affected social dynamics in the East. A conventional view, promoted by Western theorists in the nineteenth century, was that as capitalism spread across the world, it subordinated an ever-expanding zone to its own principles, thereby exposing the populations within that zone to a common set of constraints and compulsions. The fact that these populations were now subjected to the same pressures, and often the same practices, was taken as grounds for placing them within a common analytical framework. This strategy was most famously deployed by Marx and his followers, but postcolonial theorists are correct in their surmise that its use extended far beyond the Marxists. The result was the creation of something like a global

---

61   *PE* 243.

historiography of capitalism. As Chakrabarty observes, under its auspices, the story of regions as diverse as modern India or Japan or Egypt could fall under the same broad category of the history of capital.

This is the view that Chakrabarty rejects in *Provincializing Europe*, on arguments that are, as I have shown in this chapter, built on a series of misconceptions. Once we correct for his foibles, it is revealed to be entirely legitimate to write a universal history of East and West—what Chakrabarty terms "capitalist history." But this means nothing more than that in *some* of their practices, agents in Bombay, Nairobi, Detroit, and Cairo are all subjected to a common set of constraints.

Thus, I have defended both the success of a universalizing *process* and the utility of certain universal *categories* that map onto that process. The foundation for my defense of capitalism's universalization is that it does not require the subordination of every social practice in order that it may occur. All it requires as a matter of necessity is a change in the specific social relations that govern economic reproduction. Of course, this involves a wide array of relations, many of which are not directly economic. But it also omits a vast array of practices. It is not that these more distal practices will be entirely unaffected by capitalist dynamics. They will feel some impact of the economic transformation, if only because of the central role of economic reproduction—for agents at a micro level, and for society at a macro level. The changes in this sphere will therefore radiate outward, implicating other relations in many ways. The point is, the nature and weight of their impact, as well as the direction of change, cannot be prejudged once we have moved away from the core activities.

It is therefore entirely reasonable to affirm what Chakrabarty denies—that once capitalism is in place, and so long as it remains in place, we know the constitutive principles that will govern social development. This is not a sign of an illicit determinism; it is a recognition of the real effects of certain social structures. Or, to put it differently, the theory is no more deterministic than reality.

CHAPTER TEN

The Nation Unmoored

Capitalism, as was argued in the preceding chapter, exerts powerful structural pressures on the character of social institutions. It is this very property that is questioned by Dipesh Chakrabarty when he accuses Marxists of claiming to know the "constitutive principles" of future institutions.[1] He sees any such claim as issuing from an unwarranted determinism that imposes an artificial closure on the infinitely malleable future. I argued that it is in not only justified to see the future as constrained, but that it would be quite bizarre if it were not— if capitalism is real, and if it does actually limit the choices available to agents, then it simply follows that it also places limits on the range of institutions that will be compatible with it.

In this chapter, we will examine another Subalternist attempt to deny the limiting effects of capitalism: Partha Chatterjee's theory of colonial nationalism, as framed in his *Nationalist Thought and the Colonial World* of 1986.[2] Chatterjee has gained notoriety for describing these nationalisms as a *derivative discourse—* an ideology that purports to be critical of Western domination but is in fact unable to escape its grip. Anticolonial nationalism[3] is burdened by the contradiction that even while it rejects the chief claims of colonial ideology, the ideology of rule, it does so while accepting the foundations on which the colonial masters maintained their dominance. It appears to reject Western domination but in fact closes off the possibility of escaping it. It is, in this respect, trapped within the framework it seeks to displace. Existing theories of nationalism cannot appreciate this aspect of anticolonial nationalism, maintains Chatterjee, because they view it as a replication of the phenomenon as it appeared in the West. So, as with other issues we have examined in this book, a call goes out for a new theory, a new framework, an overturning of the existing canon.

For Chatterjee, one of the signs that colonial nationalism is still prisoner to Western ideology is its adoption of a modernizing agenda for the nation-state. We will see that he regards the modernizing perspective to be a ruse, a part of the very same discourse that was used to justify Western domination. For nationalists such as Nehru to accept it is, Chatterjee insists, a sign that they have been unable to break free of colonial ideology. This presumes, of course, that the turn to

---

1 See above, 240.

2 Partha Chatterjee, *Nationalist Thought and the Colonial World* (London: Zed Books, 1986). Hereafter cited as *NTCW*.

3 Chatterjee typically uses the expression "colonial nationalism." In this chapter I use "colonial nationalism" interchangeably with "anticolonial nationalism."

modernization was not undertaken because of a recognition of real constraints imposed by global capitalism—that there really was a possibility of refusing to modernize, and yet still build a viable national political economy. It is to presume that capitalism does not in fact limit the range of choices available to national elites. Chatterjee's argument, in other words, is much the same as Chakrabarty's denial that we can know the "constitutive principles" of the future.

I intend to show that Chatterjee's theory of nationalism fails in large measure because it denies the reality of capitalist constraints. It treats rational decisions as having been ideologically driven and, in so doing, vastly exaggerates the role of ideas and grossly undervalues the effects of actually existing structures. But that is not all. Chatterjee's theory is also a quite brazenly Orientalist depiction of the East-West divide. He does not merely present the turn to modernization as the product of Western indoctrination, but treats the deployment of reason—rational argument, objectivity, evidence—as Western and hence as colonial. In his theory, any nationalist who relies upon Reason— by which he means all those faculties I just listed—remains trapped within colonial discourse. Once again, we see rationality, logic, science, and objectivity as being internal to the West and alien to the East. Chatterjee's theory of nationalism is probably the most thoroughly Orientalist of all the arguments we have examined so far.

10.1 THE TWO DIMENSIONS OF ANTICOLONIAL NATIONALISM

There are two distinct components to Chatterjee's theory of nationalism. One is a historical sociology of nationalist *movements*, the other an analysis of the movements' *ideology*. The distinctive part of his work is embedded in his take on the second component: nationalism's ideological content. As for the sociology of the nationalist movement, his is much the same as Guha's, but with the references to Gramsci more visibly on display. Chatterjee bases both components of his argument entirely on the Indian experience, but it is important to note that he intends for them to be valid across the colonial world. His is a *general* theory of nationalist ideology—an important point, because even while he insists on its general relevance, he presents no evidence to support this claim. There is not even a mention, let alone a discussion, of any other colonial experience. It is up to us, therefore, to weigh his claims against the actual experience of the rest of the world.

THE PASSIVE REVOLUTION

Chatterjee takes the nationalist movement to be an instance of what Gramsci called a passive revolution.[4] The basic elements of a passive revolution are best

---

4   The basic source for this is Gramsci's analysis of the Risorgimento in the *Prison*

understood if contrasted with the classic bourgeois revolutions. Whereas in the classic bourgeois revolutions the capitalist class is understood to have launched a full-scale, frontal assault on the old order, this strategy is abandoned by its counterparts in later periods. In later periods, as evidenced in the revolutions of 1848 and in the Italian Risorgimento, the bourgeoisie draws back from directly attacking landed property. It does so because it lacks the social power to achieve leadership over the nation—to successfully "speak for all the people," as Guha might have said. Because of its meager legitimacy, it cannot trust that the movement it is leading against the feudal order will confine its goals to the eradication of landed property, while leaving capitalist property intact. The bourgeoisie in this situation differs from the leaders of the classic revolutions, in that it fears unleashing popular energies against the ancien régime. Capitalists therefore opt for a more cautious approach, in which they gradually chisel away at the base of landed power over a longer period of time. The key to this is the capture of state power, since it is with the levers of this power that the bourgeoisie slowly achieves its transformation of the class structure. Chatterjee summarizes it thus:

> [I]n situations where an emergent bourgeoisie lacks the social conditions for establishing complete hegemony over the new nation, it resorts to a "passive revolution," by attempting a "molecular transformation" of the dominant classes into partners in a new historic bloc and only a partial appropriation of the popular masses, in order to first create a state as the necessary precondition to the establishment of capitalism as the dominant mode of production.[5]

To achieve state power, the bourgeoisie must still undertake a mass mobilization, much as it did in the classic revolutions of 1640–8 and 1789. But this mobilization faces special challenges. It cannot just unleash popular anger against the ancien régime, for it does not trust its own abilities to set limits to the movement's ambitions. This is what it means to fail as a hegemonic class. Instead, therefore, it has to be a carefully modulated, *contained* mobilization, one that endows the leadership with real political leverage but is limited in its social and political goals.

Notebooks. See Antonio Gramsci, *Selections from the Prison Notebooks*, eds. Quintin Hoare and Geoffrey Nowell Smith (London: Lawrence and Wishart, 1971), 44–122. The literature on Gramsci peaked in the 1980s and suffers from fact that it was heavily overlaid with the Althusserian framework in vogue at the time, as well as the political debates around Eurocommunism. But a lucid, jargon-free introduction to the concept is provided by Joseph V. Femia in his *Gramsci's Political Thought: Hegemony, Consciousness, and the Revolutionary Process* (Oxford: Oxford University Press, 1981). A recent attempt to extend the concept to Latin America, albeit with uneven success, is Adam David Morton, *Unravelling Gramsci: Hegemony and Passive Revolution in the Global Political Economy* (London: Pluto Press, 2007).

5 *NTCW* 30.

Chatterjee's claim is that the "passive revolution is the general form of the transition from colonial to postcolonial rule in the 20th century."[6] His project is to explore the *content* of the ideology that facilitates the onset of this transition—the ideology of anticolonial nationalism. But the content itself needs to fulfill certain basic functional requirements if it is to succeed in the dual ambition of the anticolonial passive revolution: to push out the colonial power while preserving the power of domestic ruling classes. The ideology must be mobilizational, but also an instrument of *control*. It must successfully articulate some of the concerns of the popular classes, but also preclude those classes from achieving real power through genuine participation in the nation's political life. This is the challenge handed to anticolonial nationalism in the twentieth century. Its success as a discursive formation depends on its success in achieving both ends—mobilization and control.

This argument is quite similar to the one proposed by Ranajit Guha about the nature of the bourgeois revolution in India. Recall that, for Guha, the Indian bourgeoisie resorted to a mobilizational strategy that reached out to the masses but refused to allow them real political initiative. It kept them within bounds acceptable to the domestic elites. Chatterjee's description of nationalist ideology essentially recapitulates the argument set forth by Guha in the first installment of *Subaltern Studies*, and which he later developed in *Dominance without Hegemony*. For both authors, the limits of ideology as a mobilizing instrument flow directly from the constraints under which it emerges—the fact that it expresses the interests of a bourgeois class that has not, and cannot, achieve real hegemony over the movement that it leads. The conservatism of the ideology reflects the historic failure of the class it serves, the national bourgeoisie.

Since we have already uncovered irreparable flaws in Guha's argument about anticolonial nationalism, we are forced to ask whether these flaws also undermine Chatterjee's work. Actually, they do not. Guha's description of the nationalist movement in India was in fact perfectly sound, as was observed in chapter 4. Where his argument fell apart was in its counterfactual claims—that the Indian path to modernity deviated from a standard established by Western capitalists, and that therefore the Indian bourgeoisie failed as a modernizing agent. In fact, as I showed earlier, Indian capitalists did more or less exactly what their European counterparts had done, and the modernization that Guha associates with the latter—the integration of the two spheres, the rise of liberal democratic culture—was an achievement of the subaltern classes. Chatterjee's argument would fail if it rested on the counterfactual implicit in his analysis— the contrast between the "active" revolutions in England and France, and the "passive" revolution in the colonial world. But, unlike Guha, Chatterjee does not rest his argument on the counterfactual. He bases it on the descriptive

6   *NTCW* 50.

component, on what the bourgeoisie actually did. And this is the part that is defensible. Chatterjee simply asks, Given that the bourgeoisie did not have any inclination to frontally attack the landed classes, what sort of ideology would it construct as a mobilizing tool?

This raises a second question: whether Chatterjee's analysis adds anything new to the existing analyses of colonial nationalism. What made Guha's analysis interesting was its counterfactual—but it was the very thing that sank his argument. Once we abandon the contrast with Europe, what remains is the anodyne and utterly conventional claim that the leadership of India's anticolonial movement worked hard to maintain narrow limits on the movement's ambitions. Radical scholars have been pointing this out for decades.[7] Attaching a sophisticated label to it—"passive revolution"—adds little of substance. It is of course true that inasmuch as the movements were under bourgeois leadership, their ideology would respect at least some forms of property: their ideological universe would be a function of their political ambitions. And so if the nationalist leadership was committed to some form of elite compromise, it follows that the mobilizing ideology in this revolution would have to be functionally suited to these aims. Chatterjee's project—to analyze the content of the ideology— would certainly be of *descriptive* interest. It would tell us how the leadership concocted a discourse that suited its purposes. However, it would tell us little of *theoretical* interest. It would merely describe another instance in the succession of conservative nationalisms, which differs from the others only in details.

THE IDEOLOGY OF THE PASSIVE REVOLUTION

Yet there is some novelty in Chatterjee's theory. He does not simply argue that nationalist ideology is politically committed to maintaining elite dominance. He makes a stronger, more controversial argument—that nationalist ideology also ensures the *continued subordination* of the erstwhile colony to the West generally, even after independence. This, too, may sound familiar: in the postwar era, many radical intellectuals argued that formal independence had not delivered the goods to the erstwhile colonies, because they remained dominated by advanced countries through informal mechanisms of control. National independence, they claimed, just changed their status from colonies to neocolonies. Chatterjee's argument might seem reminiscent of this line of criticism.

---

7 The pioneer in the political analysis of Indian nationalism was surely M. N. Roy, one of the founders of Indian communism. An early and interesting example of his work is his 1922 book *India in Transition* (Bombay: Nachiketa Books, 1971); more illuminating were his highly influential series of articles in the 1920s and 1930s, which are now available in the multivolume *Selected Works of M. N. Roy*, ed. Sibnarayan Ray (Delhi: Oxford University Press, 1987). Also relevant are the influential analyses by the first generation of Marxists on postcolonial India: R. P. Dutt, *India Today* (Bombay: People's Publishing House, 1949); and A. R. Desai, *Social Background of Indian Nationalism*(Bombay: Popular Book Depot, 1954).

But while there is a surface-level convergence between the two arguments, they are quite different. The argument from neocolonialism locates the source of domination in various means of economic and political manipulation by the advanced world—unequal exchange, profit repatriation by corporations, technological dependence, and so on. For Chatterjee, the mechanism of subordination is located at a more fundamental level. It is in the very *intellectual framework* to which nationalism adheres—the Enlightenment legacy of science, rationality, belief in progress, etc., which he assimilates under the rubric of Reason (with a capital R). In short, nationalist ideology perpetuates the colony's subordination through its embrace of Reason. And although Chatterjee's argument draws on the Indian experience, he does not mean it to be a history of Indian nationalism. It is, he insists, valid for the colonial world as a whole, a theory of anticolonial nationalism writ large.[8]

So, there are two dimensions to Chatterjee's analysis of anticolonial nationalism. The first is his specification of the political character of the movement, that it takes the form of a passive revolution. The second is his argument about the mobilizing ideology of the movement. He advances the view that this ideology not only enables the domestic elite to maintain its power over subaltern classes by prioritizing elite interests over the interests of the poor, but also perpetuates the West's informal domination over the colony, even after decolonization, through its promotion of Reason. It is this latter dimension of his analysis that gives it its distinctiveness, and it is to this part that we now turn.

10.2 NATIONALISM AND THE CUNNING OF REASON

Anticolonial nationalism sets itself the goal of creating a national identity, even before the capture of state power. It must do so, because the leitmotif of the national movement is the anticipation of this power. As the mobilizing ideology for a movement committed to the building of a new nation-state, nationalism identifies itself as the expression of a new nation in the making. This nation may be defined along many dimensions—cultural, religious, linguistic, regional— but during the anticolonial struggle, it must define itself above all through its rejection of colonial discourse. The most visible component of nationalist ideology, therefore, is its negation of colonial claims to superiority or to the legitimacy of colonial rule. All existing theories of colonial nationalism agree on this. But what they fail to note, Chatterjee insists, is that the supposed negation of colonial ideology by nationalists obscures their acceptance, at a more fundamental level, of certain core elements of colonial discourse. Thus, while nationalism rejects colonial claims to Western superiority, it nonetheless accepts the foundations on which their dominance is based.

---

8   *NTCW* 50; see also *NTCW* 80.

THE PROBLEMATIC AND THE THEMATIC

To establish the subordinate status of nationalist ideology, Chatterjee breaks it down into two dimensions. The first is its substantive claims about the world—its historical sociology, cultural analysis, political philosophy. Chatterjee refers to this dimension as nationalism's *problematic*. The second dimension is the deeper, metatheoretical framework that is used both to generate the substantive claims and to defend them. This Chatterjee calls nationalism's *thematic*. He explains it thus:

> [W]e wish to separate claims of an ideology, i.e. its identification of historical possibilities and practical or programmatic forms of its realization, from its justificatory structures, i.e. the nature of evidence it presents in support of these claims, the rules of inference it relies on to logically relate a statement of the evidence to a structure of arguments, the set of epistemological principles it uses to demonstrate the existence of its claims as historical possibilities, and finally, the set of ethical principles it appeals to in order to assert those claims are morally justified. The former part of a social ideology we will call its *problematic* and the latter its *thematic*.[9]

To break free of colonial ideology, nationalism must reject both its problematic and its thematic. But this is where nationalism fails in its ambitions. Some nationalists claim to be overturning colonial claims to superiority, while in fact accepting the sociology or historiography utilized by the colonizer (the problematic). Another possibility is that nationalists might overturn the sociology, but accept the underlying rules of inference or normative framework that colonizers use to justify the sociology (the thematic).

Of the two components of colonial discourse, Chatterjee contends, the underlying metatheory is the more insidious in its functioning. Nationalists are quick to challenge the political ideology of colonial rule, because this is the component that is the most visible and easiest to challenge. But they are prone to overlook the thematic. This is important because the thematic *imposes limits* on the sociology or the political strategy that nationalism generates at the level of the problematic. Hence, if the thematic is left untouched, it has the effect of unduly narrowing the range of possibilities that nationalists explore when they think about the postcolony's future. They remain trapped within the parameters imposed by colonial discourse. Chatterjee observes that

> the very logical and theoretical structure of the thematic may influence the formulation of the problematic, constrain the identification of political possibilities, make some possibilities appear more desirable or feasible than others. Indeed, the

---

9   *NTCW* 38.

thematic will tend to apply a closure on the range of possibilities, and many possibilities will be ignored and some not even recognized.[10]

This, then, is the chief weakness of nationalist discourse. Even in its most developed form, wherein it repudiates the gamut of arguments used by the colonizer to defend his rule, it continues to rely upon the very forms of reasoning that Western powers imposed on the colonies. It remains derivative of colonial forms of thought. Chatterjee sums up his verdict thus: "A different discourse, yet one that is dominated by another: that is my hypothesis about nationalist thought."[11]

THE MODALITIES OF NATIONALIST DISCOURSE

The general problem of anticolonial nationalism—its entrapment within the framework of colonial ideology despite its rejection of many of the latter's claims—is embodied most clearly in the thought of Bankim Chandra Chattopadhyay. Bankim represents one of the three streams of anticolonial thought examined by Chatterjee, the other two being represented by Gandhi and Nehru. Bankim rejects colonial claims to moral or cultural superiority. He concedes that Western culture has an advantage in scientific and technological pursuits, but he insists that, on the spiritual plane, it is the East that is superior. The best way forward for a national reawakening, he argues, is for the colonized world to embrace the domain in which it has the advantage, while conceding the realm of science to West—"true modernity for the non-European nations would lie in combining the superior material qualities of Western cultures with the spiritual greatness of the East."[12]

There is an obvious sense in which Bankim's is a very limited rejection of colonial ideology. Even while he calls for Indians to reject Western rule, he seems to accept much of the content of colonial ideology. First, he fails to question the colonial problematic: he accepts that there is an essential cultural gulf separating East from West, so that the former is the repository of spiritual enlightenment, while the latter is the natural home of rational, scientific thought. In other words, he accepts the basic Orientalist description of the East.[13] His innovation is to invest the distinction with a different moral valence than does the dominant power. Whereas colonial ideology impugns the spirituality of the Eastern mind as a sign of its backwardness, Bankim praises it as superior to Western culture. The bifurcation between the rational West and the

---

10   NTCW 43.

11   NTCW 42.

12   NTCW 51.

13   See also the analysis in Sudipta Kaviraj, *The Unhappy Consciousness: Bankimchandra Chattopadhyay and the Formation of Nationalist Discourse in India* (Oxford: Oxford University Press, 1995).

spiritual East remains intact, with Bankim merely urging that Indians embrace the latter pole.

While this shows a failure to break out of the dominant problematic, Chatterjee argues that Bankim's thought suffers from an even deeper complicity with colonial discourse—it pertains to the very *form* in which Bankim presents his views. This is the level of the thematic. Like his European rulers, Bankim offers his argument in logical, rational form, as objective facts, appealing to the scientific mind-set of the modern Westernized intellectual. Hence, "the entire mode of reasoning in Bankim involves an attempt to objectify; the project is to achieve positive knowledge." When he contests the Europeans' disparaging characterization of Indian culture, "it is always as another scientist with a superior command over the facts . . . he never questions the 'objectivity' of the facts themselves or that they could be 'objectively' represented."[14] Chatterjee concludes, "Bankim's method, concepts, and modes of reasoning are completely contained within the forms of post-Enlightenment scientific thought."[15] The fact that colonial minds rely on rational argument, evidence and logic when making a case is meant to show that they are unable to escape the trap of Western domination.

Bankim represents nationalism's "moment of departure" for Chatterjee—the stage at which it is still in formation, still in its infancy. Its most mature form, the "moment of arrival," is embodied in the thought of Jawaharlal Nehru, one of the progressive leaders of the Indian National Congress and India's first prime minister. Nehru differs from Bankim in that he rejects all essentialist characterizations of the East as spiritual, otherworldly, nonrational, and the like. He therefore also rejects the notion that the East has to concede to the West a permanent advantage in economic, scientific, or military affairs. For Nehru, Indian culture was no less capable of scientific, rational thought than was the West. The reason it had to undergo two centuries of subordination to England was conjunctural circumstance—that England was the first country to industrialize, to build a superior military state, and to utilize these advantages in pursuit of geopolitical domination. Had India been allowed to follow its own course, it would have built upon its own scientific and economic abilities, to take its place in the global order.[16] But colonialism derailed India from what would have been its own path of modernization. Hence, unlike Bankim, Nehru cedes no

---

14   *NTCW* 58; see also *NTCW* 80.

15   *NTCW* 58

16   Though encased in a clunky historical account, Nehru's argument for England's emergence is a standard one, and has the merit of locating the emergence in structural changes rather than in some essential cognitive or cultural superiority. Through most of his analysis of Nehru's thought, Chatterjee accuses him—wrongly—of teleology. But now, when Nehru is clearly offering a causal and nonteleological argument, Chatterjee finds even this objectionable, apparently because of its reliance on conjunctures. I frankly admit to an inability to comprehend what Chatterjee is claiming here. See *NTCW* 133–8, esp. 136–7, for his objections.

ground to Europe on Indian culture's capacity for scientific endeavor. He rejects the essentialist bifurcation of East from West.

If the problem with nationalists like Bankim is that they embed their criticism in a basically Orientalist sociology, then surely Nehru's approach should represent a heroic alternative. If nationalism's entrapment within colonial discourse stems from its implicit acceptance of Orientalism, then Nehru's emphatic rejection of the latter should present a way out of the quagmire. For Chatterjee, however, Nehru's escape from the colonial paradigm is only partial. This is because Nehru rejects only the first level of colonial discourse—its basic sociological framework. What he does not reject is the second level, its thematic, its fundamental mode of reasoning—the Enlightenment belief in rationality, logic, objectivity, and universal laws. On these matters, Nehru is no more able to extricate himself from the dominant discourse than is Bankim. Just as Bankim remains prisoner to Reason, so too does Nehru. But in the latter's case, this belief in science leads to rather more serious consequences. Nehru's valorization of Reason leads him to accept some of the actual *values* of the Enlightenment, part of its normative framework, of which Bankim was perhaps more skeptical. Chief among these is the importance given to economic modernization and scientific progress. Chatterjee describes the problem thus:

> Nationalism sought to demonstrate the falsity of the colonial claim that the backward peoples were culturally incapable of ruling themselves in the conditions of the modern world. Nationalism denied the alleged inferiority of the colonial people; it also asserted that a backward nation could "modernize" itself while retaining its cultural identity. It thus produced a discourse in which even as it challenged the colonial claim to political domination, *it accepted the very intellectual premises of "modernity" on which colonial domination was based.*[17]

Nehru represents nationalists' internalization of the modernization dogma. Chatterjee attributes this to his immersion in post-Enlightenment philosophies, which inculcate a deep faith in the virtues of reason, progress, science, and rationality. Not only does Nehru accept that these have an intrinsic value—that they should be pursued by any culture worthy of the name—but he also accepts that they are the key to any nation's material welfare. Hence, he takes it as given that the postcolony must adopt a path of industrialization and scientific advancement, because this is what conforms with the iron laws of history.[18] The result is that Nehru is unable or unwilling to countenance any other futures for the postcolony. Notice that this is what Chatterjee takes to be the role of the colonial thematic—it imposes a closure on the range of possibilities that Nehru

---

17   *NTCW* 30. Emphasis added.
18   *NTCW* 138–46.

is able to consider. Nehru cannot bring himself to ask: "*why is it* that non-European colonial countries have no historical alternative but to try to approximate the given attributes of modernity."[19] He simply takes it as a given that the attributes of modernity must be approximated, because history demands that it be so.

It is not just that the colonial thematic prevents Nehru from considering alternative paths for India's development. Chatterjee suggests that by passively accepting modernization as an imperative and closing off other options, Nehru also ends up perpetuating the West's superiority. On this point, there is a deep and abiding ambiguity about Chatterjee's argument. It is not entirely clear whether he thinks that a modernizing stance leads to nationalists' *treating* the West as if it were superior—that is to say, acting *as if* the West were on a higher moral/cognitive plane—or if it leads to India's *actual* subordination to the West. If the former, then the diagnosis would be that nationalism propagates a kind of internalized racism, a view that the East should slavishly follow the West. This would be a claim about nationalism's effects on Indians' identities. But if it is the latter, actual subordination, then it implies a further consequence, namely, that by closing off other political possibilities, nationalism *in fact* locks the East into a subordinate position in the global order. This would be an effect not just on Indians' self-perception but on their actual capacities relative to those in the West.

Which of the two is more consistent with Chatterjee's view? There is no doubt that Chatterjee does see nationalism as perpetuating the *idea* of the West as superior, because of its acceptance of the modernizing drive:

> Nationalist thought, in agreeing to become "modern," accepts the claim to universality of this "modern" framework of knowledge. Yet it also asserts the autonomous identity of a national culture. It thus simultaneously rejects and *accepts the dominance, both epistemic and moral, of an alien culture.*[20]

Here Chatterjee seems to be saying that colonial discourse induces nationalists to treat Western culture as superior to its own. This invokes the image of an internalized racism. The West has produced the Enlightenment, with its modern framework of knowledge, as well as modern industry and science. In seeking to modernize, nationalists seek to pursue the same path as did the West before them. But this leads them also to attach great value to its culture and its modes of reasoning. Hence, insofar as the East's drive to modernize entails the acceptance of Enlightenment forms of reasoning and the validity of the "modern" frame of knowledge, it also generates the view that the West's practical

---

19   *NTCW* 11. Emphasis added.
20   Ibid.

reasoning is superior to its own. On this description, nationalists' commitment to modernization leads to them to treat the West as if it were more deserving of their respect than their own.

But in fact Chatterjee holds to the stronger view: that nationalism's valorization of the modern perpetuates the East's *actual* and *material* subordination to the West. Let us revisit a passage quoted in an earlier paragraph, and continue here with what follows:

> [W]hy is it that non-European colonial countries have no historical alternative but to try to approximate the given attributes of modernity when that *very process of approximation means their continued subjection under a world order* which only sets their tasks for them and over which they have no control? . . . It is not possible to pose this theoretical problem within the ambit of bourgeois-rationalist thought, whether conservative or liberal. For to pose it is to place *thought itself*, including thought that is supposedly rational and scientific, within a discourse of *power* . . . It is to raise the possibility that it is not just military might or industrial strength, *but thought itself, which can dominate and subjugate.*[21]

Chatterjee's point seems to be that once the colonial thematic is internalized, it locks the postcolony into a position of actual subordination to the West. It seals the West's dominance over the postcolony in the global order. But equally important, he clearly suggests that the *intellectual* failures of nationalism are every bit as important as military or economic factors in perpetuating this subordination—hence his assertion that ideology can have the same effects as military or industrial factors *in perpetuating domination.* Chatterjee thus graduates here from the proposition that nationalism's intellectual failings promote a belief in the moral superiority of the West, to the more ambitious claim that these failings secure the West's actual dominance.[22]

---

21   *NTCW* 10–11. Emphasis added.

22   If Chatterjee did not believe that the colonial thematic *actually* locked the postcolony into its subordinate position, then his criticism of Nehru would make little sense. If the only thing that modernizing nationalism does is propagate the *impression* that the West is superior, without reinforcing its *actual* dominance, then the distortive effects of nationalism would dissipate over time. The various modernizing strategies it implements would have the effect of reducing the gap between Western and Eastern levels of development. Once this happened, it would be difficult to maintain the ideology of Western moral and cultural superiority, since it would be obviously false and would cease to command much of an audience. Nehru's endorsement of a modernizing agenda would be vindicated, as would his insistence on the scientific capacities of Eastern culture. The only way Indians would continue to believe in the West's superiority, even after the postcolony successfully modernized, would be if Indians were incapable of distinguishing between fact and fiction. So, for Chatterjee's critique of Nehru to hold water, he has to commit to the view that modernizing nationalism *in fact* ensures the postcolony's continued subordination.

ELEMENTS OF A CRITIQUE

We now have some appreciation of the distinctiveness of Chatterjee's analysis. It is presented in a wrapping that is quite familiar to students of colonial history, particularly in its Indian variant: nationalist ideology was radical in its tone, but conservative in its ambitions. It had to appeal to the masses in order to mobilize them against the colonial rulers, but it also had to contain their passions, lest they turn against the local propertied classes. This was the essence of the passive revolution, as Chatterjee understands it. This description of the nationalist movement is no different from the criticism that Marxists have been making for decades;, if that were all there was to it, it would hardly merit attention. But inside this familiar wrapping is an added component, which is genuinely novel and deserves further scrutiny. It amounts to the claim that the real limits of nationalist thought rested not on its class affiliations, but in its internalization of Western *discourse*.

Having extracted the novel elements of Chatterjee's theory, we can begin to assess it. Let us first ask whether nationalists really were in the grip of colonial discourse, in the form of either its problematic or its thematic. Chatterjee uses Bankim as an example of nationalists who were trapped in both, and Nehru as an exemplar of those unable to escape the thematic. I will not dispute the argument that Bankim's political and social analysis was Orientalist in substance. I agree that his characterization of the East as spiritually oriented, and the West as rational, is a simple internalization of colonial descriptions, even if he reverses their polarity. What I do dispute is Chatterjee's analysis of modernizing nationalism. For him, modernizers such as Nehru were, in their own way, through their acceptance of the Enlightenment thematic, ensnared within colonial categories. It was because of the limits imposed by this framework that they accepted a modernizing agenda. The colonial thematic promoted certain objectives—modern industry, scientific advancement, rational management—while it obscured the value of other, nonmodernizing ones. By trapping nationalists in what Chatterjee calls the "bourgeois-rationalist" modes of thinking,[23] the colonial thematic prevented a truly autonomous discourse from taking shape.

This argument raises two questions. One concerns Chatterjee's explanation for why nationalists hewed to Reason and modernizing strategy. He maintains that Nehru opted for modernization because he was trapped within colonial forms of reasoning. He believes that this failure to break out of received modes of thought was a result of ideological conditioning. For his argument to hold, he must show that Nehru's advocacy of this approach was caused by his internalization of the colonial thematic, *not* its prudential merits. In other words, Chatterjee has to contend with the possibility that there may have been good reasons to modernize, rooted in real-world constraints and compulsions. Whether this was so is an empirical question. We would need to assess the

---

23 *NTCW* 11.

grounds on which Nehru made his choices, and determine if they have real merit. If they do, then the burden would shift to Chatterjee to explain why we should regard the choices as products of the colonial thematic. Why could we not take them instead to be choices appropriate to the circumstances?

The second issue of interest is Chatterjee's prognosis of the likely *effects* of nationalism's discursive commitments. He suggests that nationalism's internalization of Reason will consign the East to permanent domination by the West. We need to examine whether it is the case that a modernizing strategy, wrapped in the broader commitment to Reason, has in fact tightened the screws on the postcolony's domination by advanced countries. Chatterjee offers no real argument as to why one must lead to the other. Nor does he ever really explain how colonial discourse cements the postcolony's subordinate status. The key seems to be that its content—the attributes of Reason—are Western in origin. In the course of the present chapter, we will examine whether the historical record supports Chatterjee's contention to any real extent.

Before proceeding, though, it seems worth underscoring how extravagantly Orientalist all this sounds. Why, one might ask, does Reason have to be the provenance of the West? It is one thing to say that particular discoveries were made in Europe; it is also accurate to describe the West as more advanced in scientific achievements or in institution building. But in Chatterjee's usage, Reason does not refer to current scientific practices or to the institutions that promote them. As we have seen, it refers to the very idea of rationality, objectivity, economic progress, and the like. Chatterjee uses the concept to refer to certain ways of thinking, which he then assigns to the West. The West is the domain of reason and rationality, while to the East such forms of cogitation are emblems of an "alien culture." Even more, accepting their importance only assures the East's continuing subordination to the West. But why would this be true, unless the Eastern mind was irredeemably disadvantaged in the use of Reason? Once again, a Subalternist theorist is offering what appears to be a fantastically Orientalist description of the East-West divide, even as he claims to be criticizing that very discourse. We will not dwell on this, however. The reason to reject the argument is not that it is offensive, but that it is wrong. And I will now proceed to show just how wrong it is.

10.3 NATIONALISM AND THE MODERNIZING IMPERATIVE

Let us begin by addressing whether nationalist leaders adopted a modernizing agenda because they had internalized the Enlightenment ethos. Chatterjee thinks that political elites were under the grip of the colonial thematic, and that is why they embraced industrialization, scientific research, modern administrative techniques, and similar practices. But there is another possibility, which he never considers—that the reason they accepted modernization as an imperative was because it *really was* an imperative. In the modern epoch, where capitalism has begun to exert its influence on global affairs, state managers have compelling reasons to build a more productive and stable economic order. If this is so, we would predict that regardless of their biographical details—that is, whether or not they matured in a colonial setting—they would tend to view modernization as something of a compulsion. If we look to the historical record in the twentieth century, it should be clear that this explanation for the turn to modernization in the Global South is at least as plausible as Chatterjee's. In fact, this alternative explanation would seem preferable to Chatterjee's, as I am about to argue. In other words, even if Nehru had never been exposed to the colonial thematic, indeed, even if he had detested the idea of modernization, he would have had good reason to accept it anyway—which is why he and so many other leaders did so.[24]

There are, I contend, two kinds of reasons that modernization was treated as something of an imperative by twentieth-century nationalists. One issued from the international forces impinging on nation-states in the modern era. These can be grouped as *pressures from above*. The other set of factors were more local, and were related to the exigencies of political mobilization—*pressures from below*. In most cases they operated together. But whether singly or in combination, they made it eminently rational for political elites to promote modernization.

PRESSURES FROM ABOVE

Two distinct but related pressures can be grouped under this category—one military or geopolitical, the other economic. Both hit late-developing countries especially hard. But it was not just newly independent nations that felt the pressure to modernize along these two dimensions. Even European nations, which never underwent colonial subjugation, felt compelled to adopt a similar agenda.

Geopolitical pressure

For political elites—the agents who molded nationalist movements—the military dimension was probably the one they cared about most, since they were not directly involved in surplus extraction. Their main concern was political stability, against both domestic and international sources of disruption. On the international front it was geopolitical rivalries, expressed most pointedly through military conflict, that demanded attention. Warfare had been a concern for all states through the late medieval and early modern era. But with the onset of the bourgeois epoch, there occurred two changes that brought about a sea

---

24   An emphasis on the material basis for national consciousness is also, if I understand it correctly, the gist of the argument in Manu Goswami, *Producing India: From Colonial Economy to National Space* (Chicago: University of Chicago Press, 2004).

change in the calculus of power. The first was a transformation in the sheer scale of resources needed to succeed in warfare. The important shifts had started early, in the noncapitalist zones, with the construction of absolutist states. Wielding armies and military equipment that dwarfed the size of the earlier generation of feudal kingdoms, Spanish and French absolutisms set new benchmarks for the level of resources that states needed to muster in order to survive as viable political entities.[25] By the eighteenth century, concerted efforts at revenue generation and political centralization were under way across the European continent.[26] Yet while the pressures imparted by continental absolutisms were felt across the board, they were given even greater force by the rise of Great Britain. Unlike earlier powers, which squeezed ever greater resources from a creaky and arthritic agrarian base, British power grew out of an altogether new kind of foundation—a dynamic and self-expanding capitalist economy. England rose to preeminence by combining a centralized, fiscal-military state—the inheritance of the Revolution of 1688—with the most rapidly expanding economy in world history.[27]

England's rise changed the rules of the game for international relations. Until the French Revolution, states had measured their power in terms of population and geographic area—each of which was taken to be a direct measure of geopolitical leverage.[28] This was a calculus suited to political conflict in a precapitalist setting, where states had to generate revenue from a stagnant economic base, and growth in per capita income was either glacially slow or nonexistent. In such a setting, the most common way to expand revenue was to expand the size of the exploitable population, and thus larger states could presume to be the more powerful ones. But with the rise of England, this changed. Now increases in revenue could come, not just from an expanding population or geographic area, but from increasing per capita income, brought about by epoch-making increases in labor productivity. Once the Revolution of 1688 reformed Britain's fiscal apparatus so that it could harness the income streaming forth from its dynamic economic base, it overturned the rules of the geopolitical game.[29] A small island country, which had been a geopolitical

25 Two detailed studies of the transformation of warfare under absolutism are John A. Lynn, *Giant of the Grand Siècle: The French Army, 1610–1715* (Cambridge: Cambridge University Press, 1997); and David Parrott, *Richelieu's Army: War, Government and Society in France, 1624–1642* (Cambridge: Cambridge University Press, 2001)

26 See Jan Glete, *War and the State in Early Modern Europe: Spain, the Dutch Republic and Sweden as Fiscal-Military States* (London: Routledge, 2001).

27 John Brewer, *The Sinews of Power: War, Money and the English State, 1688–1783* (New York: Alfred A. Knopf, 1989); Patrick K. O'Brien, "Fiscal Exceptionalism. Great Britain and Its European Rivals," in Donald Winch and Patrick K. O'Brien, eds., *The Political Economy of British Historical Experience, 1688–1914* (Oxford: Oxford University Press, 2002).

28 H. M. Scott, *The Birth of a Great Power System, 1740–1815* (London: Pearson-Longman, 2006), 118–20, 138, 156.

29 On England's power being of an altogether new kind, see Benno Teschke, *The Myth of*

backwater through the seventeenth century, established itself as a preeminent global player by the end of the Seven Years War, and the one of the two global superpowers by 1815, along with Russia.[30] Political elites now understood that it was not enough just to expand their resource base; they would also have to transform it along capitalist lines. They had to *modernize* if they wanted their states to survive as viable political entities.

For nationalist leaders, the external threat was no idle worry. It does not need repeating that their countries *had been colonized*. They knew, firsthand, the cost of military weakness or economic dependence. For the countries that had escaped outright colonization, military intimidation was a common experience. In the nineteenth century, England did not shy away from forcing its products into weaker nations through military or naval actions.[31] China, Japan, Egypt, Greece, Paraguay—all felt the force of England's gunboat diplomacy.[32] In the twentieth century, almost contemporaneous with the Indian nationalist movement, the Middle East was being sliced up by the Great Powers, their prize for defeating the Ottomans in World War I.[33] The arc of militarism culminated in the orgy of World War II, which began with Hitler's *colonial drive* to extend the Reich beyond its traditional borders and seize control of the Central European heartland[34] and ended with another round of the Great Powers dividing up large swaths of the world, this time in Eastern Europe and East Asia.

As claimants or aspirants to state power, nationalist leaders had to respect the vicissitudes of geopolitical conflict. What this meant in a capitalist world order was that they had to attend to resource generation from the domestic economy. They could not rely on the benefits of population or landmass alone, though of course these remained valuable assets. The main route to amassing power could be only through the fostering of a more productive and more dynamic economic base—through modernizing.

1648: Class, Geopolitics, and the Making of Modern International Relations (London: Verso, 2003).

30   The geopolitical shifts are analyzed in the two most important studies of the period, Paul W. Schroeder's monumental *The Transformation of European Politics, 1763-1848* (Oxford: Oxford University Press, 1994), 3–52, and Scott, The *Birth of a Great Power System*, 8–28, 144–56; 222–43.

31   This was the imperialism of free trade, analyzed to great effect in John Gallagher and Ronald Robinson, "The Imperialism of Free Trade," *The Economic History Review* ser. II, 6:1 (1953), 1–15.

32   The best overview of British informal empire, and its use of force, is P. J. Cain and A. G. Hopkins, *British Imperialism, 1688-2000* (New York: Longman, 2002).

33   For a good scholarly synthesis, see D. K. Fieldhouse, *Western Imperialism in the Middle East, 1914–1958* (Oxford: Oxford University Press, 2006); a good popular read is David Fromkin, *A Peace to End All Peace: The Fall of the Ottoman Empire and the Creation of the Modern Middle East* (New York, Henry Holt, 2001).

34   See the brilliant analysis in Adam Tooze, *The Wages of Destruction: The Making and Breaking of the Nazi Economy* (Oxford: Oxford University Press, 2006).

Domestic capitalists

The second pressure from above was more domestic in origin: the demands coming from local capitalists in late-developing countries where industrialization had taken root. Even though no bourgeoisie, after 1789, was willing to launch a full-scale attack on the agrarian order, this did not prevent them from demanding that the state find ways of encouraging local industrial expansion. The reason was simple. Newly established firms in late-developing countries faced the daunting task of having to compete against rivals from more advanced countries, which were much better placed: they had more experience, better technology, better infrastructure, credit facilities, sales networks, and so on. Capitalists in the late-developing countries argued, correctly, that they would be unable to survive against their more advanced competitors unless their states set up protective barriers that restricted the entrance of goods produced by those more efficient foreign producers, a measure known as import-substitution, and also developed domestic economic institutions that would rapidly enable domestic firms to effectively compete with their rivals in more advanced regions. These two demands quickly became the core elements of the development strategy for recent entrants into the global economy.

Capitalism exerted pressure for the state to develop local economic and scientific capabilities—to be a bourgeois state not only indirectly, through its defense of property rights, but more directly, by actively fostering more rapid accumulation.[35] This is another way of saying that political elites were compelled to undertake a modernizing mission. They were expected to develop domestic technology, so that firms would not have to rely on foreign know-how; they were asked to create new financial institutions, so that firms could raise money for the massive investments they had to make in order to match their foreign competitors. States had to build a rationally planned infrastructure, so that transportation and power bottlenecks would be removed. None of this would have been possible unless nationalist ideology accepted modernization as an outright imperative, to ensure that the effort was appropriate to the sheer magnitude of the task.

The call from the bourgeoisie to modernize dovetailed neatly with the political elites' own interests. Not only did it add to their reasons for adopting such an agenda, but, more important, support from local capitalists gave state managers a political base within the domestic ruling class, which had the crucial effect of stabilizing the policy regime. Late developers adopted a modernizing strategy on the strength of an alliance between political elites and domestic capitalists. The reason this was important was that an industrializing agenda could, and sometimes did, encounter resistance from landed oligarchies, who saw the turn to industrialization as a threat to their own power—and indeed,

---

35   For a more extended discussion of this logic, see my *Locked in Place: State-Building and Late Industrialization in India* (Princeton: Princeton University Press, 2003), chap. 2.

they were correct in their surmise. No state could have simply overridden this resistance had it not secured support for itself from some substantial element within the ruling classes. [36]

PRESSURES FROM BELOW: THE MASS MOVEMENT

The third source of pressure, though not as significant as the first two, did have to be accommodated to some extent. This was the pressure from popular sectors for some kind of attention to their material welfare. The main reason that elites had to take this factor into account was that nationalism, especially from the mid-nineteenth century onward, had increasingly become a mass movement. This was the case as early as the Revolutions of 1848, which had a patriotic, nationalist flavor in some regions, and was most certainly true from the 1880s onward, resoundingly so from the 1920s, as nationalism became reincarnated as anticolonial mobilizations. No mobilization, on a mass scale, in conditions of dire poverty, could elicit sustained participation from the laboring classes if it failed to address their material deprivation. Eric Hobsbawm makes this point to great effect in his bravura analysis of modern nationalism, noting that as late as the closing decades of the nineteenth century, the reach of purely cultural nationalism did not extend much beyond the middle classes, whether in Europe or elsewhere.[37] Hence, he sourly concludes, "the socialists of the period, who rarely used the word 'nationalism' without the prefix 'petty-bourgeois,' knew what they were talking about. The battle-lines of linguistic nationalism were manned by provincial journalists, schoolteachers, and aspiring subaltern officials."[38] Indeed, this summation aptly describes the early organizers of the Indian National Congress, as well as many other anticolonial nationalist groups.[39]

What turned these middle-class agitations into genuine movements was the entry of the workers and peasants, en masse. And this, in turn, was inconceivable until nationalists learned to incorporate subaltern material interests into the political agenda. It was only when they opened their

---

36   For Germany in the early nineteenth century, see Jeffry M. Diefendorf, *Businessmen and Politics in the Rhineland, 1789–1834* (Princeton: Princeton University Press, 1980); for Latin America, see the overview in Victor Bulmer-Thomas, *The Economic History of Latin America since Independence* (Cambridge: Cambridge University Press, 1994); a provocative analysis of the Argentine experience—one of the few recent studies to examine the politics of national capitalists in the South—is James P. Brennan and Marcelo Rougier, *The Politics of National Capitalism: Peronism and the Argentine Bourgeoisie, 1946–1976* (University Park: Pennsylvania University Press, 2009).

37   E. J. Hobsbawm, *Nations and Nationalism since 1780: Programme, Myth, Reality* (Cambridge: Cambridge University Press, 1990), 116–17.

38   Ibid., 117.

39   The authoritative study of the early INC remains S. R. Mehrotra, *The Emergence of the Indian National Congress* (New York: Barnes and Noble, 1971). For a good synthesis of the literature, see Sekhar Bandyopadhyay, *From Plassey to Partition: A History of Modern India* (Delhi: Orient Longman, 2004), 184–226.

program to the concerns of laboring classes that their movement acquired a genuine mass base. Again, Hobsbawm: "the *combination* of national and *social* demands, on the whole, proved very much more effective as a mobilizer of independence than the pure appeal of nationalism, whose appeal was limited to the discontented lower middle classes."[40] Once nationalists incorporated these demands into their agenda, the drive for independence acquired two ingredients indispensable to making it work, not just as a movement, but as a social coalition that might sustain the postcolonial state—a much-needed consensus within the highest reaches of the ruling circles, and a deep social base within popular groups.

Subaltern interests were always just that—interests that occupied a subordinate place on the modernizing agenda. Elites did not view them as they did the pressures from above. Whereas the latter were seen as intrinsically desirable by the core members of the power bloc—political elites and capitalists—this was not true for the social agenda. Items on the social agenda were acceded to only because they were a necessary evil. They had to be included if the movement, and then the new postcolonial regime, was to secure a mass base for itself. So, whereas the policies called for by geopolitics and global competition were accorded first-order priority, those that reflected pressure from below were, at best, second-order. On this, Ranajit Guha's complaints against the nationalist leadership, which we examined in chapter 2, are on target: leaders took on subaltern demands grudgingly, and in bad faith. But this does not erase the fact that the concerns did have to be accommodated to some extent, even if the accommodation fell short of the popular classes' expectations.

Now we come to the key point: there was simply no way to accommodate subaltern demands for improvements in their living standard, while keeping domestic capitalists on board, *except* through a modernizing agenda. If workers and peasants were calling for steady rises in their standard of living, and if these calls were to be incorporated into the policy regime, then the only way to do so, *without hurting elite interests*, was through a growing economy. Unless the social surplus continued to expand, increases in wages and salaries would eat into the component of national income that went to the ruling classes. The only way to marry rising welfare for working people to ruling class interests was by engineering steady economic growth. This therefore added a *third* reason for nationalists to adopt a modernizing agenda, in addition to the pressure coming from military conflict and economic competition.

We now have an explanation for why nationalists chose to adopt a modernizing form of nationalism. They did so because the capitalist world economy imposed some powerful constraints on the national economies that

---

40 Hobsbawm, *Nations and Nationalism*, 125. Emphasis added. See also the synthesis in John Breuilly, *Nationalism and the State* (New York: St. Martin's Press, 1982).

comprised it. Political elites felt them directly, in the viability of their states, while capitalists felt them through the viability of their enterprises. And both components of the ruling bloc felt them through mass pressure for welfare improvement. This suggests that the reason nationalists took to modernization was not that they had passively accepted the Enlightenment worldview, but because it was a rational response to their circumstances. It may not have been the *only possible* response. There may even have been others, better suited to the conditions and more closely aligned with nationalist preferences. What made the modernizing response rational, however, was not that it was optimal but that it was adequate to the constraints.[41] It follows that whatever other path might have been chosen, whatever mix of policies was adopted, it, too, would have had to manage those pressures.

The forgoing argument places an analytical burden on Chatterjee's shoulders. If he wishes to maintain that nationalists hewed to a modernizing agenda because they were trapped within the colonial thematic—that it was this discourse that made modernization attractive—then he has two routes available. He could *deny* that the constraints, as outlined above, existed. He would then need to show that market competition and geopolitics do not in fact impose pressure on states to develop their economies, to modernize. If no such pressures existed, then of course it becomes possible to present the turn to modernization as a misperception of reality, and hence the product of indoctrination. Chatterjee's other option is to *accept* that the constraints exist, that states are in fact pressured to adapt in some way to the rigors of capitalism. But if he accepts this, then the only means for showing that Nehru was blinded by modernizing discourse would be to show that it led him to ignore the possibility of other, *nonmodernizing* models of governance that were not only available but would also have been capable of negotiating the pressures of the global system. Further, these models would have had to be free of Enlightenment modes of thinking—unencumbered by Reason. Chatterjee would now have to elucidate what such an alternative might have looked like, and make a plausible case for its viability, in the sense of being capable of dealing with the pressures of global capitalism. But if he fails to provide either of these arguments—a denial that postcolonies were constrained, or an affirmation that plausible nonmodernizing alternatives existed—then his critique of modernizing nationalism loses its force. We would then be free to conclude that Nehru, and others like him, chose a modernizing path because it was a reasonable response to existing conditions.

In the next section I examine whether Chatterjee provides the necessary arguments to make this case. I then take up the second claim he makes, that

---

41 See my discussion of rationality in chap. 8 above, where I defend a satisficing model of rationality.

nationalists' embrace of a modernizing path had the perverse effect of simply locking the post-colony into its subordinate position in the global order.

10.4 THE MISSING COUNTERFACTUAL

The most striking aspect of Chatterjee's argument is that he neither denies that the constraints of a capitalist world economy existed, nor provides any examples of alternative, nonmodernizing models as means of negotiating those constraints. In other words, he provides *neither* argument needed to make his theory plausible. He simply castigates Nehru for falling prey to a modernizing discourse. His typical strategy is to argue by innuendo—hinting that Nehru was ignoring some very obvious alternatives, which, however, Chatterjee refuses to describe. Many of the passages he culls from Nehru's writings are ones in which Nehru offers real justifications for the desirability of a modernizing strategy. But Chatterjee passes over these in silence, because he does not appear to see any need to demonstrate that they are mistaken. For the most part, he is content simply to point to their Enlightenment credentials as proof of their wrongness. What this leaves us with is an *assertion*, with no support, that nationalism was a derivative discourse, trapped in a foreign ideology.

For example, Nehru makes a case that if India is to industrialize along capitalist lines, policy makers will have to respect benchmark levels of productivity, encourage scientific research, foster managerial talent, and so on. He sees these measures as necessary because circumstances demand them: they are not derived from first principles, but from facts about the world. Consider the following passage, which Chatterjee quotes from Nehru's *Discovery of India*. In it, Nehru questions the idea that India can base its development path on cottage industry, as recommended by nationalists such as M. K. Gandhi. Nehru agrees that there is some space for handicrafts and small enterprise, but he suggests that they have to be ancillary to large-scale enterprises. This is not because he has a personal preference for big industry; it is because he thinks that in order to survive in world markets, Indian firms will have to respect minimum levels of size and scale. They will have to perform on a level comparable with that of their rivals in the West, or they will be swept aside in the competitive struggle. He concludes that policy makers can certainly encourage both forms of enterprise, large as well as small. However, he declares,

> One [kind of enterprise] must be dominating and paramount, with the other complementary to it, fitting in where it can. The economy based on the latest technical achievements of the day must necessarily be the dominating one. If technology demands the big machine, as it does today in a large measure, then the big machine with all its implications must be accepted . . . the latest technique has to be followed,

and to adhere to outworn and out-of-date methods of production, except as a temporary and stop-gap measure, is to arrest growth and development.[42]

Nehru's justification for a turn toward high-tech and large industry is clear—large industry and sound technology must be promoted because small firms cannot effectively compete against them. He might be wrong here; perhaps small firms using outmoded technology can in fact survive direct competition against state-of-the art modern machinery. But even if Chatterjee thinks Nehru is wrong, the burden of proof is on Chatterjee to *show* that he is. If he cannot, then Nehru can justifiably claim that his argument stands. Indeed, he might plausibly argue that *Chatterjee* is the one in the grip of an ideology, since he refuses to assess Nehru's case on its merits, dismissing it instead on *a priori* grounds. It is therefore surprising to find that Chatterjee offers no argument that would incline us to question the case for modern industry. He simply attaches labels to Nehru's arguments—"scientific," "rational," and "Marxist" are the ones he uses in this context—indicating that they fit into an Enlightenment worldview. He then moves on, with a wink and a nod, as if pedigree is proof enough of falsity.[43]

Chatterjee's failure to consider the practical argument for modernization is especially surprising if considered in light of his discussion of Gandhian nationalism. Gandhi represents the third variant of nationalist discourse, after those by Bankim and Nehru. For Chatterjee, this variant stands out because it seems to wrest thoroughly free of colonial discourse, both at the level of the problematic and of the thematic. Gandhi rejects the basic political sociology generated by colonial ideologues, which splits the world into a dynamic West and a static, otherworldly East. In this, he is much like Nehru. But unlike Nehru, he also rejects the modernizing ethos of post-Enlightenment thought, as well as the modernizing discourse of liberal and Marxist philosophies. Whereas Nehru is committed to rapid economic development based on large industry, mechanized agriculture, scientific management, and the like, Gandhi rejects the entire paradigm of modern growth.[44] In this respect he is, for Chatterjee, the more successful in escaping the colonial thematic.

But Gandhi's success is more impressive yet. Not only does he reject the modernizing ethos as a framework for national development; he also rejects the "modern" framework of knowledge that Chatterjee sees as central to the colonial thematic.[45] His liberation is thereby effective not simply on the political, but also on the epistemic, plane. Thus, when pressed to defend his political strategy,

---

42 Jawaharlal Nehru, *The Discovery of India* (New York: John Day, 1946), 414, quoted at *NTCW* 144.

43 *NTCW* 144–5.

44 *NTCW* 86–90.

45 *NTCW* 11.

or moral theory, or historical sociology, Gandhi remains undeterred if the weight of evidence is not in his favor. In fact, observes Chatterjee, "he does not feel it necessary to even attempt a historical demonstration of the possibilities he is trying to point out. Indeed, he objects that the historical mode of reasoning is quite unsuitable, indeed irrelevant, for his purpose."[46] So, unlike Nehru, he refuses to offer a defense of his recommendations by appealing to historical dynamics or constraints. He is skeptical of the knowledge claims made by science, even in the matter of natural laws.[47] Hence, he stands apart from other nationalists in that he "[does] not share their confidence in rationality and in the scientific mode of knowledge."[48] Chatterjee concludes, naturally, that Gandhi represents the variant of nationalist discourse that fully extricates itself from the dominant ideology:

> Gandhi is not operating at all within the *problematic* of nationalism . . . [What] is more striking, but equally clear, is that Gandhi does not even think within the *thematic* of nationalism. He seldom writes or speaks in terms of the conceptual frameworks or the modes of reasoning and inference adopted by the nationalists of his day, and quite emphatically rejects their rationalism, scientism, and historicism.[49]

The choice of words is interesting here. In an earlier chapter, Chatterjee warns that intellectuals like Bankim should not be dismissed simply on the grounds that they were conservative, compared with other, more forward-looking leaders. Conservatives and progressives alike were "prisoners of the rationalism, historicism, and scientism of the nationalist thematic."[50] Gandhi's genius is that, unlike the other nationalists, he is unencumbered by the Enlightenment thematic. As a result, he "emphatically rejects their rationalism, scientism, and historicism." In passages thirteen pages apart, Chatterjee uses the same three descriptors to highlight Bankim's ensnarement in, and Gandhi's singular liberation from, Reason.

We might thus expect that Chatterjee would endorse Gandhian nationalism as the authentic representative of anticolonial discourse, as the framework that might free the postcolony of its subordinate status. But in fact he is highly critical, even dismissive, of Gandhi's model. Especially noteworthy are the grounds on which he dismisses it. By the final years of colonial rule, on the eve of Independence, Gandhi had lost much of his leverage within the nationalist movement. He became relegated to the sidelines—a marginal, even tragic figure

---

46   *NTCW* 93.
47   *NTCW* 96–7.
48   *NTCW* 96.
49   *NTCW* 93.
50   *NTCW* 80.

within the organization he helped bring to power. Nehru and other modernizing nationalists largely ignored his pleas for upholding peasant production,
rural handicrafts, and village self-sufficiency, and his call for moral regenera-
tion. He had fulfilled his function, brought the masses to the Indian National
Congress, and it was now time to launch the project of building a bourgeois
order. One might have expected, at this point, a rousing defense from Chatterjee of the Gandhian program, as the road not taken, the bellwether of an
alternative development model. Instead, he joins in the dismissal of Gandhi.
And he does so on the grounds that Gandhi's program was unable to cope with
the realities of the day, both political and economic. In other words, Chatterjee
rejects Gandhian nationalism because it ignores the material compulsions—the
objective constraints—of a modern capitalist political economy.[51]

Chatterjee's dismissal of Gandhian nationalism suggests that he is at least
willing to consider the relevance of material constraints. But when he comes to
Nehru, this willingness evaporates. He neither denies that capitalism imposes
real pressures on late-developing political economies, nor lays out an alternative to Nehru's model. In other words, he presents Nehru's views as if they were
purely an artifact of ideology, without even considering the possibility of their
having been driven by prudential concerns—despite the fact that Nehru repeats,
again and again, that his adoption of the modernizing agenda is driven by these
very considerations, and despite the fact that Chatterjee produces quotes in
which Nehru is making just this point. On top of that, Chatterjee dismisses the
Gandhian model—the only possible alternative to the modernizing model—
largely on the same grounds on which Nehru would have rejected it. This places
an even heavier burden of proof on him, of which he appears entirely unaware,
to demonstrate that modernizing nationalism was in fact an artifact of ideology.

The fact that Chatterjee fails adequately to defend his argument does not
necessarily mean it is indefensible. One way to salvage it is to see if there might
have been strategies available to the postcolonies that could pass muster on the
criteria Chatterjee lays down—that they be free of the scientism, historicism,
and rationalism of colonial ideology. Hence, even if Chatterjee fails to support
his own theory, perhaps we could save it by doing the work on his behalf. The
problem with this mission, however, is that his criteria make it just about impossible to imagine what such a strategy might look like. This is not because there
are no arguments out there for a nonmodernizing model of governance for
postcolonies; over the course of the twentieth century, there have been repeated
attempts to defend various such models.[52] Nor is it that these models happen to

---

51   NTCW, 102–120, Akeel Bilgrami has noted this contradiction in Chatterjee in his
perceptive essay "Two Conceptions of Secularism: Reason, Modernity, and the Archimedean
Ideal," *Economic and Political Weekly* 29:28 (Jul. 9, 1994), 1749–61.

52   A good discussion of some such models occurs in Gavin Kitching, *Development and
Underdevelopment in Historical Perspective: Populism, Nationalism and Industrialization* (London:

be unviable, which they certainly are. The problem for Chatterjee is that if we accept his criteria, we are forced to reject *the very idea* of a strategy.

Let me repeat: the reason we cannot generate a national strategy that would pass muster with Chatterjee's theory is that *his position undermines even the possibility of a national strategy*. For elites to adopt a strategy of development is, by definition, to envision a certain end point—a desired state of affairs in the future—and to then manipulate the available resources in such a fashion as to achieve that desired end point. The manipulation of resources, whether political, economic, cultural, or otherwise, cannot be undertaken except through a reliance on what Chatterjee calls Reason—rational deliberation, neutral assessment of facts, objective knowledge, and so on. But this is precisely what Chatterjee *proscribes* on the grounds that it is a symptom of the Western, post-Enlightenment forms of reasoning at the core of the colonial thematic. Consequently, if the only permissible strategy is one that cannot rely on rules of logic, evidence, rational deliberation and the like—all those forms of thought assimilated into Reason—then it rules out not just this or that strategy, but the very possibility of strategy altogether.[53] Hence, even if we could hit upon a nonmodernizing approach to dealing with the pressures of global capitalism, it is hard to fathom how Chatterjee could endorse it. For such an approach to be effectuated, national elites would have to judge its merits, think of ways to implement it, prioritize its various demands on national resources, and integrate it with existing institutions—all of which would require the very modes of thought that Chatterjee impugns as alien to the Eastern mind and as the essence of Western domination. We would be guilty of reproducing the colonial thematic.

It is safe to conclude that Chatterjee's characterization of nationalism as a derivative discourse falls flat. Or more accurately, his portrayal of conservatives such as Bankim is partly correct, in that they did in fact reproduce Orientalist conceptions of the East in their doctrines. But he provides no reason for believing that modernizing nationalists, too, were trapped in colonial discourse. Or again, more accurately, they may have been trapped in it, but not along the lines he describes. He never shows—as he is obliged to—that the program advocated

---

Methuen, 1982).

53 Note that this calls for a shift even in Chatterjee's critique of Gandhi. Chatterjee rejects Gandhi's program because it is incapable of generating an adequate strategy for implementation, and because it would require the dismantling of many institutions already central to the Indian political economy. That is of course true. But on the grounds laid down by Chatterjee, the main problem in Gandhi's doctrine is not that it calls for too much state intervention, or that it is impracticable, but that it would depend on a careful marshalling and balancing of resources to sustain the rural handicrafts and peasant self-sufficiency he covets. In so doing, it would have to mobilize Reason every bit as much as Nehru's model. The only difference is that the ends served by Reason would be different in the two programs. Gandhi's program, therefore, has to be rejected not because it is faulty, but because *it is a program*.

by nationalists such as Nehru was a product of ideology rather than a rational response to real constraints. If anything, his criticism of Gandhi's philosophy gives indirect support to the Nehruvian agenda, inasmuch as he rejects Gandhi on grounds similar to those invoked by Nehru himself.

10.5 MODERNIZATION AS PRISON HOUSE?

Chatterjee's main argument with regard to nationalism is that, even in its most advanced form, it continued to operate within the domain of colonial discourse. But there is also Chatterjee's second claim, about the *effects* likely to follow once nationalists succumb to the Enlightenment discourse. Recall that the main effect of nationalism's internalization of the colonial thematic is that it limits the range of possibilities that elites are willing to consider. The thematic screens out political and economic options that are actually available to the postcolony and that would improve its position. The options that nationalists do consider, therefore, are ones that fail to challenge Western dominance. This leads to the second part of his argument: that in adopting the modernizing framework, in trying to approximate the economic and scientific success of the West, nationalists merely ensure "their continued subjection under a world order which only sets their tasks for them and over which they have no control."[54] Not only does Chatterjee believe that the pursuit of economic and scientific modernization is an effect of colonial ideology, he also holds that in adopting this path, nationalists consign their countries to continued subordination to the West.

Is the effect of colonial nationalism, then, indeed to lock the postcolony into subordinate status? To the contrary, if we look at the empirical record we find no warrant for Chatterjee's claim. It is true that many countries in the Global South have continued to remain subordinate to the West, even as they have tried to modernize. So it is certainly legitimate to maintain that a modernizing agenda does not guarantee economic or geopolitical improvement. It must be combined with other enabling conditions for it to generate success. But this merely tells us that, as a matter of normative orientation, the adoption of this agenda is not sufficient for the postcolony to advance. It does not overturn the view that even though the pursuit of modernization may not be *sufficient*, it is still *necessary* for the postcolony to improve the welfare of its inhabitants and to improve its position relative to the West. The fact is, in the era of decolonization, parts of the Global South have dramatically improved their material conditions. And all these regions—without exception—have done so through a conscious, highly ambitious *program of modernization*. Indeed, the most successful cases, in Northeast Asia, have developed through a kind of hyper-modernizing orientation—a state-led, carefully planned, consciously directed

---

54   *NTCW* 10.

strategy that has consistently promoted scientific research and technological advancement. It is hard to imagine a more dramatic exemplification of the very strategy that Chatterjee seems to proscribe—a strategy that, indeed, he would predict to be disastrous.

Not only is it true that every country to have improved its lot has been a modernizer; it is also true that the *only* countries to have thus improved have been those that have taken on a modernizing path. That is to say, the only countries to have escaped from, or loosened, neocolonial domination have been those that embraced Reason. This is a fact common across the class frontier. Hence, on one side of that divide we have Russia and China, which modernized on the basis of a centrally planned, command economy, and on the other side we have Korea, Taiwan, Chile, Argentina, and a handful of others, which did so by maintaining capitalist property relations.[55] The two groups differed enormously in their cultures and economic institutions, but were bound together on one particular axis—they embraced the very orientation that, to Chatterjee, would be anathema, and they produced results that, under the terms of Chatterjee's theory, can only appear anomalous.

Hence, not only is Chatterjee unable to explain why nationalists adopted a modernizing agenda, but he also errs in his prediction of its effects. It is thus safe to conclude that they had good reason to move in that direction, and to the extent that they succeeded at all in escaping their domination in the world order, it was through modernization.

To sum up our assessment of Chatterjee's theory of colonial nationalism, readers should first recall its two components: an argument about nationalism being a form of the passive revolution, and another argument about its being contained by colonial discourse. As has been demonstrated above, the second component cannot withstand scrutiny. There may have been many ways in which colonial rule distorted the agenda and the ambitions of nationalist movements, and indeed, I have endorsed Ranajit Guha's description of the Indian National Congress's failings in this regard.[56] But that argument is one that Marxists have made for decades, and is the least original of the Subalternist collective's contributions. Whatever the convergence between nationalism and colonial ideology, it did not occur along the lines proposed by Chatterjee. He suggests that the adoption of a modernizing agenda was a consequence of nationalists' internalization of Western modes of thinking, and that this agenda

---

55   On Russia, see the recent revisionist study by Robert C. Allen, *Farm to Factory: A Reinterpretation of the Soviet Industrial Revolution* (Princeton: Princeton University Press, 2004); on China, a solid recent overview is Barry Naughton, *The Chinese Economy: Transitions and Growth* (Cambridge: MIT Press, 2007).

56   Just to reiterate: I have argued that Guha's characterization of the INC as a party of bourgeois order, only weakly committed to democratic governance, is accurate. Where he stumbles is in his suggestion that this is in any way a departure from some historic norm.

in turn locked the postcolony into a subordinate position. As we have seen, however, there is no reason to believe either claim. Modernization was, as Nehru correctly perceived, an imperative that the postcolony had to respect. It was not the effect of a discourse. Further, modernization was not what made the postcolony subservient to the West, but rather its *failure* at modernization. Indeed, to the extent that any of the countries of the global South have escaped domination and improved their position, it has been by embracing the very agenda that Chatterjee warns against. Hence, his argument about the derivative character of nationalism fails to convince. All that is left standing is the least original part of his theory: the argument about passive revolution.

10.6 THE DISAPPEARANCE OF MODERNIZING NATIONALISM

In later years, Chatterjee modified the argument from *Nationalist Thought and the Colonial World*, but not in a direction that enhanced its plausibility. The chief flaw in the 1986 incarnation was that it ignored the structural constraints that nationalists tried to negotiate, treating their preferences as pure effects of ideology. This made it impossible for Chatterjee to make sense of the most widespread form of colonial nationalism, the kind embodied by Jawaharlal Nehru. In his later writing, Chatterjee's treatment of the subject takes an interesting turn. Whereas in *Nationalist Thought* he described colonial nationalism as consisting of three distinct tendencies, each embodied respectively in the thought of Bankim, Gandhi, and Nehru, this complexity largely disappears by the time *The Nation and Its Fragments* was published. Now nationalism is whittled down to a single, simple essence, which becomes the centerpiece of Chatterjee's description.

Chatterjee begins his later discussion by introducing an argument from Benedict Anderson, to the effect that colonial nationalists worked on a model of the nation that they borrowed from Western nationalisms. Anderson describes this as a "modular" concept of the nation-state, easily encapsulated and transportable from one setting to another. Chatterjee objects that this conception treats anticolonial nationalists as passive imitators of Western models: "If nationalisms in the rest of the world have to choose their imagined community from certain 'modular' forms already made available to them by Europe, and the Americas," he asks, "what do they have left to imagine?"[57] In other words, Anderson's theory ignores the specificity of colonial nationalisms by assimilating them into the broader model that originated in Europe. "The most powerful as well as the most creative results of the nationalist imagination in Asia and Africa are posited not on an identity but rather on a *difference* with

---

57   Chatterjee, "Whose Imagined Community?" in *The Nation and Its Fragments: Colonial and Postcolonial Histories* (Princeton: Princeton University Press, 1993), 5.

the 'modular' forms ... propagated by the modern West," writes Chatterjee.[58] Theorists like Anderson are unable to recognize the distinctiveness of colonial nationalism because they view it primarily through the prism of the state, as an ideology that develops in the pursuit of state power. It is seen as a political ideology, aimed at comprehending, and then mastering, the art of statecraft. This makes it another variant of the modernizing political discourse that the West created as it forged the modern nation-state. But to view colonial nationalism as a political ideology, Chatterjee argues, is a mistake. The essential elements of this discourse are forged long before it even contemplates the pursuit of power. It is worth quoting at some length the passage in which he presents his thesis:

> By my reading, anticolonial nationalism creates its own domain of sovereignty within colonial society well before it ever begins its political battle with the imperial power. It does this by dividing the world of social institutions and practices into two domains—the material and the spiritual. The material is the domain of the "outside", of the economy and of statecraft, of science and technology, a domain where the West had proved its superiority and the East had succumbed. In this domain, then, Western superiority had to be acknowledged and its accomplishments carefully studied and replicated. The spiritual, on the other hand, is an "inner" domain bearing the "essential" marks of cultural identity. The greater one's success in imitating Western skills in the material domain, therefore, the greater the need to preserve the distinctiveness of one's spiritual culture. *This formula is, I think, a fundamental feature of anti-colonial nationalisms in Asia and Africa.*[59]

Chatterjee does not qualify this description in any way, as perhaps capturing *some* aspects of nationalism or as pertaining to *one* variant of it. He presents it as a description of nationalism *tout court*. The description itself is a familiar one—although he does not say so, it is a rendering of the conservative, Orientalist portrayal developed by Bankim in nineteenth-century Bengal. Recall that Bankim's argument accepted the West's superiority in scientific and economic knowledge while insisting on the East's greater depth in all matters spiritual. Chatterjee seems now to have distilled anticolonial nationalism to this particular variant, which, in the earlier version, was just one of three—the most primitive, "the moment of departure." Moreover, Chatterjee presents this newer version not simply as representative of the Indian experience but of anticolonial nationalisms across Africa and Asia. It is now the model of twentieth-century nationalisms in the colonial world. No evidence is produced to support this claim nor is there any discussion of the actual experiences of other countries, or even of the thinking of their most prominent ideologues. Chatterjee simply

---

58 Ibid. Emphasis in original.
59 Ibid., 6. Emphasis added.

asserts, as was the case in *Nationalist Thought* as well, that the theory is valid for the generality of anticolonial nationalisms.

There is no denying that some nationalists did draw up an inner and an outer domain, as Chatterjee describes them, and did assert the inviolability of the latter. But it is quite untenable to present this maneuver as representative of colonial nationalisms in the twentieth century. As evidenced above, it is not even representative of Indian nationalism, because it omits the variant that, in the end, became the official ideology of the Indian state: the modernizing nationalism embodied in Nehru's thought. One can certainly make a case that, for all its secularism and Westernization, the leadership of the Indian National Congress made far too many concessions to traditional religious leaders. They incorporated innumerable customary, and often illiberal, practices into the legal code, as concessions to religious communities. But this is an instance of modernizing nationalism accommodating to a conservative nationalism—in other words, it is a case where the dominant ideology incorporates into its universe elements of the subordinate one. It cannot be described as the conservative variant, of the kind embodied by Bankim, displacing the modernizing one. The nationalism that emerged out of the Indian independence struggle was still basically the Nehruvian form, however irresolute or compromising it might have been. And Chatterjee's description fails to capture its essential elements.

If Chatterjee's more recent portrayal fits imperfectly with the Indian experience, it is even less plausible when we look at Asia, Africa, or the Middle East. It is hard to see the nationalism of, for instance, Sukarno, Nasser, Sun Yat-sen, the Arab Ba'ath parties, Yasir Arafat, and Nelson Mandela as anything other than the bourgeois, modernizing variant to which Nehru ascribed. They all made compromises with traditional practices, to be sure. But it would be a stretch to describe them as setting up an "inner" and an "outer" domain, and valorizing the reproduction of the former. All of them proclaimed a commitment to modernization, both in the material domain and the spiritual one. Indeed, in many of these cases, the dominant nationalisms not only expressed a commitment to modernization but found themselves at loggerheads with conservative variants that fit Chatterjee's description. Nowhere was this more evident than in the Middle East, where Saudi Arabia led a decades-long campaign to undermine the secular, modernizing nationalism of Nasser and the Ba'ath parties, which it saw as a threat to its own rule. This campaign is inexplicable unless the reality of modernizing nationalism is appreciated—which is what Chatterjee's revised theory seems to preclude.

But the theory is weakened still further if we move beyond the bourgeois nationalisms just described and consider the other variant that emerged in this era, the anticapitalist nationalisms of the postwar decades. How can Chatterjee's definition accommodate the nationalism of Ho Chi Minh, or Samora Machel, or Mao Zedong, or Amilcar Cabral, or any of the anticolonial movements inspired by socialism? How could these be described as having constructed an inner domain and an outer domain, as having declared the inviolability of the former and having built their ideology around it? The ideologies of all these nationalisms were committed to a thoroughgoing critique, even a rejection, of what Chatterjee subsumes into the "inner" domain. Indeed, they expressed a rather open disdain for the very idea of the spiritual. These nationalisms set the terms, not just for other anticolonial movements of their time, but for progressive movements more generally, across the world. And yet, by Chatterjee's description, they either did not exist or do not count as nationalisms.

In sum, I believe we are justified in proffering the following judgment: Chatterjee's new theory of nationalism cannot possibly work, since it is unable to accommodate the dominant trend in the anticolonial ideologies of the twentieth century, which was to *reject* the sanctity of the "inner" domain. What he presents as the defining characteristic of nationalism was but a single tendency within it—a subordinate one at that.

10.7 CONCLUSION

Partha Chatterjee's view is that while nationalism promised to construct a distinct identity for the postcolony, and from that, to derive a path of independent development, it failed to do so. Even while nationalism strove to break free of colonial domination, the *terms* on which it undertook its mission ensured that while it might manage to throw off the formal apparatus of rule, it would not break free of Western domination. In order truly to break free, it would have had to reject colonialism's ideological apparatus, root and branch. Although it did succeed in jettisoning certain of colonialism's more superficial elements, nationalism remained wedded to some of its more subtle mechanisms of control. The key here was the commitment to Reason—to the promotion a scientific, rational worldview. It was this baseline prejudice that made nationalists accept a modernizing agenda for the postcolony, and so committed were they to Reason that they never questioned the wisdom of such an agenda. They took it on because they viewed it as natural, even inevitable. It was the ticket to a nation's taking its place on the world stage. But their fidelity to this doctrine merely guaranteed the continued subordination of the postcolony to the West. It meant participating in a system of production and exchange they could not control, in a game they could not win. In short, it meant acceptance of their continued subjugation to an alien culture. Nationalism could not live up to its promise because it lacked the means to break out of the ideological parameters constructed by the colonizer. Its failure stemmed from its status as a derivative discourse.

I hope I have shown in this chapter that this characterization of nationalism is a fantasy. There were excellent reasons for nationalists to accept the modernizing path to development. It was a rational response to the circumstances in which they found themselves as they tried to negotiate their nation's insertion into a global capitalist economy. Chatterjee's argument works only if we assume away all the pressures that capitalism imposes on the political economies of emerging nations, and his denial of this basic fact brings us back to the weakness that runs through the entirety of the Subalternist enterprise: the tendency to obscure, or deny altogether, the properties of capitalism. As we have seen, Guha obscures the real history of the European bourgeoisie by turning them into liberal democrats; Chakrabarty pretends that interpersonal coercion is alien to capitalist power relations; Chakrabarty pretends that the existence of History 2 means that capitalism has not yet universalized, meaning that even the most advanced bourgeois economies cannot be considered capitalist. We can now add Chatterjee's theory of nationalism to this list. The only way his argument about nationalists' entrapment in colonial discourse can be taken seriously is if we pretend that capitalism does not exist.

While Chatterjee evacuates capitalism from its proper place in a theory of nationalism, he substitutes for it an inflated assessment of the role of ideas. The turn to modernization is presented as an *intellectual* failure—the failure to break out of the colonial thematic. The clear implication is that, had they been more thorough in their rejection of colonial ideology, nationalists might have been able to consider models of nation-building that were free of the modernizing urge. But what might this strategy have been? If, because of the blinders imposed by the colonial thematic, the nationalists missed seeing some model of development out there in the world, then surely we are entitled to a glimpse of its properties. Yet Chatterjee offers none. His argument relies on innuendo instead of evidence. I have suggested that this analytical strategy is not accidental. Chatterjee *does not* offer a strategy for the postcolony because he *cannot*. The moment he might do so, it would be easy to show that his strategy, too, was a prisoner to the colonial thematic, since it, too, would have to rely on Reason in some way, shape, or form.

At the very end of *Nationalist Thought and the Colonial World*, Chatterjee seems to realize that his framework might be flawed. His argument suddenly takes a rather startling turn. Until this point, he has located the weakness of nationalist thought in its failure to reject Reason. Now, however, he adds a crucial qualification: nationalism was flawed not because of its embrace of Reason per se, but because it never "challenged the legitimacy of the marriage between Reason *and capital.*"[60] This sentence appears on page 168, in a book 170 pages long.

So, we are now to understand that the problem with nationalism was not that it was a prisoner to Reason as such, but that it put Reason at the service of capital. If this is what Chatterjee would have us believe, the implication is clear:

---

60   *NTCW* 168. Emphasis added.

Enlightenment theories, scientific rationality, objectivity, universalism, and so forth are not the true problem, so long as they are emancipated from the rule of capital. The flaw of nationalism, therefore, would be that it was bourgeois in character, not that it hewed to a Western sensibility. This sounds very much like a traditional Marxist critique of elite nationalism. Is this what Chatterjee was arguing all along? It seems unlikely. To begin with, this lone, isolated comment is outweighed by the numerous instances, scattered across his book, in which he inveighs against the Enlightenment tradition as a whole, not merely the bourgeois stream within it. He carefully levels his main criticism against the idea of modernization itself, never hinting that he intends to limit his argument to *capitalist* modernization.

If it were capitalist modernization that Chatterjee wished to attack, this ought to have shown up in his actual criticisms of Bankim, Nehru, and Gandhi. But it figures not at all. Those criticisms are far more consistent with the view he announces at the outset of the book, and which he continues to reiterate until the final two pages—that the problem with nationalism was its acceptance of Reason itself, not Bourgeois Reason. It would be difficult to impugn Nehru's advocacy of modern industry and science—which Chatterjee not only does, but puts at the heart of his argument—if we were worried only about his defense of capitalism. Even if Nehru had been a card-carrying Communist, or any other kind of anticapitalist of the day, he would *still* have advocated for modernization. But Chatterjee's criticism is directed centrally at Nehru's acceptance of the modernizing imperative, which he sees as a product of the colonial thematic, not as a sober appreciation of reality. If we turn to his views on Gandhi, here, too, it is difficult to see how Chatterjee could have been arguing against only Bourgeois Reason. If he wanted to emancipate Reason from capital, then would he not have wanted to *defend* Reason against its detractors? Yet his endorsement of Gandhi's philosophy is based explicitly on Gandhi's *rejection* of Reason—not in its bourgeois form, but in *any* form. He praises Gandhi for being the only major figure in the nationalist movement to escape the prison house of colonial discourse, not because Gandhi extricates Reason from capital—which of course he did not—but because he quite "emphatically rejects their rationalism, scientism, and historicism." Chatterjee never takes up Gandhi's defense of the propertied classes, his ambivalence toward trade unions, his philosophy of trusteeship, or the like, all of which ought to figure prominently in an argument that purports to indict nationalism for its marriage of Reason to capital.

What do we make, then, of this last-minute overture to anticapitalism? At the very least, we can say that it lacks conviction.[61] More cynically, we might surmise that Chatterjee is anticipating, and trying to deflect, the very sort of critique I have leveled here. But a throwaway reference to capital, inserted at the

---

61   See also Bilgrami, "Two Conceptions of Secularism," 1,758.

very end of a book-length argument, only ends up in tension with everything the author has said up to that point. To take it seriously would call for a drastic overhaul of his entire presentation of the dilemmas and pitfalls of colonial nationalism. Since there is no sign that Chatterjee is now casting aside everything he said previously, the reader's most reasonable reaction is to gently but firmly set aside his eleventh-hour embrace of Reason, and move on.

Chatterjee's theory of nationalism embodies both of the failings I have attributed to the Subaltern Studies project—that it obscures, or denies altogether, capitalism's influence on the colonial world, and that it resurrects many of the most objectionable Orientalist myths about the East. One cannot but be impressed by the alacrity with which Chatterjee associates Reason with the West and describes the embrace of rationality and science by nationalists as their submission to "an alien culture." In many ways, *Nationalist Thought and the Colonial World* announced the turn in Subaltern Studies away from its roots in cultural Marxism and toward the greener pastures of poststructuralist irrationalism. That fork in the road appeared more than two decades ago. The collective's most illustrious members have never looked back since.

CHAPTER ELEVEN

Conclusion: Subaltern Studies as Ideology

Postcolonial theory is a diffuse and nebulous body of thought. I have focused on *Subaltern Studies* because it is acknowledged, both by its leading exponents and by commentators, as the most successful exemplar of postcolonial theorizing in historical and social analysis. My premise has been that if the theory has real value for social analysis—in a domain beyond its home in literary theory—then this value should be apparent in the work of those historians most famously associated with it. Furthermore, and to its credit, the Subaltern Studies project has produced a body of work that is quite tightly wrapped around a shared set of assumptions and propositions. This makes it possible to engage *Subaltern Studies* somewhat systematically—unlike so much of the literature bearing the theory's imprimatur. Toward this end, in the opening chapter of this book I assimilated most of the project's core ideas into a set of six theses, which I examined in the succeeding chapters. These theses, it should be noted, are culled not just from my own reading of the Subalternist oeuvre, but from the summary statement by Dipesh Chakrabarty, one of the collective's leading members.

The two main virtues attributed to postcolonial theory are that it offers a new theory of global modernity—especially pertaining to the non-West—and that it is the new face of radical critique. Often the theory is presented as the inheritor of the great radical traditions of the twentieth century, but shorn of their analytical and critical infirmities. The obvious target here is Marxist theory. For more than a hundred years, across the globe, it was the Marxist tradition that carried the banner of radical analysis. Its analytical categories formed the lingua franca of political analysis, and its anticapitalism formed the core of radical critique. Postcolonial theory presents itself as Marxism's successor in both dimensions, the critical and the analytical. Its theoretical framework supposedly remedies the usual laundry list of ills attributed to Marxist theory—its determinism, teleology, Eurocentrism, reductionism, and so forth. In addition, its critical core supposedly aligns more closely with the aspirations of subaltern groups, particularly in the non-West. In all the best-known works produced by the Subaltern Studies collective, even though the Enlightenment tradition as a whole is routinely impugned, it is Marxism that takes the brunt of the attack.

Analytically, perhaps the core thesis of postcolonial studies is that a deep structural chasm separates East and West, so much so that it undermines any framework claiming universal applicability. As one of its most prominent streams of theory, Subaltern Studies has become famous in large measure for its

defense and elaboration of this thesis. It is the basis for the collective's indictment of Western theory as hidebound and parochial, blind to the specificities of
postcolonial nations, and hence in need of drastic overhaul. In the preceding
chapters, I have focused on three areas in which this divide supposedly obtains.
The first has to do with the bourgeoisie in the East, the putative failure of which
is taken as an expression of a deeper failure, that of capital's universalization.
Second is the ostensible distinctiveness of power relations in the East, which,
Chakrabarty claims, depart fundamentally from those generated by capitalism
in the West. Third is the matter of Eastern political psychology, which, we are
told, is unmoved by matters of individual interest. These are the East's dimensions of difference, and it is their purported uniqueness that motivates the call
for a drastic rethinking of social theory.

While my burden has been to show that the Subalternist collective has
failed to establish their case in any of these domains, I have chosen to complement my critical analysis with a positive account of how capital, power, and
agency actually work. Four basic elements tie my alternative argument together.
The *first* is that the universalization of capital is real, *pace* the claims of the
Subalternist collective. The colonies' political dynamics did not attain a fundamentally different kind of modernity than did the Europeans'. More precisely,
their modernity may have been different, but not in the ways that postcolonial
theory insists. Theirs is a modernity that, over time, became no less reflective of
capitalist imperatives than the French or German. The *second* is that the universalizing drive of capital should not be assumed to homogenize power relations,
or the social landscape more generally. In fact, capitalism is not only consistent
with great heterogeneity and hierarchy, but systematically generates them.
Capitalism is perfectly compatible with a highly diverse set of political and
cultural formations. The *third* proposition is that the universalizing drive of
capital comes up against some universal facts about human psychology, and
these facts are what explain subaltern resistance to capital's drive to establish
exclusionary political orders, to dominate them in the labor process, to rely on
interpersonal coercion, and so on. The modern epoch is driven by the interaction between these two universalisms, not just the one. This overturns the
Subalternist insistence on the unique political consciousness of non-Western
agents. Which brings us to the *final* point: that the universalizing categories of
Enlightenment thought are perfectly capable of capturing the consequences of
capital's universalization and the dynamics of political agency—indeed, these
categories are essential to their analysis. If these four propositions are true, it
means that at least some of the European theories, Marxism in particular, need
not be charged with Eurocentrism simply because they originated in the West.
The dynamics that they place at the heart of their framework are in fact cross-
cultural, common to East as well as West. Hence, Marxist theory may be wrong,
but not because it is Eurocentric.

These basic counterarguments have been advanced through a critical examination of the six theses central to the Subalternist project, which I described in Chapter 1. The theses' multiple infirmities announce the failure of Subaltern Studies as substantive theory. But I have argued that the project also fails as a platform for social critique. Not only are the six theses mistaken, they are also deeply ideological. The irony of the project is that, while it presents itself as the new face of radical critique, as the leading edge of criticism in an age of global capitalism, its arguments resurrect key pillars of conservative ideology. In chapter 1, I proposed that these apologetics could be assimilated into two broad kinds: the tendency to obscure or deny basic properties of capitalism, and the valorization of some profoundly Orientalist constructions of Eastern cultures. Let me now draw together our findings, which have been dispersed across the preceding chapters, so that we may better appreciate the ideological tenor of *Subaltern Studies*.

11.1 OBSCURING CAPITALISM

Subaltern Studies can be neither a theory of globalizing capitalism nor its critique, since it systematically misrepresents how capitalism works. We have seen instances of this tendency in virtually every chapter.

- *Subalternists attribute to the bourgeoisie a democratic mission that it in fact rejected and fought against.* The idea that modern democratic culture derives from the beneficence of capitalists is central to Ranajit Guha's work. We saw in chapter 5 that Dipesh Chakrabarty, too, accepts this argument; indeed, the premise runs through much of the Subalternist literature. It is of course wholly mistaken. But it also has a multiplier effect. Many of the downstream mistakes of the Subaltern Studies framework can flow directly from this prior mistake. Two central errors are that the violence and authoritarianism of so many postcolonial countries can be traced to the fact that their capitalist classes failed to live up to the achievements of their European predecessors (chapters 2–4); and the argument that democratic consciousness within the working class requires the prior transformation of political culture by the bourgeoisie (chapter 8).

- *Subaltern Studies accepts a highly romanticized story about power relations in capitalism.* By doing so, it obscures how power actually functions in capitalist societies. More important, Subalternist theorists mistakenly urge that the forms of domination that obtain in postcolonial formations are *not* capitalist, and that they cannot therefore be analyzed through the categories developed by political economy (chapter 5). In this argument, coercion and violence within the employment relation are seen as departures from capitalism, whereas in fact they are, and have been, employers' *preferred* mode of power through most of capitalist history. Subaltern Studies airbrushes out the violence out of modern capitalism.

- *It underestimates capitalism's ability not only to tolerate heterogeneity— "difference"—but to actively promote it.* Subalternist theorists, along with many of their fellow travelers in postcolonial studies, seem to assume that for capital to universalize, it must also homogenize. This simple notion is the foundation for the entire argument in *Provincializing Europe*—its critique of abstract labor, its analysis of History 1 and History 2, and of course its tortured analysis of historicism (chapter 9). It is also the basis on which they reject Marx's concept of abstract labor (chapter 6). Doubtless it is true that capitalism does dissolve many sorts of social differences. But it also sustains and generates difference. Both of these outcomes are perfectly consistent with capitalism. In their insistence that the index for capital's universaliza- tion is the extent of social homogenization, the Subalternists end up denying capital's existence even in those areas where it has taken deep root, and pronounce as anomalous those outcomes which are a direct consequence of capitalist dynamics.

- *It fails to recognize the pressures that capitalism exerts on national institu- tions, and hence overestimates the role of ideology.* This is most clearly evident in Chatterjee's diagnosis of modernizing nationalism (chapter 10). Chatterjee explains the turn to modernization as a consequence of nation- alism's internalization of Western ideology—not as a rational response to economic and geopolitical pressures. Thus, he simply denies what so many nationalist leaders saw as self-evident—that whatever else the postcolonial state did, it would have to find a way to develop the local productive forces. I showed in chapter 10 that his argument falls flat. But just as important is that it also obscures real facts about the constraints that capitalism imposes on national political strategies.

There are two important consequences of these errors. The first is rather straightforward: postcolonial theory, as developed by Subaltern Studies, simply misdiagnoses the trajectory and internal dynamics of modernization—not just in the East, though this is quite spectacularly the case, but also in the West. It fails to recognize the real dynamics that drive political change, misidentifies the relevant actors, attributes to them preferences or interests that they do not have, and refuses to recognize the constraints under which social actors make their choices. This is a rather dramatic failing for a theory that purports to supplant the reigning theories of social change. Flowing from this mistaken historical analysis is the second consequence: because of their fascination with Grand

Theory, Subalternist theorists are not content simply to generate a (flawed) historical sociology. They proceed to justify their sociology by generating a rather confused metatheory about determinism, agency, abstraction, explanation, and the like. Thus, in order to justify his culturalism about jute workers' mobilizations, Chakrabarty spins a dubious theory about the role of needs in social agency; and because he mistakenly equates universalization with homogenization, he creates a category called "historicism," thereby inventing a whole family of Enlightenment conceptual errors that do not in fact exist. The confusion is therefore not just about what *happened* in history, but also about *how to think about* what happened in history.

In the process, capitalism turns into something quite mysterious within Subalternist theorizing. Even though the word appears with numbing regularity in their analyses, it is shorn of its central causal properties. Their "capitalism" generates a bourgeoisie that bears little or no resemblance to the actual historical actor; it creates power relations that capture only a small subset of actual forms of domination wielded by capital; it lacks the abiding structural power that we have seen it actually exercise; it is attributed with a totalizing force so awesome that every known instance of capitalism must of necessity fall short of the concept—which impels Chakrabarty to announce that the very idea of its universalization is a mistake. Naturally, if a theory cannot make basic sense of how capitalism works, then the very idea of its supplanting Marxist or other radical analyses cannot be taken seriously. Subaltern Studies realizes at least tacitly that, much as in Marx's time, the central issue in our own time is still the juggernaut of global capitalism. This is probably why they cannot exorcise the *word* from their lexicon, even if it bears little resemblance to the *concept* as we know it. And it is what makes their failure all the more striking: in their hands, the most powerful social and structural force in the world becomes a wisp of smoke, something so ghostly that one becomes not quite sure it exists.

11.2 RESURRECTING ORIENTALISM

While Subaltern Studies fails in its analysis of capitalism, it also cannot be the leading edge of anticolonial or anti-imperial critique, because it resurrects the worst instances of Orientalist mythology.

- *Subaltern Studies insists that Eastern agents operate with an entirely different political psychology than do Western agents.* This is perhaps the oldest canard in the Orientalist worldview. It is not hard to fathom why it occupies pride of place among imperial ideologues—there is no more effective justification for denying people their rights and freedoms than the claim that those people simply do not *value* those freedoms, or that they are not motivated by their material needs—in sum, that they do not deserve the same protections that we do because they do not "think like us." One of the most enduring contributions of anticolonial and anti-imperialist movements of the past century has been to reveal the ideological character of these notions—and yet, in the name of radical critique, these are the very claims that Subaltern Studies revives. We witnessed this most dramatically in chapters 7 and 8, which dealt with the political psychology of the laboring classes.

- *It assigns science, rationality, objectivity, and similar attributes to the West, instead of regarding them as common to both cultures.* This is the central argument in Partha Chatterjee's analysis of colonial nationalism, but it lurks in much of Dipesh Chakrabarty's work as well. Hence the bizarre conclusion that for the East even to embark on a political strategy guided by Reason is to consign itself to perpetual subordination.

- *Its celebration of the local, the particular—whether as History 2, or as the "fragment"—ends up justifying an exoticization of the East.* This is most evident in the work of Dipesh Chakrabarty, subjected to critique in chapter 10, who builds an entire social ontology in defense of the exotic. Notice that this flows directly from the mistaken understanding of capitalism. Because capitalism is wrongly taken to require complete homogenization, any departure from the homogenizing drive is seen as resistance to the abstract logic of capital: any practice not reduced to the abstract logic of capital is thereby a resistance to capital. The minute examination of such practices can then be linked to emancipatory theory, and so, offsets the intrepid area specialist in search of the myriad "particularities and incommensurabilities" of his region, whether India, or Bolivia, or Turkmenistan. The more marginal, and the more mysterious, the better. The various practices are all construed as ways of being, or better yet, ways of *knowing*, that have escaped the totalizing grasp of capital, and hence presented as potential escape routes from it. Traditional Orientalism is thereby repackaged as resistance to capital.

One could list other features of postcolonial theory that essentialize the East. The point of this discussion, however, is not so much to formulate an exhaustive list of such misdemeanors as it is to emphasize some of the more obvious instances.

In light of the preceding findings, we can firmly reject any claim for the value of postcolonial theory as an analytical framework or as anti-imperial critique. Consider the description offered by Robert J. C. Young in his widely used text *Postcolonialism: An Historical Introduction*, in which he assimilates postcolonial theorizing into the tradition of socialist and anticolonial movements. He characterizes it as a form of critique that "incorporates the legacy of the syncretistic traditions of Marxisms that developed outside the west in the course of anti-colonial struggles"; it is "a form of activist writing that looks back to the political commitment of anti-colonial liberation movements and draws its inspiration from them, while recognizing that they often operated under conditions very different from those that exist in the present."[1] To underline his point, Young traces the lineage of postcolonial theory not just to Lenin and Rosa Luxemburg, but to Marx and Engels themselves. Moving forward, he draws a line that runs from the anticolonial writings of Marx, through Lenin's "Draft Theses on the National and Colonial Questions," to the revolutionary writings of Mao, Cabral, Nkrumah, and thence to Derrida and Subaltern Studies. The road from Marx leads straight to Subaltern Studies.

By now it should be clear that Young's description is spectacularly mistaken. Certainly, a good case can be made for a connection between the anticolonial writings of Cabral and Nkrumah, even those of Fanon, and the socialism of Lenin or Marx. Whatever the particularities of their thought, they were all deeply committed to the reality of capitalist universalization and to the basic humanity that binds together laboring classes in the East and West. All proclaimed fidelity to the Enlightenment project, to science, rationality, and universal emancipation. But we have just seen, in intricate detail, that Subaltern Studies and, by extension, postcolonial theory are either in tension with, or simply reject, these as nostrums. It is not that Subalternist theorists disagree with given elements of the theory offered by anticolonial socialism—it is that their theory is *fundamentally at odds* with it. For example, by Partha Chatterjee's description, the socialism of all the leading anticolonial theorists of the twentieth century means that they were all prisoners of the colonial thematic; they could not be taken seriously as anti*colonial* theorists until they rejected humanism and universal ethics, confidence in science, in rationality and objectivity—in other words, until they rejected their *socialism*. Given its irrationalism, its embrace of an Orientalist sociology, and its romanticization of capitalism, postcolonial theory has little or no connection to the theoretical lineage invoked by Robert Young. How could it, when that lineage is its favorite target of critique?

11.3 HOW TO PROVINCIALIZE EUROPE

Obviously, my verdict on the merits of Subaltern Studies is not favorable. What, then, remains of the impulse to "provincialize Europe"? One reason postcolonial theory is so attractive to so many people in the academy is its hostility to Eurocentrism, and its related commitment to appreciate the specificity of the colonial experience. Readers might wonder if my critique and counterarguments amount to the view that there is in fact nothing specific about colonial

---

1   Robert J. C. Young, *Postcolonialism: An Historical Introduction* (Oxford: Blackwell, 2000), 10.

capitalism or the political culture it generated. Nothing could be further from the truth.

What is objectionable about postcolonial theory is not that it insists on "provincializing Europe," but that, in the name of this project, *it relentlessly promotes Eurocentrism*—a portrayal of the West as the site of reason, rationality, secularism, democratic culture, and the like, and the East as an unchanging miasma of tradition, unreason, religiosity, and so on. Theirs is a world in which capitalism transforms the West but loses its nerve in the East, where materialist categories are therefore appropriate to the West but only an essentializing culturalism is workable for the East. It should be obvious that, in the name of displacing Eurocentrism, postcolonial theory ends up resurrecting it with a ferocious intensity.

By way of an alternative, I would like to make only two points. The first is that the way to provincialize Europe is not by continually harping on some unbridgeable gap that separates East from West, but by showing that both parts of the globe are subject to *the same basic forces* and are therefore part of *the same basic history*. The forces I refer to are what I have called the two universalisms— the universal logic of capital (suitably defined) and social agents' universal interest in their well-being, which impels them to resist capital's expansionary drive. These forces impinge on both East and West, even if they do so with different intensities and in different registers. This means that there *is* a universal history, in which East and West are both full-time participants. But while both East and West are part of the same history, and subject to the same forces, it does not follow that they lose their distinguishing characteristics. In chapter 9 we saw that recognizing the reality of capital's universalization is perfectly consistent with an appreciation for the persistence of difference. It is unnecessary to rehearse those arguments here. But if we accept them, then we can also agree that a recognition of the two universalisms does not automatically generate a blindness to difference.

Now the second point. *The history of Marxian analysis in the twentieth century is the history of doing just this—understanding the specificity of the East.* There is probably no project to which Marxist theorists have devoted more energy and time since the first Russian Revolution of 1905 than to understand the peculiar effects of capitalist development in the non-West. Perhaps this seems shocking at first blush, especially in light of the unceasing claims from postcolonial theory to the contrary. The fact is, owing to the peculiar fate of socialist movements—namely, that they gained the most traction in the less-developed parts of the world—Marxists were driven from the outset to train their lenses on the backwaters of global capital, every bit as much as on the developed West. If we draw up a list of the main theoretical innovations to come out of the Marxist tradition after Marx's death, we see that many of them are attempts to theorize capitalism in backward settings: in the first half of the century, there was Lenin's theory of imperialism and the "weakest link," his analysis of agrarian class differentiation, Kautsky's work on the agrarian question, Trotsky's theory of uneven and combined development, Mao's theory of New Democracy, Gramsci's distinction between state legitimacy in Eastern and Western Europe. All of these were attempts to understand social reproduction in parts of the world where capitalism was *not* working in exactly the way Marx described it in *Capital*. In the years of the New Left, there came dependency theory, world-systems theory, Cabral's work on the African revolutionary path, the theory of the articulation of modes of production, the Indian "modes of production" debate—and the list goes on.

I mention this in part because Marxism is the favorite target of postcolonial theorists' accusations against the Enlightenment tradition. They invite us to believe that Marxism looks at the East only as a blurred reflection of the West, where any departures from the Western model are mere anachronisms, bound to vanish in due course, inasmuch as the East is supposed to follow passively in the tracks laid down by the West. Yet the history of Marxian analysis is exactly the opposite—it exhibits an enduring appreciation of the fact that Eastern societies seem to be driven by logics that require fresh analysis and even, at times, a modification of received categories.

To offer just one example: Trotsky's theory of uneven and combined development was an explicit *rejection* of the argument that later developers would simply replicate the developmental path of the early ones. For Trotsky, the fact of their later insertion into the capitalist vortex meant that such societies would be able to import the most recent innovations in certain spheres, while preserving a whole gamut of older social relations in others. There is no implication of homogeneous time, no historicism, no "stageism"—indeed, the theory is immune to virtually every accusation that Subalternist theorists make against the Marxian tradition.[2]

Similarly, Kautsky's classic work on the agrarian question ends up making a case for why the peasantry will not simply be dissolved by the forces of agro-industry or urban capitalism—rather, they will be incorporated into the circuits of capital, thus giving smallholders a place within the order that their counterparts lost within the early developers.[3] Here, too, there is no stageism, no historicism, no presumption of homogenization. Or take a theory of more recent vintage, the articulation of modes of production. In this approach, capitalism does not obliterate all History 2s, nor does it resolutely lurch from stage to predetermined stage. Instead, it forms an uneasy accord with archaic modes of production, so that instead of displacing them it cohabits with them over

---

2   A short representation is found in Trotsky's introduction to his *The History of the Russian Revolution*.

3   See Karl Kautsky, *The Agrarian Question*, trans. Pete Burgess (London: Zwan Publications, 1988), 2 vols.

long periods of time. This was a theory developed by French anthropologists focusing mainly on the study of Africa, and was made famous in the English-speaking world by theorists such as Harold Wolpe, who mobilized it to study the peculiar capitalism of South Africa.

Many of these theories, of course, are deeply flawed and can be criticized on various grounds, but never on the grounds that Subaltern Studies associates with Enlightenment—especially Marxian theories. If they are wrong, it is not because they are teleological, or deterministic, or stageist. Indeed, every one of these theories was developed as an *explicit rejection* of these very modes of thought. On the other hand, all of them have something significant in common: they affirm the two universalisms, and thus provincialize Europe far more effectively than anything coming out of the stable of postcolonial studies. Whatever their flaws, none of these theories grounded in Enlightment principles is Eurocentric, none of them essentializes the East, and none can be accused of Orientalism.[4] This being the case, the project of developing theory that effectively analyzes the specificity of the East is more likely to emerge from the research program associated with the Enlightenment than with postcolonial theory. And here is the reason: postcolonial theory obscures the very forces that drive the political dynamics in that part of the world (the two universalisms), while simultaneously promoting conceptions of it that are systematically misleading.

The aim to provincialize Europe, then, is wholly laudable. The problem with postcolonial theory is not that it is committed to this agenda, but rather that it is incapable of ever carrying it out.

11.4 ENVOI

My argument amounts to the contention that postcolonial theory impedes the development of an adequate analysis of the modern epoch, whether in the East or the West. Is there any chance it will be displaced from its exalted status in the near future? Interestingly, if ever there was a time when the sheer force of events should suffice to undermine a theory, it is now. Two facts about the current conjuncture would seem to deliver a decisive and devastating blow to the postcolonial studies framework, while affirming the arguments I have leveled against it. The first of these is the global economic crisis that began in

---

4   As for Marx's own Orientalism, I believe he was guilty of this at times. But the Subalternist accusations against him, which portray him as an apologist for imperialism, are so off-base that they suggest a genuine ignorance of his work. Luckily, a superb recent book lays this matter to rest once and for all. See Kevin B. Anderson, *Marx at the Margins: On Nationalism, Ethnicity, and Non-Western Societies* (Chicago: University of Chicago Press, 2011). Compare Anderson's impressive scholarship to the ill-conceived and rather baseless accusations of Gyan Prakash in his "Postcolonial Criticism and Indian Historiography," *Social Text* 31/32 (1992), 14–15.

2007–8, and the second is the series of revolts in the Middle East known as the Arab Spring.

The global economic crisis has brought into relief the basic fact that the entire world is now part of the same universal history, subject to the same underlying forces. There is no more dramatic illustration of capital's universalization than the fact that the entire world has been engulfed by its effects. This is not the first time this has happened, of course. Crises in the history of capitalism have always been global in their impact. But it is the first time such a cataclysm has hit since postcolonial theory arrived on the scene. For the first time since the 1980s, *everyone* is talking about capitalism—not alterity, or hybridity, or the fragment, but the ubiquitous, grinding, crushing force of capital. This certainly makes for a friendlier environment for the arguments I have been developing in this book, and which others will no doubt make in the years to come.

Even more devastating than the economic collapse, however, is the Arab Spring. It is hard to imagine a more dramatic confirmation of the two universalisms than the demands that came from the streets of Tunisia, Egypt, or the other centers of revolt. These were demands for bread, rights, jobs, and democracy. In fact, without exception, commentators were taken aback by the centrality of secular, universalistic, and materialist demands in the movements. This is not the first time such demands have been seen in the Middle East; secular nationalism was the main political ideology of the region in the middle decades of the twentieth century. But since the 1970s, it was Islamists of varying stripes that had gained traction within civil society. The growth of religious political organizations, and the steady enervation of secular Left forces, had been one of the conditions that lent credibility to the new Orientalism espoused by postcolonial theory. Yet when the Spring's mass movements exploded onto the scene, the Islamists were largely marginal to them. Their banners were hard to find.[5] What the masses of young revolutionaries called for was liberty, justice, and dignity—demands one should expect, if postcolonial theory is to be believed, only in the streets of Paris or New York. And if that were not enough, when the United States and Europe experienced a series of mass mobilizations against austerity during the months after the Arab Spring, the youth in the

---

5   Committed Orientalists will no doubt point to the political gains of Islamists since those heady days as being a problem for my argument. The victories by Islamist parties in the elections, the critics would say, show the deep roots of religious consciousness in the Middle East, and the marginality of universalistic motivations. This argument readily fails. The balance of votes in an election is the result of numerous factors. It is not a key to the wellsprings of a national culture. The most salient explanations of a party's electoral success are political, not cultural. So, in Egypt, the most powerful explanation for the Muslim Brotherhood's success is that it was the most well-organized party in opposition, with national organizational presence, deep roots in communities, etc., while the newer, secular parties were much weaker organizationally. In any case, the Muslim Brotherhood itself supported many of the universalistic demands made by the crowds in Tahrir Square, and reaffirmed its commitment to them after its electoral success.

streets of Barcelona, New York, and Athens carried signs saluting their counterparts in Cairo and Tunis, citing them as inspirations. How could this be? How could calls for jobs and rights in the West take inspiration from the Orient, if the latter are not even supposed to be motivated by such matters?

Hence, one can make the argument that the past five years have created optimal conditions for the recognition of postcolonial theory's shortcomings. But will it be displaced? *In fact, I doubt we will witness its eclipse anytime in the near future.* Postcolonial theory came to prominence during a period of massive political defeats for the Left, all across the world.[6] Indeed, I rather doubt there has ever been a time since the birth of the modern Left that its forces were as enfeebled as they have been since the 1980s. It is now a commonplace that the turn to irrationalism within the self-styled "radical" intelligentsia was very closely tied to their retreat into the academy.[7] But it was not just that this brought about a change in intellectual culture, narrowly conceived. Over the past quarter century, enormous resources have been sunk into the material *infrastructure* that sustains the theory. There are journals wholly committed to it, chairs in humanities departments dedicated to its propagation, sections in disciplinary societies that convene annually with hundreds of attendees, book series at publishing houses with enormous lists and promises of forthcoming volumes. None of this will come to an end anytime soon simply because the theory happens to be deeply flawed.

And this brings up the second obstacle. By now, not only have lavish material resources been plowed into the field, but hundreds of scholars have built their reputations on it. This institutional network is staffed by academics whose professional life now orbits around the ideas propagated by the theory. Apart from the first generation of postcolonial theorists, the second generation, their students, constitutes a bulwark against the possibility of critique—and hence the possibility of one's own reputation becoming sullied. For scholars from the Global South, who have now for decades promoted the Orientalism central to postcolonial theory, the prospect of exposure is especially devastating. There are now legions of intellectuals who have staked their reputations on this theoretical framework, who have made their careers on extolling its virtues and its deep insights. Put these factors together, and one should expect that the response to the political developments of the past couple of years will be twofold: to bend and twist the theory so that it might appear capable of accommodating

6   Much of the analysis in the next paragraphs is a highly condensed presentation of my argument in "On the Decline of Class Analysis in South Asian Studies," *Critical Asian Studies* 38:4 (Dec. 2006), 357–87. Readers should refer to that essay for a more detailed accounting of the conditions that gave rise to, and have sustained, postcolonial theory over the past decades.

7   See the early analysis by Perry Anderson in his *In the Tracks of Historical Materialism* (London: Verso, 1983), and the brilliant distillation by Terry Eagleton in his *The Illusions of Postmodernism* (London: Verso, 1999), chap. 1.

developments that rather directly undermine its basic propositions; and to violently attack any concerted critique issuing from the outside.

For those familiar with the literature on the history of science, my prognosis ought not to come as a surprise. Decades ago, Thomas Kuhn described the process of theoretical development in the history of scientific thought.[8] He showed that when scientific theories meet with empirical anomalies or even outright disconfirmation, they are not easily displaced by their rivals. They are able to survive for long periods, in large part because of the resources that can be deployed to defend them, and because the reputations of so many scientists hang on the success of the flawed theories. What I have described in the case of postcolonial theory is much the same phenomenon, except that it is occurring in the moral sciences. If anything, the absence of experimental conditions, along with the more dubious intellectual culture of the social sciences and humanities, makes the likelihood of rapid displacement even more remote.

None of this is to suggest, however, that the situation is hopeless. Quite the contrary. The times in which we live do offer a tremendous opportunity to expose the flaws of the theory and even to displace it. My point is simply that if this is going to happen, it will not happen on its own. It will take some time and a great deal of effort. All the more reason to begin now.

---

8   Thomas S. Kuhn, *The Structure of Scientific Revolutions*, first published in 1962. My invocation of Kuhn should not be taken as an endorsement of the more controversial parts of his argument in *The Structure*—namely, the strong version of the theory-dependence of observation and the attendant claims for the incommensurability of theories.

Index